AMERICAN

TRADE

POLITICS

FOURTH EDITION

INSTITUTE FOR INTERNATIONAL ECONOMICS

AMERICAN

FOURTH EDITION

TRADE

I. M. DESTLER

POLITICS

Washington, DC
June 2005

I. M. (Mac) Destler, visiting fellow, is a professor at the School of Public Policy, University of Maryland. He was formerly senior fellow at the Institute and senior associate at the Carnegie Endowment for International Peace and at the Brookings Institution. He has taught at Princeton University, the University of Nigeria, and the International University of Japan. He is the author or coauthor of numerous works on American trade and foreign policymaking, including *Misreading the Public: The Myth of a New Isolationism* (Brookings Institution Press, 1999), *Renewing Fast-Track Legislation* (1997), *The National Economic Council* (1996), *Dollar Politics* (1989), and *Our Own Worst Enemy: The Unmaking of American Foreign Policy* (Simon and Schuster, 1984).

**INSTITUTE FOR
INTERNATIONAL ECONOMICS**
1750 Massachusetts Avenue, NW
Washington, DC 20036-1903
(202) 328-9000   FAX: (202) 659-3225
www.iie.com

C. Fred Bergsten, *Director*
Valerie Norville, *Director of Publications
  and Web Development*
Edward Tureen, *Director of Marketing*

Typesetting by BMWW
Printing by Kirby Lithographic Company, Inc.

Printed in the United States of America
07 06 05   5 4 3 2 1

Library of Congress Cataloging-in-Publication Data

Destler, I. M.
   American trade politics / I. M. Destler.—
   4th ed.
   p. cm.
   Includes bibliographical references and
   index.
   ISBN 0-88132-382-9
   1. United States—Commerical policy.
I. Title.

HF1455.D48 2005
382'.3'0973—dc22   2005043367

To My Mother

Katharine Hardesty Destler (1909–2003)
Who Got Me Interested in Politics

Contents

Tables

Figures

Preface

Since its original publication in 1986, Mac Destler's *American Trade Politics* has become recognized as the standard work in its field. The book's first edition won the Gladys M. Kammerer Award of the American Political Science Association for the year's best book on public policy. Subsequent editions carried the story through the enactment of major trade legislation in 1988 and the completion of the NAFTA and Uruguay Round agreements in the early Clinton administration. Throughout, Destler's analyses have linked economics and politics and placed contemporary trade-political struggles in broad historical perspective.

This fourth edition carries the story through 10 more contentious years, ending in early 2005. The author finds that, while US trade continues to expand and traditional business-generated protectionism has declined, trade policy has faced new obstacles. A backlash against globalization (the focus of a separate, major Institute project directed by J. David Richardson) has generated contention about whether and how trade agreements should address labor and environmental standards. Bitter conflict between Republicans and Democrats in the House of Representatives has undercut the long tradition of bipartisan support of new trade legislation in the Committee on Ways and Means. Meanwhile, the US trade deficit has ballooned to unprecedented levels, generating deep concerns about China, the nation with the largest share of that imbalance.

This book tells the story of these and other developments: the role and record of the decade-old World Trade Organization; the continuing contention over procedures available to limit trade, such as the antidumping law; and the increased US emphasis on concluding bilateral free trade agreements. Destler concludes the new edition with an argument that blends substance and politics. The United States should complete its transition to globalization by negotiating away remaining trade barriers. But this should go hand-in-hand with much more generous and effective domestic policies to compensate Americans hurt by economic change and enable them to participate competitively in the new, globalized economy. This is the route, Destler argues, to maximum economic gains for Americans. And it constitutes a politically balanced program that ought to appeal to both political parties.

The first three editions of *American Trade Politics* were published jointly by the Institute with the Twentieth Century Fund (now The Century Foundation), which supported Destler's initial research. This collaboration was critical to the book's development and dissemination, and though the Institute has now assumed sole responsibility, we wish to acknowledge TCF's key contribution throughout the life of the project.

The Institute for International Economics is a private, nonprofit institution for the study and discussion of international economic policy. Its purpose is to analyze important issues in that area and to develop and communicate practical new approaches for dealing with them. The Institute is completely nonpartisan.

The Institute is funded by a highly diversified group of philanthropic foundations, private corporations, and interested individuals. Major institutional grants are now being received from the William M. Keck, Jr. Foundation, the New York Community Trust, and the Starr Foundation. About 18 percent of the Institute's resources in our latest fiscal year were provided by contributors outside the United States, including about 8 percent from Japan.

The Institute's Board of Directors bears overall responsibilities for the Institute and gives general guidance and approval to its research program, including the identification of topics that are likely to become important over the medium run (one to three years), and which should be addressed by the Institute. The director, working closely with the staff and outside Advisory Committee, is responsible for the development of particular projects and makes the final decision to publish an individual study.

The Institute hopes that its studies and other activities will contribute to building a stronger foundation for international economic policy around the world. We invite readers of these publications to let us know how they think we can best accomplish this objective.

C. FRED BERGSTEN
Director
May 2005

Author's Note

As we approach the midpoint of 2005, much in American trade politics has that old, familiar ring. The trade deficit has reached new heights: In the first quarter, US buyers imported, incredibly, more than $9 in goods for every $5 they sold overseas! Members of Congress of both parties are targeting China, whose unprecedented bilateral imbalance with the United States is facilitated by the relatively low, fixed value of its currency. Meanwhile, an important US trade deal—the free trade agreement with Central America and the Dominican Republic (CAFTA-DR)—is facing serious challenge in the House of Representatives.

Yet what strikes the author of this fourth edition of *American Trade Politics* is not continuity but change. In the 10 years since Congress approved the Uruguay Round agreements that established the World Trade Organization, business protectionism has faded, social concerns over globalization have grown, and partisanship on Capitol Hill has become ever more rancorous. As set forth in parts III and IV, these developments have complicated the trade-political landscape and suggested new approaches to both analysis and prescription.

To do justice to these changes, this book includes three added chapters that interpret events since 1995 and a concluding set of recommendations that departs substantially from those in prior editions. Yet the new can only be fully understood in the context of the old from which it has sprung. Hence this book preserves the main lines of trade history and analysis from earlier editions. It is more explicitly chronological, divided now into sections covering rough time periods. I hope this will help the reader understand both the roots of the current situation and the potential opportunities for constructive change.

The book remains one man's interpretation of 70 years of American trade policy experience. It is informed by considerable research, including interviews and discussions with many trade policy practitioners and criticism sustained in four Institute study group sessions convened specifically for this fourth edition. Hard information has been sought where available—in carrying forward, for example, as thorough as possible a count of unfair trade practice cases brought to the US Department of Commerce since 1980 and adding a similar count of WTO cases brought by or against the United States. (The underlying case lists supporting this data can be accessed at www.iie.com.) Ultimately, however, the most important events are *sui generis*, so their aggregation into larger patterns becomes a qualitative, interpretive enterprise. The true test of this edition, like the first three, will be whether it captures the issues and patterns of trade politics accurately enough to shed useful light on the difficult policy and procedural choices the United States now faces.

During my work on this edition, I have accumulated still more debts. Again the greatest is to Institute Director C. Fred Bergsten, who has served simultaneously as the book's greatest supporter and the author's most cogent critic. The Institute for International Economics continues, in its splendid new building, to provide a congenial work environment and stimulating colleagues. I also owe a profound debt of gratitude to the University of Maryland and its School of Public Policy, my principal professional home for the past 18 years. And my wife, Harriett Parsons Destler, continues to provide support and encouragement, even as she pursues her own distinguished career in international health policy with the US Agency for International Development.

Any author of a book like this needs able research assistance, and for this edition I have been blessed with the support of two exceptional University of Maryland students: Tomoyuki Sho and Andrew Mosley. In particular, they have both done painstaking work pulling together trade case data and helping in its analysis. Their contributions to this edition have been fully equivalent to those of Diane Berliner for the first edition, Paul Baker for the second, and Steven Schoeny for the third. And I owe continuing gratitude to the Century Foundation, which launched me on this venture and copublished the first three editions.

Like its predecessors, this edition has also benefited from colleagues' criticisms of draft chapters, often conveyed in Institute study group sessions. In addition to several who prefer to remain anonymous, I would like to thank Thelma Askey, Martin Baily, Claude Barfield, Eric Biel, Lael Brainard, Bill Cline, Kimberly Ann Elliott, Bill Frenzel, Monty Graham, Paul Grieco, Morris Goldstein, Randy Henning, Robert Hoffman, Gary Horlick, Gary Hufbauer, Kent Hughes, Steven Kull, Brink Lindsey, Cathy Mann, Thomas Mann, Greg Mastel, Scott Miller, Ted Moran, Judge Morris, Marc Noland, Robert Pastor, Adam Posen, Timothy Reif, J. David Richardson, Howard Rosen, Jeff Schott, Susan Schwab, Bruce Stokes, Dan Tarullo,

Ted Truman, Alan Wm. Wolf, and Li Zhang. Prior editions list many others who helped at earlier stages of this work, whose names I would repeat here but for concerns over space.

On a sadder note, I would like to acknowledge two special individuals. Professor Hideo Sato of the University of Tsukuba was for many years my close colleague and collaborator in analyses of US-Japanese trade relations. Congressman Robert Matsui was generous with time and insights about the changing House of Representatives. Severe illness brought each down before his time, but their societies are the better for them. So am I.

Finally, let me express my special thanks to the Institute's director of publications, Valerie Norville, and her able associates: Ed Tureen, Marla Banov, and Madona Devasahayam. They have brought this book to the finish line despite all impediments interposed by the author. The flaws that remain are his alone.

I. M. D.

ORIGIN: 1934–70

1

The Root Problem: Political Imbalance

Seventy years ago, an assistant professor at Wesleyan University published a book on the politics of trade. Its full-blown title was *Politics, Pressures and the Tariff: A Study of Free Private Enterprise in Pressure Politics, as Shown in the 1929–1930 Revision of the Tariff.* The author sought to explain why, in enacting the now-famous Smoot-Hawley bill, the United States Congress had ignored the warnings of experts and had raised import duties to record levels. The reason, he found, was that the combined power of special interests seeking import protection had dominated the legislative process. The "history of the American tariff," he concluded, "is the story of a dubious economic policy turned into a great political success. The very tendencies that have made the legislation bad have made it politically invincible."[1]

The book became a classic, and its author rose to the pinnacle of his profession. He became president of the American Political Science Association in 1956–57, and, to this day, the E. E. Schattschneider Award is presented biennially by that organization "for the best doctoral dissertation in the field of American government."

As prophecy, Schattschneider's book was a failure. He found "no significant concentration of forces able to reverse the policy and bring about a return to a system of low tariffs or free trade." Yet before his manuscript had even reached print, Congress passed the Reciprocal Trade Agreements Act of 1934, which began a historic shift of US policy toward lower trade barriers. But if the author wrongly concluded that the tariff was "politically invincible," he was right on target in his depiction of the root

---

1. E. E. Schattschneider, *Politics, Pressures and the Tariff* (New York: Prentice-Hall, 1935), 283.

political problem that advocates of international trade would have to overcome. "Although . . . theoretically the interests supporting and opposed to tariff legislation . . . are approximately equal," he wrote, "the pressures upon Congress are extremely unbalanced. That is to say, the pressures supporting the tariff are made overwhelming by the fact that the opposition is negligible."[2]

■ ■ ■

Most people benefit from international trade, for the same general reasons that most people benefit from the division of labor within nations and within localities. By participating in a broader community within which individuals and groups sell what they can produce with the greatest (comparative) efficiency, people can secure a far greater quantity and variety of goods than each individual could possibly obtain if he had to produce every one himself. There are, of course, many instances when blocking or limiting trade can bring advantages to particular groups at the expense of the broader society. But the more these groups succeed in enforcing such restrictions, the lower the standard of living and the slower the pace of economic growth for the community as a whole.[3]

As with communities, so too with nations. Specific interests can gain from import restrictions, and economic theory even recognizes cases in which a trade barrier might leave an entire nation better off, albeit at the expense of other nations.[4] In most circumstances, however, open trade—by maximizing economic efficiency—enhances the welfare and the standard of living of the nation and of the wider world.

But the costs of international trade are concentrated. They bear particularly on those firms and workers whose home markets will be diminished by foreign competition. Trade policy must respond to their concerns as well, and some form of action constraining some imports will typically be part of that response. Free trade purists deplore this, seeing a "slippery slope" on which protection for one industry leads to protection for others. But free trade, however attractive it may be as a goal, has yet to be achieved as practical policy.

A more attainable aim has been not to avoid all import restrictions but to keep those who seek them from dominating the policy process. Through much of American history, these special interests did dominate:

---

2. Ibid., 285.

3. For development of this argument, see Mancur Olson, *The Rise and Decline of Nations: Economic Growth, Stagflation, and Social Rigidities* (New Haven, CT: Yale University Press, 1982).

4. Douglas A. Irwin, *Against the Tide: An Intellectual History of Free Trade* (Princeton, NJ: Princeton University Press, 1996).

Trade policy responded to their concerns all too well. The reason for this was highlighted in Schattschneider's book: There was a chronic political imbalance between those who benefit from trade protection and those who pay the costs.

It was an imbalance in intensity of interest and, as a result, in political organization. Producers and workers threatened by imports tend to be concentrated, organized, and ready and able to press their interests in the political arena. Those who benefit from trade are generally diffuse, and their stake in any particular trade matter is usually small.

It was also an imbalance between clear, present benefits and possible future benefits. Exporters who might profit if increased US imports allowed foreigners to buy more from us are unlikely to expend the same effort to achieve a conjectural gain as their adversaries will to preserve a current market.

Finally, it was an imbalance between those who are doing well and those who are facing trouble. Firms with expanding markets and ample profits tend to concentrate on business; their worry is that government may get in their way by placing constraints on their flexibility and their profits. It is the embattled losers in trade who go into politics to seek trade protection.

Under our Constitution, the Congress has primary responsibility for regulating "commerce with foreign nations." Congress is a decentralized institution, particularly susceptible to pressure from organized interests. So if it "does what comes naturally," if the politics of benefit-seeking and logrolling goes unimpeded, the result will be a high level of trade barriers, to the benefit of certain groups and the detriment of the nation as a whole.

For a politician who must respond to concentrated interests, a vote for lowering trade barriers is therefore, as one former official put it, an "unnatural act."[5] If he or she is to vote this way—and if Congress, more generally, is to divert or turn back the pressures for trade protection—counterweights have to be built into our policymaking system. These counterweights can be ideas, such as the view espoused by Cordell Hull, Franklin D. Roosevelt's secretary of state, that liberal trade promotes peace among nations. They can be processes: means of setting tariffs that insulate Congress from direct responsibility. They can be institutions: an executive branch agency that measures its success in terms of how well it copes with trade-restrictive pressures and thus allows international commerce to flourish.

During the years following Schattschneider's classic statement of the problem, the main story in American trade politics was the development of just such antiprotectionist counterweights, devices for diverting and

---

5. "Outline for Remarks by William R. Pearce, before the Committee on Foreign Relations" (Des Moines, Iowa, 11 December 1974), 6. Pearce was Deputy Special Representative for Trade Negotiations in 1972–73.

managing trade-restrictive pressures. Such devices, taken together, constituted what this book labels the "1934 system" of trade policymaking, a system that not only has opened up the US market and fueled our postwar prosperity, but also has served as a pillar of our global economic leadership. The fact that during this period the United States was pursuing, credibly and persistently if not always consistently, policies that aimed to reduce its own import barriers made it possible for this country to take the lead internationally and to press others to do likewise. Thus our domestic trade policymaking system was a necessary foundation for building an international regime of relatively open trade under the auspices of the General Agreement on Tariffs and Trade (GATT), negotiated in the late 1940s and implemented in the decades thereafter. This international trade-negotiating process was, in turn, useful in American domestic politics as an argument against trade restrictions.

Postwar trade liberalization did not institute "free trade" or anything close to it. Visible and invisible national barriers to imports remained widespread. But it did bring freer trade, contributing to an explosion in the volume of international commerce and an era of unprecedented global prosperity and growth.

The regime of freer trade had strong domestic support. The 1934 system benefited from the rise of international economic liberalism among the emerging government and business elite. During the early years of the New Deal, liberalism was simply one contending viewpoint on trade. But in the decades that followed it became the dominant viewpoint. As the world slid into war in the 1930s, and as the war was fought and won, a powerful consensus formed among the American internationalists who took the lead in postwar reconstruction. That consensus was, in important part, Wilsonian: A world open for commerce would be a world at peace. Hull espoused this view explicitly. So did the talented new leadership generation that came to Washington during and after World War II.

In this consensus, the Smoot-Hawley Tariff Act of 1930 played the same role for economic affairs that Munich played for military matters. Just as British Prime Minister Neville Chamberlain's sincere search for "peace in our time" had only strengthened those who made war, so too had congressional use of trade barriers to aid Depression-hit American producers backfired, postwar leaders believed. Other nations had retaliated, exports had plummeted even more than imports, and the world economic catastrophe helped to spawn both Adolf Hitler's Nazi regime in Germany and aggressive militarism in Japan. Only by building a more open world could we prevent the sort of mutually destructive, beggar-thy-neighbor competition that had produced national economic disaster and international bloodshed. This meant reducing barriers to trade, and to cross-border economic transactions in general. And in the first two postwar decades, as Judith Goldstein has written, success confirmed the liberal ideology, just as the Great Depression had discredited protectionism.[6]

Public opinion polls underscored this elite support. When the Gallup organization, in June 1953, asked "a cross-section of people listed in Who's Who in America" whether they would "favor lowering tariffs from their present level," 67 percent said yes and only 11 percent expressed opposition. There were still prominent people in Washington in the 1940s and 1950s who called themselves "protectionists," just as there were still "isolationists," but they were on the defensive, politically and ideologically.

"Free trade" was never especially popular among the mass public. When Gallup polled citizens in the 1940s and 1950s about whether they favored higher or lower tariffs, a plurality did back the latter. But when a 1953 Roper poll inquired, "Would you rather see this country import more goods from foreign countries than we do, or put more restrictions on goods imported into this country from abroad," 37 percent opted for restrictions and only 26 percent for the goods.[7] What really mattered, however, was that trade was not high on the list of public concerns. So governmental leaders had the leeway to press the policies they felt were needed.

Liberal trade policies were further buttressed by a concern that was at the top of almost everyone's list: countering the threat of communism. Military alliances with Western Europe and Japan became the prime US instrument for containing the Soviet Union and the People's Republic of China.

Both the internal stability and the external alignment of our allies depended importantly on their economic recovery and prosperity. The United States provided massive aid to facilitate this recovery, permitting recipients to buy needed capital goods in the American market. But our allies' return to self-sufficiency also depended on their ability to sell in our market. To make this possible, not only did the United States grant market access, following the general nondiscriminatory trade rules of the newly established GATT regime, but it also acquiesced in substantial de facto discrimination against itself—in the maintenance of import and exchange controls while these countries recovered, and thereafter in the formation of a common market in Western Europe.

Such one-sided concessions were relatively painless for the United States because in the years following World War II, the American economy dominated the world as never before or since. It was competitive in all major industrial sectors. It was prosperous, as the anticipated postwar

---

6. Judith Goldstein, "Ideas, Institutions, and American Trade Policy," *International Organization* 42, no. 1 (Winter 1988): especially 187–88.

7. Raymond A. Bauer, Ithiel de Sola Pool, and Lewis Anthony Dexter, *American Business and Public Policy: The Politics of Foreign Trade* (Chicago: Aldine-Atherton, 1972), 85.

depression never arrived. It was insulated, with merchandise imports totaling, prior to 1960, only about 3 percent of its gross national product. And finally, exchange rate stability avoided one source of trade risk that would become important in later years.

All of these factors—the "lesson" of Smoot-Hawley, the Cold War imperative, US economic predominance, and prosperity—contributed to one crucial underpinning of the 1934 system: the fact that trade barriers were not a major source of conflict between the Republican and Democratic parties during the postwar period.

This was emphatically not the case in earlier decades. Before 1932, Republicans had used their support of the tariff to help build the broad business backing that made them the dominant party. In the early years of the Franklin Roosevelt administration, almost all Republicans opposed trade-liberalizing legislation, while the great majority of Democrats were in favor. But by the end of World War II, the business community had become less protectionist, and partisan trade divisions were waning. In the quarter century thereafter, neither party while out of office singled out trade policy as a primary point of difference with the administration in power.

This meant there could be continuity across administrations. Presidents, regardless of party, could champion liberal trade, for both foreign and domestic policy reasons. This White House support was a key to making the system work.

Such was the broad political and policy context within which American trade policy institutions developed and evolved. This system remained largely intact through the 1960s. Over the next two decades, however, it was buffeted from two sides: by economic changes that increased protectionist pressures, and by political changes that weakened the institutions erected to combat them.

The primary political change was the opening up of American political institutions. Reform in Congress, for example, made it more democratic, more responsive to the initiatives of individual members, and less capable of resisting the demands of special interests. Prominent among these interests, as ever, were elements of business and labor seeking protection from "foreign imports."

The economic changes came in three broad forms. First was the internationalization of the US economy, which placed unprecedented import pressure on US producers. Second was the relative economic decline of the United States, real and perceived, vis-à-vis its advanced industrial counterparts, particularly Japan. Third was the rapid rise of the US trade deficit in the 1980s.

With the internationalization of the American economy, trade doubled as a share of total US output of goods. This exposed more and more firms and workers to foreign competition, increasing the number of "trade losers" to whom officials would have to respond.

American anxiety about foreign competition grew as the relative position of the United States declined. The striking success of nations like Japan sowed seeds of doubt about liberal doctrine. Here was a nation that seemed committed to a "mercantilist" trade strategy, pushing exports and discouraging imports, and doing very well indeed. Other rising East Asian newly industrialized countries—Korea and Taiwan, in particular—appeared to be following Japan's example. Might they know something the United States didn't?

In this environment, many Americans became skeptical about the liberal image of a world growing more and more open, governed increasingly by common rules of nondiscrimination in trade. What they came to see was an "unfair" world where other nations played loose with the rules and "nice guys" were likely to finish last.

Compounding these problems in the early and mid-1980s was the remarkable and unanticipated rise in the international value of the US dollar. It went up 70 percent within five years, to a level 40 percent above that at which US firms were broadly competitive, before beginning to decline in 1985. The strong dollar might be good for Americans traveling abroad, but for producers it was equivalent to a 40 percent tax on exports and a 40 percent subsidy to competing imports. Foreign goods poured in as never before, and the United States suddenly faced a trade imbalance without parallel in its modern history. Imports rose to more than 50 percent above exports, and the US trade deficit swelled beyond $100 billion and kept growing. In response, restrictions on imports increased, their legitimacy grew, and protectionist proposals proliferated. The dollar's subsequent decline brought some relief for producers fighting imports and triggered a surge in American exports. But the rapid rise and slow decline of the trade imbalance left a legacy of skepticism and frustration about the benefits of liberal trade.

These political and economic changes put an enormous strain on the 1934 trade policymaking system. It eroded. It bent. But despite the fears of many, it did not break. Chapters 3 through 8 tell the story of how the system adapted to a radically different world, and how this period—1971 through 1994—ended in triumph with the creation of the North American Free Trade Agreement (NAFTA) and the World Trade Organization (WTO). The ensuing resurgence of the US economy, moreover, reestablished global US economic primacy and brought new prosperity to Americans.

Yet US trade policy was hardly home free. Chapters 9 through 11 show how globalization weakened traditional protectionism but also raised concerns about the cross-border impacts of trade, particularly on nations' labor and environmental standards. Dispute over these issues fueled a broader backlash against globalization, and led directly to President Bill Clinton's failure to win renewal of the fast-track trade negotiating authority Congress had granted to his four predecessors. Under President

George W. Bush a new threat came to the fore—bitter political polarization between Republicans and Democrats in the US House of Representatives. This broke the longstanding pattern of bipartisan trade cooperation in the key trade committee, Ways and Means, such that the 215 to 214 vote in 2001 giving the president trade negotiating authority was the closest ever, and the most partisan since the 1930s.

Such a narrow mandate has weakened US capacity to pursue liberal trade policies at home, and undercut US policy leadership abroad. So have the record-breaking trade deficits that have ballooned in the new millennium. By 2005, the newly reelected Bush administration faced a daunting set of trade challenges: unfinished global and regional negotiations; negotiating authority up for Congressional renewal; several WTO findings against US trade law and practice requiring implementation by a skeptical Congress; continuing polarization on Capitol Hill; and a public anxious over job losses and seeing trade as a prominent reason for them.

How should Americans respond? This book will conclude with comprehensive and indeed ambitious prescriptions. But first it will examine in detail how our trade policymaking system has worked over the years, and how it has changed in response to evolving pressures and needs.

Hence this book begins its analysis by setting forth the main features of the "1934 system" for managing trade pressures as that system evolved in the decades since that year's epochal legislation. Subsequent chapters focus on changes in the primary institutions and processes that deal with the politics of trade (Congress, the executive branch, quasi-judicial procedures); changes in the broader economic and political environment; and how US policymakers concluded a particularly challenging trade policy epoch with establishment of NAFTA and the WTO. We then turn our attention to major changes in American trade politics since 1994, setting the stage for a final chapter that reflects on what all this means and what might be done about it.

2

The 1934 System:
Protection for Congress

Seventy-five years ago, the United States Congress took final action on the most famous trade law in American history. The Tariff Act of 1930, better known as "Smoot-Hawley," amended "specific tariff schedules for over twenty thousand items, almost all of them increases."[1] It established "the highest general tariff rate structure that the United States [had] ever experienced," with duties actually collected reaching, by one estimate, 60 percent of the value of dutiable imports.[2]

What followed is well known. The law quickly "occasioned," as one contemporary critic put it, "more comment, more controversy, more vituperation in the national as well as in the international sphere than any other tariff measure in history."[3] Country after country raised tariff barriers in retaliation. World trade stagnated: for the United States, imports dropped from $4.40 billion in 1929 to $1.45 billion in 1933, and

1. Robert A. Pastor, *Congress and the Politics of US Foreign Economic Policy, 1929–1976* (Berkeley: University of California Press, 1980), 77–78.

2. John M. Dobson, *Two Centuries of Tariffs: The Background and Emergence of the United States International Trade Commission* (Washington, DC: US International Trade Commission, December 1976), 34.

3. Joseph M. Jones, Jr., *Tariff Retaliation: Repercussions of the Hawley-Smoot Bill* (Philadelphia: University of Pennsylvania Press, 1934), 1.

exports plunged even more: from $5.16 billion to $1.65 billion.[4] The Great Depression—already well under way in 1930—deepened and became truly global. World War II followed less than a decade later.

Not as well remembered today is the fact that Smoot-Hawley was the last general tariff law ever enacted by the United States Congress. From the "Tariff of Abominations" denounced by Andrew Jackson and John C. Calhoun in 1828 through the McKinley Tariff of 1890 and the Fordney-McCumber Act of 1922, such comprehensive tariff bills had been prime congressional business and the level of US import barriers one of the hottest issues between the Republican and Democratic parties. The tariff, "more than any other single topic, had engrossed [congressional] energies for more than a hundred years."[5] And high rates of duty had been the rule, not the exception.

But barely four years after Smoot-Hawley, our national legislature enacted an entirely different sort of trade law. The Reciprocal Trade Agreements Act of 1934 began a movement of tariffs in the opposite—downward—direction, by authorizing the president to negotiate and implement pacts with other nations in which each agreed to cut tariffs on items of interest to the other. With this authority, the president could reduce any US tariff by up to 50 percent without further recourse to Congress. And the authority was renewed in 1937, 1940, and 1943.

Secretary of State Cordell Hull lost no time in exploiting this authority. By 1945, the United States had entered 32 such bilateral trade agreements with 27 countries, granting tariff concessions on 64 percent of all dutiable imports and reducing rates by an average of 44 percent.[6]

In the immediate postwar period, trade negotiations went multilateral. The reciprocal negotiating authority was updated in 1945 to allow further reductions of up to 50 percent from that year's rates. Under American leadership, the General Agreement on Tariffs and Trade (GATT) was negotiated. Its articles provided guidelines for national trade policies and a framework within which the United States and its major (primarily Euro-

---

4. US Department of Commerce, Bureau of the Census, *Historical Statistics of the United States: Colonial Times to 1970, Part 2* (Washington, DC: US Department of Commerce, 1975), 884. Much of this fall, of course, reflected the Depression's sharp price and output decreases. But even after adjustment for these changes, exports fell, as a share of total US goods production, by more than 20 percent between 1929 and 1933.

5. James L. Sundquist, *The Decline and Resurgence of Congress* (Washington, DC: Brookings Institution, 1981), 99.

6. John H. Jackson, Jean-Victor Louis, and Mitsuo Matsushita, *Implementing the Tokyo Round: National Constitutions and International Economic Relations* (Ann Arbor: University of Michigan Press, 1984), 141; and John W. Evans, *The Kennedy Round in American Trade Policy: The Twilight of the GATT?* (Cambridge, MA: Harvard University Press, 1971), 7.

pean) trading partners could enter a series of global negotiating "rounds" resulting in further tariff cuts.

This approach began to flag in the 1950s: Item-by-item tariff negotiations produced diminishing returns; protectionist pressures regained strength in the United States; and the European Common Market, created in 1957, posed a new challenge. Congress responded in 1962, on President John F. Kennedy's recommendation, by authorizing negotiations to cut tariffs across the board. The resulting "Kennedy Round," completed in 1967, produced further cuts in US protective duties averaging 35 percent.[7]

Smoot-Hawley remained on the books, in form still the basic US trade law. But because of negotiations authorized by subsequent Congresses, its average tariff level on dutiable imports had been reduced from 60 percent in 1931 to 10 percent in 1970 (and 5.7 percent in 1980).[8]

Total US exports did not return to their pre-Depression level until 1942. But thereafter they grew rapidly: to $10.2 billion in 1950, $20.4 billion in 1960, and $42.6 billion in 1970.[9] The parallel figures for imports were $8.9 billion in 1950, $14.7 billion in 1960, and $40 billion in 1970.

The increase in global commerce was even greater. This trade expansion was a prime contributor to a remarkable era of world prosperity. It also contributed to something the 20th century had not previously seen: decades of peace on the European continent.

How was it possible, politically, for the United States to reduce its own trade barriers and persuade the world to do likewise? As noted in the opening chapter, E. E. Schattschneider had demonstrated how politics must drive Congress to respond to producer pressures and raise levels of protection. By what political magic had "Schattschneider's law" been repealed?

The short answer is that Congress legislated itself out of the business of making product-specific trade law. There were exceptions, of course. But, as a general rule, Congress as a collective body was as assiduous in avoiding specific trade barriers after 1934 as it had been in imposing them the century before.

A new system for trade policymaking came into being. Like any ongoing set of policy processes, it was not created by any one actor at any sin-

---

7. Evans, *The Kennedy Round in American Trade Policy*, 283.

8. Dobson, *Two Centuries of Tariffs*, 34; US Department of Commerce, Bureau of the Census, *Statistical Abstract of the United States, 1982–83* (Washington, DC: US Department of Commerce, 1982), 844.

9. US Department of Commerce, *Historical Statistics of the United States*, 884, and US Department of Commerce, Bureau of the Census, *Statistical Abstract of the United States, 1984* (Washington, DC: US Department of Commerce, 1985), 831. These data differ slightly from the Commerce Department data employed later in this study in discussions of contemporary US trade flows.

gle time. It evolved, not only because of creative leadership from men like Cordell Hull, but also because it served the political interests of those senators and representatives most responsible for trade policy.[10]

Protecting Congress from Trade Pressures

Article I of the United States Constitution grants Congress sole power "to regulate commerce with foreign nations." It also provides Congress authority "to lay and collect . . . duties," and the tariff supplied about half of federal revenues as recently as 1910.[11] The Constitution grants the president no trade-specific authority whatsoever. Thus, in no sphere of government policy can the primacy of the legislative branch be clearer: Congress reigns supreme on trade, unless and until it decides otherwise.

Beginning in the mid-1930s, Congress did decide otherwise, changing the way it handled trade issues. No longer did it give priority to protecting American industry. Instead, its members would give priority to protecting themselves: from the direct, one-sided pressure from producer interests that had led them to make bad trade law. They would channel that pressure elsewhere, pushing product-specific trade decisions out of the committees of Congress and off the House and Senate floors to other governmental institutions.[12]

---

10. In recent years, there has been a lively scholarly debate about the relative importance of these process changes in the redirection of US trade policy. Michael J. Hiscox argues that although "the RTAA [plausibly] helped to produce more liberal policy outcomes," its enduring success was due less to the institutional changes than to two *"exogenous* changes in [societal] trade policy coalitions that altered the preferences of Republicans and Democrats enough to cement the new system in place" (*italics* in original). "The Magic Bullet? The RTAA, Institutional Reform, and Trade Liberalization," *International Organization* 53: 4, Autumn 1999, 670, 690. Karen E. Schnietz, by contrast, sees the RTAA as "arguably the most important piece of trade legislation of this century" but challenges standard explanations of *why* it was enacted (e.g., since few of them changed their votes between 1930 and 1934, members of Congress did not "learn" from Smoot-Hawley that congressional logrolling had disastrous economic consequences). "The Institutional Foundation of U.S. Trade Policy: Revisiting Explanations for the 1934 Reciprocal Trade Agreements Act," *Journal of Policy History* 12, vol. 4 (2000): 417–20.

While differing with this author on a number of matters, Sharyn O'Halloran gives central place to the specifics of congressional delegation in her "new institutionalist" analysis. See her *Politics, Process, and American Trade Policy* (Ann Arbor: University of Michigan Press, 1994), especially chapter 5.

11. Dobson, *Two Centuries of Tariffs*, 31. In fiscal year 1984, by contrast, customs duties constituted just 1.7 percent of total federal budget receipts.

12. Implicit in the pages that follow is an assumption about congressional motivation at variance with much of the "new institutionalist" literature on Congress, which assumes that members' policy behavior aims overridingly at influencing policy outcomes. Elsewhere I seek to make this explicit, arguing that this is "not a necessary means to their broader goal:

The instruments for accomplishing this goal developed and changed with time, and political protection was never, of course, the sole congressional motive. What moved some legislators was a conviction that trade regulation had become too complicated and too detailed for Congress to be handling its specifics. For Secretary of State Cordell Hull and some of his fellow Democrats—historically the lower-tariff political party—the aim was to reduce trade barriers in any way that was practical. As a Tennessee congressman during World War I, the secretary himself had become convinced that "unhampered trade dovetailed with peace; high tariffs, trade barriers, and unfair economic competition, with war."[13] And without the combination of his determination and an economic crisis that produced lopsided Democratic majorities in Congress, the historic shift of 1934 would not have come about—at least not then. Twenty years later, a landmark trade policymaking study could report that protectionists "shared in the consensus that somebody outside Congress should set tariff rates or impose and remove quotas."[14] But no such bipartisan consensus existed in the 1930s.

The shift did not mean that legislators abdicated all responsibility for trade. They continued to set the guidelines, regulating how much tariff levels could be changed, by what procedures, and with what exceptions. Individual members also remained free to make ample protectionist noise, and to declaim loudly on behalf of producer interests that were strong in their states or districts. In fact, they could do so more freely than ever, secure in the knowledge that most actual decisions would be made elsewhere.

The year 1934 was not the first in which Congress delegated specific trade authority to the president. The US Tariff Commission had been created in 1916 as a nonpartisan, fact-finding agency. And the "flexible tariff" position of the Fordney-McCumber Act of 1922 empowered the president, at the commission's recommendation, to raise or lower any tariff by up to 50 percent in order to equalize the production costs of domestic firms and foreign competitors. (If fully applied, which it never was, this provision would have eliminated "comparative advantage," the primary

---

to maintain and enhance political standing at home and in Washington." See Destler, "Constituencies, Congress, and US Trade Policy," in Alan V. Deardorff and Robert M. Stern, *Constituent Interests and U.S. Trade Policies* (Ann Arbor: University of Michigan Press, 1998), 93–108.

13. *The Memoirs of Cordell Hull*, vol. 1 (New York: Macmillan, 1948), 81. Karen E. Schnietz argues that, more generally, "Democrats hoped the RTAA would institutionalize low tariffs" through two features highlighted here (delegation to the president, reciprocal tariff negotiations) and one not explicitly addressed in this book: removal of the prior requirement that the Senate ratify trade agreements by a two-thirds vote. "The Institutional Foundation of U.S. Trade Policy," 418, 429–38.

14. Raymond A. Bauer, Ithiel de Sola Pool, and Lewis Anthony Dexter, *American Business and Public Policy: The Politics of Foreign Trade* (Chicago: Aldine-Atherton, 1972), 39.

economic reason for trade since it is such differences in production costs that make trade profitable!)[15]

But as long as Congress was expected to pass comprehensive bills adjusting tariffs every few years, such measures could never keep protectionist wolves from the Capitol's doors. For those affected knew that Congress would shortly be acting on their specific products, in a process that gave priority to their interests. This could only encourage them to press all the harder, for greater and greater protection. As Hull put the matter,

> it would have been folly to go to Congress and ask that the Smoot-Hawley Act be repealed or its rates reduced by Congress. This [approach had], with the exception of the Underwood Act in 1913 . . . always resulted in higher tariffs because the special interests enriched by high tariffs went to their respective Congressmen and insisted on higher rates.[16]

What was required was a system that would make the buck stop somewhere else. In 1934, the legislative and executive branches began to construct such a system.

The central need was obvious: to delegate specific tariff setting. But meeting this need required answers to two basic questions. First, how could Congress rationalize giving up such a major power? And second, would not whoever was delegated this power be subject to the same unbalanced set of pressures, with similar policy results?

The "Bargaining Tariff"

The need for a rationale for the delegation of congressional power was answered by linking tariff setting to international negotiations, a clear presidential prerogative. To borrow the phrase of Joseph M. Jones, Jr., a strong advocate of this approach, the United States moved decisively from an inflexible, statutory tariff to a "bargaining tariff."[17] The president could reduce rates by up to 50 percent, but only after negotiating bilateral agreements in which the United States "got" as well as "gave."[18]

Another way that Congress rationalized the delegation of authority was by making it temporary. As Dean Acheson noted many years later,

---

15. Dobson, *Two Centuries of Tariffs*, 87–95.

16. *Memoirs of Cordell Hull*, vol. 1, 358.

17. Joseph M. Jones, Jr., *Tariff Retaliation*, 303.

18. The delegation of tariff-setting authority to encourage "reciprocal" concessions was not unprecedented. The barrier-raising McKinley Tariff Act of 1890 gave the president authority to adjust tariffs on sugar and other specified commodities according to the "reciprocity" shown American exports by particular Latin American countries. See David A. Lake, *Power, Protection, and Free Trade: International Sources of U.S. Commercial Strategy, 1887–1939* (Ithaca, NY: Cornell University Press, 1989), especially 100–02.

unlike almost all of the New Deal economic legislation once regarded as radical, the executive power to negotiate trade agreements has not been permanently incorporated in American legislation, but only extended from time to time for short periods with alternating contractions and expansions of scope.[19]

By its answer to the first question—the rationale for delegating power— the Reciprocal Trade Agreements Act of 1934 also addressed the second: how to avoid unbalanced trade pressures. In the process of trade negotiation, "getting" and "giving" were defined in terms of producers, not consumers. But the "bargaining tariff" shifted the balance of trade politics by engaging the interests of export producers, since tariff reductions could now be defended as a means of winning new markets for American products overseas. Export interests had long been an influence on US trade policy, but usually they were no match for producers threatened by imports. The bargaining tariff strengthened the exporters' stakes and their policy influence, creating something of a political counterweight on the liberal trade side.

Thus, partly as a genuine objective (we did want other countries to lower their trade barriers) and partly as a political device, the "bargaining tariff" was an essential ingredient in the emerging American trade policy-making system. And since, from the 1920s onward, the United States regularly extended bilaterally negotiated tariff cuts to its other trading partners (under the unconditional "most favored nation" [MFN] principle), country-by-country deals were an effective means of reducing trade barriers across the board.

In 1934, legislators could grant the new authority tentatively, experimentally. Hull had wanted it to be unbounded in time, but Congress limited it to an initial three years (however, the agreements negotiated during this period would remain in effect indefinitely). Hull also would have liked to bargain multilaterally, but he settled for "the next best method," bilateral negotiations, because "it was manifest that public opinion in no country, especially our own, would at that time support a worthwhile multilateral undertaking."[20] Yet in one crucial respect the executive authority to negotiate trade agreements was unconstrained by the traditional limits: Congress did not insist on approving the specific agreements that were negotiated.

In subsequent decades, presidents would employ tariff-negotiating authority more ambitiously—to negotiate multilaterally (after World War II) or to bargain on general tariff levels rather than item by item (the Kennedy Round). Always there were limits in time and in the range of negotiation. Nevertheless, Congress continued to respond to new trade policy demands by shifting the basic pressure and responsibility onto the president.

---

19. Dean Acheson, *Present at the Creation: My Years at the State Department* (New York: W. W. Norton, 1969), 10.

20. *Memoirs of Cordell Hull*, vol. 1, 356.

The "Bicycle Theory" and "Export Politics"

One political effect of trade negotiations was to divert some trade policy-making attention from the problems of the American market to the benefits of opening up markets overseas. In fact, the very existence of ongoing negotiations proved a potent rationale for deferring protectionist claims. It gave negotiators (and their congressional allies) a strong situational argument: to impose or tighten an import barrier now, they could assert, would undercut talks aimed at broader American trade advantages. Conversely, the unavailability of this argument in periods between major trade negotiations strengthened the hands of those seeking protection. Trade specialists came to label this phenomenon the "bicycle theory": The trade system needed to move forward (liberalize further) or else it would "fall down" into new import restrictions. It could not stand still.

Even in the absence of major negotiations, trade officials sought ways to shift from "import politics" to "export politics." From the late 1960s to the mid-1990s, for example, every US administration has had to cope with severe pressures generated by rising sales from Japan. Although interest group pressures were typically tilted toward curbing imports, officials have regularly, with congressional cooperation, shifted the focus to exports, to opening up the Japanese market. Responding to arguments that other countries' trading practices were unfair, US trade negotiators did not have to defend those practices or point to the beams in our own eyes. Instead, they could demonstrate their toughness by demanding market-opening concessions from our trading partners.

But to delegate power over specific trade barriers with reasonable confidence, Congress needed more than an international negotiating process. It also needed two sorts of executive agents: a *broker* who would be responsive to legislators' concerns domestically even while pushing for bargains internationally, and *regulators* who would technocratically apply statutory import relief rules to a set of exceptional cases.

The Executive Broker

In preparing Smoot-Hawley, the House Ways and Means Committee "accumulated 11,000 pages of testimony and briefs in forty-three days and five nights," but no one came to speak for the executive branch.[21] At hearings for the 1934 act, by contrast, seven of 17 witnesses represented the Roosevelt administration.[22] Congress would not have adopted such a law without executive branch leadership. And if the new American trade policymaking system were to work, Congress needed a focal point for trade

---

21. E. E. Schattschneider, *Politics, Pressures and the Tariff* (New York: Prentice-Hall, 1935), 36.

22. Pastor, *Congress and the Politics of US Foreign Economic Policy*, 88.

policy management within the executive branch, an official who could balance foreign and domestic concerns.

For the first decade, the position of trusted executive agent was admirably occupied by a man from Capitol Hill, Secretary of State Cordell Hull. While he tilted trade policy in the market-expanding direction as much as was politically feasible, he retained his sensitivity to congressional concerns. He moved immediately and aggressively to exploit the new bargaining authority. At the same time, he never forgot that the hand that had granted this authority could also take it away.

Hull resigned in 1944, leaving a gap on the trade scene that would not be filled in any durable way for nearly 20 years. In the immediate postwar years it did not really matter. Europe and Japan were devastated. Triumphant and economically dominant, the United States was in a position to sell abroad far more than the world could sell us in return. Thus, it was logical—and politically feasible—for trade policy to be subordinate to the broader American foreign policy of constructing a free world coalition founded on a liberal world economic order. And it was logical for the State Department, staffed by such talents as Under Secretary Will L. Clayton, to continue to play the lead trade-negotiating role.

But in the 1950s, as resurgent international competition once again began to threaten American industries, attacks on State stewardship increased. The department was charged with favoring foreign interests over American interests, with bargaining away US commercial advantages in the interest of good political relations or other diplomatic goals. For a time, State managed to keep the primary negotiating responsibility, and it could play this role aggressively when its senior economic official was someone like Under Secretary C. Douglas Dillon. However, in 1953, President Dwight D. Eisenhower found it necessary to join Congress in setting up a commission, chaired by Clarence B. Randall, to develop recommendations for his overall trade policy. Randall was then brought into the White House as a special trade adviser to implement the commission's report. And the Kennedy administration developed its major trade expansion program in the White House, under a temporary staff headed by Howard C. Petersen.

So when, to meet the challenge of the new European Economic Community (EEC), that administration went to Congress seeking broad new authority to reduce tariff rates across the board (not item by item), it was not surprising that House Ways and Means Chairman Wilbur D. Mills (D-AR) raised the question of whether State could be trusted with this new authority. Should it not be given instead to a negotiator who would be responsive at least equally to domestic clients? No existing agency was a good candidate. The Commerce Department was, in Mills' view, incompetent. Moreover, Mills and another well-placed critic of State, Senate Finance Committee Chairman Harry F. Byrd, Sr. (D-VA), thought Commerce insufficiently responsive to agricultural interests. So perhaps there should be a new presidential negotiator who could balance domestic and foreign concerns.

Mills proposed, therefore, that the president designate a special representative for trade negotiations (STR). An important figure in developing and brokering this idea was Myer N. Rashish, a Mills aide in the late 1950s, who was serving as Petersen's White House deputy in preparing the Trade Expansion Act. Rashish suggested that the Petersen office itself was an appropriate model. He believed that conflicting bureaucratic interests made it impossible for the administration to initiate such a reorganization proposal; however, if Mills proposed it, the president would consider reorganization an acceptable price to pay for the broad new negotiating authority he was seeking. And Kennedy did accept it, but reluctantly; like most presidents, he resisted efforts to establish special-purpose offices in "his" Executive Office.[23]

Organizationally, the STR was an anomaly. Though it was housed in the Executive Office of the President, few of its heads had close personal contact with the chief executive (Robert S. Strauss was the prime exception). For presidents were politicians who, like members of Congress, wanted to limit their direct responsibility for decisions that went against important trade constituencies. Neither was trade negotiating the normal type of White House activity. In fact, it was the sort of day-to-day operating function usually housed in a cabinet department. But no appropriate department existed.

The White House location offered flexibility, balance, and (sometimes) power. During the Kennedy Round, STR Christian A. Herter and his deputies, W. Michael Blumenthal and William M. Roth, enhanced their leverage by initiating close working relationships with State—which then retained authority for most trade negotiations outside the Kennedy Round—and with the international economic component of the National Security Council staff. (In the early 1970s, when influence in such matters shifted to the economic side of the White House, STR William D. Eberle and his deputies William R. Pearce and Harald B. Malmgren made their

---

23. Congress not only created its own agent in 1962; it protected and strengthened the special representative a decade later. When the Nixon administration proposed to place the STR under its Council on International Economic Policy (CIEP), Ways and Means responded by voting to make the office of the STR (not just the representative) statutory, in an amendment to what became the Trade Act of 1974. By the time the Senate finished its work, the office had been placed formally in the Executive Office of the President, and, on the proposal of Finance Committee Chairman Russell B. Long (D-LA), its head was given cabinet rank. Long underscored legislators' sense that they owned a piece of this White House trade operation when he suggested, during the confirmation hearings of Jimmy Carter's STR, Robert S. Strauss, that "it might be a good idea for us to ask" the secretaries of state and treasury to meet with his committee "so that there can be no misunderstanding" about which official was to have trade primacy (US Congress, Senate Committee on Finance, *Hearing on Nominations*, 95th Congress, 1st session, 23 March 1977, 4).

presidential connection through George P. Shultz, secretary of the treasury and "economic czar" of the Nixon administration.) But whatever the specific relationships of the STR, the White House location—combined with special status and separation from the White House political staff—offered him flexibility in working with legislators across as well as along party lines, drawing in some interests to balance others, and keeping the trade policy game as open as possible.

The office of the STR allowed executive branch trade officials to do what Hull had done three decades before: employ their leeway to tilt trade policy in the liberal, market-expanding direction. Sensitive to the political winds, they could lean at least moderately against them, recognizing that congressmen who bucked interest group demands to them did not always require their full satisfaction. The STR-led executive branch certainly advocated US interests in international negotiations—it had to do so to retain credibility at home. But the role of such negotiations in US trade politics was to keep the game open, to limit protection, and to respond to the trade problems of specific industries with market-expanding solutions.

Domestically, American trade policymakers were noninterventionist. Unlike their counterparts in Japan's Ministry of International Trade and Industry (MITI), for example, they did not aspire to nurture those industries at home that promised future competitiveness abroad. But when it came to international trade barriers, they were definitely not policy neutral. They wanted to limit such barriers insofar as was possible. This made them trade policy activists, for when they feared being trapped by one-sided pressure for protection, they would look for countervailing interests and encourage them to weigh in on the other side. This approach created frequent tension with legislators championing particular industries. But most congressional trade leaders, most of the time, sympathized with the broad objective of liberal trade and, free of direct responsibility themselves, often connived with their executive counterparts to steer the political game in the direction of trade expansion.

"The Rules"

As legislators worked with executive branch leaders to construct a system to protect themselves from trade pressures, they also employed a different sort of administrative institution, one modeled on quasi-judicial regulatory procedures. For there remained broad agreement that, under certain exceptional circumstances, American industries ought to have recourse to trade protection. Unless "objective" procedures could be devised to provide such protection, these industries would demand specific statutory action. Thus, US law and practice maintained a set of "trade remedies" designed to offer recourse to interests seriously injured by imports and to those up against what were considered "unfair" foreign practices.

Some major legal trade remedies originated well before the Reciprocal Trade Agreements Act of 1934. A law dating from 1897 required the secretary of the treasury to impose a special, offsetting duty if he found that foreign governments were subsidizing exports with a "bounty or grant." The Anti-Dumping Act of 1921 called for similar measures if foreign sellers were found to be unloading goods in our market at prices below their home market price. (After World War II, GATT Article VI authorized and regulated national antidumping and countervailing duty [CVD] measures.)

There remained the problem of industries injured by import competition that they did not, or could not, claim to be "unfair." If, for example, a US tariff reduction led to an unexpectedly large surge in particular imports, should not competing domestic producers have the right to seek at least temporary trade relief? Congressional trade specialists generally thought they should; Congress was worried about the uncertainty inherent in the international negotiations it had authorized, and wanted some form of insurance for domestic interests. So in the 1943 agreement with Mexico, the United States, drawing on pre-1934 precedents, included an "escape clause" allowing an affected industry to appeal for temporary import relief if it could prove injury from the results of US trade concessions. This approach was incorporated in Article XIX of the GATT.[24]

Seeking to avoid statutory constraint, State officials proposed to include such a clause in all future US trade agreements, and President Harry S. Truman issued an executive order in 1947 setting forth procedures by which injured firms could seek relief. This deferred statutory action for a while, but by 1951 Congress had found this insufficient, so legislators incorporated a general "escape clause" provision in an act extending presidential trade-negotiating authority.

By making protection the "exceptional" recourse in the "normal" process of trade-barrier reduction, the escape clause kept the quasi-judicial form of the old flexible tariff but turned the substance on its head. Protection-minded legislators sought to counter this with so-called "peril point" requirements that were incorporated in the 1948 law and intermittently thereafter. These required the Tariff Commission to estimate the point beyond which tariffs could not be reduced without "peril" to specific industries; their aim was to pressure the executive not to negotiate rates below that level.

If regularly followed, the peril point principle would have made protection the norm and trade liberalization the exception. And in fact, with

---

24. For background on US and GATT law, together with case examples, see John H. Jackson, *Legal Problems of International Economic Relations: Cases, Materials and Text, American Casebook Series* (St. Paul: West Publishing Co., 1977), 617–64.

this and other devices, Congress in the 1950s slowed the momentum of trade liberalization to a crawl: by grudging, sometimes single-year extensions of presidential negotiating authority; by escape clause criteria that made it fairly easy for industries to qualify for relief; by a 1958 provision allowing Congress, with a two-thirds vote in both houses, to compel the president to implement a Tariff Commission escape clause recommendation; and by limiting the range of future tariff reduction. In the "Dillon Round" negotiation of 1960, for example, authority for tariff cuts was limited to 20 percent. In fact, only a 10 percent reduction was achieved.

The Trade Expansion Act of 1962 brought major revision and codification to the escape clause. An interest seeking relief had to demonstrate serious injury, the major cause of which was an increase in imports due to US tariff concessions. If the Tariff Commission found that a particular interest met this rather tough test, the president had a choice whether or not to accept the commission's recommendations for tariff or quota relief. If he did not, Congress could override his negative decision by a majority vote in both houses. But while the administration had to swallow this "legislative veto" provision, it was able to beat back a Senate floor amendment adding a "peril point" requirement. (And in fact the veto was never exercised.)

During congressional debate, President Kennedy illustrated the political utility of the escape clause by implementing a Tariff Commission recommendation to increase tariffs on Belgian carpets and sheet glass. When the European Community retaliated, Kennedy stuck to his decision, adding that if his bill were already law, he "could have then offered an alternate package [of compensating tariff reductions] which . . . would have prevented retaliation."[25] He was thus able simultaneously to demonstrate his readiness to help injured industries and to argue that trade-liberalizing legislation offered a better way to do so.

The 1962 act also added an innovative approach to injury from imports—that of "trade adjustment assistance" (TAA). The idea was originally suggested, it appears, in a Council on Foreign Relations planning paper prepared during World War II, and it was given broad public exposure when proposed to Eisenhower's Randall Commission by David J. McDonald of the United Steelworkers union in 1953. The TAA idea offered an alternative, or a supplement, to tariff relief. Workers or firms hurt by imports could apply for government financial, technical, and retraining assistance—including relocation allowances—that would help the firms to become more competitive and the workers to move to other lines of endeavor. The political aim was to weaken support for trade restrictions by offering a constructive alternative to those hurt by imports.

The Randall Commission had rejected the idea, by a 16 to 1 vote. But it was picked up by several senators in the 1950s, including one John F. Kennedy. When he became president, Kennedy favored its adoption on

---

25. Pastor, *Congress and the Politics of US Foreign Economic Policy*, 114.

both substantive and political grounds, since it was something to offer AFL-CIO leaders to help secure labor support of his Trade Expansion Act. TAA was, moreover, consistent with his administration's emphasis on worker retraining as a response to unemployment.

By the 1960s, therefore, a number of administrative remedies were available to companies and workers injured by increased import competition. Substantively, their goal was equity—an established set of procedures, available to all, offering insurance against damage from trade liberalization or offsets for trade-distorting foreign practices like subsidies. Politically, the administrative remedies were another means by which Congress could divert trade pressures elsewhere. Legislators could say to those seeking statutory remedies, "Have you looked into the escape clause?" or "It sounds like a dumping case to me—can I make an appointment for you at Treasury so you can learn the procedure for relief on that?" Rather than trying to arbitrate the many trade claims, legislators could point to "the rules" under which firms and workers were entitled to relief. And officials of the executive branch could do likewise.

But in practice, the administrative remedies could not satisfy the largest trade-impacted industries. These industries wanted greater assurance of relief, and their political power gave them reason to believe they could do better by applying direct pressure at both ends of Pennsylvania Avenue.

Deals for "Special Cases"

International negotiations brought executive branch officials and export interests more effectively into trade politics; remedy procedures offered the injured a recourse other than going to Congress for new legislation. There remained the "special cases": those large, import-impacted interests that saw in open trade more threat than promise, and that were powerful enough not to settle for such relief as the regular rules might afford. The trade policymaking system also needed means to cope with them, or they might join together in a protectionist coalition and overthrow the liberal order. And even if that were beyond their immediate reach, they could certainly do much to impede an administration's trade-expanding initiatives.

In the postwar period, the most important "special case" was textiles (including apparel), followed by certain agricultural products[26] and steel. Oil

---

26. Agricultural interests sometimes won specific statutory protection for products like meat and sugar through legislation that moved through the House and Senate agriculture committees (which never fully joined in the tradition of congressional self-denial on trade). At other times they won import relief through executive action under legal authorities like Section 22 of the Agricultural Adjustment Act of 1933, which authorized the president, on the recommendation of the Tariff Commission and the secretary of agriculture, to impose quotas or fees to the extent that imports were interfering with a domestic commodity program designed to buttress prices and limit production.

imports were a prime issue until a 1955 statutory compromise authorized the president to restrict imports in cases in which they threatened to impair national security, and President Eisenhower imposed oil import quotas four years later. The auto industry remained committed to open trade until the late 1970s. But the textile-apparel coalition, with its 2.5 million workers and firms located in every state of the union, had sufficient concern about trade and sufficient political power to threaten the general trade policy-making system unless its specific interests were accommodated.

For the first nine postwar years, the textile industry was relatively inactive. It shared the benefits of the artificial economic dominance the war had provided the United States. So confident were its leaders that in 1946, they endorsed and cooperated in a mission to Japan—a fierce prewar trade competitor—to aid in reconstructing that country's textile industry during the American occupation. But in 1955, suffering a depressed market at home and resurgent sales from across the Pacific, and seeing in the debate over reciprocal trade renewal an opportunity to make the industry's weight felt,

> [t]extiles entered the legislative battle in full force. Letters poured in on the congressmen from the textile districts. The Georgia and Alabama delegations, long-time mainstays of Southern free-trade sentiment, went over to the protectionist side.[27]

At that time, US cotton textile exports exceeded imports, and the latter were less than 2 percent of domestic production. But if the industry's substantive case for relief was a bit overstated, its power was taken very seriously. In the House of Representatives, it took an enormous personal effort by House Speaker Sam Rayburn (D-TX) to beat back efforts to open up the trade authority bill of 1955 to protectionist amendments. A year later, a proposal for rigid textile quotas failed by just two votes in the Senate. The Eisenhower administration got the message, and Japan was pressured to limit its cotton textile exports. When the US textile industry found this "voluntary" Japanese restraint insufficient, Congress added Section 204 to the Agricultural Act of 1956, authorizing the president to negotiate bilateral export limitation agreements with foreign governments on "textiles or textile products." The Eisenhower administration moved promptly to exercise this authority.[28]

For a comprehensive survey of "special protection," see Gary Clyde Hufbauer, Diane T. Berliner, and Kimberly Ann Elliott, *Trade Protection in the United States: 31 Case Studies* (Washington, DC: Institute for International Economics, 1986).

27. Bauer, Pool, and Dexter, *American Business and Public Policy*, 60.

28. For an extended treatment of textile policymaking, especially vis-à-vis Japan, see I. M. Destler, Haruhiro Fukui, and Hideo Sato, *The Textile Wrangle: Conflict in Japanese-American Relations, 1969–1971* (Ithaca, NY: Cornell University Press, 1979).

What was clear to President Eisenhower was clearer still to President Kennedy. As senator from a declining textile state, he knew both the industry's power and its interests. As presidential candidate, he had promised action to control textile imports from Hong Kong and elsewhere, which—now that Japanese sales were limited—were growing in volume. As president, he wanted to deliver on this promise. He recognized also that unless this key industry was appeased, Congress was unlikely to approve general trade-expanding legislation.

The result was a special multilateral deal for the industry, known officially as the Long-Term Arrangement Regarding International Trade in Cotton Textiles (LTA). This pact was completed in 1962 under GATT auspices, although it constituted a massive exception to normal GATT rules. The LTA set guidelines within which importing nations could negotiate detailed, product-by-product quota agreements with exporters. And once negotiations for the LTA were well under way, the American Cotton Manufacturers Institute returned Kennedy's favor by endorsing his trade legislation: "We believe that the authority to deal with foreign nations proposed by the President will be wisely exercised and should be granted."[29]

This pattern was repeated eight years later, albeit at considerably greater international cost. At industry insistence, the Nixon administration embarked on a fractious, three-year negotiation with Japan, eventually threatening use of the "Trading with the Enemy Act" to force that nation to broaden its export restraints to include textiles of wool and man-made fibers. (Then, in 1973, this too was multilateralized in the Multi-Fiber Arrangement [MFA], which succeeded the LTA. Not entirely by coincidence, Congress completed action on President Nixon's trade expansion proposal the following year.)

And in the late 1960s, with the steel industry feeling growing import pressure, the State Department shepherded an arrangement among Japanese, European, and American producers to limit the volume sales of the major foreign exporters to the US market. This arrangement was abandoned in the 1970s, in part because of uncertainty about its legality under American antitrust law, and in part because dollar devaluation (plus an economic boom) brought a temporary easing of US steel-trade problems.[30]

These special deals circumvented both national and international rules. Typically, they involved pressuring foreign governments—primarily Japan in the 1950s and 1960s—to enforce "voluntary" export restraints (VERs). This device got around the domestic rules for proving injury and

---

29. Bauer, Pool, and Dexter, *American Business and Public Policy*, 79.

30. But in 1977, the Carter administration would respond to renewed pressure from the steel industry with a new form of an ad hoc import limit, the "trigger price mechanism" (TPM). See Hideo Sato and Michael Hodin, "The U.S.-Japanese Steel Issue of 1977," in I. M. Destler and Hideo Sato, eds., *Coping with U.S.-Japanese Economic Conflicts* (Lexington, MA: D. C. Heath, 1982), 56–70.

limiting the duration of protection. For the United States, VERs had the international benefit that, unlike measures taken directly against imports, they were not subject to the GATT proviso allowing other nations to impose equivalent trade restrictions unless the United States offered "compensation" in the form of offsetting tariff reductions. In both of these ways, they undercut the 1934 policymaking system, for they showed how easily its rules could be avoided by those with power to do so.

Yet at the same time, special deals reinforced the protection for Congress that was the system's political foundation. They kept industry-specific protection out of US trade statutes. They gave executive officials significant leeway to cooperate with exporting countries in working out the form that protection would take, thus limiting the risk of retaliation. They let congressmen play the role they preferred: that of making noise, lobbying the executive branch for action, but refraining from final action themselves. (And for foreign firms they had one major benefit that tariffs or US import quotas did not have—they allowed them to raise their prices, thus pocketing the "scarcity rents" available because they were selling fewer goods than the market wished to buy. This was the real "compensation" provided, and it was one that directly benefited the industry hurt by the restraint.)[31]

Strong Congressional Committees

Last but not least, Congress needed internal safeguards. For the various means of diverting trade pressures shared one fundamental weakness: Congress could always override them by enacting a trade-restrictive statute, since it did not, and could not, yield that fundamental power to make any law "to regulate commerce with foreign nations." Thus, since the political interests of an individual senator or representative continued to be tilted in the direction of supporting the claimant for protection, there was always the danger that, if forced to an up-or-down vote, legislators would impose statutory trade restrictions.

There was therefore a need for internal procedures and institutions that would keep this from happening. Insofar as possible, product-specific bills and amendments had to be kept off the House and Senate floors.

This required strong committees. Fortunately, trade policy had long been the province of two of the most powerful congressional panels: Finance in the Senate and Ways and Means in the House. They were the tax

---

31. C. Fred Bergsten and his colleagues have argued for replacing VERs with tariffs or auction quotas that would allow the United States to capture these rents. See C. Fred Bergsten, Kimberly Ann Elliott, Jeffrey J. Schott, and Wendy E. Takacs, *Auction Quotas and United States Trade Policy*, Policy Analyses in International Economics 19 (Washington, DC: Institute for International Economics, September 1987). VERs were outlawed in the Uruguay Round Agreement of 1994.

committees, and their jurisdiction over foreign commerce derived originally from the tariff's revenue function. From the 1930s onward, their power was enhanced by jurisdiction over Social Security. As tax committees, they had broad authority, close links to domestic interests, and the reputation for being hard-nosed, realistic, and slightly conservative. Unlike Foreign Relations in the Senate or Foreign Affairs in the House, they were unlikely to be disparaged by their colleagues as soft on foreign interests. Because they had other major legislative fish to fry, they were content with a system that delegated trade details, and satisfied with considering major trade authority bills just once every few years.

Particularly pivotal was the House Ways and Means Committee. In comparison with the House of Representatives, the Senate was smaller, more informal, and more personality dependent in its mode of operation. It had always allowed individual members more sway—more opportunity to delay action with unlimited debate, more leeway to propose amendments to legislation being considered on the floor. Once an influx of liberal activists broke down the informal dominance of southern seniors in the 1960s, the Senate became a very open place, where leaders reigned but did not rule. Senate rules did not require an amendment to be "germane" to the pending legislation. Therefore if a trade-restrictive amendment was suddenly sprung on the floor for attachment to a semirelated bill, the Finance Committee chairman often lacked the ability to block it.

But the Ways and Means chairman could. Because of its size, the House was inevitably more dependent than the Senate on formal institutions, rules, and procedures. And after the power of the House leadership had been limited by the revolt against Speaker Joseph G. Cannon (D-IL) in 1910, committee chairmen—chosen by seniority—rose to dominance. In fact, "the zenith of committee government occurred between the years 1937 and 1971,"[32] precisely the period when the 1934 system flourished. A strong and skillful Ways and Means leader could virtually ensure that the full House considered only those trade proposals that his committee wished to place before it. He could also place a strong personal imprint on whatever his committee recommended.

The most artful practitioner of this power was Wilbur D. Mills (D-AR), Ways and Means chairman from 1958 to 1974. He kept his committee relatively small by House standards—25 members—and resisted the formation of subcommittees. Working closely with these members, he dominated his panel not by arbitrary action—although he valued and used the chair's prerogative—but by his superior grasp of both substance and politics. He was always listening: to committee members, to lobbyists, to administration leaders, and to staff experts. In his committee, he knew how

---

32. Roger H. Davidson, "Subcommittee Government: New Channels for Policy Making," in Thomas E. Mann and Norman J. Ornstein, eds., *The New Congress* (Washington, DC: American Enterprise Institute, 1981), 103.

to put together bills that had consensus support. And he was determined not to take the slightest risk that a Ways and Means bill would lose on the House floor, or that it would be subject to an amendment the committee could not abide.

On trade, this meant playing the game of protecting his colleagues: blocking floor votes, diverting pressure elsewhere, pushing an administration to work out special deals when the heat got too strong. And while Mills was a free trader by personal conviction, he was clever enough not to seem insensitive to import-affected petitioners. He would listen to them sympathetically and make sure that they had access to the proper procedures. Simultaneously, he would maneuver to avert statutory protection of any sort for specific products.

A classic example of how Mills made the system work was his response to mounting textile-industry pressure in the years following the Kennedy Round. In 1968, a junior South Carolina senator, Ernest F. Hollings (D), proposed as an amendment to the Johnson administration's pending tax bill that statutory quotas be established for textile and apparel products. The full Senate approved the amendment, and the vote was not close. Mills, in alliance with the White House and the State Department, refused to accept it when the bill went to the Senate-House conference committee; he insisted, as a matter of constitutional propriety, that such provisions should originate in the House (trade was tariffs; tariffs were revenue measures). Senate conferees receded, as they did normally in such cases in those days, and so the quota proposal died without House members ever having to vote on it.

But Mills did not rest here. Realizing that the rise of then uncontrolled imports of man-made fiber textiles meant that the industry was very likely to win some form of protection eventually, Mills began to advocate it—in the nonstatutory form of restraints negotiated with Japan and the other major East Asian suppliers. And while his goal was to prevent direct congressional action, he buttressed the Nixon administration's bargaining position by introducing his own quota bill. If "voluntary" restraints were not achieved, Mills declared repeatedly, Congress would be forced to act.

Mills was playing a game familiar to trade practitioners: hyping the "protectionist threat" from Congress so as to create pressure on foreign governments to come to terms and to render legislative action unnecessary. The administration, in turn, was supposed to talk about the threat of legislation but stop short of supporting it. However, President Richard M. Nixon broke this unwritten rule in June 1970 when, frustrated by Japan's failure to carry through on high-level promises to come to terms, he "reluctantly" endorsed the statutory quota bill Mills had introduced.

The chairman was now in a bind. He had no choice but to move forward with a "Mills bill" that he did not really want enacted. But it somehow took until late November for the House to complete floor action, and although supporters rushed the bill to the Senate floor in December, they were unable to force a vote. Finance Chairman Russell Long played his part by attaching to the bill a controversial Social Security–welfare reform package, so that it was subject to twin filibusters: by liberal traders and by welfare reform critics. The bill died when the 91st Congress adjourned.

Then, in early 1971, in order to avoid having to travel the same road again, Mills encouraged the Japanese textile industry to develop its own unilateral plan to restrain exports. It did so, and though the limits were far less stringent than those the administration had been seeking, Mills endorsed the plan immediately upon its announcement.

In the end, this Japanese industry plan did not resolve the US-Japan textile dispute. But it did achieve both of Mills' objectives: removing the threat of legislation and providing some relief to the US industry.[33] Thus Mills protected the Congress. He also protected the nation's capacity to pursue generally liberal trade policies.

The fact that it regularly diverted proposals for statutory protection of specific industries did not mean that Congress never employed its independent legislative authority in matters of trade. When, every few years, presidents proposed major trade-negotiating legislation, Ways and Means and Finance were anything but administration rubber stamps. They held lengthy hearings; they reworked executive branch drafts from beginning to end. But the most thorough academic study of the House panel pointed out that in the typically closed Ways and Means markup sessions, "executive department representatives not only attend . . . but are an integral, active part of the discussion."[34] And markups focused on adjusting the details of the system of delegation—setting the range and limits of negotiating authority and refining the rules for trade remedies. With rare exceptions, general trade bills did not include product-specific protection.

Trade as a Nonparty Issue

As it operated in the decades following its inauguration, the 1934 system provided protection for Congress with a range of devices: the bargaining tariff, the executive broker, the quasi-judicial "trade remedies," the "special deals," and the strong congressional committees that worked with liberal-leaning executive branch leaders to make the system work. It also benefited enormously from the fact that trade was not a primary focus of partisan political competition.

This had not been true for most of American history. Schattschneider went so far as to argue that "the dominant position of the Republican

---

33. See Destler, Fukui, and Sato, *The Textile Wrangle,* especially chapter 11.

34. John F. Manley, *The Politics of Finance: The House Committee on Ways and Means* (Boston: Little, Brown, 1970), 348.

party before 1932 can be attributed largely to the successful exploitation of the tariff by this party as a means of attaching to itself a formidable array of interests dependent on the protective system and intent upon continuing it."[35] In the early Roosevelt administration, the great majority of Democrats had supported the reciprocal trade legislation, and virtually all Republicans had opposed it. (In 1934, 1937, and 1940, no more than five Republican votes were cast in favor of reciprocal trade in either house.)

But beginning with the wartime extension of 1943, and increasingly in the late 1940s and 1950s, Republicans began to support final passage of liberal trade legislation, although they often backed restrictive amendments.[36] And by the early 1970s, members of the GOP were increasingly aligned in favor of liberal trade, as was logically consistent with their general skepticism about intervention in the domestic economy.

By this time, the Democrats had begun to move in the opposite direction. Policy logic might have inclined them toward protectionism in the 1930s, since in the New Deal they were the party that became committed to aggressive intervention in the US economy. Instead, throughout the 1940s and 1950s they maintained their low-tariff tradition as exemplified by Cordell Hull (who had fought New Deal interventionists seeking to restrict trade), even though textile-industry pressure created a shift among representatives from the South, historically the strongest free trade region. And after President Kennedy had appeased that industry, members of his party voted overwhelmingly in support of his Trade Expansion Act of 1962. Only when organized labor left the liberal trade camp in the late 1960s did substantial numbers of northern Democrats begin to defect.

Thus, in the quarter century after World War II, neither party, while out of office, singled out trade policy as a primary point of difference with the administration in power. This contributed to cooperation on Capitol Hill: Ways and Means, whose deliberations over taxes were characterized by sharp party division, handled trade in a bipartisan, consensus manner as the issue "lost its partisan character nationally."[37] Presidential candidates would, of course, target appeals to particular interests—Kennedy sought votes from textile states with industry-specific promises in 1960, and Nixon, bested in that encounter, emulated him eight years later. But the basic open-market orientation of overall policy was not challenged. "Protectionism" remained a discredited concept, and while a politician who advocated it might win gratitude from specific interests, he would lose respect in the broader public eye.

---

35. Schattschneider, *Politics, Pressures and the Tariff*, 283.

36. For the main votes through 1958, see Pastor, *Congress and the Politics of US Foreign Economic Policy*, 97.

37. Richard F. Fenno, Jr., *Congressmen in Committees* (Boston: Little, Brown, 1973), 207.

This meant that presidents of both parties could tilt in favor of open trade, as they had to for the system to work. There were variations in their degrees of personal commitment: on balance, Gerald R. Ford's was greater than Richard M. Nixon's, and Lyndon B. Johnson and Jimmy Carter were more devoted free traders than John F. Kennedy. But all proved willing to play the role of tilting policy in the liberal direction—in the decisions they made themselves and in the appointments they made to key trade positions. And all proved able to play this role, for they knew that they were not thereby subjecting themselves to broad, partisan assault. They could take some of the interest group heat. This continuing presidential commitment made it possible for the Congress to buck responsibility, and for the "brokers" in the bureaucracy to do their trade-expanding work.

The System's Advantages and Limits

Operating within the broader context just described, the 1934 system had enormous advantages—not just for trade, but also for the major governmental participants. The president could generally treat trade policy as a component of US international leadership. Yet he could occasionally respond to specific industry constituencies, and he could avoid making very many decisions against particular producers, except those taken in broader negotiations that brought compensating benefits to other producers.

If presidents could pick and choose among trade issues while tilting generally in the liberal direction, members of Congress had even greater leeway. The majority were free to make noise, give "protectionist" speeches, or introduce bills favored by particular constituencies, secure in the knowledge that nothing statutory was likely to result. Or they could respond sympathetically to constituents and point to all the possibilities for help available elsewhere, sending them "downtown" to the Tariff Commission or the STR. Members of the trade committees could use their potential influence over trade legislation to press the executive branch to do something for particular constituencies on either the export or the import side. All could avoid final responsibility for product-by-product trade action, and thus avoid the choice between what they felt to be good politics and what they believed to be good policy.

For the senior trade officials of the executive branch agencies, the system was cumbersome, inefficient, and frustrating on a day-to-day basis. There were always interest groups to respond to, or interagency battles to fight, or technical problems to thrash out with foreign officials who had their own full agendas of political and operational problems. But over the longer term the system "worked"; maneuvering within it, trade officials could manage issues and negotiations so as to limit trade restrictions.

They could give priority to bargaining about foreign trade barriers. They could bring in countervailing interests if a US industry's campaign for protection threatened to overwhelm them. And with timely domestic brokering, they could prevent the formation of a protectionist coalition seeking broad, Smoot-Hawley–type restrictions. Thus they could avoid negative actions that might reverse the continuing growth of trade that was bringing profit to producers worldwide.

Finally, the 1934 system benefited from the checks and balances built into our governing charter. Since the prime need was to prevent restrictive action, it proved helpful that much in our Constitution is designed to inhibit rash governmental action of any kind. Division of power between branches and within the Congress means that bad proposals might be stopped at several points. A president could resist or veto legislation. A strong House committee chairman might kill it. The two houses might not agree on details. This constitutional bias was particularly important in those relatively rare instances—like that of textiles in 1969–71—when a president became so committed to achieving a particular trade restriction that his support for the overall liberal system was compromised. For it meant that an adroit legislator—like Wilbur Mills—could come to the rescue.

The system had, of course, important limits. It never provided "free trade," nor did its proponents seriously claim it did. What they sought and achieved was relative openness, but the exceptions could prove significant and expandable. On textiles, for example, what began as "voluntary" Japanese restraints on sales of cotton products grew, by stages, into an elaborate network of bilateral agreements that subjected sales of any textile or apparel item from any substantial developing country to tight quota limits.

The system was weak also in the area of agricultural trade. Here the controlling legislation went through the House and Senate agriculture committees, and the farm legislators did not always play by the same rules. Despite an increasingly favorable overall trade balance in agricultural products, the United States imposed quotas on imports of products such as sugar, cheese, and beef. In fact, to reconcile such restrictions (and broader US crop production programs) with GATT rules against quotas, the United States sought and obtained in 1955 a waiver exempting such measures from GATT coverage. Later, as heavy subsidies and quota restrictions came to deny American farmers substantial markets in Europe and Japan, they had cause to rue this precedent, regularly cited by European Union trade negotiators defending their agricultural trade barriers.

Another limitation was that, nationally and internationally, the system dealt primarily with direct trade measures such as tariffs and quotas, tending to neglect broader national policies that had an important trade impact. There had been one major effort to go further, by creating an International Trade Organization (ITO). The Havana Charter, signed in March 1948, provided for an organization that would not be limited to regulating trade barriers but would also address such matters as international commodity agreements and domestic full-employment policies. But when the charter came up for legislative ratification, its broad scope alienated not only congressional protectionists but also protrade "perfectionists" who feared it would encourage government actions that inhibited business enterprise. The ITO charter was never ratified.[38] So these issues had to be addressed ad hoc, under the auspices of a GATT originally conceived as a temporary arrangement.[39]

The system also depended, to a considerable degree, on favorable economic conditions for the nation as a whole and for specific industries. Textile protection began in a decade—the 1950s—when that industry faced stagnant domestic and international demand. Increased demand for trade restrictions tended to rise with the level of unemployment and the overvaluation of the dollar.

And the system could be shaken if a key player departed from the script. After Richard Nixon "reluctantly" supported statutory quotas for the textile industry in 1970, the House voted to enact them.

The System's Contradictions

More important than these particular kinds of limits, which no system could have avoided, were some deeper contradictions. In several respects, the 1934 system of trade policymaking would become the victim of its success, as its accomplishments weakened the instruments that had made success possible.

The "Bargaining Tariff" as Vanishing Asset

As long as the primary trade policy business involved the traditional barriers—tariffs and quotas—international negotiations could focus on limiting and reducing them. This made for efficient international negotiations, as national delegations had clear and measurable things to trade off against one another. They could point to concrete results and monitor implementation without great difficulty. And the prospect of barrier reduction abroad served as a brake on pressures at home—protection for an industry could be denied or limited on the grounds that it would undercut the chance to gain export benefits for other industries.

---

38. William Diebold, Jr., "The End of the ITO," *Essays in International Finance* 16 (Princeton, NJ: Princeton University Press, October 1952), especially 11–24.

39. In fact, trade bills in the 1950s regularly included a clause reading as follows: "The enactment of this Act shall not be construed to determine or indicate the approval or disapproval by the Congress of the Executive Agreement known as the General Agreement on Tariffs and Trade." See Jackson, *Legal Problems of International Economic Relations*, 408–10.

Tariff negotiations also facilitated the delegation of congressional power. Legislation could specify in advance the range of permitted reductions, and the executive branch could negotiate and the president proclaim them without Congress having to ratify their specifics. And to the degree that trade policy was tariffs, the jurisdiction of the "tax" committees, Finance and Ways and Means, was hard for Hill competitors to contest.

However, the more trade negotiators accomplished, the lower were the remaining tariffs. Attention shifted to nontariff trade distortions, which were harder to define and whose removal was more fractious to negotiate internationally; it was hard to point to clear, measurable results.

Domestically, there were two major complications. First, Congress could not simply authorize a negotiation and let an administration take it from there, since legislation could not fully anticipate the sorts of changes in US law that would be required to implement an agreement. So Congress would have to enact trade legislation at both ends of the process. Second, to the degree that trade negotiations explicitly involved many things other than tariffs, the control of the trade committees would be weakened. They would be under pressure to share jurisdiction; subjects like product standards and government procurement regulations were the province of other, competing committees.

International Openness Versus Domestic Intervention

The demise of tariffs as the key trade issue exacerbated another contradiction built into the postwar GATT regime—that between the drive to lower economic barriers among nations and the increasing governmental intervention within them.[40] For if one lesson of the Great Depression was the folly of protectionism, an even more powerful one was that national economies, left to themselves, would not necessarily provide full employment, much less ensure equitable income distribution and personal economic security. So almost all "capitalist" governments entered the postwar period determined to conduct activist, interventionist economic policies at home. Their electorates expected them to do so and held them accountable for the results.

As long as trade policy involved tariffs—a distinct, separable instrument—nations could reconcile barrier reductions with activist policies at home. They could be "liberal" on cross-border transactions and interventionist within the home market. But their "domestic" economic actions had a considerable impact on trade, and the lowering of tariffs made this impact more visible. Inevitably, American producers began to focus less on tariffs and more on other nations' domestic steps: the subsidies benefiting

---

40. See John Gerard Ruggie, "International Regimes, Transactions, and Change: Embedded Liberalism in the Postwar Economic Order," *International Organization* (Spring 1982): 379–415.

Europe's state-owned steel companies, or the buy-Japanese policies of the government telecommunications agency in Tokyo.

The many asymmetries in what various governments were doing made it hard to put together packages of "reciprocal" national concessions on nontariff trade issues. Pressures on nations to change their domestic subsidy, regulation, and procurement policies struck at the policy tolerance that had been a central, if largely implicit, element of the international consensus that created and maintained the GATT. For many nontariff barriers (NTBs), like product standards or systems of taxation, negotiations raised sensitive questions of national sovereignty.

Within the United States, attention to NTBs fueled charges of "unfairness," the political Achilles' heel of the liberal trade consensus at home. From the numerous specific cases in which foreign governments intervened in trade to the disadvantage of particular American producers, it was easy to construct a broad general argument that Uncle Sam had become "Uncle Sucker"—that our competitors were taking away with oft-invisible domestic policies the trade opportunities they apparently granted in tariff negotiations.

Success as Multiplier of Trade Pressures

To the degree that the postwar regime brought about expanded trade, it created another problem for the policymaking system. For it increased the number of "losers"—producer interests adversely affected by foreign competition and driven to seek help. It was one thing when the major trade-impacted industries were few and predictable: textiles, steel, shoes. But when imports rose from less than 5 percent of GNP to more than 10 percent, the ranks of the "injured" multiplied. Large industries previously ranked among America's finest—consumer electronics, automobiles, and machine tools—began coming to Washington with their problems. The system, accustomed to facing only a handful of specific pressures, now had to cope with a basketful.

There were also, of course, an increasing number of American producers who were profiting from the export side of international trade, not to mention importers and retailers with a stake in foreign products. But for all the traditional reasons, they did not so readily join the political arena. If trade "losers" go regularly into politics to seek relief, trade "winners" generally stick to business. Trade officials and politicians could work to involve them, and they regularly did so, but this only increased their leadership burden.

The Dilemma of the Rules

A final contradiction was one built into the trade remedy procedures. These procedures were, in principle, an important escape valve, diverting pressures at least temporarily away from Congress (and the executive branch). Yet to remain credible, they had to result—reasonably often—in actual trade relief.

Viewed from overseas, actions granting such relief were viewed as departures from liberal trade policy, signs that the United States was "going protectionist." The fact that our foreign competitors were imposing their own (often less visible) trade restrictions did not seem to lessen their propensity to express alarm about ours. Moreover, if the trade-remedy procedures regularly resulted in restraining trade, they would in fact have a protectionist result. Thus, relief procedures that were credible domestically weakened US trade leadership internationally.

In the 1960s this dilemma was resolved, under the Trade Expansion Act of 1962 (TEA), by rules that made escape clause relief hard to obtain, and by lax administration of the countervailing duty and antidumping laws. In the short run, this facilitated US international trade leadership, but it brought petitioners back to congressional doorsteps. And relief under the new TAA program, which might have absorbed some of the pressure, proved as hard to qualify for as relief under the escape clause. So the TEA approach proved unsustainable: in the 1970s legislators, seeking continued protection for themselves, would respond by rewriting the trade-remedy laws so that relief would be easier to obtain. This would help domestically, but it undercut US international trade leadership. Particularly sensitive abroad were those cases in which US petitioners alleged unfair foreign trade practices.

■ ■ ■

From the 1930s through the 1960s, the main story of American trade policymaking was the story of the construction and elaboration of a pressure-diverting policy management system. No one planned the 1934 system in its entirety. It evolved from a mix of strong executive and congressional leadership and ad hoc responses to particular pressures. It gave the American body politic not only an unaccustomed capacity to resist new trade restrictions, but remarkable success in reducing old ones, as evidenced by a series of negotiations that culminated in the Kennedy Round agreements of 1967.

This chapter has sought to describe the "1934 system"—how we got it and how it worked. The next section of this book, however, sets forth how this system was shaken in the 1970s and 1980s, not only by pressures and contradictions such as those described above, but also by more turbulent economic times—for the United States, its major competitors, and the international trading system. The next chapter examines the global changes to which trade policy has been forced to respond. Thereafter, we look at the response of specific US institutions and processes—Congress, the executive branch, the quasi-judicial rules, and the broader domestic political system.

II

EROSION AND ADAPTATION: 1971–94

3

A Tougher World: Changes in the Context of Trade Policy

The 1970s and 1980s brought far-reaching changes to the world economy. US firms and workers became much more exposed to foreign competition in both home and overseas markets. The relative world position of the United States declined, as European rivals were joined by Asian ones—first Japan, then rapidly industrializing countries such as Korea. The rules of the international trading regime, the General Agreement on Tariffs and Trade (GATT), grew less effective. The advanced industrial economies, buffeted by two oil shocks, entered a period of stagflation, combining rapid price increases with sluggish growth. Fixed exchange rates among currencies could not hold, and the world moved to a floating rate regime, featuring massive financial flows and severe and protracted misalignments. Last but not least, the collapse of the Soviet Union in 1991 reinforced the long-standing trend toward tripolarity in the global economy. The United States had to share power with the European Union and Japan. And all three needed to cooperate without the glue that Cold War security alliances had theretofore provided.

15 August as Prologue

The new era was heralded by a US policy action both dramatic and unexpected. On 15 August 1971, at the urging of Treasury Secretary John B. Connally, President Richard M. Nixon took several related steps aimed at reducing the international value of the dollar. He suspended the US commitment to support its currency by selling gold reserves on demand; he called upon other major nations to raise the value of their currencies against the dollar; and, to get everybody's attention, he imposed a temporary 10 percent "additional tax" on imports. The aim, Nixon declared, was to ensure "that American products will not be at a disadvantage because of unfair exchange rates. When the unfair treatment is ended, the import tax will end as well."[1]

The financial context of the 15 August actions was the increased vulnerability of the dollar in foreign exchange markets. Since the late 1950s, the United States had been running regular deficits in its international balance of payments, and these deficits had generated intermittent concern, in Washington as well as overseas, about the dollar's long-term strength. Under the Bretton Woods system, the dollar was the unit against which other nations defined their currency values, and concern about the dollar was therefore synonymous with concern about the viability of the broader international monetary system. Until 1971, the dollar's value had been sustained by a variety of cooperative efforts among the US, European, and Japanese central banks. The speculative pressure that summer, however, was of an entirely new order of magnitude.[2]

The trade context of 15 August was a shift in the overall US export-import balance. Merchandise trade surpluses had been a constant feature of the postwar American economic landscape, averaging more than $5 billion annually in the early 1960s. In 1968 and 1969, however, the US surplus dropped below $1 billion, and critics like Senate Finance Committee Chairman Russell B. Long (D-LA) argued that US commercial trade was actually in deficit, since export statistics included more than $2 billion financed by foreign aid.

---

1. This action was aimed importantly at getting the US economy moving, without worsening inflation, before the 1972 election. It also included, therefore, domestic economic stimulus measures and wage and price controls.

For an account of the Nixon decision in historical perspective, see Robert Solomon, *The International Monetary System 1945–1976: An Insider's View* (New York: Harper and Row, 1977), chapters 11 and 12. For comprehensive analyses of the forces behind this major policy change, see John S. Odell, *U.S. International Monetary Policy: Markets, Power, and Ideas as Sources of Change* (Princeton, NJ: Princeton University Press, 1982), chapter 4; and Joanne Gowa, *Closing the Gold Window: Domestic Politics and the End of Bretton Woods* (Ithaca, NY: Cornell University Press, 1983). For a thorough analysis of American policy interests during this period, see C. Fred Bergsten, *The Dilemmas of the Dollar: The Economics and Politics of United States International Monetary Policy* (New York: New York University Press for the Council on Foreign Relations, 1975), especially part 2.

2. "In the first nine months of 1971 . . . US liabilities to foreign monetary authorities increased by more than $21 billion." Solomon, *International Monetary System*, 184. These authorities' increased dollar holdings reflected the movement of other holders out of dollars into other currencies. The average annual increase in such foreign official dollar holdings in the late 1960s, by contrast, was only $637 million. *Economic Report of the President*, 1974, table C-88.

An increasing number of economists saw the trade shift as evidence that the dollar had become overvalued. Its exchange rate with other currencies reflected a postwar preeminence that no longer existed. American industry and labor were experiencing greater foreign competition as a result, and official Washington was under new pressure for trade restrictions. Hardly was the ink dry on the Kennedy Round tariff-cutting agreement of 1967 when a range of industries began pushing for new protection. These included textile and apparel manufacturers, alarmed by the growing imports of man-made fiber products, and steel firms and workers concerned about competition from resurgent European and Japanese competitors. Organized labor, which had endorsed the Kennedy Round, was arguing by 1970 that a new competitive situation had "made old 'free trade' concepts and their 'protectionist' opposites increasingly obsolete." Labor now called for policies aimed at *"orderly* expansion of world trade."[3] As recounted in chapter 2, these pressures, combined with the Nixon administration's mismanagement of the textile issue, led the House of Representatives to pass a restrictive import quota bill in November 1970.

The overvalued dollar put the United States in an economic policy bind. Through the 1960s, devaluation was considered impractical—even unthinkable—because it would undercut the dollar-based exchange rate system established in 1944 at Bretton Woods. President John F. Kennedy told his advisers he did not want the subject mentioned outside his office; for Kennedy, devaluation "would call into doubt the good faith and stability of this nation and the competence of its President."[4] The traditional medicine for righting one's trade balance without devaluation was to depress overall demand. This would, however, drive up unemployment and generate increased pressures for trade restrictions. (And in fact, the Johnson administration did the opposite in the late 1960s. Its inflationary policies—increasing spending for the Vietnam War years before new taxes were enacted to finance it—made the trade balance worse.)

The United States could also support the dollar with measures that would limit capital outflows and discourage other activities requiring its conversion to foreign currencies. The Kennedy and Johnson administrations employed a variety of devices to this end: an interest equalization tax, limits on foreign direct investment, reduction of the value of duty-free goods that traveling Americans could purchase overseas, even a "balance of payments" program to cut official US overseas staffing. But these palliatives had no durable impact.

---

3. Statement of the AFL-CIO economic policy council, as reported in the *New York Times*, 22 February 1970. Emphasis added.

4. Theodore G. Sorensen, *Kennedy* (New York: Harper and Row, 1965), 408.

Nixon and Connally broke the United States free from this bind in a way that was deeply disruptive of the postwar economic system. Not only was the content of their actions unsettling; their rhetoric generated strong doubts in foreign capitals about whether the United States could still be counted on to support the international monetary and trade regimes its leaders had fostered. Connally actively provoked such anxieties, in part to increase US leverage: Europeans and Japanese might yield more if they saw their concessions as the only way to bring a suddenly rogue America back onto the international economic reservation.

Within four months and three days, however, agreement was reached on a new set of exchange rates that effectively devalued the dollar by about 10 percent against other major currencies. Within two years, the dollar went down substantially further, and the major trading nations were forced to abandon the system of fixed exchange rates altogether. By the mid-1970s, in fact, it seemed that the net effect of the "Nixon shocks" had been not to bury international economic cooperation but to give it new life. Realignment of exchange rates restored the US capacity to pursue open trade policies and to press others to do likewise. The US trade balance began to improve in early 1973, just as legislation to authorize the new Tokyo Round made its way through the House of Representatives. With their competitiveness thus buttressed, firms and workers were less disposed to press for protection against foreign products and more conscious of the opportunities a new trade round might bring. When the oil crisis hit later that year, the floating rate regime made it easier for the world to make the wrenching adjustments forced by the fourfold increase in the price of that critical commodity.

Nonetheless, the world Americans faced after 15 August 1971 was clearly one of greater economic insecurity and turmoil. Seven intertwined features of this world stand out:

- increased exposure of the US economy to trade;

- the relative decline of the United States, real and perceived;

- the rise of new (particularly East Asian) competitors;

- the erosion of the GATT international trade regime;

- the worsening of "stagflation," with the United States and its European trading partners facing a combination of slow economic growth, high unemployment, and rapid price increases;

- the move to floating, and oft-misaligned, exchange rates; and

- beginning in 1989, the end of the Cold War and the emergence of a tripolar economic world.

All of these developments put new strains on an American trade policy-making system shaped in more insular economic times.

The Trade Explosion

In 1960, exports of US merchandise to the rest of the world totaled $19.7 billion; in 1990, they totaled $387.4 billion (table 3.1).[5] During this same period, US global merchandise imports shot up from $14.8 billion to $498.4 billion. The numbers are in current prices and ballooned by inflation, but on a price-deflated, constant-dollar basis exports rose more than sixfold, and imports nearly eightfold.[6] Perhaps the most important indicator, however, was the growth of trade in proportion to the US economy. In 1950, the United States exported just 6.3 percent of its total production of goods. This percentage rose modestly for two decades—to 7.7 percent in 1960 and 9.2 percent in 1970. Then it shot up to rates more than double that: 19.1 percent in 1980 and 18.2 percent in 1990. The corresponding figures for imports were 5.6, 5.8, and 8.7 percent for the earlier years, and 21.3 percent and 23.2 percent for 1980 and 1990.[7]

The expansion of trade with the United States' primary overseas trading partner was even more dramatic. In 1960, the United States sold $1.4 billion in goods to Japan and bought $1.1 billion. By 1990, it was exporting $48.6 billion and importing $89.7 billion.[8] When adjusted for price increases, this amounted to an elevenfold increase in US exports to Japan over this period and a nineteenfold increase in imports.

The causes of the trade explosion were many: reduced international transportation and communication costs; reductions in tariff barriers; the broader internationalization of the US economy; and the ballooning cost of oil imports, which required an expansion of foreign sales to pay for them. A thorough examination of these causes goes beyond the scope of this book. But the effects of the trade explosion are an important part of our story, and they were substantial.

First and perhaps most significant, the expanded inflow of foreign products brought an inevitable political response. Measured by any standard, US firms were facing significantly more import competition in the

---

5. Though this portion of the book covers developments only through 1994, table 3.1 offers—for reader convenience—trade balance data through 2004. Figure 3.1 later in this chapter does the same for exchange rates. The resurgence of the dollar and the trade imbalance in 1998 is addressed in chapter 9.

6. US Commerce Department data, as reported in *Economic Report of the President*, 1991, table B-102, and US Congress, Joint Economic Committee, *Economic Indicators*, June 1991, 36. The growth of real exports and imports is calculated from the constant (1982) dollar figures in table B-21 of the *Economic Report of the President*, 1991.

7. Percentages obtained by dividing total merchandise exports (or imports) by total production of goods, as reported in *Economic Report of the President*, 1991, tables B-102 and B-6, and US Congress, Joint Economic Committee, *Economic Indicators*, June 1991, 36.

8. US Department of Commerce data.

Table 3.1 US merchandise exports, imports, and trade balance, 1960–2004
(billions of current dollars)

Year	Exports	Imports	Balance
1960	19.7	14.8	4.9
1961	20.1	14.5	5.6
1962	20.8	16.3	4.5
1963	22.3	17.0	5.2
1964	25.5	18.7	6.8
1965	26.5	21.5	5.0
1966	29.3	25.5	3.8
1967	30.7	26.9	3.8
1968	33.6	33.0	0.6
1969	36.4	35.8	0.6
1970	42.5	39.9	2.6
1971	43.3	45.6	−2.3
1972	49.4	55.8	−6.4
1973	71.4	70.5	0.9
1974	98.3	103.8	−5.5
1975	107.1	98.2	8.9
1976	114.7	124.2	−9.5
1977	120.8	151.9	−31.1
1978	142.1	176.0	−33.9
1979	184.4	212.0	−27.6
1980	224.3	249.8	−25.5
1981	237.0	265.1	−28.1
1982	211.2	247.6	−36.4
1983	201.8	268.9	−67.1
1984	219.9	332.4	−112.5
1985	215.9	338.1	−122.2
1986	223.3	368.4	−145.1
1987	250.2	409.8	−159.6
1988	320.2	447.2	−127.0
1989	359.9	477.7	−117.8
1990	387.4	498.4	−111.0
1991	414.1	491.0	−76.9
1992	439.6	536.5	−96.9
1993	456.9	589.4	−132.5
1994	502.9	668.7	−165.8
1995	575.2	749.4	−174.2
1996	612.1	803.1	−191.0
1997	678.4	876.5	−198.1
1998	670.4	917.1	−246.7
1999	684.0	1,030.0	−346.0
2000	772.0	1,224.4	−452.4
2001	718.7	1,145.9	−427.2
2002	681.8	1,164.7	−482.9
2003	713.1	1,260.7	−547.6
2004	807.6	1,473.1	−665.5

Note: Data reported on balance of payments basis.

Sources: Economic Report of the President, 2005; US International Trade in Goods and Services, March 2005.

1970s and 1980s than at any previous point in the 20th century. Of course, exports also rose during this period. But the firms that benefited from exports were by no means comparably aggressive in the political arena, though exporters (and import users) did act to limit protectionism when their own specific interests were at stake.

Furthermore, there was great disparity in the impact of the trade explosion on various industries and regions. During the 1970s—the period of greatest relative increase in US trade—producers of farm and high-technology products reaped great benefits. Overall, "in high-technology industries in which U.S. comparative advantage continue[d] to increase," the US trade surplus "grew from $15 billion in 1973 to $52 billion in 1980."[9]

But those who made standard producer and consumer goods suffered, whether their business was steel or autos or television sets. And the suffering was regional as well as sectoral. In the United States as a whole, employment in manufacturing stayed roughly the same between 1973 and 1980. But in the rust belt states from New York to Michigan, it declined by 10 to 15 percent. Within the highly unionized basic industries concentrated in this region, laid-off workers faced, on the average, substantial drops in their income levels even after they found new jobs outside those industries. As William H. Branson has noted, this meant that the greatest adjustment was being forced upon those very "workers and companies . . . in the best position to bring pressure on trade policy."[10] With their plight as concrete evidence, they could claim that a major American achievement of the earlier 20th century, the bringing of industrial workers into the middle class, was now being threatened by foreign competition.[11]

---

9. Robert Z. Lawrence, *Can America Compete?* (Washington, DC: Brookings Institution, 1984), 95. Between 1980 and 1985, as spelled out later in this chapter, virtually all US product sectors, including agriculture and high-technology industries, were hurt by the rise in the dollar, and many were helped, in turn, by its subsequent decline.

10. William H. Branson, "The Changing Structure of U.S. Trade: Implications for Research and Policy," paper prepared for the Washington Conference of the National Bureau of Economic Research, 9 March 1984, photocopy.

11. Defining a middle-class income as within 30 percent of the median for the economy, Lawrence finds that, according to census data, the proportion of manufacturing workers earning such incomes declined from 44.6 percent in 1969 to 39.3 percent in 1979. Lawrence, *Can America Compete?*, 80.

More generally, "the earnings of less skilled American men began dropping in real terms after 1973 and fell precipitously during the 1980s." This was "a striking break with [the] historical pattern," for "[f]rom 1900 through the 1960s the real earnings of less skilled American workers grew substantially." See McKinley L. Blackburn, David E. Bloom, and Richard B. Freeman, "The Declining Economic Position of Less Skilled American Men," in Gary Burtless, ed., *A Future of Lousy Jobs? The Changing Structure of U.S. Wages* (Washington, DC: Brookings Institution, 1990), 31.

The "Decline" of the United States

The nation that was suddenly more exposed to world trade was also comparatively less well off. As late as 1960, the incomes per capita of the United States' major "trilateral" competitors—France, Germany, Japan, and the United Kingdom—ranged from 30 to 68 percent of its own. By 1979, their per capita incomes had risen to between 64 and 86 percent of that of the United States.[12] The US share of world trade had also declined, albeit much less dramatically, and in the context of rapidly growing absolute trade flows. In 1950, US international commerce accounted for fully one-third of the trilateral total. This portion dropped to 27 percent in 1960, 23.5 percent in 1970, and 22.1 percent in 1980.[13]

As these last statistics suggest, most of the decline in the US share of world production and trade took place before the 1970s. Moreover, a major goal of postwar US foreign policy had been to restore its European and Japanese allies to economic health. After 1970, broad indicators suggest that the United States held its own economically vis-à-vis western Europe; for example, between that year and 1989, the US index of industrial production rose 76 percent, compared with just 48 percent for the European Community. And while Japanese industrial production grew by 110 percent over the same period, the difference between the real annual economic growth rates of the United States and Japan was only 1.7 percent a year over 1976–90—compared with an average annual difference of 7.9 percent in the 1960s.[14]

By these broad indicators, the US "decline" came mainly in the 1950s and 1960s, and could be seen as an inevitable correction of the abnormal and unsustainable preeminence created by World War II. But the full impact was felt in the 1970s and 1980s. Industrial sectors that were once world leaders came under intense trade-competitive assault: first steel and consumer electronics, then automobiles, then microelectronics. By the late 1980s, concern about the apparent erosion of America's economic and geostrategic position had made Paul Kennedy's heavy work of world history into a surprise best-seller.[15] And such concerns were reinforced by a

---

12. Irving B. Kravis, Alan Heston, and Robert Summers, *World Product and Income: International Comparisons of Real Gross Product* (Baltimore: Johns Hopkins University Press [for the World Bank and the United Nations Statistical Office], 1982), 15. Figures are for "gross domestic product per capita," in terms of actual purchasing power.

13. Calculated by Robert O. Keohane from the *UN Yearbook of International Trade Statistics,* 1981. See his *After Hegemony: Cooperation and Discord in the World Political Economy* (Princeton, NJ: Princeton University Press, 1984), 199.

14. *Economic Report of the President,* 1991, tables B-107 and B-110.

15. Paul Kennedy, *The Rise and Fall of the Great Powers: Economic Change and Military Conflict from 1500 to 2000* (New York: Random House, 1987). Kennedy's argument triggered nu-

separate phenomenon that was frequently, albeit oversimply, interpreted as reflecting an *accelerating* decline. This was the onset of regular merchandise trade deficits.

Every year from 1894 through 1970, the value of the goods the United States sold on world markets exceeded the value of those that Americans bought. The inflow of funds from these merchandise trade surpluses was offset, in important part, by an outflow of funds for investment overseas. But beginning in 1971, the year of Nixon's policy bombshell, the pattern changed: the United States ran a merchandise trade deficit that year, and in all but two of the 20 years thereafter. And the numbers looked increasingly alarming. The negative balance of $2.3 billion in 1971 was succeeded by records of $6.4 billion in 1972, $33.9 billion in 1978, and $159.6 billion in 1987.[16] Bilateral deficits with the United States' most-watched trading partner, Japan, grew apace, with records of $4 billion in 1972, $11.6 billion in 1978, and $56.3 billion in 1987.[17]

The deficits of the 1970s were not unreasonable for a mature industrial economy. What the United States was doing, essentially, was using the income from its foreign investments to finance a higher level of consumption than its current production would have allowed. Once it ceased being a consistent net capital exporter, simple mathematics dictated that modest "structural" trade deficits (amounting to less than 10 percent of total US trade) would be its normal condition, to offset net returns on overseas investment.[18] And the United States could do this while still running, on the average, an approximate balance in its current account, which includes not only merchandise trade but also services and investment income. In other words, US trade deficits were no larger than what its overseas earnings could finance; the United States was not going into debt to pay for imports.[19]

However, this was hardly the way the deficit was characterized in US politics. Rather, it was treated as offering clear evidence that the United

---

merous rebuttals, including those by Joseph S. Nye, Jr., *Bound to Lead: The Changing Nature of American Power* (New York: Basic Books, 1990), and Henry R. Nau, *The Myth of America's Decline: Leading the World Economy into the 1990s* (New York: Oxford University Press, 1990).

16. *Economic Report of the President*, 1991, table B-102.

17. Japan Economic Institute of America, *Yearbook of U.S.-Japan Economic Relations in 1982* (Washington, DC: JEI, 1983), 129.

18. No one, of course, "decided" that the United States should do this, and it could have made its future returns even greater by continuing the substantial net capital exports of the 1950s and 1960s.

19. The same could not be said of the genuinely alarming trade deficits of 1984 and thereafter, addressed later in this chapter.

States was losing out in the world marketplace.[20] This had several related and constraining effects on executive branch policymakers and on the broader political environment.

First of all, it undercut the argument—already very weak in American politics by 1970—that the United States should absorb costs to its specific trade interests in order to help maintain the broader international trading system (and US alliances that were intertwined with that system). The belief that "we could no longer afford" such generosity was hardly limited to Richard Nixon's demanding Secretary of the Treasury, John Connally; in the 1970s and 1980s, it became nearly universal.

Second, merchandise trade deficits increased political receptivity for claims that American firms and workers were facing unfair foreign competition, broadly defined. In many instances, foreign governments subsidized products destined for export and restricted imports more than the United States did for comparable products. One plausible—albeit analytically incorrect—explanation for trade deficits was that foreign markets were less open than the US markets.[21] Once we equated negative trade balance figures with a decline of the United States, it was more comfortable to blame this on foreign nefariousness than on domestic inadequacies.

Third, deficits placed American trade negotiators on the defensive because they suggested a negative market judgment on prior US trade bargaining: the United States had not been tough enough with foreign governments, and its producers were being battered as a result.

All of these constraints forced US negotiators to assume a more demanding international trade posture, by pushing for more concessions overseas and offering fewer in return, at a time when US power in the world was diminished. This seemed, at a minimum, a recipe for increased

---

20. Russell Long (D-LA), chairman of the Senate Finance Committee throughout the 1970s, argued persistently that the Commerce Department's preferred method of valuing imports— "customs value," or f.a.s. (free alongside ship)—led to understatement of the real US trade deficit, because it excluded the cost of shipping those imports. To get people to use what he considered the "right" numbers, Long attached to the major trade legislation of 1979 a provision requiring that import statistics be reported on the c.i.f. (cost, insurance, and freight) basis "no later than 48 hours before the release of any other government statistics" on imports or the balance of trade (Trade Agreements Act of 1979, section 1108 [a]). He expected the numbers released first to the press to become the ones most used—and his expectation was borne out. Thus, during the height of the trade imbalance, the annual deficit number commonly cited was inflated by roughly $18 billion, and the monthly number by about $1.5 billion.

This requirement was repealed by the Omnibus Trade and Competitiveness Act of 1988, section 1931 (a), enacted after Long's retirement. This returned Commerce Department reporting to the practice, preferred by most economists, of treating shipping as a service.

21. For discussion of why, in a floating exchange rate regime, the US trade balance is not fundamentally a function of market openness here or overseas, see Catherine L. Mann, *Is the US Trade Deficit Sustainable?* (Washington, DC: Institute for International Economics, 1999), especially chapter 6.

trade conflict, as US leaders were driven to ever more demanding exercises in "export politics."

The Rise of New Competitors

The relative decline of the United States meant, by definition, the rise of other nations. Foremost among them was Japan. That story is well known, and it is underscored by the dramatic rise in US-Japan trade that was noted earlier in this chapter. But a few other numbers are worth recalling as well.

In 1960, after recovery from World War II, per capita income in Japan stood at just 30 percent of the US level in terms of purchasing power—about equal to that of Mexico, a bit below that of Spain. Nineteen years later, it had grown to 71 percent of that of the United States, placing Japan squarely in the middle of the more prosperous Western European nations—ahead of Italy and Britain, if still behind France and Germany.[22] And Japan advanced further in the 1980s—by the comparative measure of the Organization for Economic Cooperation and Development (OECD), Japanese GNP per capita had reached 76 percent of the US level by 1989.[23] Between 1960 and 1980, Japan's share of total world GNP increased from 3 to 10 percent.[24] By 1989, at current exchange rates, Japan's GNP had reached 54 percent of the US level.[25]

Japan achieved this rise through phenomenal annual increases in national production and trade. Between 1960 and 1970, its real GNP rose an average of more than 11 percent a year.[26] Its merchandise exports grew even faster: by 17.2 percent annually in the 1960s and by 8.5 percent (from a much larger base) between 1970 and 1982.[27] Japan's share of world

---

22. Kravis et al., *World Product and Income*, 15.

23. Calculated from Organization for Economic Cooperation and Development, *Main Economic Indicators* (Washington, DC: OECD, July 1991), 175. The OECD figure for 1980 was 67 percent.

24. Keizai Koho Center, *Japan 1984: An International Comparison* (Tokyo: Japan Institute for Social and Economic Affairs, 1 September 1984), 9.

25. By 1989, income per capita in Japan already exceeded that in the United States if converted at current exchange rates. But analysts generally found Japan's cost of living (at these rates) to be 40 to 75 percent higher than that in the United States. Hence purchasing power parity (PPP) comparisons, like those developed by Kravis et al. and those employed by the OECD, are preferable. For a comprehensive analysis, see Robert Summers and Alan Heston, "The Penn World Table (Mark 5): An Expanded Set of International Comparisons, 1950–1988," *The Quarterly Journal of Economics* 106, no. 2 (May 1991): 327–68.

26. *Economic Report of the President*, 1991, table B-110.

27. World Bank, *World Development Report* (Washington, DC: World Bank, 1984), 235.

exports rose from 3.5 percent in 1960 to an estimated 8.3 percent in 1985.[28] No other major nation had had growth rates anything like these.

Any large country rising so rapidly was bound to cause problems for the world trading system. In fact, Japan had been perceived as a special trade problem, and its products subjected to a range of discriminatory barriers, well before its era of double-digit growth began.[29] But there were other problems in absorbing Japan as one of the preeminent players in the world trading system. As the first non-Western nation to achieve industrial success, Japan was culturally different. This traditionally closed and close-knit society had maintained substantial formal barriers to imports throughout the 1960s. The pace at which these barriers were dismantled always lagged behind that which Japanese export success would have allowed; the de facto opening of Japan's markets seemed to lag even further, though the strong yen of the late 1980s brought an enormous surge in imports. Moreover, in contrast to the aggressive business behavior of Japanese firms, the standard style of the Tokyo government in trade diplomacy was not to take the initiative but to await foreign pressure for trade liberalization and to open up markets, bit by bit, in response to this pressure.[30]

Hence, there developed a widespread perception of Japan as a "free rider" on the international trading system, exploiting market opportunities abroad while only grudgingly making changes at home. It also seemed clear that Japanese producers benefited from some special form of government-business cooperation, although experts differed sharply over its precise nature and impact. By the 1970s and 1980s, when American firms complained about what they perceived to be unfair trade practices—whether producers dumping television sets or governments promoting development of future export industries—Japan was most often their target. They could compete against companies, US business executives argued, but not against the government of a major economic power. Making matters more sensitive was the fact that Japan was the first

---

28. Percentages computed from International Monetary Fund, *International Financial Statistics: Supplement on Trade Statistics*, no. 15, 1988; and International Monetary Fund, *Direction of Trade Statistics Yearbook*, 1990.

29. Gardner Patterson devoted an entire chapter to the various ways that other major trading nations developed special barriers against Japan in *Discrimination in International Trade: The Policy Issues* (Princeton, NJ: Princeton University Press, 1965).

30. American trade negotiators, by contrast, were prone to take the initiative, in part to channel trade pressures in the export-expanding rather than import-restricting direction. Hence, "officials in both governments" have recurrently employed "intense, highly visible United States pressure as a catalyst for Japanese policy change." Report of the Japan-United States Economic Relations Group, prepared for the President of the United States and the Prime Minister of Japan (Tokyo and Washington, January 1981), 101. See also I. M. Destler and Hideo Sato, eds., *Coping with U.S.-Japanese Economic Conflicts* (Lexington, MA: Lexington Books, 1982), especially 279–81.

nation since the rise of mass-production manufacturing processes to challenge the United States for industrial preeminence across a wide range of industries. Books that highlighted this phenomenon, like Clyde Prestowitz's *Trading Places*,[31] won wide circulation and broad credence.

Trade concerns triggered by Japan were magnified by the rise of "new Japans": nations that were following Japan's rapid-growth, export-expanding path. The most impressive single example, perhaps, was the Republic of Korea, whose exports increased annually by 35 percent in the 1960s and by 20 percent in the 1970s, and whose growth in income paralleled Japan's, albeit at lower levels.[32] Taken together, the share of world trade of the "four tigers" of East Asia—Hong Kong, Korea, Singapore, and Taiwan—rose from 1.9 percent in 1963 to 7.7 percent in 1988.[33] Thus, from the 1970s onward, American firms faced a trading world very different from the bipolar (US-EC) one of the Kennedy Round.

The Erosion of the GATT

Even as these new competitors were emerging, the system of rules for regulating international trade was weakening. In the first two postwar decades, the GATT had provided a surprisingly effective framework for negotiating trade liberalization and disciplining import restrictions. But thereafter it came under siege.[34]

One reason for its erosion was the identity of the new competitors. The GATT had originated as a North American–European enterprise, shaped by leaders who drew common lessons from the prewar (and wartime) experience. Nations from these two continents continued to provide the GATT's primary political leadership through the 1970s, but the rise of other nations meant that the lead trading states now formed a less homogeneous community, making it harder to maintain agreement on trade policy norms. And since the new competitors were slow to assert leadership

---

31. Clyde V. Prestowitz, Jr., *Trading Places: How We Allowed Japan to Take the Lead* (New York: Basic Books, 1988). A superb retrospective look at this period of US trade policy and politics is provided by an Australian analyst, John Kunkel, in *America's Trade Policy Towards Japan* (London: Routledge, 2003).

32. By the estimates of Kravis et al., gross domestic income per capita for Korea rose from 8.15 percent of the US level in 1960 to 24.8 percent in 1979. *World Product and Income*, 15. Korean export statistics are drawn from World Bank, *World Development Report*, 1984, 235.

33. Marcus Noland, *Pacific Basin Developing Countries: Prospects for the Future* (Washington, DC: Institute for International Economics, 1990), 5.

34. For a good summary of the original GATT system and its evolution, see Miriam Camps and William Diebold, Jr., "The Old Multilateralism and What Became of It," *The New Multilateralism: Can the World Trading System Be Saved?* (New York: Council on Foreign Relations Press, 1983), chapter 1.

in multilateral trade negotiations, there was a growing divergence between the locus of trade-political activism and the locus of trade-economic power.

A second reason for the GATT's weakening was, ironically, its enormous success at what it did best: multilateral tariff-cutting negotiations. As noted in chapter 2, the remarkable postwar reductions in customs duties forced international trade relations onto the harder ground of nontariff trade barriers: harder to measure and negotiate, more intertwined with issues of domestic policy and national sovereignty, and not well defined by the original GATT rules. The Tokyo Round, or MTN, of the 1970s resulted in agreement on a number of "codes" addressing such subjects as subsidies, dumping, product standards, and government procurement. But not all GATT members accepted the obligations of these codes, and enforcement procedures proved slow and cumbersome. The Uruguay Round initiated in 1986 sought to establish GATT-type rules for international investment and services transactions—another task much more complex than the tariff cutting of earlier periods.

A more general problem for the GATT was the erosion of its bedrock principle of nondiscrimination, the core notion that each national government would grant equal treatment to the products of all others adhering to the GATT system. The European Community was one enormous exception; by definition, its members agreed to grant one another more favorable (i.e., duty-free) market access than they granted to outsiders. Tariff preferences for less developed countries were another exception. The Canada–United States Free Trade Agreement of 1988 was yet another, as was the North American Free Trade Agreement (NAFTA) that followed five years later.

Governments discriminated in restricting imports as well as in admitting them. Under the GATT escape clause, Article XIX, members were allowed to impose temporary import barriers for the products of trade-injured industries. But they were supposed to do this on a nondiscriminatory basis. In practice, Article XIX was increasingly circumvented by "voluntary" export restraints (VERs) or orderly marketing agreements (OMAs), in which specific exporting nations agreed to limit their sales. Such arrangements became the norm for trade in textiles and apparel; they spread to steel and automobiles; and, in particular, they were employed to limit the sales of such rapidly rising competitors as Japan and the East Asian newly industrialized countries (NICs).

For American trade policymakers, the erosion of the GATT weakened one important postwar source of leverage in domestic trade bargaining: the argument that a particular restrictive action would undercut the international trading system from which the United States derived great benefits. For the more the international trade regime was viewed as ineffective and riddled with exceptions, the less credible were claims that US interests were served by following its rules.

Stagflation

The GATT also faced growing strain because, from the 1970s to the mid-1980s, the United States and its advanced industrial trading partners were beset with what became known as "stagflation": slow growth and high unemployment coexisting with high inflation. The United States sowed the seeds of the stagflation era when, for several years, Lyndon B. Johnson refused to seek a tax hike to finance the Vietnam War. Richard M. Nixon made matters worse with his overstimulation of the American economy in the election year of 1972. In both cases, the United States pursued fiscal and monetary policies that increased overall demand at a time when production was at or near capacity. The immediate result was price rises, which proved contagious. By early 1973, inflation in the United States was running at double-digit levels.

Then came the October War in the Middle East. Seizing the opportunity presented by tight supply conditions, members of the Organization of Petroleum Exporting Countries (OPEC) quadrupled the price at which they offered their crude oil on world markets. This generated enormous new inflationary pressure, driving up costs for productive enterprises and gasoline-dependent consumers. At the same time, the oil shock depressed demand in all the advanced industrial countries, since paying for needed oil imports at the new prices forced a massive shift of funds from consumer to producer countries. The world plunged from a 1973 boom to a 1974 recession—the deepest of the postwar era. In 1979, revolution in Iran led to the second oil shock, a near tripling of the OPEC export price. Again, inflation rates rose and the world economy plunged into recession.

Once under way, stagflation proved endemic. The higher the US rate of inflation became, the greater the level of unemployment that was needed to wring expectations of future inflation out of the economy. Hence, in 1979, the Federal Reserve Board under Chairman Paul A. Volcker began to pursue consistently tight money policies, even as growth flagged and the number of jobless increased. What economists and journalists came to label the "misery index"—the sum of the unemployment and inflation rates—rose to new heights.

Statistics once viewed with alarm came to be seen as normal, even encouraging. In the United States in 1957, a 3.6 percent rise in the consumer price index (CPI) had alarmed the Eisenhower administration; for more than a decade thereafter, the country did not again see a year-to-year increase above 3 percent. But the 1970s and early 1980s brought four years of double-digit price inflation, and President Ronald Reagan could claim victory when the 1983 CPI was "only" 3.2 percent above that of 1982.[35] Prior to 1975, the highest annual postwar rates of civilian unemployment

---

35. *Economic Report of the President*, 1985, tables B-54 and B-55.

were 6.8 percent in 1958 and 6.7 percent in 1961. By 1982, unemployment reached 9.7 percent. Expectations in the United States were so reduced that, in a year when unemployment averaged 7.5 percent, Reagan could be credited with an impressive economic recovery and ride to a landslide reelection victory.[36]

The trade problems of key industries were exacerbated by their failure to adjust to this less congenial environment. Management and labor continued to negotiate hefty wage increases, notwithstanding slower domestic growth and stiffer international competition: "In 1970 hourly compensation for auto and steel workers was about 30 percent higher than the average compensation in manufacturing. By 1981 the difference had grown to 70 percent for steel workers and 50 percent for auto workers."[37] Only after both industries faced massive layoffs were significant wage and benefit concessions forthcoming.

Coming together with stagflation, as both cause and effect, was a decline in the rate of economic growth. Not only did the United States experience five negative growth years between 1970 and 1982 (there were none from 1959 to 1969), but its average GNP growth also fell by a percentage point despite an exceptional increase in the labor force.[38] This reflected a sharp decline in productivity growth. As a result, the average real wages of the American worker stopped growing around 1973, in dramatic contrast to their near doubling over the 25 previous years.[39] Moreover, income inequality rose over the 1970s and 1980s.[40] Nor were such changes affecting the United States alone. All advanced industrial nations found the going harder after the early 1970s. Average Japanese growth of 4.4 percent in 1971–83 might look good to Americans and Europeans, but it was a big drop from the 11.7 percent of the decade preceding.[41] The worsening in US unemployment looked mild when set against the much steeper proportionate rises in Germany, France, Canada, and above all

---

36. Ibid., table B-29. By the end of 1985, Reagan (and the US economy) were beginning also to benefit from an oil glut, precipitating a sharp decline in oil prices and undermining the always tenuous OPEC effort to buttress prices through national production quotas. In the ensuing years, driven by sharp US growth in 1984 and moderate growth thereafter, the average civilian unemployment rate declined to 5.3 percent in 1989 before rising with the 1990–91 recession.

37. *Economic Report of the President*, 1984, 92.

38. Average US GNP growth was 3.8 percent from 1961–70, and 2.7 percent from 1971–84. Yet the labor force grew by 29 percent over 1971–80, much more than in either previous postwar decade. See *Economic Report of the President*, 1991, tables B-109 and B-32.

39. The best work on this subject is Frank Levy, *Dollars and Dreams: The Changing American Income Distribution* (New York: Russell Sage Foundation and W. W. Norton, 1988).

40. Bartless, *A Future of Lousy Jobs?*, 1.

41. *Economic Report of the President*, 1991, table B-110.

Britain, whose jobless rate leaped from 3 percent in 1970 to 12 percent in 1984![42]

The mid- and late 1980s did bring some good economic news for Americans. Inflation fell substantially: from 1982 through 1989, it never exceeded 4.6 percent, whereas it was above that level every year from 1974 through 1981. US economic growth averaged 3.5 percent over 1984–90, compared with 2.5 percent over 1976–83. There was a rebound in the productivity growth of manufacturing (though not services) industries. And toward the decade's end, Europe also experienced a surge in growth, as did Japan.

But by 1990–92, the United States was back in recession, a problem that in short order also beset Europe and Japan. Thus, other nations would not be very receptive to American demands that they give the United States more in international trade talks than they were likely to get in return.

Floating Exchange Rates and Dollar "Misalignment"

The monetary regime within which the United States faced these new difficulties was no longer the Bretton Woods system of fixed exchange rates pegged to the dollar, but one in which the dollar's relative price—the single most important determinant of US producers' trade competitiveness—was being set and reset, day by day, in foreign-exchange markets.[43]

As noted at the outset of this chapter, the end of Bretton Woods initially made life easier for US trade policymakers. The "Nixon shock" of 15 August 1971 had begun the process, and devaluations of roughly 10 percent followed in December 1971 and February 1973. Renewed currency speculation forced the major trading nations to move to a floating-rate regime a month later, in March 1973. After that, the markets generally kept the real (inflation-adjusted) value of the dollar at or below the March 1973 level through the Nixon, Ford, and Carter administrations.[44] American exports benefited; import competition eased somewhat; and the management of trade-restrictive pressures was somewhat less of a burden. And it was at a time of dollar weakness, with US exports expanding rapidly, that the world completed (and Congress approved) the Tokyo Round agreements aimed at reducing nontariff barriers to trade.

---

42. Ibid., table B-108.

43. For a general analysis of the challenges this posed for US policymakers, see I. M. Destler and C. Randall Henning, *Dollar Politics: Exchange Rate Policymaking in the United States* (Washington, DC: Institute for International Economics, 1989), especially chapters 1–4.

44. In fact, the markets brought the dollar sharply down in the early Carter administration, necessitating a "dollar defense" initiative on 1 November 1978 to reverse this fall.

However, in the first half of the 1980s, this exchange rate situation reversed itself with a vengeance. From its level in 1980 to its peak in late February 1985, the trade-weighted value of the dollar rose an incredible 67 percent by the MERM index of the International Monetary Fund (see figure 3.1), and 88.2 percent by the index of the Federal Reserve.[45] At this point, the dollar was roughly 40 percent above the level that would have brought balance to the US current account. In terms of trade competitiveness, this was a severe and protracted currency misalignment that had been unseen—and unforeseen—by postwar economists, businessmen, and politicians.[46]

Beginning in March 1985, the dollar turned around again. Given a major push by a joint declaration by the finance ministers of the Group of Five nations (France, Germany, Japan, the United Kingdom, and the United States) in the Plaza Agreement in September 1985, the dollar had plummeted by the end of 1987 to roughly its 1980 level, and it moved within a far narrower range in the years thereafter—as figure 3.1 shows. With both the decline and the subsequent stabilization came renewed cooperation in exchange rate management among the finance ministers and central banks of the advanced industrial nations.[47]

How could the exchange rate shift so much? How was the dollar able to reach a level that rendered many American products uncompetitive, as it had by early 1982, and continue to rise for three more years despite burgeoning US trade deficits, only to plummet over the next three years? A critical underlying source of such currency fluctuations and misalignment was a revolution in world capital markets.

Many international economists had favored a floating exchange rate system well before the world was forced to accept one. Generally, they expected that trade transactions would dominate foreign-currency markets. Since the trade competitiveness of major countries was generally slow to change, this meant that relationships among the strong currencies would

---

45. Destler and Henning, *Dollar Politics*, 22–25. MERM stands for the Multilateral Exchange Rate Model.

46. For a definition of currency misalignments, see John Williamson, *The Exchange Rate System*, POLICY ANALYSES IN INTERNATIONAL ECONOMICS 5 (Washington, DC: Institute for International Economics, September 1983, rev. June 1985), 12. For a proposal to reduce them, see Williamson and Marcus H. Miller, *Targets and Indicators: A Blueprint for the International Coordination of Economic Policy*, POLICY ANALYSES IN INTERNATIONAL ECONOMICS 22 (Washington, DC: Institute for International Economics, December 1987). For a comprehensive contemporary analysis of the dollar misalignment's macroeconomic causes and trade consequences in the 1980s, see Stephen Marris, *Deficits and the Dollar: The World Economy at Risk*, POLICY ANALYSES IN INTERNATIONAL ECONOMICS 14 (Washington, DC: Institute for International Economics, December 1985, rev. August 1987).

47. See Destler and Henning, *Dollar Politics*, chapter 4, and Yoichi Funabashi, *Managing the Dollar: From the Plaza to the Louvre* (Washington, DC: Institute for International Economics, 1988, rev. 1989).

Figure 3.1   US nominal effective exchange rates, 1980–2004

annual average (2000 = 100)

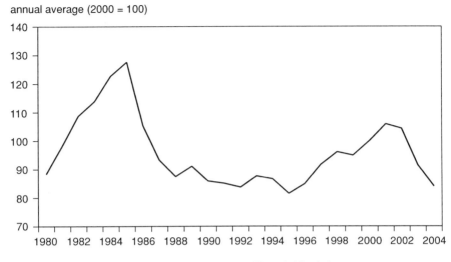

Source: International Monetary Fund, *International Financial Statistics.*

be rather stable.[48] Shifts in exchange rates would be gradual, and a function primarily of shifts in trade flows.

What no one anticipated was the impact of the dramatic increase in the magnitude and international mobility of investment capital, particularly "short-term" funds seeking the most rewarding current situation. As one informed observer characterized matters in early 1985: "The flow of money was now dwarfing the growth of world trade. In 1984, for example, world trade in goods and services was on the order of $2 trillion, while global capital transfers reached $20–30 trillion."[49] This meant that exchange rates were increasingly driven not by trade transactions, but by whatever might cause those who controlled capital to shift funds from one currency to another. Portfolio managers, responsible for large pools of investment money, became critical participants in the world economy. And while no school of economics could model their behavior with much confidence, they seemed to be motivated primarily by two factors: differences in real interest rate returns between countries, and anticipation as to how, in the near term, a currency's value was likely to move.

---

48. This would not, of course, apply to the currencies of countries experiencing very high inflation.

49. Jeffrey E. Garten, "Gunboat Economics," *Foreign Affairs* 63, no. 3 (America and the World, 1984): 453. As Garten's broad range suggests, estimates of the magnitude of capital flows were necessarily imprecise.

When a major country like the United States pursued policies the markets perceived as inflationary—likely to reduce the currency's value and hence the "real" returns on dollar assets—that currency's value plummeted. The swing was exacerbated by the herd instinct of money managers, whose rewards come from calling the day's market correctly. Thus the dollar sank in 1977 and 1978.

When, conversely, the United States began its "riverboat gamble"[50] with Reaganomics in 1981, the situation turned around. The United States now needed foreign funds to finance its suddenly mammoth budget deficits. And real US interest rates were strong, spurred by this expanded government borrowing and by the tight-money policies of Federal Reserve Chairman Paul A. Volcker, who had come into office in 1979 determined to squeeze inflation out of the US economy. Foreign money therefore flowed in and drove the dollar skyward. By the end of 1984, a dollar would buy more than twice as many French francs, British pounds, and German marks as it had in October 1978. The dollar could even buy about 40 percent more Japanese yen.

US producers of traded goods found their competitive position demolished, as the currency misalignment made foreign goods far cheaper for Americans to buy and American products very dear for purchasers overseas. Exports stagnated, with the total for 1986 actually below that of 1980. Imports surged. The overall US trade deficit ballooned to $67 billion in 1983 and $159.5 billion in 1987. As former Federal Reserve Chairman Arthur F. Burns noted at mid-decade, such 12-digit deficits were "awesomely different from anything experienced in the past," by any country.[51]

The strong dollar was not the sole cause of the enormous shift.[52] But Secretary of State George P. Shultz stated the consensus view when he blamed it for "over half . . . of the deterioration in the US trade account."[53] From the perspective of producers of traded goods, the strong dollar of the mid-1980s was a devastating source of competitive disadvantage. It was something about which they, as individual economic agents, could do absolutely nothing. And it was something against which traditional intergovernmental trade bargaining was impotent as well.

But the trade balance *was* responsive to exchange rate change. And just as the rise of the dollar brought unprecedented trade pain, its rapid fall

---

50. The phrase is that of Howard Baker, then majority leader of the US Senate, who guided the Reagan program to enactment.

51. "The American Trade Deficit," *Foreign Affairs* 62, no. 5 (Summer 1984): 1068.

52. The other major sources were the developing-country debt crisis, which sharply curtailed exports to Latin America, and the fact that the US economy grew more rapidly, in 1983 and 1984, than those of its major trading partners.

53. "National Policies and Global Prosperity," address at the Woodrow Wilson School, Princeton University, Princeton, NJ, 11 April 1985, photocopy.

brought substantial relief. By the end of 1987, the dollar could buy only half as many yen—or marks—as it could in early 1985. With this new price advantage, US exports, stagnant for six years, doubled between 1986 and 1992. Imports maintained their rapid growth for a while, and the annual trade deficit did not begin to decline until 1988. By 1991, however, it had finally dropped well below the $100 billion annual rate; import growth had slackened (with recession an important cause), while the export boom continued.[54]

But if the monthly trade deficits were now lower, deficits they remained. And the United States was still borrowing overseas to finance them.

Economic Tripolarity and the End of the Cold War

Finally, Americans had to digest the fruits of a great victory: the end of the Cold War and the demise of their longtime Soviet adversary. For over 40 years, that global political-military confrontation had dominated American foreign policy. It had also muted economic conflicts, since leading US trade competitors were also its most critical Cold War allies.

Now, suddenly, the Cold War was won, with the collapse of the Warsaw Pact in 1989–90 and the disintegration of the Soviet Union in 1991. The United States emerged as the sole military superpower, flexing its military muscle by leading a United Nations coalition in reversing Iraq's conquest of Kuwait, and extracting major financial contributions in support of this campaign from Tokyo and Bonn. Yet simultaneously it found the going harder on economic issues, as illustrated by the December 1990 breakdown in the Uruguay Round multilateral trade talks, and the rise in trade and economic frictions with Japan.

---

54. The dollar began falling in early 1985, but as Paul R. Krugman noted, "through much of 1987 [trade] imbalances continued to grow, leading to widespread assertions that the traditional international adjustment process no longer worked." In fact, Krugman concludes, the US "export boom . . . happened just about when and in the magnitude that the traditional [economic] models would have predicted." *Has the Adjustment Process Worked?* POL-ICY ANALYSES IN INTERNATIONAL ECONOMICS 34 (Washington, DC: Institute for International Economics, October 1991), 1–3, 46. Stephen Marris, on the other hand, writes that "the actual improvement in the US trade balance was about 30 percent less than it should have been according to the D&D model, reflecting an overestimation of the benefits from devaluation (common to most models of the US trade balance extant at the time)." See his essay, "Why No Hard Landing?" in C. Fred Bergsten, ed., *International Adjustment and Financing: The Lessons of 1985–1991* (Washington, DC: Institute for International Economics, 1992), 250. The "D&D model" is that in Marris' *Deficits and the Dollar.* Robert Z. Lawrence concludes that the experience of the 1980s offers "little support for the pessimists who have claimed that U.S. trade flows would not respond to exchange rate changes." See his "U.S. Current Account Adjustment: An Appraisal," *Brookings Papers on Economic Activity* 2 (1990): 382.

As recounted earlier in this chapter, the relative US economic position had been receding for decades. But mutual security dependence had kept Europe and Japan responsive to US trade leadership, and made leaders in all three inclined to compromise on trade issues in order to preserve the free world coalition. As Robert Gilpin noted, "Difficult economic issues dividing the three centers of world capitalism could frequently be resolved through appeals to the need for unity against the common Soviet enemy."[55] Now trilateral economic relations had lost their "security umbrella."[56] Leaders would need to pursue trade and trilateral cooperation for its own sake, or not pursue it at all.

A Tougher World

As these seven changes were intertwined, so too were their political effects. Explosion in the volume of trade meant greater import competition for American producers, and greater pressure for trade restrictions, even in the 1970s when the dollar was comparatively weak. The dollar misalignment of the early and mid-1980s compounded the political problem: It increased the volume of imports and consequent protectionist reaction, while demoralizing export interests because it curtailed their gains from open trade. The dollar decline of 1985–87 brought needed relief, economically and politically. But frustration continued.

The diminished relative position of the United States joined with stagflation and recession to cast a shadow on future American economic prospects. Such unhappy economic outcomes discredited, to a degree, arguments for a continuing commitment to open trade. And the end of the Cold War eliminated the necessity to compromise with allies on economic issues in order to maintain the grand anti-Soviet alliance. More generally, as successive presidents found themselves embattled with economic woes, they had less leeway to press market-opening measures at home, and felt more pressure to restrict imports or to demand that US trading partners buy US exports.

Stagflation and American "decline" were accompanied by the growing visibility of unfair foreign trade practices, as well as unequal market access in specific product areas. There was an understandable tendency to blame at least some of the "decline" on these foreign trade practices. The weakening of the GATT made it harder to achieve effective remedies for unfair practices within the multilateral system, and pressure for unilateral

---

55. "The Transformation of the International Political Economy," Jean Monnet Chair Papers (San Domenico, Italy: The European University Institute, 1991), 12.

56. C. Fred Bergsten, "The World Economy After the Cold War," *Foreign Affairs* 69, no. 3 (Summer 1990): 96–112. See also the articles by Theodore C. Sorensen and Peter Tarnoff in the same issue.

responses therefore increased. Reinforcing such pressure was the threatening nature of the United States' new competitors—Japan and the NICs—whose trade was growing at historically unprecedented rates, who clearly benefited from some form of government-business cooperation, and whose aggressiveness in exports preceded and exceeded their willingness to open their markets to imports.

Changes of this magnitude would have posed severe problems for the 1934 system even if it had retained its basic postwar character and strength. But it too was changing. This was due in part to the new international economic realities, but also in part to developments that were specific to US politics.

We turn now to these domestic system changes—the primary focus of part II of this book. And we begin with the United States Congress, that central constitutional authority whose interest in protecting itself from trade pressures was the key element in the effectiveness of the old trade order.

4

A Less Protected Congress

In the early postwar decades, the United States Congress was remarkably restrained in the exercise of its constitutional authority to "regulate commerce with foreign nations." Individual senators and representatives engaged in a great deal of trade rhetoric; they lent their names to hundreds of bills proposing trade restrictions for industries that were strong within their constituencies. Congress periodically passed general trade laws to extend, expand, and limit presidential negotiating authority, including the reciprocal trade act renewals in the 1950s, as well as larger authorization acts like those of 1962 and 1974. There were also times when Congress failed to deliver on important executive commitments: to the International Trade Organization charter of 1948, for example, or to the Kennedy Round antidumping agreement signed almost 20 years later.

But product-specific legislative output was sparse. Senators and representatives consistently referred particular cases elsewhere: to the Tariff Commission for assessing injury to petitioning industries, for example, or to the executive for negotiating tariff cuts or arranging limits on the inflow of particularly sensitive commodities. Bills proposing statutory protection for textiles or shoes or steel typically died in committee, often without so much as a hearing. With the exception of a few agricultural quotas, Congress almost never legislated specific import protection.

As outlined in chapter 2, such "voluntary restraint" by Congress was the central domestic political prerequisite for US international trade leadership. By delegating responsibility to the executive and by helping fashion a system that protected legislators from one-sided restrictive pressures, Congress made it possible for successive presidents to maintain and expand the liberal trade order.

Congressional restraint depended, in important part, on the capacity of legislative leaders to control the action by preventing floor votes on product-specific restrictions. In the words of one prescient analyst in 1974, the House Ways and Means Committee and its chairman were "in effect . . . hired to put a damper on particularism in tax and tariff matters."[1]

However, during the postwar period, Congress was changing. Power was spreading out among the 535 individual members; thus the legislative calendar and output were less subject to leaders' control. This change accelerated in the 1970s, particularly in the House of Representatives. At the same time, trade was becoming more important to the American economy.

Then, in the 1980s, this less-protected Congress was hit with unprecedented trade-political pressure, generated mainly by unprecedented trade deficits. And the Reagan administration was slow to respond. So legislators of both political parties seized the initiative, demanding tougher executive action to enter resistant foreign markets, and passing the first congressionally initiated omnibus trade bill since before Smoot-Hawley.

Counter to many predictions, Congress still did not "go protectionist." Nor did legislators reclaim their constitutional power to impose product-specific trade barriers. They continued to delegate broad powers to the executive—in the 1988 act and in the 1991 vote renewing "fast-track" negotiating authority for the multilateral Uruguay Round and for free trade negotiations with Mexico. But they did so more grudgingly, with more detailed demands and timetables, which constrained administration flexibility. They thus put more pressure than ever on the executive branch, making open US trade policies more dependent than ever on the latter's policy commitment and leadership skill.

■ ■ ■

The tragedy of one man came to symbolize the demise of the old order. In October 1974, even as the Senate Finance Committee was quietly marking up the authorizing legislation for the Tokyo Round, the chairman of its House counterpart became involved in a scandal that would force his resignation. For years, Wilbur D. Mills (D-AK) had been the consummate insider. The central congressional figure on trade and tax policy, he was perhaps the most powerful member of his chamber, yet he was little known to the general public. In a parliamentary regime, he might well have become prime minister. But in the United States, his one quest for national recognition was in a belated campaign for the 1972 Democratic presidential nomination. This campaign had peaked with a 4 percent vote in the New Hampshire primary, and Mills won a total of 33.8 delegate votes at the convention the following August.

---

1. David R. Mayhew, *Congress: The Electoral Connection* (New Haven, CT: Yale University Press, 1974), 154.

Now Mills' name would become a household word because of a bizarre incident that exposed his heavy drinking and involvement with a woman not his wife.[2] It came at a time when Mills' influence was already in decline. Suffering from a back ailment, he had missed most of the House Ways and Means markups of the Tokyo Round authorization bill the year before. Now his career and reputation publicly disintegrated. He won reelection in November, but the sudden scandal reduced his usually overwhelming majority to 59 percent. By December, he had declared himself an alcoholic and announced that he would not continue as Ways and Means chairman in the next Congress. Two years later, he retired from public office.

Mills was succeeded as chairman by Al Ullman (D-OR). He was replaced by no one. His talented Senate counterpart of the 1970s, Finance Chairman Russell B. Long (D-LA), would develop a formidable personal reputation, as would Long's successors, Robert J. Dole (R-KS) and Lloyd Bentsen (D-TX). In the 1980s, virtuoso politician Dan Rostenkowski (D-IL) would restore some of the old luster to Ways and Means. But, from the 1960s onward, the Senate was too freewheeling and democratic to permit the sort of personal policy dominance that Mills had exercised. In the 1970s the House became so as well.

Congressional Reform and the Weakening of Ways and Means

Even before the Arkansan's public fall from grace, the "excessive power" of Ways and Means had been "a major target of reorganization."[3] This was part of a broader challenge to the power of committee chairmen by congressional reformers.

American politics was opening up, and more and more legislators owed their election not to party machines but to personal entrepreneurship. They did not want to run the turtle's race between seniority and senility by serving quietly as apprentices for the 20 to 30 years it might take to move up the ranks to chair a major committee.

By the end of 1974, it was clear that new House members no longer had to wait. They could aspire to policy influence almost immediately. The post-Watergate election had brought no fewer than 75 new Democrats into the House. Adding to them the newly elected Republicans and the turnover in the 1972 election, more than one-third of the House members in January 1975 had not been there three years before.

---

2. A car in which Mills was riding was stopped (for speeding, without lights) by a National Park Service police cruiser, at which point the woman ran from the car and leaped into the nearby Washington Tidal Basin. The episode received extensive press coverage, particularly in the *Washington Post*, as the "full story" was gradually revealed.

3. Roger H. Davidson and Walter J. Oleszek, *Congress Against Itself* (Bloomington: Indiana University Press, 1977), 179.

The freshmen joined the veteran reformers to activate the long-moribund Democratic caucus. Exploiting a recently adopted requirement for caucus votes on all House committee chairs, they ousted three and threatened others. The caucus took particular steps to cut the powers of Ways and Means. Its Democratic members were stripped of one special source of power over their colleagues: the role of "committee on committees," deciding who would fill vacancies on all House panels. Ways and Means was also expanded from 25 to 37 members, making close management in the Mills mode harder for a successor to accomplish.

Not all reform ideas were adopted. One major internal review group, the "Bolling Committee," proposed in 1974 to take away substantial chunks of jurisdiction, moving authority over trade and tariffs, for example, to House Foreign Affairs. This proposal was set aside, and Ways and Means' substantive sphere remained largely intact.

Nevertheless, like other committees, Ways and Means was forced to form legislative subcommittees with separate staffs. This meant that, in the future, its chairman would share primary trade responsibility with the chairman of the Trade Subcommittee. The committee was also subject to new House rules making markups of bills generally open to the public. Bills were subject to procedural changes that made "open rules"—allowing floor amendments—the norm, so that on-the-record, roll-call votes on such amendments were now far easier for proponents to obtain.

In both its sources and its goals, the congressional reform movement was unrelated to trade. But the reformers' twin objectives—decentralization of power and openness of procedures—nonetheless struck at the heart of the old American trade policymaking system. Open US trade policy had been founded, in part, on closed politics, on a variety of devices that shielded legislators from one-sided restrictive pressures. It had prospered under congressional barons—Mills above all—who had enough leverage to manipulate issues and to protect their colleagues from those up-or-down votes that forced a choice between conviction and constituency. As noted in chapter 2, the system did not protect Congress all of the time; for example, agriculture was partly outside its domain. In addition, as illustrated by the "Mills bill" episode of 1970 (see chapter 2), an unfavorable sequence of events could overcome barriers to congressional action. Still, the 1934 system had succeeded in keeping the great bulk of product-specific protectionist proposals from coming to roll-call votes on the House floor.

This was the very sort of thing that reformers wanted to change. Although they were not thinking specifically of trade, their overall goal was to force policy choices out in the open by publicizing House actions and members' stands. Believing that "special interests" benefited from the closed system, they reasoned that if Congress were democratized and its operations exposed to the sunshine, then the larger public interest would prevail.

There was both truth and oversimplification in this critique of the cozy old system. Closed procedures could indeed benefit special interests. But they also could offer insulation to members who wanted to resist such interests but were reluctant to do so under the watchful eyes of their lobbyists. For while anyone could attend open meetings, it was typically the lobbyists who did. They came, they saw, and they reported back on what members were doing for (or against) their particular causes. More open floor procedures also offered new opportunities for special interests to press their proposals.[4]

Three textile episodes, spread over three decades, illustrate how more open House processes offered advantages to those seeking protection. In the spring of 1968, to buttress his candidacy for his first full Senate term, Senator Ernest F. Hollings (D-SC) won adoption of a stringent proposal for statutory textile quotas cosponsored by no fewer than 67 colleagues, attaching it to major Johnson administration tax legislation. However, as noted in chapter 2, this proposal stopped at the House door, for Mills, supported by the administration, refused to accept it in conference. The Senate Finance Committee cooperated; indeed, it generally counted on its House counterpart to kill such initiatives. (And Johnson, according to someone who served in his White House, added a personal flourish, making Hollings "an offer he couldn't refuse." He told the junior senator that if he pushed for another Senate floor vote the administration would defeat him and then spread the word around South Carolina that Hollings had bungled the textile industry's case.)

In 1978, Hollings won Senate adoption of another extreme industry proposal, one that would require an 11th-hour withdrawal of all the textile tariff reductions offered by the United States in the nearly completed Tokyo Round.[5] Senate Trade Subcommittee Chairman Abraham A. Ribicoff (D-CT) declared that this could "ensure the failure of the negotiation." Again the vehicle was a bill that the administration needed, one that renewed the lending authority of the Export-Import Bank. But now a weaker Ways and Means Committee, in a decentralized House, could not

---

4. John F. Witte draws a similar connection between congressional reform and special-interest tax provisions. See his "The Income Tax Mess: Deviant Process or Institutional Failure?" paper prepared for delivery at the 1985 Annual Meeting of the American Political Science Association, New Orleans (1 September 1985).

5. The industry was hardly in dire straits. The system of negotiated quota agreements had been broadened in the early 1970s from cotton products to those of all major fibers, and this had helped keep the total volume of textile imports in 1976–78 at about 6 percent below its peak in 1971–73.

prevent a floor vote on the proposal. So a much more elaborate procedural shuffle had to be devised to sidetrack the proposal.[6]

In 1985, with imports really surging, the textile industry was able to move a highly restrictive quota bill to the House floor through the Ways and Means Committee, notwithstanding the opposition of the chairmen of both the full committee and the trade subcommittee. Sponsored by Representative Ed Jenkins (D-GA), the bill would have imposed quotas on a global and on a country-specific basis. With nearly 300 members signing on as cosponsors, the Ways and Means leadership elected to send it to the floor without recommendation, in the expectation that President Ronald Reagan would veto the measure. Reagan did, and a motion to override failed by eight votes.[7] Similar bills were passed—and vetoed—in 1988 and 1990.

The textile industry campaign of 1978 contributed to the failure of the Carter administration to win enactment that same fall of legislation needed to complete the Tokyo Round of multilateral trade negotiations (MTN): extension of authority to waive enforcement of countervailing duties.[8] The chairman and the ranking Republican of the Ways and Means Trade Subcommittee then conceded defeat, declaring in a public letter to Special Trade Representative Robert S. Strauss that the countervailing duty waiver could not be passed in the next Congress unless the textile exclusion was attached. To prevent this, the administration was forced to buy off that industry with policy concessions in early 1979.

If congressional reform thus weakened the key committees, so also did changes in the content of trade policy. Senate Finance and House Ways and Means were, first and foremost, revenue committees. By historical precedent and recurrent argument, their trade authority was derived from tariffs—the main means of raising revenue during most of the republic's

---

6. The Export-Import Bank measure was formally abandoned, its provisions attached to another bill at 4 a.m. on the last day of the 95th Congress. The textile-tariff proposal was brought to the House floor and adopted overwhelmingly, but as an amendment to a bill President Jimmy Carter could afford to veto—one authorizing the sale of Carson City silver dollars. By design or coincidence, this bill was one of the last two of the session to be formally "enrolled" and sent to the White House, and the presidential veto thus could be delayed until after the mid-term election (the other straggler, also vetoed, provided for meat import quotas).

7. The veto took place in December 1985, but in an unusual action, industry supporters won postponement of an override vote until the following summer, in a successful effort to toughen the administration's stance in the talks for extension of the Multi-Fiber Arrangement.

8. Europeans had insisted from the start that they would not negotiate under threat of such duties being imposed under the old, pre-GATT US law, which did not require that petitioning industries prove injury from imports, at the same time as they were working out a new subsidy-countervail-code agreement under which the United States would impose such a test. Although the Trade Act of 1974 had granted a five-year authorization for the Tokyo Round, it only provided a four-year authority for waiving countervailing duties. This expired on 3 January 1979, just as the negotiations were reaching their climax.

existence. Tariffs' declining importance in trade policy undercut this juris-dictional rationale. The rise of nontariff trade issues in the 1970s—such as government procurement, product standards, and subsidies—inevitably brought other committees into the substance of trade policy.

How then could Congress play its role in the trade system? On one major type of business—authorization and implementation of major trade agreements—it showed considerable creativity by developing new rules for expedited action that led to the overwhelming 1979 vote in favor of the MTN. On product-specific issues, however, Congress had become more vulnerable to special-interest pressures.

Renewing the Delegation of Power: The "Fast-Track" Procedures

From the Reciprocal Trade Agreements Act of 1934 through the Trade Ex-pansion Act of 1962, the means by which Congress delegated authority for trade negotiations remained basically the same. Successive statutes authorized executive officials to negotiate (within specified numerical limits) reductions in US tariffs, in exchange for reductions by US trading partners. When a deal was finally struck, it could be implemented by presidential proclamation, without further recourse to Capitol Hill.

For American trade negotiators, this arrangement had enormous ad-vantages. It gave them maximum credibility abroad, since their power to deliver on their commitments was not in doubt. It also increased their leverage with affected industries at home. Those fearing the effects of par-ticular tariff cuts could and did appeal for congressional backing, but since no formal ratification of the final trade agreement was required, the ultimate decision rested at the northwest end of Pennsylvania Avenue. In theory, of course, lobbyists could prevail on Congress to vote an exception for their product—as the textile industry sought to do in 1978. But this was very much an uphill fight, for it went against the whole system of delegating power and protecting legislators.

When a nontariff trade barrier (NTB) was at issue, however, there was no comparable system of advance authorization, and therefore no assur-ance that what US representatives negotiated abroad would become law at home. This weakness of the 1934 system was revealed rather dramati-cally in the final stages of the Kennedy Round. In exchange for related foreign concessions, the Johnson administration made two important nontariff commitments in 1967: to participate in a new GATT antidump-ing code and to eliminate the system of customs appraisals called the American Selling Price (ASP), which inflated the duties of certain cate-gories of US imports. Congress had authorized neither of these agree-ments; in fact, the Senate passed a sense-of-Congress resolution in 1966 opposing their negotiation. And Congress implemented neither of them.

In fact, it rendered US adherence to the antidumping code meaningless by insisting that whenever it conflicted with domestic law, the latter would prevail.[9]

These precedents were hardly encouraging. With tariffs now at a fraction of Smoot-Hawley levels, future trade rounds would focus increasingly on NTBs. How could US negotiators be credible internationally? And how could Congress be insulated from pressure to reject or rework what the executive branch had wrought?

The Nixon administration confronted this problem in early 1973 when it sought legislation to authorize a trade round giving priority to nontariff distortions. Not surprisingly, it proposed a procedure nearly identical to that for tariffs. Congress would authorize talks to bargain down NTBs; the president would implement the agreements reached by proclaiming the necessary changes in US domestic statutes, which would go into effect unless either house of Congress vetoed the measure within 90 days. The process was similar to that inaugurated in the New Deal for executive branch reorganization: The president could put forward "reorganization plans," which became law unless the House or the Senate objected.

The House accepted this legislative veto proposal; the Senate did not. It was, argued senior Finance Democrat Herman E. Talmadge of Georgia, "not the way we make laws." This procedure might be all right for government organization, but for substantive policy he was convinced that such an open-ended delegation of power to amend statutes was unconstitutional. Talmadge saw no alternative to affirmative congressional action, after the fact, on all specific, nontariff changes in American law resulting from trade negotiations. And his Finance Committee colleagues agreed.

This seemed to render negotiations impossible: How could foreign governments deal seriously with the United States if Congress might reject or amend the outcome or never take definitive action at all? However, negotiations between leaders from the office of the special representative for trade negotiations (STR), Talmadge, and Finance Committee staff yielded an alternative that the senator found acceptable. This was a statutory commitment to an up-or-down vote, within a specified period of time, on any legislation implementing an NTB agreement submitted by the president.

As finally enacted, the Trade Act included an elaborate procedural timetable aimed at ensuring expeditious legislative action. After consulting with the relevant congressional committees, the president would give notice of intent at least 90 days before entering into any NTB agreement.

---

9. For detail and documentation on this episode, see Michael J. Glennon, Thomas M. Franck, and Robert C. Cassidy, Jr., *United States Foreign Relations Law: Documents and Sources*, vol. 4, International Economic Regulation (London: Oceana Publications, 1984), 1–38.

Once he did so, Congress would act within 60 days of his submitting the implementing bill, under rules barring committee or floor amendments.[10]

This was not a perfect solution for executive negotiators, for they could not assure their foreign counterparts that Congress would deliver. But they could promise a prompt and clear answer.

These new procedures were adopted to facilitate negotiations abroad. Yet, although no one fully realized it at the time, they would also reshape the policy process at home. Specifically, on trade agreements, the procedures allowed the new, "open" Congress to replicate its closed predecessor. With the legislative process limited in scope and time, the stance of the trade committees, Finance and Ways and Means, was once again likely to prove decisive. To be confident of favorable floor actions, the STR's office needed the committees' overwhelming support of the agreements negotiated. This meant paying attention to committee members and aides, whom the legislation made official observers and advisers at the negotiations.

In practice, the Hill's substantive contribution was limited for most of the MTN. But as the end of the talks approached in the spring of 1978, the senior trade expert on the Finance Committee staff, Robert C. Cassidy, Jr., posed a procedural challenge. He began pressing for a major congressional role in the drafting of the nonamendable MTN implementing legislation that the president was to propose. Politically, he argued, enactment of such legislation would require a joint commitment by the STR and the trade committees. Operationally, this could best be accomplished if they developed that legislation together.

Insofar as possible, Cassidy proposed, they would replicate the normal legislative process. In sessions with STR Robert Strauss and other executive branch representatives that came to be labeled "nonmarkups," Finance and Ways and Means would advise separately on the implementing bill's substance. They would then reconcile their differences in a "nonconference." Finally, the drafting of the actual statutory language would be an interbranch process, with congressional legal aides working with counterparts in executive agencies much as they did on normal trade legislation. Only then would the president send the formal, nonamendable implementing bill to Capitol Hill.

There was some initial skepticism at the staff level in STR: Did they really want to give Capitol Hill that strong a role in drafting the president's bill? But ties between trade office and Finance staff were strong—STR

---

10. For details, see I. M. Destler, *Renewing Fast-Track Legislation* (Washington, DC: Institute for International Economics, POLICY ANALYSES IN INTERNATIONAL ECONOMICS 50, September 1997), 1–2, 6–8; Matthew J. Marks and Harald B. Malmgren, "Negotiating Nontariff Distortions to Trade," *Law and Policy in International Business* 7, no. 2 (1975): 338–41; and Glennon, Franck, and Cassidy, *Foreign Relations Law*, especially 41–65. The maximum time period for action on an "implementing revenue bill" was slightly longer: 90 days.

General Counsel Richard R. Rivers had worked for that committee prior to 1977—and so STR acquiesced. But "unofficially," by one authoritative report, "STR said they still hoped to carry on the bill drafting process without too much congressional interference."[11] So Finance senators summoned STR Strauss and won his personal assent to this procedure, which was quickly confirmed in an exchange of letters. Ways and Means, never a formal party to the arrangement, followed it in practice.[12]

In return for this considerable concession on procedure, the executive branch won near-total congressional approval of the substance of the MTN agreements it negotiated, which were implemented through a single legislative package, the Trade Agreements Act of 1979.[13] On the most sensitive issue—how tough an injury test would be applied in US countervailing duty cases—the code commitment to a "material injury" test survived a strong industry challenge. So strong was Strauss's credibility by this time that he reportedly clinched his argument by declaring that "the French want it" this way. "I don't know why and [Deputy STR Alan Wm.] Wolff doesn't know why and Rivers doesn't know why, but I need you to go along!"[14]

Congressional action was expeditious as well. On 4 January 1979, President Jimmy Carter gave the required 90-day notice of intent to conclude the MTN. By 6 March, the Senate Finance Committee had begun its series of nine "nonmarkups," and by 16 May, the House Ways and Means Subcommittee on Trade concluded its 15th such session. Representatives of the two then joined in a "nonconference" on 21–23 May. All these meetings were closed to the public, although hearings were held in both com-

---

11. Glennon, Franck, and Cassidy, *Foreign Relations Law*, 161.

12. See Robert C. Cassidy, Jr., "Negotiating About Negotiations," in Thomas M. Franck, ed., *The Tethered Presidency* (New York: New York University Press, 1981), 264–82; I. M. Destler and Thomas R. Graham, "United States Congress and the Tokyo Round: Lessons of a Success Story," *World Economy* (June 1980): 53–70; Destler, "Trade Consensus; SALT Stalemate: Congress and Foreign Policy in the Seventies," in Thomas E. Mann and Norman J. Ornstein, eds., *The New Congress* (Washington, DC: American Enterprise Institute, 1981), 333–40; and documents in Glennon, Franck, and Cassidy, *Foreign Relations Law*, 153–99.

13. In only one case did its congressional consultations force the administration to alter a previously negotiated accord: the House Small Business Committee protested the proposal to open up to international bidding US government contracts reserved for minority-owned enterprises. Strauss responded by substituting other opportunities for foreign firms to sell to US agencies.

14. One interesting example of a substantial change in US policies resulting from the MTN was the wine gallon concession, in which American negotiators agreed to thoroughgoing revision of a method of computing excise taxes on distilled spirits that dated from the mid-19th century and that had the effect of penalizing imports. For a full description, see Gilbert R. Winham, *International Trade and the Tokyo Round Negotiation* (Princeton, NJ: Princeton University Press, 1986), chapter 7.

mittees and press releases reported major committee decisions as they were made.

Most interesting perhaps was the fact that this quasi-legislative process cut the full Senate and House out of the main action. When a 373-page "committee print" containing proposed statutory language was finally circulated on 1 June, all the major decisions had been made. With a few changes, these same words were what the president proposed to Congress in his nonamendable bill 18 days later. Both chambers passed the bill in July, by votes of 395 to 7 and 90 to 4. One who voted no, reformist Representative A. Toby Moffett (D-CT), gave testimony to how effectively the broad membership had been excluded when he protested that "the speed with which we were expected to get on with this bill did not provide ample opportunity for full analysis."[15]

The Carter administration, with STR Robert Strauss in the lead, had constructed a carefully balanced MTN package that responded to all major US trade interests. Some observers actually felt that Strauss had been too responsive, and cited the overwhelming approval margins as evidence. Ranking Ways and Means Republican Barber B. Conable (R-NY) recalled warning him, "You're buying a landslide," giving away too much. In terms of congressional process, however, the key was that the "fast-track" provisions protected the bulk of legislators from product-specific pressure in 1979 just as effectively as the bargaining tariff, and the closed rule barring House floor amendments, had done in the 45 years previous. The administration, in alliance with the primary trade committees, shouldered the main political burden for the members at large. And the main congressional trade players clearly were pleased with the process, for they included in the implementing act a provision that extended this procedure for negotiating and implementing NTB agreements through 3 January 1988.

Still, there were important differences between the new NTB process and the old one on tariffs, and these differences had policy consequences. One was the fact that Congress now had to pass legislation at both ends of a negotiation. For the Kennedy Round tariff agreements, the Trade Expansion Act of 1962 had sufficed. The Tokyo Round required the Trade Act of 1974 to get it going and the Trade Agreements Act of 1979 to conclude it successfully.

This meant that during the talks, US negotiators had to worry about the danger that unhappy industries might join together and mobilize a congressional majority to block the implementing bill. In fact, negotiators felt they had to prevent even the formation of such a coalition, since once one came together there was no telling how widely it might spread. Thus, in addition to mobilizing maximum support from export interests that stood

---

15. *Congressional Record*, Daily Edition, 13 July 1979, E3582.

to gain from a successful MTN, the STR had to show particular sensitivity to the demands of the more powerful among the potential losers, the import-affected industries.

So pressure for special deals increased. Textiles, which had already gotten its Multi-Fiber Arrangement during the run-up to the 1974 act, won a tightening of its implementation vis-à-vis the major East Asian exporters and mainland China. The steel industry won adoption of the trigger price mechanism (TPM), through which the US government pledged to initiate antidumping action if foreign products were sold at prices below certain specified minimum levels.

Further policy concessions were included in the 1979 law itself. Though generally consistent with the MTN codes, its drafting was much more than a pro forma implementation exercise. In fact, it grew to exceed the 1974 law in its length, and the key committees used their leeway to press purposes well beyond those the MTN required. As will be recounted in chapter 5, Senate Finance held up final action until President Carter submitted a proposal to reorganize the trade bureaucracy. Even more important for trade policy, steel industry ally John Heinz (R-PA) joined with trade law reformer John C. Danforth (R-MO) to bring about a comprehensive rewriting of the countervailing duty and the antidumping laws, with effects to be set forth in chapter 6.

Finally, the content of the codes meant that Finance and Ways and Means had to acknowledge more explicitly than ever that trade regulation reached into the jurisdictions of numerous competing committees. The 1974 act foreshadowed this recognition, for the fast-track procedures provided only that an implementing bill be referred to "the appropriate committee" in each chamber. The decision to use a single implementation bill for the entire MTN meant that Ways and Means kept its primacy on MTN legislation, and in practice it even proved possible to get the other committees to waive their claim to joint referral. But in return, Trade Subcommittee Chairman Charles A. Vanik (D-OH) invited members of the relevant committees to participate in nonmarkups affecting their jurisdictions. Senate Finance went even farther, passing entire titles on to sister committees and adopting their recommendations as its own.

Most important was the fact that the fast-track procedures solved only half of the "Congress problem" insofar as trade was concerned. They established a new mechanism for authorizing and implementing major international, trade-expanding agreements. Thus, they extended the possibility of US leadership in negotiating such agreements into the posttariff trade world. In 1984, Congress would authorize negotiation of bilateral agreements under this procedure, enabling the Reagan administration to negotiate free trade arrangements with Israel and Canada and win expeditious, overwhelming fast-track approval. And in 1988 and 1991, as discussed later, Congress again extended the fast-track time period, both for the Uruguay Round multilateral talks and for negotiations with Mexico.

But this procedure did nothing to divert the many other product-specific restrictive proposals that individual members had always put forward and always would. As Congressman Conable phrased it a few months before his retirement at the end of 1984, "Congress has become a participatory democracy. So you can't stop bad proposals as easily as you used to."[16]

Industry-Specific Proposals: The Automobile Case

The textile episodes offer one illustration of Conable's point. Few congressional trade leaders believed that the textile industry needed further protection, but they lacked both the authority and the mechanisms to prevent it.

This did not mean that Congress had become eager to pass statutory restrictions. In most instances, the aim of particular quota bills was still not to get them enacted into law but to demonstrate the sponsor's allegiance to a particular industry, or to pressure the executive branch, the appropriate foreign government, or both. Congress was still acting as a lobby to influence decisions made outside its halls.

In the early 1980s, the most dramatic and visible example was the struggle over trade in automobiles. The second oil shock of 1979 brought gasoline lines and a doubling of the price of motor fuel. As a result, demand shifted sharply toward small, high-mileage models. American carmakers were unprepared for this shift: Their sales fell off sharply, and imports, three-fourths of which came from Japan, expanded to meet the new demand.[17] Ford and General Motors suffered record losses, and Chrysler needed a governmental rescue to avert bankruptcy. US auto unemployment exceeded 300,000, out of a total of almost 1 million directly employed in the industry.[18]

Long the symbol of US economic supremacy, the auto industry was suddenly in very dire straits. The congressional response went through three distinct stages. The first, extending through most of 1980, was one of spotlighting the problem and hoping that established remedies would produce a solution. Vanik's Trade Subcommittee held hearings, sending a clear signal that some form of protective action might have to be taken. At

---

16. Personal interview, 31 July 1984.

17. In absolute numbers, the growth of imports was moderate, from 2 million in 1978 to 2.4 million in 1980. But their market share shot up from 17.7 percent to 26.7 percent, as sales of American-made vehicles plummeted during the same two years from 9.3 million to 6.6 million, the lowest figure since 1961. See Gilbert R. Winham and Ikuo Kabashima, "The Politics of U.S.-Japanese Auto Trade," in I. M. Destler and Hideo Sato, eds., *Coping with U.S.-Japanese Economic Conflicts* (Lexington, MA: Lexington Books, 1982), 76.

18. "The U.S. Automobile Industry, 1980," Report to the President from the Secretary of Transportation, January 1981, 83–85.

the same time, legislators supported the United Auto Workers (UAW) in its campaign to get Japanese automakers to build plants in the United States. The June submission of an escape clause petition by the UAW and Ford offered the hope that "the rules" could provide the needed relief. While the US International Trade Commission (USITC) deliberated, President Carter encouraged provision of generous adjustment assistance for laid-off workers, and his electoral rival, Ronald Reagan, promised in September to "try to convince the Japanese that . . . the deluge of their cars into the United States must be slowed."[19]

But the USITC decided in November, by a three-to-two vote, that it could not recommend relief because the major causes of the industry's woes were other than imports. Congress then moved quickly into the second stage, that of pressing for the issue to be treated as a "special case." Vanik rushed to schedule hearings and won House passage, before December adjournment, of a special resolution authorizing the president to negotiate an orderly marketing agreement with Japan.

In the new 97th Congress, the initiative shifted to the Senate. Vanik, a pragmatist frequently sympathetic to trade-impacted industries, had retired and was succeeded as subcommittee chair by liberal trade champion Sam M. Gibbons (D-FL). On the other side of the Hill, the surprise Republican capture of the Senate made John Danforth chairman of the Finance Subcommittee on International Trade. Automobiles were an important industry in his home state of Missouri, and he lost no time: He held hearings before Reagan's inauguration in January and introduced a bill in February that would impose statutory quotas on Japanese automobile imports for three years.

The aim was not to pass the bill but to pressure the Japanese, and to ensure that Reagan's general campaign promise won out over the liberal trade views of his senior economic advisers. Tokyo was, in fact, willing, but the Japanese Ministry of International Trade and Industry needed strong American pressure as leverage against its auto industry. The Reagan administration, however, wanted to minimize its own formal responsibility for any restrictive outcome. The result was a "look no hands" approach that confused Tokyo and increased the need for congressional threats. Finance Chairman Robert J. Dole (R-KS) claimed that he could count two-thirds of the Senate in support of the quota bill, enough to override a presidential veto, and Danforth scheduled a markup for 12 May.

All of this positioning had the intended result. On 1 May, with US Trade Representative William E. Brock in Tokyo, the Japanese government announced a "unilateral" commitment to limit exports for two to three years. This met the Finance Committee's demand for a "multi-year effort,"[20] and

---

19. Winham and Kabashima, "The Politics of U.S.-Japanese Auto Trade," 115.

20. Finance Committee Press Release 81–89, 29 April 1981.

in fact the restraints were extended every year through March 1993. It also enabled USTR Brock to satisfy the Japanese political need, by assuring them that, in the light of the plan, there was now no prospect of the quota legislation passing Congress. Danforth could declare the plan "an important step in the right direction," and set aside his bill.

The second phase thus produced modest protection for autos, and this solution lasted, politically, for about a year. But the US recession deepened, helping move the auto issue into the third phase, in which politics now spilled over outside the trade committees' control.

The impetus came from the United Auto Workers, a union long committed to open trade. Beset with growing unemployment and frustrated by the slow response by Toyota and Nissan to his campaign for Japanese investment in the United States, UAW President Douglas A. Fraser began in 1980 to suggest "local content legislation" as a long-term solution. But the real push came two years later. The continuing recession had caused US auto sales to plunge further, and despite the slightly lower sales forced by export restraints, the Japanese share of the US market edged further upward. The UAW responded with a bill that mandated a rigid domestic-content formula: The larger the number of cars a company sold here, the greater the portion of their total value would have to come from the United States, up to a maximum of 90 percent. Had it become law, this bill would have slashed future imports of autos and auto parts to a fraction of current levels.

Brock called it "the worst piece of economic legislation since the 1930s," and Danforth exaggerated very little in declaring that "the overwhelming majority" of members saw it as "perfectly ridiculous."[21] By making the bill a litmus test of the allegiance of labor Democrats, however, the UAW was able to win House adoption of a modified domestic-content bill by a 215 to 188 vote in December 1982. In November 1983, a House with 26 more Democrats passed a somewhat stronger bill by a slightly smaller margin, 219 to 199 votes. On both occasions, northeastern and midwestern Democrats voted almost unanimously in favor. The bill never reached the Senate floor, however, and the issue gradually faded from the trade scene as the US auto industry regained sales and strength, albeit at lower levels of employment.

Committee Competition and Policy Entrepreneurship

As important as the progress of domestic-content legislation was the process by which it was achieved. By drafting the legislation as a measure to regulate domestic production, its proponents managed to get it referred to the sympathetic Committee on Energy and Commerce. Ways and Means, the panel with established trade jurisdiction, was limited to sponsoring parallel hearings and urging rejection of the bill—suggesting a further erosion of the procedural checks on industry-specific trade legislation.

---

21. *Congressional Quarterly Almanac*, 1982, 56.

Energy and Commerce was chaired by an aggressive old-timer, John D. Dingell (D-MI), who had come to the House in 1955. But by 1982, its next eight ranking members, in terms of seniority, were members of the reformist class of 1975. They were, for the most part, policy activists in the Democratic party mainstream. With energy fading as a national concern, trade policy was a natural focus for their talents.

Ways and Means had also expanded in 1975, as noted at the outset of this chapter. But competition for seats on that committee was much keener, so in 1982 the most senior of its 1975 arrivals remained number seven on the committee (Gibbons, who chaired the Trade Subcommittee, had come to the House in 1963). And the energies of several of the more aggressive mid-level members—James R. Jones (D-OK, sixth in seniority), Richard A. Gephardt (D-MO, 12th) and Thomas J. Downey (D-NY, 13th)— were divided between Ways and Means and the Budget Committee.

The net result in the early 1980s was a certain imbalance of initiative and energy. Dingell and his committee were aggressive and policy active. Ways and Means continued in the more passive gatekeeper role, but without the power and procedural tools it had possessed a decade before.

Dingell's committee was far from seizing control of trade policy. In fact, when Dan Rostenkowski (D-IL) became Ways and Means chairman in 1981, Dingell faced an adversary whose political skills and concern for "turf" were at least equal to his own. In 1985, Rostenkowski himself would seize the initiative by cosponsoring a trade-restrictive bill targeted at Japan and other nations running large surpluses with the United States. And from then into the 1990s he was clearly the most important House figure on trade policy. But Energy and Commerce was an active contestant, and it pushed Ways and Means toward activism as well. It gave the Gibbons Trade Subcommittee strong reason to take initiatives about which some senior members were ambivalent, like toughening the trade-remedy laws to demonstrate seriousness about the trade problems of important constituencies.[22]

Activism in competing committees was also consistent with another congressional trend. Trade issues were becoming, to a greater extent, entrepreneurial issues, as members increasingly saw the subject as worthy of investment of their discretionary time.

Since the 1950s, there had been a sharp rise in policy entrepreneurship on Capitol Hill, particularly among liberals. Senators and representatives would adopt particular issues as their own, seeking both to improve government policy and to enhance their personal reputations. But through the mid-1970s, it is striking how seldom they made trade policy a vehicle for their ambitions. It was seen as a dull, "no-win" issue. Free trade was unappealing to the mass public; protectionism was anathema to the policy community. So neither broad stand was attractive for presentation to

---

22. As an aide to a relatively protectionist senator put it in an interview, "We always figured that the way to get Gibbons to do something was to get Dingell to do something."

a general national or party audience. Legislators (and presidential candidates) generally limited themselves to trade "noise" targeted at specific constituencies. Broader trade advocacy was left to idiosyncratic legislators like Senator Vance Hartke (D-IN), cosponsor of the Burke-Hartke quota bill of 1971. Its fate did not inspire emulation. Nor did the fate of Hartke himself, who was beaten decisively in his 1976 reelection contest.

Even on a central question like trade with Japan, activism was late in coming. It was not until 1977, for example, that a congressman, Democrat Jim Jones of Oklahoma, moved to concentrate his energies on this broad subject, forming a Ways and Means Task Force on US-Japan Trade. And one apparent reason why Senator Lloyd Bentsen (D-TX) suggested a surcharge against Japanese imports in 1979 was that despite the enormous rise in that country's sales to the US market, the senator's staff judged that none of Bentsen's 99 colleagues had yet made Japan "his" issue.

This could not, of course, continue. As detailed in chapter 3, trade was simply becoming too important to the American economy. So congressional debates reflected increasing trade advocacy: between 1975 and 1980, by one measure, the frequency of House and Senate floor references to trade went up by 70 percent.[23] And a comprehensive count, based on computerized bill summaries supplied by the Congressional Research Service (CRS), indicates a gradual increase in the number of trade-restrictive bills introduced in the House of Representatives: from 127 in the 96th Congress (1979–80) to 137 in the 97th and 144 in the 98th.[24] These included proposals to impose steel quotas or link wine import restrictions

---

23. This figure was arrived at by comparing the number of columns under "Foreign Trade" in the *Congressional Record Index*, adjusted for the index's overall length.

24. This computation draws on the computerized CRS bill digest file. If one counts only those bills whose primary purpose was to restrict trade, and whose primary apparent motivation was to benefit US producers (for example, excluding bills to bar purchases of Iranian crude oil, Ugandan coffee, etc.), this modest trend disappears: the numbers drop to 62, 56, and 57, respectively. There was a clear upsurge in 1985, however. In the first nine months of that year, 49 such bills were introduced, compared with just 30 in the same period two years earlier.

After this analysis was completed, Raymond J. Ahearn of CRS published a count that was more comprehensive in its coverage, and more detailed for 1985. Using a broader definition of trade, this computer search found 1,089 trade bills introduced in the 96th Congress, 1,150 in the 97th, 1,401 in the 98th, and 879 in 1985, the first year of the 99th. Bill-by-bill inspection of the 1985 group to eliminate nongermane legislation reduced the total to 634, of which 99 were significantly and directly protectionist in purpose and effect. There were also 51 routine bills adjusting tariffs upward, 77 "potentially protectionist" bills that would make it easier to obtain quasi-judicial trade relief, and 109 bills to "restrict trade to achieve nonprotectionist objectives." See Raymond J. Ahearn, "Protectionist Legislation in 1985" (Washington, DC: Congressional Research Service, 31 March 1986, processed).

At this author's request, Ahearn updated his general bill count in 1991: totals were 1,248 for the 99th Congress (1985–86), 1,455 for the 100th (1987–88), and 1,429 for the 101st (1989–90). Over this period—and for the first seven months of the 102nd Congress—trade bills were between 11.5 percent and 12.9 percent of total bills submitted (Ahearn to Destler, memorandum, 12 August 1991).

to wine export opportunities, and even, in one case, a proposal to establish a dollar ceiling for the bilateral US-Japan trade imbalance.

Many proposals have been in the "export politics" tradition of seeking to solve problems through trade expansion, opening foreign markets. But even here, several of the most prominent, in the words of two expert analysts, "break sharply with traditional US trade policy."[25] In their original form, the "reciprocity" bills sponsored by Danforth and Heinz sought to require restrictions on access to US markets in sectors where major trading partners denied US products comparable market opportunities. More generally, as Raymond J. Ahearn and Alfred Reifman noted at mid-decade, "the most common congressional approaches were based on unilateral standards of reciprocity, discrimination, and the threat of retaliation. Successive administrations have opposed similar approaches on the grounds that they violate US international obligations, undermine US global leadership, and are economically counterproductive."[26]

Reinforcing such congressional approaches was a spreading belief that the United States needed to recognize that the liberal trade ideal was impractical and outmoded and to adopt a more sophisticated, interventionist approach to international trade, comparable to that of its trading partners. Intellectual staff aides put forward appealing alternate conceptions: we should no longer pretend that we or anybody else could make market openness the touchstone of commercial relations; rather we should determine the shape of the future economy we want and use trade policy as one tool to bring it about.[27]

More than once in the 1980s and early 1990s, an explosion of specific initiatives signaled to many who followed trade that Congress was at last going to reclaim direct, detailed control over "commerce with foreign nations." In late 1982, the plight of import-impacted industries was exacerbated by an overvalued dollar, with record unemployment fueling worker discontent. Frustration with US trading partners was compounded by

---

25. Raymond J. Ahearn and Alfred Reifman, "U.S. Trade Policy: Congress Sends a Message," in Robert E. Baldwin and J. David Richardson, eds., *NBER Conference Report: Current U.S. Trade Policy: Analysis, Agenda, and Administration* (Cambridge, MA: National Bureau of Economic Research, 1986), 104.

26. Ibid. See also William R. Cline, *"Reciprocity": A New Approach to World Trade Policy?* POLICY ANALYSES IN INTERNATIONAL ECONOMICS 2 (Washington, DC: Institute for International Economics, September 1982). There was some resistance among the leaders of multinational firms. The Business Roundtable warned, for example, that "an improper use of reciprocity could worsen, instead of improve, our economic vitality. If misapplied, the concept has the potential for further undermining an already vulnerable multilateral trading system by triggering retaliation." "Statement of the Business Roundtable Task Force for International Trade and Investment on Reciprocity in Trade" (19 March 1982, processed), 2.

27. See, for example, US Congress, House Energy and Commerce Committee, *The United States in a Changing World Economy: The Case for an Integrated Domestic and International Commercial Policy*, Staff Report, September 1983.

seemingly endless market-access negotiations with the Japanese, and by bitterness about European agricultural protectionism, which boiled over at a fractious GATT Ministerial Conference in November. Looking at these trends, and at the number of trade-related bills on the near-term legislative schedule, Senate Finance Chairman Robert Dole predicted that 1983 would be "the year of trade" on Capitol Hill. The *National Journal* rang in that year with a headline, "The Protectionist Congress—Is This the Year That the Trade Barriers Go Up?" "The 98th Congress," it reported, "may be dominated by legislators angered by what they view as unfair European and Japanese trade practices and eager to retaliate in kind."[28]

Two years later, the driving force was the hitherto unimaginable US trade deficit, which shot above $100 billion in 1984 and continued in 12 digits through 1990. Feeling enormous pressure from affected producers, and frustrated by the administration's neglect of both specific trade issues and the overvalued dollar, senators and representatives began in the spring of 1985 by unloading on Japan, passing strongly worded (albeit nonbinding) resolutions by votes of 92 to 0 and 397 to 19. Through this and subsequent moves toward omnibus legislation, they seized the trade policy initiative—and retained it through the end of the Reagan administration.

On each occasion, however, Congress made only marginal policy changes. While it forced greater aggressiveness in US trade policy, it refrained from taking clear control, and from imposing protectionism. It stepped back from the abyss. The ferment of 1982–83 culminated in the modest, marginally liberalizing Trade and Tariff Act of 1984. The raging trade fires of 1985–86 were dampened, by and large, in the comprehensive—but only marginally restrictive—Omnibus Trade and Competitiveness Act of 1988. And a vigorous debate in 1991, triggered by the launch of NAFTA talks with Mexico and Canada, culminated in solid—though not overwhelming—congressional endorsement of the Bush administration's multilateral and bilateral trade initiatives.

The first anticlimax came in 1983. Contrary to Dole's forecast, Congress did little on trade that year, as the long-delayed US economic recovery began, taking some of the bite out of the drive for statutory restrictions. Once again, legislators were willing to channel pressure elsewhere. Even when, in 1984, 201 representatives signed onto a steel quota bill, the predominant view was that it would serve the traditional function of pressuring the executive branch rather than find its way into the statute books. And the pressure proved successful, as President Reagan ordered USTR Brock to negotiate export restraint agreements with major foreign suppliers. The summer and fall of 1984, however, brought a surge of congressional activity, capped by enactment of the first general trade bill in five years.

---

28. *National Journal*, 1 January 1983, 18.

The Trade and Tariff Act of 1984: Pressure Contained

The closing months of the 98th Congress saw the policy context worsen.[29] By summer, most experts had come around to C. Fred Bergsten's projection that the US trade deficit would top $100 billion in 1984. This put advocates of open trade very much on the defensive and made the prospects bleak for the several relatively specialized trade bills on the legislative agenda.

These included one "must" item for the liberal trade community, trade preferences for developing countries (GSP, or Generalized System of Preferences). In the Trade Act of 1974, the United States had, pursuant to an international agreement, granted these countries duty-free access to the US market for a range of their products for a 10-year period ending on 3 January 1985. GSP had precious little support among American economic interests, even though only 3 percent of total US imports were affected— because of the exclusion of sensitive articles (for example, textiles and shoes) and ceilings on benefits available to any one country for a specific product. Organized labor opposed the program, particularly for the "big three" newly industrialized countries (NICs)—Hong Kong, Korea, and Taiwan—whose products were generally competitive in the United States without special treatment. But Third World nations attached great symbolic importance to GSP. Its abandonment would make it very hard for the United States to negotiate with these countries on matters that were important to interests here—intellectual property protection, for example, and access to their markets.

The prospects for passing GSP extension on its own were dim: The administration had been unable in 1983 to find a single House member to sponsor it. There was on the table, however, a trade proposal that was enormously popular in both Congress (it had 163 House sponsors) and the Reagan White House: a bill authorizing negotiation of a bilateral free trade agreement with Israel. On 31 July 1984, the Senate Finance Committee voted to combine the two, add a number of other proposals (including Danforth's modified reciprocity bill), and attach the whole package to a minor tariff-adjustment bill (HR 3398) that had already been passed by the other chamber.[30]

USTR Brock welcomed this development. With the House stymied on GSP, this offered the best opportunity for forward movement. Trade Sub-

---

29. The following pages draw substantially on confidential interviews with persons involved in the enactment of the Trade and Tariff Act of 1984. See appendix A of the first edition of this book (1986) for a more detailed account of its enactment.

30. This legerdemain was necessary because of the constitutional requirement that "all bills for raising revenue," and hence bills affecting tariffs, "originate in the House of Representatives" (Article I, Section 6).

committee Chairman Danforth favored it for this reason, and another: It was the best vehicle for enactment of his reciprocity proposal. But Majority Leader Howard H. Baker, Jr. (R-TN) was reluctant to allot Senate floor time to the bill. Danforth had not been able to negotiate a "unanimous consent" agreement limiting time for debate or amendments that might be proposed. The leader feared, therefore, that the bill would be tied up procedurally on the floor and loaded with protectionist baubles for a wide range of industries.

But because of a House-Senate-administration impasse on budget legislation, there was floor time available in mid-September. So Baker gave Danforth his chance. The tacit understanding was that if he lost control, the bill would be pulled off the floor, never to return.

In one sense, Baker's fears were borne out. Danforth never lost control, but to keep it—as debate extended from the anticipated two days to three, then four—he had to accept six floor amendments on Monday, 14 on Tuesday, 12 on Wednesday, and 11 on Thursday. The pattern, faintly reminiscent of Smoot-Hawley, was to bargain down but then accept industry-specific protection proposals, and among the successful floor amendments were those favoring producers of copper, bromine, wine, footwear, ferroalloys, and dairy products. When, on the second day of debate, the president made his decision to negotiate voluntary restraint agreements with steel-exporting countries, an amendment was added giving the administration legal authority to enforce such restraints.

But for three factors, the damage would have been even greater. First, on the second day, the Senate did signal that there were limits by rejecting a particularly egregious proposal to reverse a USITC decision and raise the tariff on water-packed tuna. Second, during the final two days, Danforth was supported by the personal presence of Brock, who employed his floor privileges as a former senator to involve himself aggressively in the brokering process. Third, organized labor did essentially nothing, reacting very slowly when the legislation was suddenly taken up. Labor senators proposed neither domestic-content requirements nor anything else for autos. Nor did any senator advance a labor amendment curbing GSP, which might either have passed or forced the extended debate that would have been fatal to the legislation.

So the bill survived, passing the Senate late Thursday by a vote of 96 to 0. The margin reflected the number of interests that had been temporarily "bought off" in the bill itself or through agreements negotiated on the side. An alarmed *Washington Post* lambasted the result in an editorial entitled "The Anti-Trade Bill": "The losers in every major trade case of the past year have managed to insert language to try to win in Congress what they lost in litigation."[31]

---

31. *Washington Post*, 28 September 1984.

Senate passage broke the Ways and Means logjam, and a week later that committee reported out four separate trade bills: GSP renewal, US-Israel free trade, "steel import stabilization," and "wine equity." Chairman Rostenkowski secured floor time for each under "modified closed rules" that limited amendments. Six days later, on Wednesday, 3 October, the House passed each of the four separately, defeating in the process, by a surprisingly wide 233 to 174 margin, a labor-backed Gephardt amendment that would have eliminated preferences for the big three NICs. It then attached the four bills as amendments to the Senate-passed HR 3398, along with several previously enacted bills, the most important being the "Trade Remedies Reform Act" developed by Trade Subcommittee Chairman Sam Gibbons. Interestingly, the domestic-content bill was not among them.

By this point, time for compromising House-Senate differences had grown very short: the target for *sine die* adjournment of the 98th Congress was the coming weekend. One question was whether the product-specific amendments in the Senate bill (and to some degree the House bill as well) could be deleted, rendering the bill acceptable to President Reagan. Another was whether the House conferees could be persuaded to yield on most other issues where the two bills differed—preferences, procedures for approving the US-Israel agreement, trade remedies. If they did not, Brock and the administration could not accept the bill. But what could House representatives get in return?

The answer, it soon became clear, was in the provisions with which Rostenkowski was personally most identified, those on steel. He had pushed through a bill that, in the name of implementing Reagan's just announced "national policy for the steel industry," incorporated two proposals advocated by presidential challenger Walter F. Mondale and other Democratic critics of the president's action: a market-share target of 17 percent for steel imports, and an "adjustment" condition for steel firms, which were, as a price for continued protection, required to reinvest all net cash flow in steel operations and allocate 1 percent of earnings to worker retraining. Rostenkowski insisted on retaining these, and was granted most of his demands. One by one the other issues were worked out, in a frenetic 26-hour conference punctuated by both policy and personal tensions. By the conclusion of the Senate-House deliberations Friday afternoon, 5 October, Congress had abandoned its weekend adjournment target, and the compromise bill, labeled the Trade and Tariff Act of 1984, was adopted by both houses the following Tuesday. Somehow, observed the *Washington Post* in a follow-up editorial, "most of the bad stuff got thrown out [in conference] and all of the good stuff stayed."[32]

---

32. "On Trade, a Happy Ending," *Washington Post*, 12 October 1984. Singled out for special praise was "William E. Brock, who worked mightily and, as it turned out, highly effectively to change the thrust of this bill."

It had proved possible for Congress to pass a general trade bill that extended an unpopular program (GSP), while omitting or gutting most protectionist provisions. Language designed to benefit copper, ferroalloys, shoes, and dairy products was deleted or neutralized. On preferences, in fact, the bill represented a move in the liberal-internationalist direction, in comparison with the 1974 law that it replaced, by encouraging the administration to negotiate with the NICs for market access and intellectual property rights, and offered the NICs inducements as well as penalties.[33]

But the bill had restrictive provisions as well.[34] Most serious was one that originated in the administration—the new steel policy. The White House had suggested, in a way that the industry read as a promise, that it would seek to limit total steel imports to a certain level. This cleared the way for the bill to incorporate a global import ceiling, something even the textile industry had been unable to achieve. It was written as a bipartisan compromise—between the 17 percent ceiling favored by Mondale and the 20.2 percent Reagan target—reflecting only the "sense of Congress." But the bill included a future threat, of "such legislative actions concerning steel and iron ore products as may be necessary," if the Reagan program did not "produce satisfactory results within a reasonable period of time."[35] And the entire steel title was enacted hastily, without hearings or serious review of the language in either body.

Still, in 1984, Congress was able to enact a modest, balanced trade law. Legislative success that year was the product of a confluence of particular personalities: Brock, Danforth, and Rostenkowski. Each, in a different way, wanted the omnibus bill to pass, and each was skilled in moving it forward. Each was willing to limit rewards for special interests, and each proved indispensable to its success.

But the way the bill moved through the Congress underscored the weakness of the old institutional checks, particularly in the House. With Ways and Means deadlocked, the Senate had to move on the legislation first, something Wilbur Mills would never have allowed. This exposed the

---

33. The Reagan administration used this leverage to win policy concessions—getting Singapore, for example, to revamp its intellectual property laws. Then, in the spring of 1988, it revoked trade preferences for Singapore anyway, together with those for Hong Kong, Korea, and Taiwan.

34. For example, it included technical changes in the trade-remedy laws, using such obscure labels as "cumulation," which tilted them in favor of domestic claimants. It also included a watered-down but still objectionable precedent on wine, allowing producers of grapes to challenge wine imports and thus provoking a confrontation with the European Community. The Community won a GATT panel ruling against this law in 1986, and the United States complied, but only because "the law expired." See Robert E. Hudec, "Thinking about the New Section 301: Beyond Good and Evil," in Jagdish Bhagwati and Hugh T. Patrick, eds., *Aggressive Unilateralism: America's 301 Trade Policy and the World Trading System* (Ann Arbor: University of Michigan Press, 1990), 157.

35. Trade and Tariff Act of 1984, Section 803.

bill to the vagaries of that freewheeling chamber and guaranteed that there would be an enormous amount of cleanup work to do in the House-Senate conference—and little time to do it.

The legislation cleared most current issues on the trade-legislative agenda. So as the 98th Congress completed its work, there was a widespread expectation that its successor would focus on other issues. But 1985 through 1988 would be the *years* of trade, the period of greatest congressional trade intensity since the 1930s. From the late-January 1985 release of figures showing a $123 billion trade deficit for calendar year 1984,[36] to the presidential signing of comprehensive trade legislation almost four years later, trade leaped to a place near the top of congressional preoccupations. Both House and Senate seized the trade policy initiative, and the second Reagan administration struggled to stay in the game.

1985–88: The Years of Trade

The initial target of congressional activism in 1985 was Japan, the nation with the largest trade surplus with the United States. Danforth and his Senate Finance colleagues felt frustrated on a number of fronts. The bilateral imbalance, conservatively measured, had shot up from $19.3 billion to $33.6 billion, making it far higher than any the United States had ever run with any country. At the same time, American negotiators seeking to open Japanese markets felt continuing frustration, even in areas like telecommunications, in which there was a long negotiating history and a strong commitment to progress from Prime Minister Yasuhiro Nakasone. And the Reagan administration was declaring itself ready to end voluntary auto restraints. Before the end of March, the Senate had passed, without opposition, a strongly worded Danforth resolution denouncing "unfair Japanese trade practices" and calling for retaliation unless Japan opened its markets sufficiently to American products to offset its anticipated increases in auto sales. The House followed with a parallel resolution, which, although it was directed more at the overall US trade imbalance and its macroeconomic causes, also singled out Japan for priority attention.

The concerns of Danforth and his Republican colleagues involved politics as well as policy. If Republicans did not find a way to get out front on trade, the issue might threaten them in the mid-term elections in November 1986. This fear gained substance in August 1985, when a Democrat

---

36. The Commerce Department reported trade figures first on a c.i.f. basis, with imports including the cost of freight, as required by the Trade Agreements Act of 1979. The "customs value" deficit figure, preferred by economists, was $107 billion, later adjusted to $112.5 billion. This study generally uses customs value trade statistics, the norm before 1980 (and after 1988), to facilitate historical comparison.

who blamed imports for lost jobs won a close race for an open congressional seat, taking particular advantage of his opponent's unthinking rejoinder questioning "what trade had to do with East Texas."

By that summer, three prominent, centrist Democrats on the trade committees—Bentsen of Senate Finance, and Rostenkowski and Gephardt of House Ways and Means—had cosponsored a bill imposing a surcharge on countries running heavy trade surpluses with the United States. Brazil, Japan, Korea, and Taiwan were the countries potentially affected. In September, House Speaker Thomas P. "Tip" O'Neill (D-MA) could declare with only modest exaggeration: "Based on what I hear from members in the cloak room, trade is the number one issue."[37]

More traditional protectionism flourished as well. A highly restrictive textile quota bill, sponsored by Representative Ed Jenkins, was originally introduced to stiffen the administration's position in the negotiations on renewal of the Multi-Fiber Arrangement (MFA), which regulated imports from developing nations and from Japan. But the bill took off, with a majority of senators and nearly 300 representatives signing on as cosponsors. Proponents got the bill through Ways and Means essentially as proposed, despite the opposition of the full committee and trade subcommittee chairs, with the latter, Sam Gibbons, reduced to declaring victory when the House passed it by "only" 262 to 159, less than the number required to override a veto.

Unable to get Finance to take up the measure, Senate sponsors Hollings and Strom Thurmond (R-SC) went around the committee, attaching the legislation to bill after bill on the floor until Majority Leader Robert Dole was forced to cooperate. And in the version passed by the Senate, quotas for shoes were added, as well as a provision calling for voluntary trade restraint on copper. President Reagan vetoed the measure in December, but in the override vote the textile industry managed to increase its House margin to 276 to 149, just eight votes short of the two-thirds required.

Legislative initiative continued also on other trade fronts. Danforth's proposal to enforce "reciprocity" on telecommunications products was reported out by Finance. A similar bill was approved by the House Energy and Commerce Committee, which challenged the supremacy of Ways and Means on trade by also drafting its own trade-remedy legislation. The House Democratic Caucus formed working groups that made their own proposals, and Senate Democrats did likewise.

But the most important drive was for new omnibus trade legislation. In November 1985, Danforth introduced S 1860, a relatively moderate, 10-title bipartisan proposal with 33 cosponsors, 13 of them from Finance. Early in 1986, the House Democratic leadership launched a more partisan campaign to make trade one of its top priorities. Ways and Means now

---

37. Quoted in the *Washington Post*, 19 September 1985.

had to move lest it lose its authority, and by early May it had reported out legislation that curbed presidential discretion in trade-remedy cases, mandated retaliation when other nations did not open their markets (with a separate, specific chapter for telecommunications products), and provided (in the famous "Gephardt amendment") for quotas in cases of countries—Japan, Taiwan, and Germany—running large bilateral surpluses with the United States. After being combined with bills reported out of other committees, the omnibus measure passed the House by 295 to 115.

The White House denounced the bill as "pure protectionism," a "rankly political" action that would be "trade-destroying, not trade-creating."[38] This was technically misleading on substance, but all too accurate about the likely results. Unlike the Jenkins bill or Smoot-Hawley, the omnibus measure did not restrict imports directly. But it revised section after section of general US trade laws to make it easier for firms to qualify for import relief and harder for presidents to deny it to them. It also represented a giant step toward unilateralism, establishing new, "made in USA" standards for defining fair and unfair trade that were not sanctioned by GATT rules or by established international practice. The bill therefore merited the label of "process protectionism." The likely outcome, had it become law, would have been a significant rise in de facto US import restrictions, though this was not necessarily the intent of all members who supported it.

Senate Republicans did not share President Reagan's unhappiness with the House bill. Indeed, many of its provisions had counterparts in Danforth's S 1860. Members of the Finance Committee would have liked to move their own trade measure, but they were preoccupied through spring and summer 1986 with major tax reform legislation. With the administration opposing any trade action that year, it proved impossible to achieve consensus among committee members on the omnibus legislation's substance and priority, and so the measure died with the 99th Congress in October 1986.

Within a month, however, executive-congressional relations were transformed. The Democrats recaptured control of the Senate, with a surprise gain of eight seats in the mid-term elections. That same month, the Reagan administration was gravely weakened by the exposure of what became known as the Iran-contra scandal. The partisan change had the more direct impact on trade politics. The reason was not that Senate Democrats were more aggressive on trade, or more protectionist, than their Republican counterparts—the difference here was marginal. What mattered was that control of that body had shifted from a leadership whose job (in important part) was to make life easier for a Republican administration, to one whose job (in major part) was to score points against it. Trade was *the* legislative issue most ready for such use, and Senator Robert Byrd

---

38. Statement by White House Deputy Press Secretary Larry M. Speakes, 22 May 1986.

(D-WV), soon to be restored to the majority leadership, lost no time in declaring that trade would be the Democrats' top priority in 1987–88.

The Omnibus Trade and Competitiveness Act of 1988

Senate Democrats were eager to move on trade, but the House had to go first. Trade bills remained revenue measures, which the Constitution ordained must originate in the House. The rule had been circumvented in 1984, but now there was no need: Jim Wright (D-TX), O'Neill's successor, was eager to move in 1987. Seeking greater substantive engagement than the typical speaker, Wright set an ambitious deadline for action by all interested committees. The omnibus bill passed in 1986 was reintroduced as HR 3 and parcelled out for reworking to 11 House committees, with Ways and Means first among equals.

Seeing the handwriting on the wall, Treasury Secretary James Baker now indicated that omnibus legislation could be useful. The Plaza Agreement of September 1985 had been followed by a steady decline in the dollar, generating expectations that the trade deficit would soon begin to shrink. Moreover, USTR Clayton Yeutter had won agreement the previous September to inaugurate the multilateral Uruguay Round, so the administration needed extension of the fast-track negotiating authority due to expire in January 1988. The administration now sent down its own draft legislation, as had its predecessors for the Kennedy and Tokyo Rounds. But in sharp contrast to 1962 and 1974, the House ignored the administration's bill,[39] and proceeded on the basis of HR 3.

By April the leadership was merging the 11 separate committee proposals. Wright insisted on excluding product-specific measures: Textiles would get a separate vote later, and an Energy and Commerce–reported measure to limit imports of high-quality digital tape recorders was excised from the omnibus legislation. The revised HR 3 passed the House, 290 to 137, on 30 April, with 43 Republicans joining virtually all Democrats in support. Included with the standard trade policy measures—such as authorization for the Uruguay Round, numerous toughenings of trade-remedy laws, strengthening of the authority of the USTR—were several new measures, including the "Bryant amendment," which required reporting of foreign investment, and provisions on exchange rates and Third World debt; worker retraining; relaxation of national security export controls; agricultural and broader export promotion; and math, science, and foreign language education. (The "omnibus" in the title was not without meaning.)

---

39. In the words of one congressional source, "They never opened the envelope." See J. David Richardson, "U.S. Trade Policy in the 1980s: Turns—and Roads—Not Taken," Working Paper 3725 (Cambridge, MA: National Bureau of Economic Research, June 1991), 46. For a detailed account by a central participant, see Susan C. Schwab, *Trade-Offs: Negotiating the Omnibus Trade and Competitiveness Act* (Boston, MA: Harvard Business School Press, 1994), chapters 4–7.

Included also was the Gephardt amendment, which required imposition of import barriers against countries that failed to reduce their large bilateral trade surpluses with the United States. Unlike in 1986, Ways and Means had not incorporated it in the provisions it reported. But Gephardt won inclusion of his amendment by a floor vote of 218 to 214. The victory helped Gephardt's newly launched presidential campaign, which many members supported. But the narrow margin signaled that the amendment was unlikely to be included in the final legislation.

Meanwhile, the Senate began its work, with new Finance Committee Chairman Lloyd Bentsen in the lead. By early May, his committee reported a bill with broad (19 to 1) bipartisan support, which excluded the Gephardt amendment but which, among its many provisions, imposed new procedural conditions on fast-track authorization for the Uruguay Round, mandated retaliation against unfair foreign trade practices, and curbed presidential discretion in escape-clause cases. Majority Leader Byrd combined this with bills reported by eight other committees, and brought it to the Senate floor in June. (One of these, from Edward Kennedy's [D-MA] Labor and Public Welfare Committee, included a provision requiring firms with over 100 employees to give 60 days' notice before plant closings.) After a month of debate, the omnibus measure passed by a vote of 71 to 27.

The Senate bill included, in a floor amendment, the Senate's alternative to the Gephardt amendment: a measure that would, after conference reworking, become known as "Super 301," and which required the USTR to name and target countries maintaining patterns of import barriers and unfair, market-distorting practices. The bill also contained a ban on all imports from Japan's Toshiba Corporation and a Norwegian defense company, a provision also added on the floor after revelation that the two companies had sold important defense-related equipment to the Soviet Union (in violation of both Japanese law and international export control arrangements). In general, this bill—like its House counterpart—was considerably less restrictive in its likely effects than the omnibus bill of 1986. Moreover, the House bill was more restrictive on some matters, the Senate on others, suggesting that the final result could prove more liberal than either.

Administration trade officials were considerably more engaged in the legislative process in 1987 than they had been in 1986. And White House comments as the bill made its way forward were certainly more moderate than the denunciations of 1986. But officials' access was asymmetric: good in the House, limited in the Senate. Deputy USTR Alan Holmer and USTR General Counsel Judith Bello had prepared the ground carefully with Rufus Yerxa and his associates on the Ways and Means trade staff, spending weekends in 1986 going over issues and possible solutions. Moreover, Chairman Rostenkowski was predisposed to cooperate with the administration. And so even though the House leadership had pushed trade for partisan advantage, Holmer and Bello had good working access to Ways and Means staff and to members' caucuses.

It was chillier for them on the north side of the Hill. Holmer had once served as Senator Packwood's administrative assistant, facilitating good relations with staff aides Leonard Santos and Josh Bolton during his chairmanship. But Packwood's successor, Lloyd Bentsen, was a much sterner critic of administration trade policy, and Jeffrey Lang, who acceded to the key Finance staff position, replicated his boss's reluctance to work closely with USTR officials. Holmer and Bello thus lacked both regular access to Finance senators and the sort of ties to Finance staff that their predecessors had developed in 1974 and 1979. So they worked with whom they could. Particularly important was longtime Danforth aide Susan Schwab, architect of his "reciprocity" legislation and an influential inside player on issues such as Section 301, telecommunications, and Japan.

In general, the administration was less happy with the Senate bill than its House counterpart: USTR Yeutter and Treasury Secretary James Baker urged Senate Republicans to vote against final passage in order to strengthen the prospects for change in conference. In any case, each house had passed a multititle, multicommittee bill roughly 1,000 draft pages in length. To reconcile the two, a 199-member conference committee was appointed—44 senators and 155 representatives. They were split into 17 subconferences responsible for separate sections.

Organizing all this brought the members into October, when a dramatic event intervened: the Dow Jones Industrial Average plunged by over 500 points in a single day. The crash of 19 October, "Black Monday," was blamed in part on the federal budget deficit, and it precipitated a White House-congressional summit on that subject. As this summit dragged on into December, it became the main policy preoccupation of Bentsen, Rostenkowski, and many of their colleagues. Black Monday also made members wary of taking *any* forceful trade action; the markets were jumpy, and anything labeled "protectionist" might drive them further down, with Congress taking the blame!

At the start of 1988, Rostenkowski and Bentsen began to refocus on trade, and they signaled that they were seeking a bill the president would sign. Their readiness to compromise with the administration was underscored when the House conferees proposed dropping all provisions in either version that were directly trade restrictive, a proposal the Senate eventually accepted. Such action was made easier by the fact that the trade deficit was at last declining, lessening the heat from import-impacted interests and giving exporters the incentive to lobby for moderation to avoid cutting short the now burgeoning boom in their foreign sales. By the end of March, Subconference I had resolved virtually all trade policy issues; a rewritten version of Super 301 supplanted the Gephardt amendment, and numerous specific authorities were transferred from the president to the USTR, although executive flexibility was maintained on the escape clause and the imposition of trade sanctions. The Bryant amendment that threatened foreign investment in the United

States was replaced by the Exon-Florio provision, which provided for executive branch review of foreign takeovers that carried national security implications: the president was authorized to block those he found inimical. The ban on Toshiba imports was narrowed to apply only to the offending subsidiary, Toshiba Machine Company, and to its Norwegian counterpart.[40] A broad range of special-interest amendments to the antidumping laws were deleted or neutralized. And fast-track authority was extended in a form the administration found acceptable.

On 20 April 1988, the full conference committee reported out a compromise HR 3, still over 1,000 parchment pages. The House passed it by 312 to 107, and the Senate followed by 63 to 36. The legislation still contained, however, the Senate-initiated provision mandating notification of plant closings by companies employing 100 or more workers. There had been frenetic negotiations on this issue, with Kennedy and organized labor pushing for retention of the provision, and many other Democrats attracted by its political message. But Reagan, backed by organized business, was threatening a veto. To prevent this, Rostenkowski and Bentsen wanted the provision removed, but they did not prevail. Speaker Wright sent the bill to the White House in a Capitol "signing ceremony" featuring television cameras and laid-off workers speaking in support of the measure.

Reagan did veto HR 3 in May, citing in particular both the plant-closing provision and a formerly obscure prohibition of certain oil exports from Alaska. The Senate override attempt fell five votes short. To trade legislators and officials, it looked briefly as if their intensive labors would come to naught. But Democrats soon found an ingenious way to have their cake and eat it too. A new trade bill was prepared, HR 4848, identical except for the excision of the plant closings and Alaskan oil provisions. The plant-closing provision was introduced as a separate measure, and brought quickly to the House and Senate floors. To Democrats' and organized labor's delight, the issue and the bill caught fire, and both chambers passed it with lopsided, bipartisan majorities. Thus put on the (antiworker) defensive, Reagan let it become law without his signature. In the meantime, the House and then the Senate were passing the slightly slimmer trade bill by overwhelming margins. On 23 August, with Reagan's signature, HR 4848 became Public Law 100-418, the Omnibus Trade and Competitiveness Act of 1988.

The 1988 law was the culmination of four years of congressional activity. It was the first major trade bill initiated by Congress since the days before Smoot-Hawley. And it was by far the longest trade bill passed by the postwar Congress: the 1,000-plus pages of parchment amounted to 467 statutory pages, compared with 173 pages for the 1979 law, 98 pages

---

40. This result was widely attributed to Toshiba's multimillion-dollar lobbying effort. But US firms using Toshiba inputs were also very unhappy with the original ban, and they made their feelings known on Capitol Hill.

in 1974, and just 31 pages for the Trade Expansion Act of 1962. The length reflected the multicommittee process and the many detailed methods by which legislators sought to constrain the executive in the management of trade policy.

There were two important things the bill did not do: It did not impose statutory protectionism, and it did not impose direct congressional control over trade. Rather, it passed the policy ball back to the statutorily enhanced USTR with multiple provisions aimed at setting the USTR's agenda and stiffening its spine. Most important were extension of fast-track authority to cover the Uruguay Round and bilateral negotiations,[41] and language centered on Section 301, which targeted "unjustifiable and unreasonable" foreign trade practices—particularly those impeding US exports. Congress wanted to make retaliation against such practices "mandatory but not compulsory," to quote the delightful phrase that originated at a Finance Committee hearing and was widely repeated thereafter.[42] But as this ambivalent language suggested, members remained more than willing to have the USTR make the tough calls.[43]

The House also accepted, in the end, continuing Ways and Means trade primacy. Speaker Wright was a force at key junctures, and his office was active in intercommittee coordination. But on the details of substance and trade policy bargaining, it was Rostenkowski who emerged supreme in the House—confident in the eighth year of his chairmanship and comfortable in bargaining with colleagues in the House, his counterpart in the Senate, leaders in the administration, and the many private interests engaged.

Ways and Means also played a central role in another important trade measure of 1988: the implementing bill for the Canada–United States Free Trade Agreement. Responding to an initiative from north of the border, and using the bilateral, fast-track authorization contained in the 1984 act, President Reagan notified Congress in December 1985 of his intention to proceed. Frustrated over the administration's lack of responsiveness to its concerns, Senate Finance took up a proposal to block fast-track treatment for the negotiations, rejecting it in April 1986 (by 10 to 10) only after

---

41. Congress imposed new conditions on fast-track authority, one of which would deny use of the procedures if both houses passed, within any 60-day period, procedural disapproval resolutions declaring that "the President has failed or refused to consult with Congress on trade negotiations and trade agreements in accordance with the provisions of the Omnibus Trade and Competitiveness Act of 1988." Section 1103(c)(1)(E).

42. Judith Hippler Bello and Alan F. Holmer, "The Heart of the 1988 Trade Act: A Legislative History of the Amendments to Section 301," in Jagdish Bhagwati and Hugh T. Patrick, eds., *Aggressive Unilateralism*, 59. They report that the phrase originated in an exchange between Chairman Packwood and former STR Robert Strauss.

43. For a broader argument on why senators and representatives may find such behavior in their political interest, see I. M. Destler, "Constituencies, Congress, and US Trade Policy," in Alan V. Deardorff and Robert M. Stern, *Constituent Interests and U.S. Trade Policies* (Ann Arbor: University of Michigan Press, 1998), 93–108.

assurances were provided on softwood lumber and other issues.[44] And the negotiations were rushed to completion in the waning months of 1987 so that Congress could be prenotified in early October, as the law required, and the agreement could be signed on 2 January 1988, the very last day that the fast-track authority allowed.[45]

Thereafter, however, the implementing process proceeded smoothly, replicating that for the Tokyo Round nine years earlier. The administration promised not to submit implementing legislation before June, provided congressional leaders agreed to act between then and adjournment in October. "Nonmarkups" were then held in February through May, followed by a "nonconference" to resolve House-Senate differences. Only after agreement was reached was the legislation formally introduced and approved, by 366 to 40 in the House and 83 to 9 in the Senate. Ways and Means' central role in tracking the details was reflected in the fact that, as one administration official later put it, the implementing bill "was written on Mary Jane Wignot's computer." (Wignot was the Ways and Means aide with specific responsibility for US-Canada trade.)[46]

With approval of the Canada-US Free Trade Agreement in September, the 100th Congress completed its ample trade work. Its successor would not do likewise: legislators in 1989–90 moved on to other issues, limiting their trade activity to monitoring implementation of their 1988 handiwork. In 1991, however, they were suddenly confronted with a new challenge: a vote on extending the fast-track deadline not just for the Uruguay Round but for free trade talks involving Mexico as well. This brought before Congress the first explicit floor consideration of the legislative procedure that constrained the authority of the rank and file over trade.

NAFTA and Fast-Track Renewal

In 1989 and 1990, trade receded on the legislative agenda. Exports continued to surge; import growth moderated; and the trade deficit shrank somewhat. Speaker Jim Wright was caught up, in 1989, with a scandal that would force his resignation. Tom Foley of Washington, a liberal trader, was

---

44. Jeffrey J. Schott, *United States–Canada Free Trade: An Evaluation of the Agreement*, POLICY ANALYSES IN INTERNATIONAL ECONOMICS 24 (Washington, DC: Institute for International Economics, 1988), 13.

45. To legislators' annoyance, and contrary to the law's intent, major substantive provisions of the agreement were defined in the period *between* the October notification and the January signing. In 1991, they extracted commitments from the Bush administration not to repeat this practice in negotiations for the North American Free Trade Agreement.

46. For more detail, see David Layton-Brown, "Implementing the Agreement," in Peter Morici, ed., *Making Free Trade Work: The Canada-U.S. Agreement* (New York: Council on Foreign Relations Press, 1990), 28–30.

the consensus choice to succeed him, and Foley was succeeded as majority leader by Richard Gephardt (D-MO). In the Senate, Robert Byrd left the majority leader position to become president pro tempore and chairman of the Appropriations Committee, with George Mitchell of Maine his successor.

Trade-minded senators and representatives watched with approval in 1989 as USTR Carla Hills named Japan a "priority foreign country" under Super 301,[47] and as Korea and Taiwan scurried to make enough trade concessions to avoid similar designation. And in 1990, many in both chambers were preoccupied with the extended budget negotiations that began in the spring and continued into late October. Aside from its now routine passage of textile quota legislation, and the equally routine failure to override President Bush's veto, Congress took little specific trade action. There were no burning statutory issues. Moreover, the enactment of the 1988 act had been a politically demanding enterprise, with Bentsen, Rostenkowski, and their colleagues compelled to respond to and balance an enormous range of pressures and interests. The years that followed offered welcome respite. And even though Super 301 expired in 1990, there was no serious congressional move to extend it.

Such legislative restraint was also consistent with the projected timetable of the Uruguay Round. The multilateral talks were intended to last four years, culminating in an agreement by the end of 1990. The 1988 act reflected and reinforced this timetable, with a bit of leeway, by providing that fast-track approval procedures would be followed if the president signed an agreement by 1 June 1991—provided he gave notice 90 days before.

But the Uruguay Round moved slowly. Agreement was particularly elusive on agriculture, where the United States had initially sought a commitment to remove all trade-distorting government policies and was still insisting on major liberalization as a prerequisite for deals on textiles, services, and the many other specific issues on the agenda. A December 1990 GATT Ministerial Conference at Brussels, designed to break the impasse, confirmed it instead.

With the multilateral talks at a stalemate, attention turned to a fallback provision of the 1988 act inserted with just such a contingency in mind. The president could, on or before 1 March 1991, seek a two-year extension of fast-track authority by declaring that progress had been made and additional time might allow the negotiations to succeed. And as the law was written, he could gain the extension unless either house voted against it by 1 June.[48] He would then have until June 1993 to sign a multilateral agreement.

---

47. Also designated were Brazil and India.

48. In general, legislative vetoes of presidential or agency actions had been rendered unconstitutional by the Supreme Court's *Chadha* decision of June 1983. But the issue here was not statutory substance but legislative procedures, over which the Constitution gave Congress full authority.

There was one complicating factor. In the spring of 1990, Mexico's re-formist president, Carlos Salinas de Gortari, broke with his country's protectionist and anti-*yanqui* tradition by asking President Bush to negotiate a bilateral free trade agreement. Bush agreed, notwithstanding the reluctance of trade advisers who would have preferred to wait until a Uruguay Round accord was in hand. He sent Congress the required notification of intent in September. When Ottawa expressed concern that a bilateral US-Mexico pact might undermine Canada's arrangement with the United States, it was agreed to include Canada in the talks, with the aim of creating a North American Free Trade Agreement (NAFTA). Bush notified Congress of this decision in February 1991.

A fast-track extension would therefore apply to the NAFTA talks as well as to the Uruguay Round. Free trade with Mexico had been in no member's mind when the law was enacted in 1988. The act did include a brief section endorsing the procedural US-Mexico "framework" agreement signed in 1987, but a free trade arrangement was considered a decade off at the very least. Still, the fast-track procedures had been broadened in 1984 to cover bilateral accords, with similar consultation caveats and the same expiration date. And the new timetable in the 1988 act applied to both as well. Hence an extension for the GATT talks would cover NAFTA as well.

This prospect alarmed organized labor and some environmental groups. The former felt particularly threatened by open trade with a "low-wage" neighbor: US workers had already lost many low-skill, mass-production jobs to foreign competition, and a Mexico deal would only exacerbate this trend. Environmentalists worried that competition with Mexico would undercut US environmental regulations by creating a "pollution haven" for US firms south of the border, leading to a relaxation of US antipollution laws for competitive purposes. Well before 1 March, both were mobilizing against fast-track extension. Their initial success drove Rostenkowski to suggest at one point that it might be necessary to somehow exclude Mexico from coverage in order to salvage authority for the GATT talks. However, the president followed the law (and his interests) in requesting general fast-track extension.

The fast-track procedures had been law for over 16 years, but this was the first time they had held center stage on the House or Senate floor. Previously, their specifics had been worked out in Finance and in Ways and Means, with Congress as a whole ratifying the committees' handiwork when it voted general trade legislation. And this time the issue *could* have been killed in committee—the law provided that a fast-track disapproval resolution could reach the House or Senate floor only if the requisite committee(s) approved. But committee and chamber leaders quickly decided that burial in committee, while perfectly legal, would be viewed as politically egregious and thus discredit both the procedures and any agreements reached thereunder. Disapproval resolutions therefore would have to go to both floors, and be voted up or down there.

With critics quick off the blocks, congressional leaders would have normally sought statutory compromise. But on its face the law made this difficult or impossible: the "sole matter" of an "extension disapproval resolution" was to be "That the [House/Senate] disapproves the request of the President for the extension . . . because sufficient tangible progress has not been made in trade negotiations."[49] Moreover, Speaker Foley resisted creative proposals to separate the Mexico negotiations from the Uruguay Round, or otherwise compromise the procedures. He saw them as a pact between Congress and the executive; if Congress changed the rules when acting on the extension, how could it demand that the administration play straight?

Bentsen and Rostenkowski, both strong backers of fast-track renewal, therefore resorted to nonstatutory bargaining. They wrote to President Bush seeking assurances on three key matters: the overall economic impact of a NAFTA; its effects on jobs and worker rights; and its impact on the environment.[50] They needed a reply by 1 May, they declared, so that Congress could consider it and vote before the 1 June deadline. Gephardt, resisting strong labor pressure and maintaining an undecided posture, wrote a separate letter raising similar concerns.

With everyone's attention on Mexico, the Uruguay Round got something of a free ride. When the Brussels ministerial conference failed, it was thought that a fast-track extension debate would turn the spotlight on those negotiations, with senators and representatives pressing the administration on why progress had been limited and why they expected the next two years to be any better. Congress might even have threatened specific conditions or minimum requirements for a Uruguay Round package. The USTR would presumably have responded by pressing its counterparts in Europe and East Asia, seeking concrete evidence of prospective gains in order to persuade Congress to continue the enterprise. But this did not happen—in fact, the tendency was for members critical of a Mexico accord to say nice things about the multilateral round, to balance their positions and avoid being labeled protectionists.

Reacting to the strong, early labor and environmentalist opposition, Bentsen and Rostenkowski pressed business leaders to get moving: if they favored fast-track extension, they had better lobby hard, or else the measure would fail. And business responded. The old protrade coalition, demoralized by the Reagan trade deficit and mobilized only for the endgame in 1985–88, was now back in full force—encouraged by the export boom,

---

49. Public Law 100-418; Section 1103(b)(5)(A).

50. Bargaining with colleagues was impeded by the fact that some key labor Democrats on Ways and Means (like Donald J. Pease of Ohio) were committed to vote against extension for Mexico. And labor followed its characteristic strategy of taking a strong stand and refusing to compromise. On trade, this had usually served to minimize labor's influence with the plant-closing provision of 1988 the major exception; it would do so in 1991 as well.

but concerned that a collapse of the Uruguay Round would unleash protectionism here and abroad. So they went "balls out" for extension, as one Washington insider put it. Mexican representatives were active and effective also, belying their long-standing reputation for inattention to the Washington power game.

Last but not least, the charge was led by a highly competent USTR, Carla A. Hills, backed by a president who wasn't about to see his Mexico initiative go under. Together, the USTR and the White House pressed business to be active; they encouraged (and received) restraint and flexibility from Mexico and Salinas; they brought in a range of arguments, from the future of the world trading system to the interests of the growing population of Hispanic-Americans.

And on 1 May, in language crafted by the USTR, the president responded adroitly to the questions posed by Bentsen and Rostenkowski. Pointing to the doubling of US exports to Mexico between 1986 and 1990, the administration declared "a NAFTA will result in greater prosperity for US workers, farmers, businesses and consumers." Moreover, since "Mexico's economy is $\frac{1}{25}$ the size of the US economy . . . scenarios of mass dislocations resulting from reduced US trade barriers are not realistic." Nonetheless, the statement promised "adjustment provisions to avert injurious effects," including transition and safeguard mechanisms and an "adequately funded" worker adjustment program providing "prompt, comprehensive, and effective services" for those who lost their jobs as a result of free trade with Mexico.[51] Bush's statement also praised and supported Mexican efforts to enforce labor standards and worker rights. On the environment, "Mexico and the United States agree that efforts to increase growth through an FTA should be complemented by cooperative efforts to enhance environmental protection." And in addition to pursuing "joint environmental initiatives," the United States would "ensure that our right to safeguard the environment is preserved in the NAFTA."[52]

The statement accelerated a shift by some environmental groups: from opposition to an accord to using the negotiations as an opportunity to advance their concerns. Labor remained in opposition, but once the outcome was clear the AFL-CIO deemphasized the final vote and scurried unsuccessfully for ways to make the outcome less clear-cut. Bentsen and Rostenkowski declared their satisfaction with the White House response. On 9 May Gephardt declared his support, with a "caveat: If the administration sends to this Congress a trade treaty that trades away American jobs,

---

51. This represented, at least potentially, a reversal of the deemphasis on trade adjustment in the 1980s. See chapter 6.

52. Quotations are from "Response of the Administration to Issues Raised in Connection with the Negotiation of a North American Free Trade Agreement," transmitted to the Congress by the president on 1 May 1991, processed, "Overview" section, 1, 3, 6, 9, and 11.

or tolerates pollution of the environment or abuse of workers, we can, and we will, amend it or reject it."[53]

When the votes came, they were anticlimactic. Ways and Means voted 27 to 9 against the disapproval resolution; Finance did likewise by 15 to 3. On 23 May the House rejected the resolution by 231 to 192, a margin that apparently overstated the bedrock opposition to fast-track extension.[54] The Senate followed the next day by 59 to 36. The split was both partisan and regional. Democrats in the House voted 170 to 91 to veto fast track, but the leadership backed it, and representatives from California, Florida, and Texas—states with large Hispanic-American populations—voted 64 to 25 in favor.

Critics got one consolation prize. Speaker Foley had resisted the idea of staging separate votes on the Uruguay Round and NAFTA, though some members complained they were being forced to oppose the former because of the latter. But the House did adopt by 329 to 85, *after* rejecting the disapproval measure, a Gephardt-Rostenkowski resolution endorsing the labor and environmental objectives included in the 1 May statement, and calling for close consultation with the administration during the Mexico negotiations.

By fall 1991, it was back to business as usual. Hills was pushing ahead on the Geneva and Mexico fronts; legislators, faced with many competing demands, were only sometimes responsive to opportunities to give advice. The House majority leader had come forth with "a new 'Gephardt amendment' that will put teeth in Super 301," again targeting Japan in particular, to "reduce the discretion the President has not to take action against priority countries and priority practices."[55] But its effect—and perhaps its intent—was more to position Gephardt and like-minded Democrats on the "tough" side of the trade debate (and to balance Gephardt's support of fast track) than to influence the legislative agenda on trade, at least in the near term. For that awaited the results of the global and hemispheric trade talks (see chapter 8).

1984 and After: The Leadership Difference

In the 1980s and early 1990s, Congress seemed ready on several occasions to reverse postwar liberal trade policies. On each occasion, it refrained

---

53. Quoted in *Congressional Quarterly*, 11 May 1991, 1181.

54. *Congressional Quarterly* reported that "the opposition total" seemed padded, "since many votes to reject the fast track were made after it was apparent that proponents had the numbers to win." The AFL-CIO vote count had shown "only 140 lawmakers solidly . . . against the fast-track extension." 25 May 1991, 1358–59.

55. Richard A. Gephardt, remarks at the Institute for International Economics, Washington, DC, 10 September 1991, 4–5.

from doing so. Product-specific protectionism, so much in prospect in 1982 and 1983, was removed from the law passed in 1984. The explosion of concern about the US trade balance in 1985–86 was brought under control by an administration that first shifted course on the exchange rate—encouraging the dollar to fall—and thereafter bargained hard on the specifics of what became the 1988 Trade Act. And despite strong early opposition, fast-track renewal passed comfortably in 1991. Frustration with the no-amendment procedure was substantial, raising doubts as to whether Congress would agree to it for a post-1993 trade negotiation. But for the present, it once again went along and delegated major authority to the administration.

On each of these occasions, members of Congress showed strong interest in trade policy, and insisted on making it tougher and more responsive to US-based economic interests—particularly on the export side. But on each occasion, Congress failed to seize authority for itself and instead passed the policy ball back to the other end of Pennsylvania Avenue. Members of Congress were less satisfied with liberal trade policies than they had once been. And with the reform in congressional procedures, they were less capable of resisting product-specific initiatives. But they wished neither to succumb to such initiatives nor to take responsibility for their consequences. Delegation to the executive was the natural way out of this dilemma.

But greater congressional skepticism and activism increased the burden on executive branch trade leaders. The changed role of Congress made the trade policymaking system even more dependent on the liberal trade commitment and the political skill of the senior officials at the other end of Pennsylvania Avenue, who now had to delve deeply into the legislative game, arguing and resisting and bargaining with trade activists on Capitol Hill.

USTR Brock and his staff performed this service in 1984, helping to protect Congress from itself. In 1985, when White House attention was elsewhere for most of the year, the administration lost the initiative, and USTR Yeutter was forced to spend the years through 1988 struggling to regain it. Hills did regain momentum for the Bush administration in 1989, but the USTR's longer-term success would depend on what it achieved in the Uruguay Round talks, which would play back into domestic trade politics. For a deeper look at this interplay, we turn now to the subject of the next chapter, the executive branch.

5

An Embattled Executive

From the 1930s onward, the key activator of liberal American trade policies has been the executive branch of government. Whether negotiating abroad or facing pressure at home, US officials responsible for international economic relations have leaned persistently in the direction of reducing barriers and expanding trade. Presidents, while only occasionally involved in day-to-day decisions, have supported trade officials in this liberal tendency and lent their names and their weight, periodically, to the major steps forward. Hence, the 1960s negotiations were dubbed the Kennedy Round. The successor talks might well have been remembered as the "Nixon Round" had not Watergate rendered that label unappealing.

Successive Congresses not only endorsed executive branch trade leadership, but also sought to centralize it in an institution that would balance domestic and international concerns. The Trade Expansion Act of 1962 created the position of the president's special representative for trade negotiations (STR). After two Nixon administration efforts to weaken or abolish it, the Trade Act of 1974 made the STR a statutory unit in the Executive Office of the President. Five years later, Congress forced the Carter administration to carry out a trade reorganization that increased the office's size and power and renamed it USTR (for Office of the United States Trade Representative). And in 1983, strong resistance from Senator John C. Danforth (R-MO), chairman of the Finance Subcommittee on Trade, helped block a Reagan administration–backed proposal to subsume the USTR in a new cabinet-level Department of International Trade and Industry.

The White House trade office proved an effective policy leadership institution. It brought the US government successfully through two ambitious multilateral trade negotiations. Its leaders got major trade bills enacted by Congress in 1974 and 1979, limited the trade-restrictive damage from the legislation of 1984 and 1988, and won congressional reauthorization of major trade negotiations in 1991. The demands of trade leadership drove the office into close relationships with the key congressional trade committees and into an interest-balancing, coping mode with private groups. The office showed greater sensitivity to protection-seeking forces than did, say, the State Department or the Council of Economic Advisers. Nevertheless, its aim was not to bury liberal US trade policy but to keep it alive.

Presidents have not given consistent backing to the White House trade representative as a person or to the USTR office as an institution. Just as Kennedy was reluctant to have Congress structuring "his" executive office, his successors have been ambivalent, more often than not, about a high-profile White House trade office with which they had limited day-to-day contact. Presidential political aides have been wary as well. In the first Reagan term, Secretary of Commerce Malcolm Baldrige was able to use his White House ties, and the added trade powers given his department in 1980, to pose a strong challenge to USTR William E. Brock.

In the 1980s, this presidential ambivalence toward the USTR was joined by a rise in piecemeal protectionism, in steps taken to shield specific industries without offsetting measures on the market-expanding side. President Reagan, committed in principle to free trade, was driven—in the words of his Treasury secretary—to "grant more import relief to US industry than any of his predecessors in more than half a century."[1] And when the record trade imbalances of the mid-1980s triggered a political storm on Capitol Hill, his administration lost the initiative to a Congress determined to enact tough new trade legislation. Despite a new aggressiveness in pressing export cases overseas, the USTR was mainly reacting at home to a flurry of congressional proposals. Only in 1989—with the legislative battle over—did a new USTR, Carla A. Hills, succeed in recovering the trade policy initiative for the executive branch. She succeeded in concluding the NAFTA negotiations, but was unable to complete the global Uruguay Round talks before her term in office expired.

■ ■ ■

From the 1930s through the 1950s, there was little statutory control of the structure and process of executive branch trade policymaking—who should lead in international trade negotiations, for example, or how the counterpart domestic negotiations should be conducted. Inevitably, then as now, a range of departments and agencies were involved, especially Agriculture and Commerce, and interagency committees were the typical

---

1. Remarks of Secretary of the Treasury James A. Baker III at the Institute for International Economics, Washington, DC, 14 September 1987.

means of handling complex policy and operational issues. Yet as late as 1960, a senior State Department official could be so dominant—domestically and internationally—that a tariff negotiation under the General Agreement on Tariffs and Trade (GATT) was given his name.[2]

But the "Dillon Round" was the State Department's last hurrah in multilateral trade leadership. When John F. Kennedy moved to break a political stalemate by going after sweeping new barrier-reducing authority—including a mandate to negotiate across-the-board (as opposed to item-by-item) reductions—Congress demanded a change in executive branch trade structure. Thus was created an "executive broker," the STR, to oversee US participation in the talks.[3]

STR's Early Ups and Downs

Section 241 of the Trade Expansion Act of 1962 established two roles for this new trade official: the STR was to be "the chief representative of the United States" during the authorized negotiations and also chairman of the "interagency trade organization" that was to manage them for the president. It said nothing about his staff or its location, however. Kennedy had insisted on having leeway to define these himself, which he did in Executive Order 11075 of 15 January 1963, placing the new unit within the Executive Office of the President. The new negotiator and his aides were clearly intended to play the "executive broker" role required by the 1934 system—between domestic interests and foreign governments, between the executive branch and Congress, and among the concerned government agencies.

During the Kennedy Round, the STR played this role with a small staff of about 25 professionals and with substantial sharing of specific analytic and negotiating tasks with State and, to a lesser degree, Commerce and Agriculture.[4] Kennedy filled the post with a prominent Republican, former Secretary of State (and Massachusetts Governor) Christian A. Herter, who had one deputy for Washington management, William M. Roth, and one for Geneva bargaining, W. Michael Blumenthal. When Herter died

---

2. The official was Under Secretary of State C. Douglas Dillon.

3. Also significant, at least as a harbinger of the future, was a provision making two senators and two representatives accredited members of the US negotiating team for the first time. The STR was also required to seek advice and information from industry, agriculture, and labor representatives. As in previous talks, the administration had to give public notice and hold hearings before agreeing to reduce tariffs for a particular industry. And the Tariff Commission was to advise on the probable impact of such reductions on particular sectors.

4. On the STR's early years, see Anne H. Rightor-Thornton, "An Analysis of the Office of the Special Representative for Trade Negotiations: The Evolving Role, 1962–1974," in *Commission on the Organization of the Government for the Conduct of Foreign Policy*, vol. 3 (Washington, DC: GPO, June 1975), appendix H, 88–104.

from a heart attack in December 1966, President Lyndon B. Johnson designated Roth as his replacement. Neither trade executive spent much time with either president; for example, to prepare for the crucial climactic stages of the talks in the spring of 1967, LBJ worked mainly through his deputy special assistant for national security affairs, Francis M. Bator. Yet with his ultimate acceptance of the final Kennedy Round package, Johnson gave his strong endorsement to what the STR-led team had wrought.

For the next four years, however, the STR went into eclipse. The big trade negotiation was over, and the role of the office in bilateral and product-specific talks was not well established. In early 1969, Richard M. Nixon's Secretary of Commerce, Maurice H. Stans, pressed to have trade-coordinating responsibilities transferred to him. Congressional and interest group opposition blocked this; agricultural interests, in particular, feared they would get short shrift. But Stans won two substantial concessions: the right to control who was appointed STR and the lead role in the major trade action of the early Nixon administration, the "textile wrangle" with Japan. The STR became a bureaucratic backwater, weakly led and devoid of presidential support.

There followed a trade policy disaster. Stans bungled the textile negotiation, as his aggressive, insensitive style provoked fierce Japanese resistance. This led to a blunder with Congress: Stans got Nixon to endorse statutory import quotas for textiles. As discussed in chapter 2, this drove Ways and Means Chairman Wilbur D. Mills (D-AR) to push a protectionist bill he privately abhorred. The bill passed the House and got as far as the Senate floor before time ran out in December 1970.[5]

The need to restore central trade policy leadership was now evident, and in 1971 the White House named a new STR, Idaho lawyer and businessman William D. Eberle. Eberle quickly recruited two strong deputies: William R. Pearce to handle the development of legislation, and Harald B. Malmgren to manage the international negotiations to prepare a new trade round.

But the STR was still not secure in the Nixon administration, for the president also established in 1971 a Council on International Economic Policy (CIEP), whose staff was headed by an assistant to the president for international economic affairs—first Peter G. Peterson, then (in 1972) Peter M. Flanigan. And in 1973 Flanigan moved, with Nixon's apparent endorsement, to have the STR formally incorporated in CIEP under his direction.

Many legislators feared that the nonpartisan, "trade expert" character of the STR would be destroyed if it were brought into a more "political" (partisan) White House operation. And they had twice seen the Nixon administration ready to sacrifice the trade representative. So House Ways

---

5. For details on these events, see I. M. Destler, Haruhiro Fukui, and Hideo Sato, *The Textile Wrangle* (Ithaca, NY: Cornell University Press, 1979), chapters 3–10.

and Means responded in 1973 by adding to the pending trade legislation a section making the STR a statutory office, something Kennedy had resisted. The Senate bill went two steps further: placing the STR in the Executive Office of the President by law, and giving cabinet rank and salary to its chief. As signed by President Gerald R. Ford, the Trade Act of 1974 included all of these provisions.

Even as these steps were being taken, the STR was asserting de facto leadership, first in drafting the administration's legislative proposals, then in lobbying the Trade Act through the House and the Senate in 1973 and 1974.[6] By the time the bill was enacted, the STR had become a congressional as well as a presidential agent. In 1975 and 1976, the office entered another in-between period, as the trade negotiations it was leading moved slowly at Geneva. But this time its position in the executive branch was stronger and more secure. And the stage was set for a major trade-brokering success story—the completion of the Tokyo Round in 1979 under the leadership of President Jimmy Carter's special trade representative, Robert S. Strauss.

Strauss and the MTN: The STR on Center Stage

Almost alone among senior Carter administration international economic officials, Robert Strauss had no prior experience with trade policy. His forte had been partisan politics. He had served as chairman of the Democratic National Committee, beginning with a party bitterly divided by its 1972 debacle and ending with Democrats surprisingly united behind the Carter candidacy. He had made an important personal contribution to this outcome with his ornery, persistent, inclusive style of interpersonal diplomacy. And along the way he had established close relationships with a number of senior senators, including Senate Finance Committee Chairman Russell B. Long (D-LA).

With his flair for the public spotlight, Strauss brought celebrity to the STR job. Skilled at political maneuvering, he led in reenergizing the Tokyo Round of multilateral trade negotiations (MTN) abroad and selling them at home. As STR aides he brought in trade or management specialists, not partisan politicos: Geneva Deputy (later to be Carter White House operations chief) Alonzo L. McDonald; Washington Deputy (and former STR General Counsel) Alan Wm. Wolff; and General Counsel (and former Finance Committee aide) Richard R. Rivers. Strauss promptly demonstrated his brokering ability by negotiating orderly marketing agreements with Korea and Taiwan on shoes, and with Japan on color television sets. He also led in bilateral, market-expanding negotiations with Tokyo.

6. For a detailed account, see I. M. Destler, *Making Foreign Economic Policy* (Washington, DC: Brookings Institution, 1980), chapters 10 and 11.

His handling of Japanese market issues in late 1977 and early 1978 illustrated Strauss's unique blend of verbal hyperbole and political adroitness. Until that fall, other administration officials had been more active than he on US-Japanese economic issues. Strauss seized the initiative by exaggerating the danger. He declared—with little if any supporting evidence—that US-Japan relations were near the "bursting point," and that Congress would likely go protectionist when it reconvened in January 1978, unless Japan made significant market-opening commitments. Turning aside an initiative from Senate staff aides to hold Finance Committee hearings on US-Japan issues—that might raise the political temperature too much, he thought—he nevertheless urged senators to be very demanding in their private conversations with Japanese trade officials.

When a newly designated Japanese minister for international economic policy flew to Washington in December, Strauss got Finance Committee senators to host a very tough private luncheon. And Strauss himself immediately and "very candidly" declared the minister's offer of tariff and quota adjustments to be "insufficient," falling "considerably short" of what was necessary. This made it possible for Strauss to find an anticipated further concession "promising," and to imply that US toughness was beginning to bear fruit. He traveled to Japan the following month to complete a revised Japanese trade agreement, and, by threatening to fly home without signing, he won further concessions on its language.

When he then reported the deal to senators at a Finance Committee hearing, the first thing Strauss did was to give *them* the credit. He thanked them, "on behalf of the entire nation," for "the strong bipartisan support" they had given to US negotiators. He described the result in expansive terms: the specific Japanese commitments in the agreement represented "an entire change of direction and change of philosophy of trade" on Tokyo's part. But he cautioned that implementation was "just beginning."

When Senator William V. Roth, Jr., (R-DE, no relation to the former STR) suggested hearings every six months to monitor progress with Japan, Strauss questioned whether that was often enough. "I think I should report to you on a more frequent basis, if you have the time in the Senate to do it." He wanted the Japanese and the Germans and the European Community "to feel some of the pressure from the Congress that I feel. You know, you are breathing down my neck every day . . . I would like to turn that red hot breath toward the people we are trading with."[7]

---

7. US Congress, Senate Committee on Finance, Subcommittee on International Trade, *Hearing on United States/Japanese Trade Relations and the Status of the Multilateral Trade Negotiations*, 95th Congress, 2nd session (1 February 1978), 9, 12, 13, 22. For a fuller discussion of those negotiations, see I. M. Destler, "United States-Japanese Relations and the American Trade Initiative of 1977: Was this 'Trip' Necessary?" in William J. Barnds, ed., *Japan and the United States: Challenge and Opportunity* (New York: New York University Press [for the Council on Foreign Relations], 1979), 190–230.

The performance was vintage Strauss—part substance, part charade—as his more savvy Senate interlocutors fully realized. But his game was their game too: He was giving them credit for toughness greater than they had actually displayed, and greater credit than they deserved for such negotiating results as were achieved. Yet while deferring to them in rhetoric, he kept the initiative for himself—just as they wanted him to do. For he was absorbing the political heat, diverting pressure from them. Strauss was also adroit with the Japanese, for although his strong words ruffled their sensitivities, they also gave Tokyo bureaucrats and politicians a credible rationale for making trade concessions. In both cases, Strauss was the consummate activist broker—keeping the game going, getting results that at least defused the immediate crisis, and spreading credit around in a way that enhanced his own central role, rather than diminished it.

Strauss was also playing another old trade game, that of "export politics." The main domestic pressures concerning Japan were coming from import-competing industries like color TVs and steel, and the Carter administration accommodated these pressures with moderate trade-restraining arrangements. But it preferred to push trade-expanding issues. Thus, it encouraged agricultural export interests and then employed these interests as pressure in winning limited, grudging Japanese expansion of beef and citrus quotas. The overall gain was small—no more than $50 million set against a bilateral trade deficit with Japan that would reach $12 billion in 1978. But to the degree that discontent with Tokyo on trade was generalized in nature, such tactics channeled this discontent into pressure for expanding exports, not restricting imports. (The Carter administration also pressed Tokyo to stimulate its economy and to allow the yen to appreciate in order to reduce Japan's growing trade surplus.)

"Export politics" also was prominent in early 1979 when the United States, in order to broaden the coverage of the MTN government procurement code, pressed Tokyo to internationalize the purchases of its government telecommunications agency, Nippon Telephone and Telegraph (NTT).[8] In that case again, US officials, with Strauss in the lead, sought to reinforce domestic interests in export expansion and to counter and limit the influence of those seeking import restriction.

A more comprehensive and structured form of brokering took place within the private-sector advisory committees that were established under the Trade Act to work with US negotiators in setting and implementing MTN goals. In response to complaints from some in the business community about their limited and ad hoc role in the Kennedy Round, Congress had added a detailed section to the 1974 law, setting forth requirements and guidelines to institutionalize "advice from the private sector." Working

---

8. See Timothy J. Curran, "Politics and High Technology: The NTT Case," in I. M. Destler and Hideo Sato, eds., *Coping with U.S.-Japanese Economic Conflicts* (Lexington, MA: Lexington Books, 1982), 185–241.

with Commerce, Labor, and Agriculture, the STR was required to organize general and sectoral committees that would, "so far as practicable, be representative of all industry, labor, or agricultural interests. . . ."[9]

Initially, some officials feared that the requirement for such elaborate private-sector consultation would prove a straitjacket, for the law even provided that the STR must inform the advisory committees—and give reasons—when he did not accept their counsel! In practice, however, the advisory network proved a great boon. Membership on the committees gave producers a forum for pressing specific concerns; film manufacturers could argue that a reduction on Japanese tariffs would increase their sales, for example. And committee members knew that trade negotiators would listen and try to respond, since each committee would report independently to the Congress on how it viewed the final MTN agreements. The advisory committee system gave Congress what its members particularly favored: a place away from Capitol Hill where they could refer petitioning interests and assure them that they would get a hearing. Each committee was broad enough (for example, "Industrial Chemicals and Fertilizers," "Nonferrous Metals") to encompass a range of firms and interests. Their exposure to one another gave committee members a broader perspective, and it gave executive officials useful leeway on whose advice they finally took. And because the advisers felt they were taken seriously—and came to understand the constraints faced by their governmental counterparts—they developed sympathy for the larger enterprise and modest personal identification with its success.

As noted by Gilbert R. Winham, broader lessons can be drawn from this experience:

> In delegating the task of constituency relations to the executive, Congress took advantage of the capacity of governmental bureaucracy to take the initiative in dealing with constituents. . . . The same [advisory group] system that organized the sectoral interests and gave them influence in government also structured the task of the executive in dealing with those interests. [It also] meant that communications with constituency groups generally occurred in an environment defined by trade bureaucracies and not by the constituents themselves. . . .
>
> To sum up, the Tokyo Round experience demonstrated that channels of access could be two-way streets: access to the executive by the private sector could also mean access to the private sector by the executive. . . .[10]

At the final stage of the MTN, Strauss's political skills were tested by a crisis that was partially of his own making. Europeans had participated in the MTN on condition that the United States not impose countervailing duties on European Community exports before the subsidies code was

---

9. Trade Act of 1974, Section 135.

10. Gilbert R. Winham, *International Trade and the Tokyo Round Negotiation* (Princeton, NJ: Princeton University Press, 1986), 315–17.

negotiated. Congress had reluctantly granted the secretary of the Treasury the authority to waive countervailing duties for four years, until 3 January 1979. But when it became clear that the MTN would not be entirely completed by then, and Strauss and his Hill allies failed to get the waiver extended before Congress adjourned for the year in October 1978, Europeans refused to continue. An intricate rescue was required. At home, the United States deferred collection of the duties, while Strauss bargained with Congress to extend the waiver retroactively.[11] In the meantime, the Europeans agreed to resume talking, but not to sign anything until the waiver extension became law, which it did in March 1979.

In the end, everything came together in one of the Carter administration's major policy successes. Nontariff barrier codes were completed to regulate government behavior on subsidies, government procurement, product standards, etc. The United States granted long-sought concessions—abandonment of the American Selling Price system of customs valuation,[12] and an injury test for the imposition of countervailing duties—in exchange for commitments on a range of trade-distorting foreign practices. Of the 38 private-sector advisory committees, 27 made positive reports to Congress, with five neutral and just six tilted toward the critical side. As recounted in chapter 4, the STR collaborated with its congressional counterparts in drafting the implementing bill, which passed overwhelmingly. A triumphant Strauss moved on to other pursuits, as did all of his senior STR colleagues.

The Executive Broker and Its Critics

Strauss was sui generis, but the way he handled trade policy was broadly consistent with the tradition of the 1934 system. He aimed to balance pressures, build coalitions, give a little here, get a little there—but above all to keep the overall American and global trade regime moving in a trade-expanding direction. For the ultimate goal of postwar US trade leaders was not maximum US advantage but openness in general, a trade world where American products and firms could compete as freely as possible with others. Trade was a positive-sum game, and liberal policies would make everyone better off, the United States included.

---

11. As described in chapter 4, part of this bargain was increased protection for the textile industry.

12. This was a provision of US customs law, long offensive to America's trading partners, that required duties on certain products (including benzenoid chemicals, rubber footwear) to be calculated by multiplying the tariff rate not by the price of the import, the normal procedure, but by the higher selling price of the competing US product. This inflated actual duties considerably.

Of course, no US trade official could argue openly for brokering as the primary function. If US trade negotiators were to keep their mandate from Congress and product interests, they had to appear tough in advancing and defending specific US commercial interests. And if aggressiveness simply meant being assertive in trade bargaining and going after those foreign trade barriers that blocked promising US trade opportunities, this was fully consistent with the postwar brokering tradition. Successive administration leaders did pursue market openness abroad even as they did so at home. This was the path to expanding the volume of trade. And "export politics" demanded it. Only by convincing industries and firms that there was money to be earned overseas could officials engage them in policy struggles, balancing the ever active forces that sought import restrictions.

There were political risks, of course. A tough, critical, and visible market-expanding campaign—like those of successive administrations toward Japan—might buttress executive credibility, but it would also fuel anti-Japanese sentiment. For in practice the best "leading indicator" of congressional activism on Japan was executive branch activism. Noisy, visible negotiations got congressional attention and drew members and their staffs into the policy game of pressing their demands. And "Japan bashing" by the executive branch legitimized Japan bashing on Capitol Hill, though up to a point this too could be useful to executive brokers, as Strauss demonstrated.

In terms of the brokering function, the flexibility of the STR arrangement was useful, as was its White House location. These features made it easier not just to engage important business interests but to bring into the balance other departments, such as Treasury or State, that were dependably antiprotectionist for economic or diplomatic reasons. But compared with other units within the Executive Office of the President, the STR was an organizational anomaly. First, unlike the coordinating staffs for broad subjects like national security or domestic policy, the STR was a special-purpose operating unit, typically distant from daily presidential business. Second, it was staffed by "professional" trade specialists, in contrast to the more partisan recruitment pattern that became the norm at the National Security Council and its domestic policy counterparts. Yet the STR did have rapid staff turnover, and hence it was not a career bureaucracy with an institutional memory like, say, the old Bureau of the Budget.

These features made the office a natural target of reorganizers. So did frustration about trade policy. As set forth in chapter 3, the relative position of the United States was, by most measures, declining in the 1970s and 1980s. Throughout the postwar period, other advanced industrial nations had grown faster, closing the gap in per capita income and individual well-being. The merchandise trade balance, consistently in surplus through 1970, was almost always in deficit thereafter. Major industries were losing international market share—and not just textiles or shoes, but steel, automobiles, and consumer electronics as well. It was easy to draw from this evidence a broader diagnosis of American industrial decline and to view "trade wars" as a prime contributor.

So there developed an alternative view of US trade policy: that priority had to be given to halting and reversing this decline. Uncle Sam had to stop being the world's nice guy. As Russell Long put it in 1974, the United States could no longer afford to be the world's "least favored nation," exposing our markets while the rest of the world employed "practices which effectively bar our products."[13] Others were taking advantage—Japan in particular—and America had to fight back. Our policy should thus give priority to the relative position of the United States, particularly in the industries of the future.

These factors combined to generate dissatisfaction with the executive branch trade structure even as Strauss was moving to his triumphant congressional votes. To some, there was a link between the disappointing market results and the dispersion of various trade functions within the executive branch. The Senate Finance Committee summarized these concerns:

> Trade is not given a very high priority in terms of commitment of resources and the attention to top governmental policy officials on a regular basis, other than the STR. Additionally, major trade functions are spread throughout the Executive branch making formulation of trade policy and implementation of trade policy haphazard and in some cases contradictory. No single agency clearly predominates [so] that people with a trade issue know where in the Executive branch they can turn . . . and whom they . . . can hold accountable. [Moreover,] present organization has failed to retain experienced trade personnel, [in contrast] with other countries who have a tough, seasoned corps of trade negotiators.[14]

The STR had established a clear lead role for major multilateral negotiations and an important one in bilateral and product-specific issues. Yet other trade responsibilities were spread about: Commerce promoted exports, Treasury handled unfair trade practice cases, Agriculture dealt with grain sales, and most major departments influenced presidential decisions on escape clause cases.

One proposal for clarifying matters was to consolidate most of these functions within a new Department of Trade. This idea got its first prominent exposure when the author of a study on US international economic policymaking showed a draft proposal to a staff aide of Senator Roth; the

---

13. US Congress, Senate Committee on Finance, *Hearings on the Trade Reform Act of 1973*, 93rd Congress, 2nd session (4 and 5 March 1974), part 1, 2. Challenges to the general trade-expanding and brokering tradition in postwar US trade policy are discussed further in chapter 7.

14. US Congress, Senate Committee on Finance, *Trade Agreements Act of 1979*, 96th Congress, 1st session (17 July 1979), Staff Report 96–249, 268–69.

aide liked it and so did his boss, who introduced it as a bill and won the cosponsorship of the chairman of the Finance Subcommittee on Trade, Abraham A. Ribicoff (D-CT).[15] So when Finance began meeting on the draft MTN results, it voted initially to recommend that the implementing legislation include a provision establishing a Trade Department.

But the Finance senators' commitment to the idea was less than it seemed: Ribicoff was of two minds, and Russell Long preferred to retain the White House office. Moreover, House Ways and Means members did not favor the departmental approach. So, in the end, a compromise was adopted. The draft trade legislation required the president to consider establishing a Trade Department (along with other options), and to submit a specific trade reorganization proposal to Congress by 10 July 1979. When that date instead found Carter on his famous retreat to Camp David, soliciting insights from a range of national leaders about what had gone wrong with his presidency, Ribicoff held up final Senate action on the MTN package. This had the intended impact. On 19 July, Carter sent forth to Congress a reorganization proposal, which, after further consultation and resubmission, became effective in January 1980.

The Carter Reorganization

The Carter reforms created, in essence, a two-tiered executive branch structure. On top was an enlarged and renamed Office of the United States Trade Representative (USTR). It was assigned "international trade policy development, coordination and negotiation functions," and it included responsibilities previously handled by State—GATT, bilateral, commodity, and East-West trade matters, as well as policy responsibility for overseeing trade-remedy cases.

At the level of trade administration, Commerce was to become "the focus of nonagricultural operational trade responsibilities." It was therefore given Treasury's authority over countervailing duty and antidumping cases, as well as State's jurisdiction over commercial attachés. The trade committees had, in fact, insisted on the former step, judging Treasury to be insufficiently aggressive in enforcing the unfair trade statutes (see chapter 6). And the adjective "nonagricultural" signaled a bow to political reality: Farm interests would never accept the transfer of responsibility and expertise for their products from the Department of Agriculture.

The USTR half of the Carter reorganization reflected the sensible principle that in restructuring government one should start with what works. The Trade Representative's office had completed the MTN with success and with a reputation for effectiveness, and it was better to build on that

---

15. For the story as told by a participant, see Stephen D. Cohen, *The Making of United States International Economic Policy* (New York: Praeger, 2d ed., 1981), chapter 8.

than to start anew. There was some risk of making its staff too large.[16] This could incline the USTR toward too much in-house detail work, at the expense of reaching out and mobilizing the resources of all agencies. And assigning it difficult tasks outside the GATT-MTN mainstream, such as East-West trade policy coordination, did not necessarily bring added strength. Still, a timely, visible reinforcement of the STR's mandate helped offset the tendency for trade policy power to disperse whenever a multilateral round was completed.

The reasons for strengthening Commerce were more ad hoc. It was there. It already handled certain operational trade functions, such as industry information and export promotion. So it seemed a logical home for other trade tasks whose current management generated dissatisfaction. Moreover, Carter did not want the White House trade office to grow too much, since this would undo his earlier reorganization, which had reduced the total number of Executive Office personnel. So those functions that required an expanded, specialized staff—enforcement of unfair trade laws, for example—were placed in Commerce.

The overall package was rationalized by an old and largely discredited public administration dichotomy—the separation of policy from operations, with the corollary that the former could control the latter.[17] The USTR, with policy leadership responsibility, would be in charge; Commerce would carry the policy out. This could work, but only if both organizations and their leaders accepted these roles and worked closely and cooperatively, with Commerce deferring to USTR direction.

Under Carter, the system performed adequately, as both agencies had to adjust to new leaders. Commerce busied itself with filling a range of new positions, including an under secretary for trade who would oversee the department's renamed and expanded International Trade Administration, with no fewer than 17 officials at or above the deputy assistant secretary level. The new USTR was former Florida governor Reubin Askew, who lacked Strauss's political mastery and close presidential ties; he proved a competent trade policy leader, however, and no single competitor rose to challenge him.

Reagan I: Commerce Versus USTR

Askew's successor, William E. Brock III, was not so lucky. Like Strauss four years earlier, Brock in 1981 had just completed a successful term as

---

16. The Carter administration, under substantial congressional pressure, increased the number of permanent USTR staff slots to 131, compared with 59 in the STR.

17. For a more general discussion of the persistence and limits of this approach to foreign policy management see I. M. Destler, *Presidents, Bureaucrats, and Foreign Policy: The Politics of Organizational Reform* (Princeton, NJ: Princeton University Press, 1972), 18–22.

his party's national chairman. And once in the trade job, he would demonstrate comparable talents on Capitol Hill.

Yet a month before Brock was named to the USTR, President-elect Ronald Reagan chose as secretary of commerce a capable, ambitious Connecticut businessman named Malcolm Baldrige.[18] In discussions surrounding the appointment, it became public knowledge that influential Reagan counselor Edwin Meese III favored abolishing USTR and giving Baldrige the primary trade responsibility. Again, the fact that the trade representative's office was an organizational oddity, a "line" unit (possessing specific policy responsibility) within the president's Executive Office staff, rendered it vulnerable to reformers who sought to streamline structure before they understood substance. Brock, one of the last cabinet-level appointees announced by Reagan, had therefore to respond in his confirmation hearings to claims by the incoming Commerce secretary that he, not Brock, would be the central trade policy figure.

Brock replied by reiterating the "indispensable" USTR function: it "must continue to be, for the President and the Congress, the government's principal architect and exponent of trade policy to insure that we act and speak as one." Three successive laws had made the trade representative chairman of the statutory interagency trade committee, so that matter was settled; moreover, he had had "fairly extended conversations with the Secretary of Commerce" and they had "a very healthy and solid commitment to the same goal": an "aggressive" trade and export policy. He was sure they would "work very effectively together."[19] Nevertheless, when the Reagan administration, under Meese's leadership, created its own (nonstatutory) network of coordinating committees, it was Baldrige who chaired the Cabinet Council on Commerce and Trade.

In practice, neither man was able to establish clear predominance in the first Reagan administration. Brock was supported by the precedent of successful leadership by previous STRs. He also had strong policy and political skills and close ties to senators and representatives, having served (as had Cordell Hull) in both chambers. Indeed, when the new Cabinet Council on Commerce and Trade held its first meeting under Baldrige's chairmanship, both the Finance and the Ways and Means chairmen reportedly phoned the president and informed him that this was against the law! Yet the commerce secretary had political resources also: a stronger relationship with Reagan (and with Meese), the new authorities

---

18. When, in a November conversation with the President-elect, Brock expressed interest in the USTR position, Reagan "expressed surprise at Brock's choice." Reagan "wasn't aware that the trade representative position was a Cabinet post." Steve Dryden, *Trade Warriors: USTR and the American Crusade for Free Trade* (New York: Oxford University Press, 1995), 265, based on Dryden's interview with Brock.

19. US Congress, Senate Committee on Finance, *Hearing on the Nomination of William E. Brock, III*, 97th Congress, 1st session (19 January 1981), 3, 10, 12, 13.

given Commerce in the Carter reorganization, and the talents of an aggressive under secretary, Lionel H. Olmer. So while Brock handled auto imports from Japan and headed the US delegation at the unsuccessful GATT ministerial talks of November 1982, it was Baldrige who brokered a voluntary export restraint agreement between American steel companies and European governments earlier that same year. Beginning in 1980, Commerce also established the first credible enforcement operation for the unfair trade laws. (The consequences are addressed in chapter 6.)

Baldrige also continued in his quest for governmentwide trade dominance. His persistence was hardly surprising, for trade was by far the most prominent of his department's substantive responsibilities, and it naturally attracted any aggressive secretary with decent White House connections. And if Maurice Stans had failed egregiously in 1969–71, Baldrige did a bit better 12 years later. In the spring of 1983, despite the opposition of Brock and almost all other senior presidential advisers, President Reagan accepted a Baldrige-Meese recommendation that the administration endorse Senator Roth's proposal for a Department of International Trade and Industry, with the USTR incorporated therein. The Commerce secretary spent much of the rest of Reagan's first term lobbying to win industry support for that reorganization.

The reemergence of the trade department proposal raised anew the question of whether the brokering function was adequate for trade leadership. Roth's Governmental Affairs Committee argued the negative in its report recommending approval of the legislation: "Trade needs a champion in government. The new Department Secretary will be this champion. The USTR was created as a broker, not an advocate." Or to quote the views of three Democrats:

> USTR was established basically to pull together our position for multilateral negotiations at a time when our major trade problem was coordinating and balancing our own diverse interests, and we had no significant industrial problems. We now have a host of other problems, and most of the negotiating action has shifted into the bilateral arena. We need a more focused effort to deal coherently with trade, industry, and competitiveness questions.[20]

Nonetheless, the Trade Department idea did not move very far on Capitol Hill. To win bipartisan endorsement by his committee, Roth had to accept organizational add-ons, including an industrial policy mechanism pushed by Democrats.[21] This served to reduce the Reagan administra-

---

20. US Congress, Senate Committee on Governmental Affairs, *Trade Reorganization Act of 1983*, 98th Congress, 2nd session (3 April 1984), Staff Report 98–374, 8, 128. The three Democrats were Thomas F. Eagleton of Missouri, Carl Levin of Michigan, and Jeff Bingaman of New Mexico.

21. For any trade-threatened sector of national significance, the secretary was to convene an "industry sector competitiveness council" representing business, labor, and government to recommend an action program.

tion's enthusiasm for the venture. Pungent opposition by Finance Trade Subcommittee Chairman Danforth delayed the bill, and ultimately prevented it from reaching the Senate floor in 1984. In the House, it never reached the markup stage. Still, the fact that the president was proposing to eliminate his organization could only damage Brock's standing and the credibility of the USTR generally.

USTR and Presidential Ambivalence

Reagan's lack of attachment to the trade office had ample precedent. Kennedy had been reluctant to establish a trade representative in the Executive Office of the President (EOP). Nixon had been willing to reorganize it out of existence. As House Trade Subcommittee Chairman Sam Gibbons (D-FL) remarked, with only modest exaggeration, "Every President that comes in wants to throw the USTR Office out of the White House."[22]

Presidents have, traditionally and understandably, resisted establishing units to serve other people's purposes in "their" White House. Presidency scholar Richard E. Neustadt, in his role as transition adviser, warned Kennedy against pressures in this direction. Citing Franklin D. Roosevelt's staffing practices, he urged that JFK start by filling only jobs "for which the President-elect, himself, feels an *immediate and continuing* need." Neustadt inveighed thereafter against "proliferating advisory staffs in your Executive Office."[23] Kennedy generally followed such advice. And 16 years later, Jimmy Carter's Executive Office reorganization similarly aimed at "limiting EOP, wherever possible, to functions which bear a close relationship to the work of the President."[24]

Kennedy did, of course, accede to the STR's creation. Carter retained it and, under congressional pressure, broadened its functions and enlarged its staff. Yet the office has never had the sort of connection to broad presidential policy business possessed by, say, the National Security Council or the Office of Management and Budget. It is too specialized, too focused on a specific slice of policy substance and ongoing operations.

Had Congress not wanted (U)STR, it is unlikely that any postwar president would have created or proposed such an EOP office on his own. Trade policy just has not loomed large enough, and presidents have seen it as, for the most part, second-order, technical business. Also, presidents

22. US Congress, House Committee on Ways and Means, Subcommittee on Trade, *Hearings on Options to Improve the Trade Remedy Laws*, 98th Congress, 1st session (16 and 17 March, and 13 and 14 April 1983), Serial 98-14, part 1, 389.

23. "Memorandum on Organizing the Transition" (15 September 1960), 7 (emphasis added), and "Memorandum on the Council of Economic Advisers: First Steps" (19 December 1960), 2. Copies obtained from Neustadt; both are available in the John F. Kennedy Library, Boston.

24. US Congress, "Reorganization Plan No. 1 of 1977," *Message from the President of the United States*, 95th Congress, 1st session (15 July 1977), H. Doc. 95–185.

frequently want protection from trade issues for the same reasons that legislators do: They don't like to say "no" to important interests or to choose among them when choice can be avoided.

This presidential coolness has limited the capacity of the trade representative to build personal ties with the man in the Oval Office. Of all who have held the office, only Strauss under Carter and Mickey Kantor under Bill Clinton were close presidential advisers, and they kept that status because they were useful on a broad range of matters.[25] Trade alone would not have given them enough to talk about with the president and his key aides; however, the general belief that they were talking regularly with the president was central to their credibility on trade, not only with business and on Capitol Hill, but in foreign capitals as well.

Conversely, those who, like Brock, could not build such strong presidential ties were vulnerable to challenge from executive branch rivals. Some managed to build a presidential base indirectly: Herter and Roth through the national security staff; Eberle and his deputies through Nixon's "economic czar," George P. Shultz. Indeed, one advantage of the (U)STR's Executive Office location is that it makes such relationships easier for its head to develop than they would be for the head of a separate executive department. On the other hand, a high-profile USTR, of the sort needed to manage major international trade talks or domestic trade crises, may be hard for a White House chief of staff to swallow, since the USTR combines independence in day-to-day actions and the White House label. She or he must swear allegiance to Congress as well as the president.

Liberal Words, Protectionist Deeds

In part because of the struggle between Brock and Baldrige, but more importantly perhaps because of recession and the burgeoning trade imbalance, the first Reagan administration developed a pattern of endorsing liberal trade in principle but providing protection in practice. The auto quotas initiated in 1981 were understandable, and probably unavoidable, given the industry's sudden crisis. However, they were followed in 1982 by "voluntary" European Community steel export restraints, and in December 1983 by toughening of restrictions on textile imports, after Baldrige persuaded the president to overturn an 11 to 1 cabinet committee vote against such a move. Brock's reputation rebounded the following September, as the USTR took the lead in explaining and implementing yet another protectionist step, perhaps Reagan's most significant: his decision to negotiate sales-limiting agreements with all major steel exporters. On the free trade side, Brock also gained by blocking or neutralizing several

---

25. The index of Jimmy Carter's *Keeping Faith* (New York: Bantam Books, 1982) has seven references to Strauss. Only two refer to his trade job, and none to the substance of trade policy.

industry-specific protectionist provisions in what became the Trade and Tariff Act of 1984 (see chapter 4). Brock was frustrated, however, by the failure of the 1982 GATT ministerial talks and the difficulty of winning endorsement, at home and abroad, for a new round of trade negotiations. And as a consequence, Brock lacked the advantage of a central trade negotiation to strengthen his hand within government and vis-à-vis private interests.

At the same time, the trade deficit was ballooning to levels previously unknown. Prominent Democrats were pushing for more protection, not less, and it looked for a while as if trade would become a central issue in the president's reelection campaign. Reagan was hardly the first incumbent to buy some insurance with sympathetic responses to politically potent industries like textiles or steel. The trade policy performance of the first Reagan administration was therefore understandable, if far from ideal.

The second Reagan administration proved very different. In the first eight months of 1985, its behavior can only be described as bizarre. As the trade pressure mounted, the administration seemed to do nothing, and seemed not even to recognize that there was any problem to address. Then, under new leadership, it launched an 11th-hour campaign to open markets abroad and stave off protection at home.

Reagan II: An Eight-Month Vacuum

First, the president agreed to a 1985 New Year's meeting with Japanese Prime Minister Yasuhiro Nakasone. But despite the urgings of his trade advisers, and despite the fact that the politically sensitive bilateral deficit was rising to an unheard-of $33.6 billion for calendar year 1984, he decided not to press trade matters with his counterpart. It was only when Nakasone brought up the subject that a bilateral negotiating agenda was established.

In March 1985, with trade-oriented businesses feeling the squeeze of yet another rise in the dollar and with Congress alarmed at a global trade deficit that had topped $100 billion and was climbing, the White House acknowledged political reality by declaring it would not push the Trade Department proposal further "at this time." But this was followed, two days later, by the announced transfer of the presumed winner in that decision. Now that he had finally established himself as the administration's most respected and politically astute trade man, William Brock was to become Secretary of Labor! What would this do to trade policymaking? There is no evidence that Reagan or his new chief of staff, Donald T. Regan, even asked this question. As *Washington Post* columnist Hobart Rowen put it at the time, "The reality is that the White House seemed to have only one thing on its mind: the need to build new relationships with the labor movement. . . ."[26]

In that same March, the administration announced it would not seek renewal of the voluntary export restraint on autos; this decision, defensible in economic terms, was made without reckoning the congressional reaction. In August, Reagan said no to the escape clause petition of the shoe industry, a case championed by Danforth. He did this without any apparent recognition that denying relief through established channels to an industry that was clearly damaged by imports was bound to increase pressure for statutory solutions.

The administration appeared no more helpful to trade-embattled industries on what most considered the prime source of their problems: the sky-high dollar. Through the summer, the president and his chief of staff tended to speak of this as a good thing, yet another sign that "America was back." Business leaders who talked to the White House (outside the USTR) about the havoc this was wreaking in their markets found themselves rebuffed; some were told, in essence, that they were crybabies and should stop asking for government help against the workings of the marketplace. This made them angry and frustrated. They felt, like many others, that the prime cause of dollar strength was government policy, specifically the Reagan budget deficits. It was hard for these companies, through their own efforts, to offset an exchange rate estimated to give foreign competitors a 30 to 40 percent cost advantage! Lacking a hearing downtown, they descended with double strength on Capitol Hill.

In the spring and summer of 1985, Congress needed more executive branch help than ever, because of its own decentralization, and above all because of the enormous trade deficit. It was getting just about none. In fact, the administration was doing the opposite of protecting Congress. It was diverting trade-restrictive pressures to Capitol Hill! Little wonder that the number of trade bills increased, as did their prominence and their progress through committees and onto the House and Senate floors. Not only were legislators genuinely concerned about the trade problem; not only did some of them see partisan advantage (or fear partisan disadvantage) in the issue; but they needed to shock the administration, to jar it back onto the activist track. As one aide to a Senate Republican involved in the spring's Japan bashing put it privately: "You don't understand. The target isn't the Japanese; it's the White House!" And rank-and-file administration trade officials were encouraging such congressional activity, since they too were trying to get the president's attention.

---

26. "Filling Bill Brock's Shoes," *Washington Post*, 28 March 1985. It took more than three months for Brock's successor, Clayton Yeutter, to be named, cleared by the administration, and confirmed by the Senate.

Reagan II: The Shift to Activism

Finally, in late September 1985, the administration unveiled a trade strategy. On Sunday the 22nd, Treasury Secretary James A. Baker III joined with the finance ministers of France, Germany, Japan, and the United Kingdom in a joint declaration calling for a weaker dollar (more precisely, for the "further orderly appreciation of the major nondollar currencies against the dollar"). The Group of Five indicated their intention to intervene in foreign exchange markets to help bring this about. The dollar dropped sharply, particularly in Tokyo, where the Bank of Japan was a heavy buyer of yen.[27]

The next day, Monday the 23rd, President Reagan gave a "fair trade" speech at the White House. He sounded his determination to fight for the rights of American producers in foreign markets, and announced an intent to press several unfair trade practice cases against Japan, the European Community, Korea, and Brazil.

This two-track strategy combined economic and political logic. Decline of the dollar would bring first the hope, then the reality, of improvement in the trade balance. Because of the J-curve effect, the impact on the nominal balance would be delayed, but the effect on the real balance—the volumes of exports and imports—would be greater than the dollar statistics showed. Since this real balance was important for trade politics, the administration could expect better political days—if it could hold off pressures in the meantime. That it would do through its new aggressiveness in opening foreign markets to American exports. But it would resist the congressional push for trade legislation—at least until dollar decline could do its work.

Orchestrating the new administration strategy were Secretary of the Treasury Baker and his deputy, Richard G. Darman. They played a close hand on exchange rate matters, over which Baker had direct authority, and used the interagency Economic Policy Council, which Baker chaired, to develop the new strategy on trade policy. Responsibility for executing the new strategy was divided between Baldrige and the new USTR, Clayton Yeutter, but without the conflict that had characterized Reagan's first term. Baldrige had lost not only the battle for a Trade Department but also his White House ally, Edwin Meese, who became attorney general, and the services of his aggressive under secretary, Lionel Olmer, who left government for private law practice. Much of the new trade strategy employed statutory authorities belonging to the USTR, and that office's congressional ties made it the main administration locutor on the specifics

---

27. For details, see Yoichi Funabashi, *Managing the Dollar: From the Plaza to the Louvre* (Washington, DC: Institute for International Economics, 1988, rev. 1989), chapter 3, and I. M. Destler and C. Randall Henning, *Dollar Politics: Exchange Rate Policymaking in the United States* (Washington, DC: Institute for International Economics, 1989), chapters 3–4.

of the trade legislation. Moreover, with Baker there was now a clearer locus of decision-making power on international economic issues, unlike during the first Reagan administration. The USTR could use the Baker process to get the go-ahead to push more unfair trade cases with foreign governments.

Yeutter came to the USTR job with prior trade policy experience, having served as assistant secretary of Agriculture and deputy STR in the Ford administration. So if he lacked his predecessors' close congressional ties and exceptional political talents, he knew a lot about trade. He also possessed seemingly boundless energy, which he employed to repair political fences. One tack he took was traditional. Following on the work of Brock and others, he chaired the cabinet-level US delegation to the September 1986 GATT ministerial talks at Punta del Este, which inaugurated the new Uruguay Round of multilateral talks on trade in goods and services. Working with Baldrige and Secretary of Agriculture Richard E. Lyng, Yeutter won agreement that the new round's agenda would include trade in agricultural products and services, subjects of particular American interest. In so doing, he demonstrated how the USTR leadership role can and should work within the executive branch.

But much of the USTR's energy in the late 1980s was directed to what critics have labeled "aggressive unilateralism": negotiations aimed at opening specific foreign markets under threat of closing our own.[28] And the core authority they employed was Section 301 of the Trade Act of 1974.

Targeting the World: Section 301

Section 301 granted the president authority to take any of a broad range of retaliatory actions against a country that "maintains unjustifiable or unreasonable tariff or other import restrictions," or "subsidies . . . on its exports . . . which have the effect of substantially reducing sales of the competitive United States product. . . ."[29] This was potentially a powerful club, but for its first decade it was generally kept in the closet. From 1975 through the summer of 1985, private firms filed 48 Section 301 petitions on matters ranging from EC wheat flour export subsidies to Japanese import quotas on leather. These led typically to consultations, inside and outside the GATT. Some brought significant changes in foreign behavior; on others, GATT review dragged on for years. But prior to the summer of

---

28. See, for example, Jagdish Bhagwati and Hugh T. Patrick, eds., *Aggressive Unilateralism: America's 301 Trade Policy and the World Trading System* (Ann Arbor: University of Michigan Press, 1990).

29. Section 252 of the Trade Expansion Act of 1962 had provided the president a more limited authority to act against "unjustifiable" or "unreasonable" foreign import restrictions.

1985, there were only two cases where the president took the retaliatory action that the law authorized.[30]

Congressional champions of Section 301 grew more and more unhappy. They had amended the law in 1979 and 1984: to establish timetables for action; to set specific criteria for judgment; to encourage the administration to initiate[31] cases on its own. But they found the response soft. In the words of Senator Danforth, the most persistent congressional champion of this authority, trade policy was "a failure" because no one ever saw "any possibility . . . that the United States [would] ever . . . retaliate."[32]

All this changed in September 1985. After an intensive internal review, the president ordered the USTR to recommend retaliation in several long-pending cases if resolutions were not reached by December. That same month, the USTR for the first time initiated three Section 301 investigations on its own, without waiting for an industry petition. The targets were Brazilian informatics (computer and telecommunications) policy, Japanese import restrictions on tobacco, and Korean restraints on access to its insurance market. The USTR initiated an additional 301 case later in 1985, and six subsequent cases during the Reagan administration. Congress was not entirely satisfied, and its moves to toughen Section 301 were, to two senior USTR officials, "the heart of the 1988 Trade Act."[33] But one purpose may have been "to ensure that future administrations continue to apply this trade remedy in the vigorous manner of the Reagan administration from 1985 through 1988."[34]

Section 301 was "export politics" pursued with a vengeance, a product of the egregious trade imbalance and frustration at foreign unfairness, real and perceived. And its most important single target was Japan. The administration worked, for policy and political reasons, to spread the pain among countries, but there was no doubt which country Congress had most in mind.

---

30. Gary Clyde Hufbauer and Joanna Shelton Erb, *Subsidies in International Trade* (Washington, DC: Institute for International Economics, 1984), 115; Thomas O. Bayard and Kimberly Ann Elliott, *Reciprocity and Retaliation in U.S. Trade Policy* (Washington, DC: Institute for International Economics, 1994). The cases involved Argentina's breach of an export control agreement on hides and EC subsidies on wheat flour exports. In a third case, involving Canadian restrictions on US television broadcasting, the president recommended—and Congress adopted—mirror legislation.

31. The word typically used in trade policy circles is "self-initiate," an expression that seems redundant and (to this ear) linguistically offensive.

32. Debate of 28 March 1985, *Congressional Record*, S35.

33. Judith Hippler Bello and Alan F. Holmer, "The Heart of the 1988 Trade Act: A Legislative History of the Amendments to Section 301," in Bhagwati and Patrick, eds., *Aggressive Unilateralism*, 49–89.

34. Ibid., 88.

Targeting Japan: From MOSS to Semiconductor Sanctions

From the Strauss era on, the US-Japan trade relationship had been the USTR's most challenging. The challenge grew through the 1980s, as the bilateral imbalance ballooned and the number of specific conflicts multiplied. In 1985, after Reagan discussed trade with Nakasone, the market-oriented, sector-specific (MOSS) talks began. These sought major Japanese concessions in four broad areas where US products seemed competitive but weren't selling: telecommunications, pharmaceuticals, microelectronics, and wood products. Hard negotiations led to significant Japanese concessions. The doubling of overall US sales to Japan between 1985 and 1989 was due mainly to the decline of the dollar, but the USTR's Advisory Committee concluded in early 1989 that in those product areas where the United States had pushed, sales had grown particularly fast.[35] There was also substantial negotiating achievement in agriculture and related products, with Japan agreeing to abandon beef and citrus quotas in 1988. The most dramatic and symbolic issue of the latter 1980s, however, was trade in semiconductors.

The semiconductor "chip" had been independently invented by two Americans in the late 1950s and had received a major early boost from official defense and space programs. US firms—based particularly in California's Silicon Valley—had led the way through the 1970s as hundreds, then thousands of electronic functions were crowded onto the tiny chips, which became indispensable to computers, telecommunications, and many other advanced industrial products.

But with government help and encouragement, Japan's integrated electronics firms began making major inroads into the semiconductor market in the late 1970s and early 1980s, particularly with the mass-produced, standardized dynamic random access memories (DRAMs). In 1983, the California-based Semiconductor Industry Association (SIA) published a report entitled *The Effect of Government Targeting on World Semiconductor Competition: A Case History of Japanese Industrial Strategy and Its Costs for America*. This report contrasted the rise in Japanese exports with the low and static share (around 11 percent) that US producers held in the Japanese market.

In July 1985, its members hit by growing Japanese competition and a severe slump in overall demand, SIA filed a Section 301 case claiming that this import resistance, encouraged by past government action, was an "unreasonable" barrier to US trade. In the months thereafter, antidumping cases were submitted by individual US firms and by the secretary of Commerce. There were conflicting interests within the US industry, of course—major chip users, like the US computer industry, benefited from

---

35. Advisory Committee for Trade Policy and Negotiations, *Analysis of the U.S.-Japan Trade Problem* (Washington, DC: USTR, February 1989), chapter 6.

high-quality, low-cost Japanese inputs. Nonetheless, anxieties about erosion of US technological leadership, spreading from private industry to the Pentagon,[36] made support of the industry's case far broader than would have been received by a "low-tech" industry of comparable size.

There followed a year of complex—and fractious—negotiations, culminating in a unique "three-market" trade agreement announced in August 1986.[37] To halt dumping in the United States, the two governments adopted a system of minimum prices and reporting of sales by Japanese firms. There was also a somewhat looser system of price monitoring in third-country markets, aimed at protecting US exports against dumping there. Last but certainly not least was a commitment to increase US-based producers' share of the Japanese market, featuring a side letter from Japanese officials declaring, in the words of one US negotiator, that "they understood, welcomed, and would make efforts to assist the US companies in reaching their goal of a 20 percent market share within five years."[38]

The arrangement had political and economic logic. To act only against dumping in the US market would mean higher-priced chips here than elsewhere, undercutting producers of computers and other downstream products, such as IBM. Moreover, if the Japanese firms—NEC, Hitachi, Fujitsu, etc.—were able to restrict foreign access to their very large home market, it would be hard for US firms to hold their own globally. Nor did these firms wish for a two-market agreement that would encourage low-priced Japanese sales in the rest of the world. The deal completed was responsive to all of these concerns. But it was also internally contradictory. Specifically, the provisions aimed at dumping in the United States undercut the expansion of US market share in Japan and third countries.

The minimum (nondumping) prices in the United States were based on each Japanese firm's cost of production, and they were periodically updated. This procedure encouraged large production runs that brought down unit costs. But these large runs also brought oversupply and falling prices within Japan (the only market where the agreement did not set minimum prices). This undercut US firms' sales there. It led also to a "gray market" in third countries, as chips were flown out of Japan in suitcases for low-price resale.[39]

---

36. See US Department of Defense, Office of the Under Secretary for Acquisition, *Report of the Defense Science Board Task Force on Defense Semiconductor Dependency* (Washington, DC: US Department of Defense, 1987).

37. For an extensive discussion of the semiconductor issue, see Laura D'Andrea Tyson, *Who's Bashing Whom? Trade Conflicts in High-Technology Industries* (Washington, DC: Institute for International Economics, 1992), chapter 4.

38. Clyde V. Prestowitz, Jr., *Trading Places: How We Allowed Japan to Take the Lead* (New York: Basic Books, 1988), 65.

39. The obvious way to combat this was for Japan's Ministry of International Trade and Industry to encourage Japanese firms to limit production, but when the Japanese had sug-

By the end of 1986 SIA was complaining that both the Japanese and third-country market provisions of the agreement were being violated. US officials expressed growing concern to Tokyo and warned of retaliation. By early spring, the Ministry of International Trade and Industry was pressing the Japanese firms to cut output, in order to drive the price up in Japan and take the profit out of the gray market. But before this could be effective, US patience ran out. Pressed by a Congress considering omnibus trade legislation, President Reagan announced in March 1987 that he would impose sanctions because of "Japan's inability to enforce" the agreement. In April, he imposed punitive (100 percent) tariffs against selected Japanese electronics imports[40] equivalent to the estimated sales lost to US firms in the Japanese market and in third countries.

The tariffs prompted shock and headlines in Tokyo: "sanctions against an ally," the first such US action against Japan since World War II. Later that year, with the third-country dumping issue resolved, Reagan removed a portion of the penalties (and as discussed in chapter 7, US users of chips shortly found themselves facing sharp price *increases*, which they blamed on the agreement). But the major portion of the sanctions, retaliation for loss of anticipated US sales in Japan, continued through the decade—until the agreement was renegotiated and extended in 1991. Japanese dominance in the DRAM market continued through the decade as well.[41]

The semiconductor issue symbolized the complexity of modern trade issues: it was a high-technology production input sold by multinational firms in global markets. Trade policy was not an ideal instrument for addressing it, but it was the one most readily available. The USTR had to show toughness to respond to semiconductor producers, but at the risk of damage to semiconductor users. And it had to keep one eye cocked toward that older political institution, the US Congress.

Working the Trade Bill: Damage Limitation

As discussed in chapter 4, the administration resisted trade legislation through 1986, then accepted it as inevitable and possibly desirable from

---

gested this during the negotiations, both SIA and the US government had opposed it—SIA because of concerns of its members about supply shortages, US officials because it was contrary to free market principles.

40. The tariffs were imposed not against semiconductors—this would have hit US users—but against selected "downstream" products that incorporated them: laptop and desktop computers, color TV sets, and power hand tools.

41. In retrospect, it is clear that both nations wildly exaggerated the importance of DRAM production to high-tech industry leadership. Flexibility and creativity proved more important—as the United States showed in the 1990s.

1987 on. One reason was the Democratic recapture of the Senate; another was that the USTR now needed extension of fast-track authority to complete the Uruguay Round. The USTR's can-do attitude toward the legislation was not universally shared in the administration: Free market devotees at the Council of Economic Advisers and elsewhere felt that any bill passed by the Congress would be far too interventionist. When a senior trade official reported conference agreement, in early 1988, to remove a number of trade-restrictive provisions, one such economist responded that the USTR was "doing too well": Now the president might actually sign the terrible thing!

But as that story illustrates, the game to the end was damage limitation: removal or modification of provisions that were clearly GATT-illegal, or that tied the executive's hands, or that tilted trade remedies further to the advantage of protection-seeking claimants. And notwithstanding his efforts, Yeutter did not possess in 1988 the congressional ties Brock had used to such advantage in 1984, and Strauss in 1979. He and his aides were thus excluded from some key conference-related meetings of the sort at which their predecessors had been included.[42] In contrast to the late 1970s, moreover, USTR people now found their best ties not with Senate Finance but with House Ways and Means, at both the member and the staff levels.

Nonetheless, their damage-limitation effort was at least a qualified success. In the most unfavorable trade-political climate since 1930, Yeutter and his aides had gotten the negotiating authority they needed, and had managed to neutralize—or modify—the most restrictive provisions. Retaliation was made "mandatory but not compulsory." And one issue on which the administration lost—congressional insistence on transferring some major trade authorities from the president to the USTR—represented a congressional vote of confidence for "its" executive broker. Rostenkowski had been particularly adamant in insisting on this transfer.

Taken as a whole, Reagan-era trade policy represented a "strategic retreat" for advocates of liberal trade.[43] The president had granted "more import relief" than any predecessor "in more than half a century,"[44] particularly during his first term. Damage had been limited during the second term, but the administration lost the trade initiative in 1985 and left office still struggling to regain it. Interestingly, Yeutter's successor would

42. Symbolic was the final bargaining of Subconference I on 31 March 1988. Senate Finance Chairman Lloyd Bentsen and House Ways and Means Chairman Dan Rostenkowski met in the Capitol, while Yeutter, Deputy USTR Alan Holmer, and General Counsel Judith Bello waited three hours in an adjacent room. Bello and Holmer, "The Heart of the 1988 Trade Act," 56 (see footnote 45).

43. William A. Niskanen, *Reaganomics: An Insider's Account of the Policies and the People* (New York: Oxford University Press, 1988), 137.

44. Remarks by James A. Baker III at the Institute for International Economics (see footnote 1).

regain it. And she would do so, ironically, by exploiting the new authorities that Congress had forced on her reluctant predecessors.

Carla Hills and Super 301

Carla A. Hills came to the USTR post a seasoned Washington professional, a lawyer who had served as assistant attorney general and then secretary of Housing and Urban Development under President Gerald Ford. She had no special trade expertise, though she and her firm had represented international clients. Nor, unlike a number of her cabinet colleagues, did she enter office with close and long-standing ties to President George Bush. Secretary of Commerce Robert Mosbacher did possess such ties and used them to seize the initiative on a controversial agreement to co-develop the FSX fighter aircraft with Japan. For a while, it seemed possible that the Brock-Baldrige experience would be reenacted.

It wasn't. Hills proved competent, tough, and credible in her new role. The Bush administration rewarded such performance more reliably than had its predecessor. Mosbacher lost some luster when he ventured closer to advocating "industrial policy" than was safe in a free-market, Republican administration, evoking the wrath of Budget Director Richard Darman and White House Chief of Staff John Sununu. And the new USTR benefited from the full negotiating agenda that Yeutter and Congress had left her.

Hills' most immediate challenge was the new amendments to Section 301. The 1988 Trade Act had transferred to the USTR from the president not only authority to determine whether foreign practices were unfair under that provision, but also to decide upon, and order, specific retaliatory action.[45] And it had added to Section 301's emphasis on specific trade practices a provision commonly known as Super 301,[46] a mandate that the USTR identify, by 31 May 1989, "priority foreign countries." These were to be named for the "number and pervasiveness" of their "acts, policies or practices" that impeded US exports, and for the US export gains that might be anticipated from the removal of these impediments.

To the surprise and pleasure of the USTR (and Congress), two important US trading partners—Korea and Taiwan—were determined *not* to be so designated. To avoid this fate, they offered trade concessions they had previously resisted. The European Community and its Common Agricultural Policy would have met the statutory criteria nicely, but naming

---

45. To appease the administration, the phrase "subject to the specific direction, if any, of the President" was added to the USTR's action authority. Of course, the USTR would be subject to such direction in any case.

46. Actually, Section 310 of the Trade Act of 1974, as amended.

Europe was judged politically counterproductive. This left Japan—the prime congressional target of Super 301—and Brazil, with which the United States had been pressing a growing range of trade complaints. Also put on the list was India—a country with highly restrictive trading practices, to be sure, but not the sort of major US trading partner Congress had in mind. To soften the blow against these countries, the USTR limited its indictment to six very specific practices and markets, of the sort it had been pressing in any case. But to appease Congress, it proposed to Japan a separate negotiation outside the 301 framework. The resulting Structural Impediments Initiative (SII) talks aimed at the sort of broader import resistance that Danforth and his colleagues had in mind, but the SII dialogue was to be two-way. Japanese could—and did—point to American structural problems as well.[47]

Over the next year, Hills worked a range of trade problems, particularly vis-à-vis Japan, taking care to be responsive to both congressional and industry complaints. By April 1990, the second (and last) Super 301 deadline, she had built the political basis for a bolder approach. Stretching the language of the law to the limit—and perhaps beyond it—she declared that the United States' "top trade liberalization priority for 1990" was neither a specific product nor a particular country, but "the successful completion of the Uruguay Round of global trade talks by December."[48] As for specific countries, Brazil had moved to "dismantle its restrictive import licensing practices," and its new government, under President Fernando Collor de Mello, was "embracing market-driven reforms." According to Hills, Japan had "moved farther and faster than any of our other trading partners in the past twelve months. . . . Given our recent successes, we believe that the most effective way to achieve such results is through cooperation, not confrontation. Therefore, we think it would be counterproductive today to initiate new Super 301 cases against Japan."

She balanced this praise with a warning: "Japan is on notice: We expect maximum efforts that yield results." And because India had refused to negotiate, it was renamed.[49] But no country was added to the Super 301 list. Members of Congress grumbled, but did nothing more:

> [I]n the week before the announcement [not to rename Japan], members had threatened to scuttle or hold hostage everything from trade agreements with the

---

47. For a comprehensive political analysis of the SII talks, see Leonard J. Schoppa, *Bargaining with Japan: What American Pressure Can and Cannot Do* (New York: Columbia University Press, 1997).

48. This and subsequent quotations are from Hills' press statement of 24 April 1990, 1, 3, and 4.

49. Forty-five days later, Hills would determine "that India's insurance and investment practices are unreasonable and burden or restrict U.S. commerce, but that retaliation is inappropriate at this time given the ongoing negotiations on services and investments in the Uruguay Round of global trade talks" (USTR Press Release 90-39, 14 June 1990).

Soviet Union to the worldwide trade pact being negotiated through the General Agreement on Tariffs and Trade (GATT). . . . But after the announcement, the air seemed to have gone at least temporarily from the balloon.[50]

Geneva Versus Mexico City?

In her first 15 months in office, Hills had built enough credibility to be able to handle Super 301 on her own terms. But the way she did so increased her stakes in a successful Uruguay Round. This was consistent with her interests, and with the US trade policy tradition dating from Cordell Hull. And it made sense economically. Multilateral trade agreements would bring the greatest trade gains with the partners of greatest importance to the United States. They would also constrain American protectionism and unilateralism. Finally, success in completing another major round would redound to the credit of the USTR.

But Hills inherited the central problem of the Uruguay Round: trade in agricultural products. This was the major area of economic activity least constrained by GATT rules, and the United States stood to gain (for many products) if markets were opened and subsidies reduced. This had been a US goal before, in the Kennedy Round of the 1960s and the Tokyo Round of the 1970s. Each began, in Dale Hathaway's words, "with a resounding declaration of the intent to reform agriculture . . . with the [United States] insisting on reform of the Common Agricultural Policy (CAP) and the Community refusing." In each, the "deadlock" was "finally broken by the United States abandoning its demands."[51] This time, it was declared US policy not to back down. Compounding the difficulty was the negotiating position initially adopted by the Reagan administration, which called for elimination of all trade-distorting measures in agriculture—tariffs, quotas, price supports, production, and export subsidies—over a 10-year period. Whatever its substantive merit, this stance was counterproductive politically: it reinforced farmer resistance to concessions in Europe, and it postponed serious dialogue internationally and domestically about real-world priorities and possibilities.

Agriculture was but one of 15 Uruguay Round subjects being addressed by negotiating groups whose settlement deadline was December 1990. And the Uruguay Round was not the only dance on the trade floor. For the Bush administration faced, to its south, a Mexican president, Carlos Salinas de Gortari, who was continuing and accelerating the trade liberalization policies begun by his predecessor, Miguel de la Madrid Hurtado. As

---

50. *Congressional Quarterly*, 5 May 1990, 1333.

51. Dale E. Hathaway, "Agriculture," in Jeffrey J. Schott, ed., *Completing the Uruguay Round: A Results-Oriented Approach to the GATT Trade Negotiations* (Washington, DC: Institute for International Economics, 1990), 51.

noted in chapter 4, Salinas came to President Bush in June 1990 and asked that the United States negotiate a free trade agreement with Mexico, as it had with Canada in 1985–88. The USTR would just as soon have waited—the Uruguay Round was business enough—but Bush decided to move forward. Canada would soon seek to join the talks, and the aim became establishment of a North American Free Trade Agreement (NAFTA).

The Uruguay Round still had priority—the administration considered it far more important as a trade policy matter, and it was scheduled to conclude before the NAFTA talks could seriously begin. Bush had pressed the matter with colleagues at the seven-nation Houston economic summit that July, recognizing that his counterparts there—French President François Mitterrand, and above all Germany's Chancellor Helmut Kohl—held the key to an agriculture breakthrough. But notwithstanding the earnest efforts promised at that meeting, there was no significant movement in the EC position that fall.

The Brussels ministerial meeting of December 1990 produced a climax quite different from what the round's architects had intended. Carla Hills flew to Europe, accompanied by a large interagency supporting cast, observers from the Hill, and a strong delegation of US private-sector representatives. Also present in the European capital were thousands of angry European farmers. Kohl had just emerged victorious from a historic, all-German election, but his need for farmer support had trumped any commitment to trade compromise, leaving him in no position to return the kindness George Bush had shown in facilitating German reunification. So the talks failed. The agriculture negotiators could not even reach consensus on the framework for an agreement, with Korea and Japan joining the Community in casting crucial, negative votes. When Hills announced that without progress in agriculture the United States would not bargain on other issues, she won cheers from the assembled US private-sector representatives.

As this response illustrated, Hills' tough stand at Brussels was helpful in Washington—for the time being. Senior members of Congress had expressed the view that she might have to "reject a bad agreement if she was to get a good agreement." And Hills had built herself a formidable reputation in the broader trade policy community. She knew the issues. She responded to specific problems raised by legislators, even when she could not offer satisfaction. Though she had never worked on Capitol Hill, she seemed to have an innate sense of what legislators wanted and needed, how much of what they demanded was real and how much was noise.

Her skill at congressional relations in-the-large was not matched by empathy in one-on-one dealings. She lacked the patience, and the personal inclination, to "schmooze" with senators and representatives as Strauss or Brock did. And when she testified at congressional hearings, she could not always mask her negative judgment on the quality of a question. These limitations created problems, according to several reports: for example, when it came time to line up votes for the renewal of the president's fast-track authority in the spring of 1991. Still, the general Washington view was that Hills was an exceptionally competent and effective USTR. One hardened observer thought she was the best ever to hold the position.

Her overriding goal was to complete the Uruguay Round, on which she had staked so much. It was the multilateral GATT round that offered the big potential gains to mobilize export constituencies, and the broadest opportunity to advance US trade policy goals. But the demands on Hills compelled her to move wherever the trade opening was. So she and her senior deputy, veteran negotiator Julius Katz, found themselves giving major energy to the NAFTA talks, a negotiation that was not central to US trade policy priorities.

A more serious threat to Hills' position was the emergence of trade as a front-burner political issue in the fall and winter of 1991–92. In the afterglow of victory in the Persian Gulf War of 1991, President George H. W. Bush's public approval rating remained above 70 percent—higher than Ronald Reagan's had ever been—through most of the year. But as the US economy stagnated and unemployment grew, he increasingly came under attack for his international preoccupations: by September, no less than 66 percent of Americans felt their president was spending "too much time on foreign problems" and not enough on domestic.[52] Two months later, in economically depressed (and traditionally protectionist) Pennsylvania, Democrat Harris Wofford won an upset Senate victory over former Bush administration Attorney General Richard Thornburgh on the slogan that Americans should "take care of our own."

The president responded with what can only be described as panic, abandoning the international leadership that had hitherto been his forte. First Bush canceled (without credible reason) a once-postponed trip to Tokyo and the Far East, which the Japanese government had been counting on to buttress the post–Cold War alliance and give a positive twist to Pearl Harbor's 50th anniversary on December 7, 1991. He then rescheduled the visit and recast it as an export-sales mission—in search of "jobs, jobs, jobs"—without time for the advance preparation that success would require. He invited 21 business leaders to join him, thus making the enterprise hostage to what *they* said and did. And as icing on the cake, he included among them the embattled leaders of the Big Three auto companies, men for whom no conceivable breakthroughs in the Japanese market could provide the short-term relief they so badly needed, and who indeed needed for the mission to be *unsuccessful* in order to build support for protectionist action at home.

---

52. ABC News poll, reported in *National Journal*, 12 October 1991, 2510.

The trip proved a disaster, made forever memorable by the president's sudden stomach ailment at a Japanese state dinner. It unleashed a torrent of Japan bashing (and America bashing) in the days and weeks that followed, together with a grassroots "buy America" campaign.[53] Suddenly, US trade policy seemed again up for grabs. The president had both legitimized attacks on Japan and undercut his capacity to counter them. And victory in the Cold War had removed the protection that military alliance had heretofore provided for trilateral economic relations: There was no longer a common enemy against which America, Europe, and Japan needed to unite.

NAFTA but Not (Yet) GATT

The trip was so mismanaged, in part, because Hills was not in charge of it: This outcome would have been inconceivable had Bush worked on trade issues with her anywhere near as much as he worked on international security issues with Secretary of State James Baker III and national security adviser Brent Scowcroft. But the furor over Japan subsided in the spring, though the episode served to increase Bush's electoral vulnerability on the economy—precisely the opposite of its intent.

The NAFTA talks continued to move faster than those under the GATT. One reason was the personal commitment of Mexican President Carlos Salinas de Gortari, whose legacy would depend on success in the talks. Another was that the prime interlocutor on the GATT, the European Community, seemed able to negotiate only during the final three months of each year. The other nine months the Europeans spent getting their internal act together, particularly on agriculture.

On NAFTA, there was no such problem. There, the pace of negotiations accelerated in the spring and summer of 1992, and the three nations reached agreement in August. After the required period for notification and consultation with Congress and affected industry groups, the North American Free Trade Agreement was signed on 17 December 1992. It provided for phased elimination of tariff and most nontariff barriers, most of them within 10 years. NAFTA also contained important measures for liberalization of investment. And its nearly 2,000 pages included detailed provisions defining "North American content" for autos and textiles, designed to give competitive advantages to North American companies. On

---

53. One feature was employers giving bonuses to workers for purchasing US-made automobiles. Americans soon discovered that it was not easy to determine what was an "American car:" many models with Big Three nameplates were in fact assembled in Canada or Mexico or across the Pacific, whereas a growing number of Toyotas and Hondas and Nissans were "made in USA."

balance, the United States gained much more than it gave, winning major Mexican tariff reductions and changes in many restrictive procedures.[54]

The GATT negotiations continued through the November election. In fact, one important meeting was held on election day in Chicago, and when it stretched on too long, Deputy USTR Julius Katz was unable to get back home in time to vote. The central issue remained agriculture, as it had been since the talks started. A long-festering US-EC dispute over EC subsidies for oilseeds producers provided the catalyst, with a threat of US retaliation against a billion dollars of EC exports bringing new urgency to the broader farm issue.[55] Finally, the trade and agriculture ministers of the United States and the European Community met at Blair House, across Pennsylvania Avenue from the White House. They reached a compromise deal on 20 November imposing significant limits on European export subsidies and modest ones on domestic support levels. Bush administration officials then pressed an eleventh-hour campaign to complete the entire Uruguay Round agreement during the November-to-January presidential transition. Without such an effort, they argued, fast-track authority for the talks would expire before the new administration could get its trade team operating effectively. And the talks received an eleventh-hour shot in the arm when the purposive Leon Brittan became negotiator for the European Community, replacing the oft-ineffective Frans Andriessen.

President-elect Clinton supported the effort publicly: "America has only one president at a time," he said the day after the election, and talks on arms control and trade should go on. But signals from his Little Rock transition team were mixed as time went on: one Bush negotiator recalls a deadly "no comment" about a story that Clinton's advisers wanted the negotiation put on hold until Inauguration Day.[56] It was arguably in the Clinton administration's interest to have Bush people close the deal: it would grease the skids for implementation and reduce the amount of old business the new team would have to address. But the credibility of the old team would have been hard to maintain in any event, even if there

---

54. For a contemporary overview and assessment, see Gary Clyde Hufbauer and Jeffrey J. Schott, *NAFTA: An Assessment* (Washington, DC: Institute for International Economics, revised edition, October 1993). For an analysis 10 years later, see Gary Clyde Hufbauer and Jeffrey J. Schott, assisted by Paul L. E. Grieco and Yee Wong, *NAFTA Revisited: Challenges and Achievements* (Washington, DC: Institute for International Economics, forthcoming).

55. For details on this dispute and its relation to the Uruguay Round, see Charles Iceland, "European Union: Oilseeds," 209–32, in Thomas O. Bayard and Kimberly Ann Elliott, *Reciprocity and Retaliation in US Trade Policy*.

56. Personal interview. *The New York Times* reported on 8 December 1992 that the Clinton transition team had "been reviewing whether to try to rein in the negotiations but had reached no conclusions."

had been perfect confidence and coordination between them and the Clinton people. And as illustrated above, there was not. So though talks continued into January, time ran out for the Bush negotiators. They and their president left their successors a mixed trade legacy—with major negotiations completed or near completed, but with heightened political concerns about the ability of the United States to compete.

The larger 1971–94 period featured, moreover, another major trade policy development: the strengthening of "the rules" under which trade-injured industries could seek relief. These are the subject of chapter 7.

6

Changing the Rules: The Rise of Administrative Trade Remedies

Administrative remedy procedures—"the rules"—were a key component in the 1934 system of US trade policymaking. In the years after 1970, they became central to the policy debate. Congress made them more accessible to trade-impacted producers, resulting in an upsurge of cases and greater import relief.

There were four major statutes. The "escape clause" offered recourse to firms and workers injured by import competition in general. The countervailing duty (CVD) law provided relief from imports subsidized by foreign governments, which the statute labeled an "unfair trade practice." The law that protected US producers from "dumping" (sales at "less than fair value") by foreign firms also used the same label to describe dumping. Finally, those hurt by trade could apply for "adjustment assistance," mainly stipends and worker retraining.

Up through the early 1970s, however, US firms found it difficult to win relief under these statutes. Eligibility criteria for the escape clause and adjustment assistance were tightly drawn, and enforcement of the CVD and antidumping laws was at best a sometime thing. So import-competing interests lobbied successfully for changes in the rules that would broaden eligibility and tighten enforcement. Their success was reflected in the many more petitions for administrative import relief that they submitted in the 1980s, and the fact that, increasingly, they were winning those cases.

Champions of these quasi-judicial procedures defended them as a way to "depoliticize" trade issues, to "run trade on economic law."[1] They were seen as a way to keep trade decisions "out of politics," and petitioners off of legislators' backs, by establishing objective import relief rules that governed the strong and the weak alike. For large cases, however, this was often not the actual result. As steel producers, in particular, moved to take advantage of these statutes, the effect—and often their clear intent—was not to lower the political temperature but to raise it. "The rules" changed from a means of diverting political pressure to a means of asserting it. Typically, the policy result was not the remedy specified in law but new "special case" protection for the claimants.

Two other trends were evident. One was the decline in use of the escape clause, with the antidumping law the primary recourse for protection. The second was the tilting of the rules for calculating foreign and domestic prices in antidumping cases, such that findings of dumping became nearly automatic.

■ ■ ■

The escape clause was originally intended to provide exceptional relief from the impact of negotiated reductions in US tariffs. In a manner consistent with Article XIX of the General Agreement on Tariffs and Trade (GATT), if producers met the statutory criteria of injury from imports as determined by the Tariff Commission,[2] it would recommend and the president could order temporary relief, including tariffs, quotas, or other import restraints.

In addition to such insurance, the rules also provided offsets to "unfair" advantages of foreign competitors, with the sanction of GATT Article VI. In accordance with a statute dating from 1897, if another government gave a "bounty or grant" to a particular industry or firm, the US government, on the petition of the American interests affected, was supposed to impose a CVD equivalent to the size of the foreign subsidy. It could impose a similar penalty on imports found to be "dumped," or sold in the US market at "less than fair value," or below the prices at which the good was sold in its home market.

Finally, there was a program to facilitate adjustment. Under the Trade Expansion Act of 1962, if firms were injured or workers lost jobs as a result of import competition, they were eligible for "trade adjustment assistance" (TAA), consisting of financial aid and retraining above and beyond normal unemployment benefits, designed to help them move into new, competitive lines of work.

---

1. Chairman Charles Vanik (D-OH), US Congress, House Ways and Means Committee, Subcommittee on Trade, *Trade with Japan*, 96th Congress, 2nd session (18 September 1980), 140.

2. The Tariff Commission was restructured and renamed the United States International Trade Commission (USITC) in 1975.

The trade policy justification for the various quasi-judicial procedures was that they provided options for those damaged by the operation of the open system. The political rationale was that they offered an escape valve, a place for congressmen and executive branch leaders to refer complaints, thus easing the pressure to take immediate trade-restrictive action themselves. There was also the promise of equity. Like other government regulatory procedures, the trade "rules" were supposed to take certain tariff and quota decisions out of the political arena, where benefits went to those with the greatest clout, and entrust them to institutions that would act "objectively," relating the rules to the facts of particular cases.

But there was one problem. In concept, such procedures appeared to give advantages to import-injured petitioners.[3] In practice, however, in the early postwar decades, those who played by these rules tended to come out losers.

Through the Early 1970s: Little Relief

Under the escape clause, the Tariff Commission investigated 113 claims between 1948 and 1962 and recommended relief in 41 cases, but the president provided it in only 15.[4] Things grew worse for affected industries after the Trade Expansion Act of 1962 tightened relief requirements. The Tariff Commission considered 30 cases in the 12 years ended in 1974. It found injury justifying import relief in only four.[5]

Petitioners did not find the countervailing duty law much more helpful. The law triggered 191 investigations between 1934 and 1968, but only 30 resulted in the imposition of CVDs. In 1968, just 13 CVD orders were in effect, with only four of them having been imposed in the 1960s.[6] There were three more affirmative findings in 1969, and just eight more between 1971 and 1974.[7]

Trade relief was similarly elusive on antidumping cases. Out of 371 processed from 1955 through 1968, only 12 resulted in findings of dumping,

---

3. J. Michael Finger et al. note that the "technical track" favors petitioners because it excludes from the review process those economic interests "who want access to foreign sources of supply." But they concluded that, through the 1970s, "this bias" toward protectionism was "not large": in 1975–79, "only 2.2 percent of US manufactured imports [were] granted relief under the [countervailing duty and antidumping] statutes, and only 3.8 percent under the escape clause." J. M. Finger, H. Keith Hall, and Douglas R. Nelson, "The Political Economy of Administered Protection," *American Economic Review* 72, no. 3 (June 1982): 454, 466.

4. Herbert G. Grubel, *International Economics* (Homewood, IL: Richard D. Irwin, 1981), 174.

5. Tariff Commission, *Annual Report*, Washington, DC, various years.

6. US Department of the Treasury, "Report of the Secretary of the Treasury," *Annual Report of the Department of the Treasury, 1968*, Washington, DC, 416.

7. Ibid., Statistical Appendices.

although 89 more were concluded by revision in the price or termination of sales.[8]

Finally, not a single petition for trade adjustment assistance for workers won favorable action in that program's first seven years. The volume of petitions went up sharply in the early 1970s, but out of 110,640 workers seeking benefits by the end of 1974, only 48,314 received them.[9]

So in the first 30 postwar years, import-affected industries that played the trade policy game by the legal rules generally lost out.

The immediate effect was to make US markets more open than they otherwise would have been, since less trade was being restricted. More important was the longer-term impact. Predominantly negative outcomes for petitioners discredited the trade remedy procedures, discouraging their use and encouraging affected interests to seek direct help from Congress or the administration. This was, of course, exactly what "the rules" were intended to avoid.

As the Kennedy Round drew to a conclusion in 1967, executive branch trade leaders recognized that to restore the credibility of these statutes, their procedures needed to be made less forbidding. Legislators were even more committed to this goal. If the 1934 system was to continue to provide "protection for Congress," other channels had to offer real relief alternatives. Otherwise, pressure on Congress to provide direct, product-specific trade protection could only increase. Indeed, such pressure built up rapidly in the late 1960s and early 1970s, as evidenced by the House vote in favor of general import quota legislation in 1970 and the introduction of the more restrictive, labor-endorsed Burke-Hartke quota bill the following year.

Twice during the 1970s, Congress responded to this pressure as one would have predicted: it changed the rules to make administrative trade relief easier for import-affected industries to obtain. It did so in 1974, as part of the Trade Act, authorizing US participation in the Tokyo Round trade negotiations. It did so again in 1979, in the Trade Agreements Act, which approved the round's results.

The Trade Act of 1974

The simplest and most straightforward action in 1974 was that governing the escape clause. The Trade Expansion Act of 1962 had required that an industry prove that it had suffered serious injury, the "major cause" of

---

8. Ibid., 416.

9. US Department of Labor, "Labor Issues of American International Trade and Investment" (prepared for the National Manpower Administration Policy Task Force), *Policy Studies in Employment and Welfare*, no. 24 (Washington, DC, 1976): 52.

which was imports due to US tariff concessions ("major cause" meant greater than all other factors combined). Section 201 of the Trade Act of 1974 lowered that threshold, requiring that imports be only a "substantial cause of serious injury, or the threat thereof" (this was defined as "not less than any other cause"). Section 201 also removed a proviso that such injury had to result from specific US tariff concessions.

Congress also sought to encourage favorable findings by increasing the independence of the Tariff Commission, which ruled on industry petitions. Members' terms were lengthened from six to nine years, and it was renamed the US International Trade Commission (USITC) "because tariffs are no longer the major impediments to trade."[10] Moreover, in cases where the USITC recommended relief, the president was required to act on that recommendation within 60 days. If he did not grant the relief, Congress could override him and enforce the USITC recommendation by majority vote of both houses.[11]

On adjustment assistance, Congress insisted that the program be expanded and made easier to qualify for, notwithstanding organized labor's disillusionment with it and the Nixon administration's skepticism about the appropriateness of a special program for workers displaced by trade. One reason few workers had previously been eligible was that the criterion was essentially the same as those for tariffs or quotas: Imports had to be the "major cause" of unemployment or underemployment. House Ways and Means Committee members thought trade adjustment assistance should be the easiest form of relief to obtain. So the law was changed to open it to workers for whom "increases of imports . . . contributed importantly to loss of jobs." The magnitude and duration of benefits were also increased.

But the primary focus of efforts to "change the rules" in the early 1970s was the alleged foreign abuses covered by the CVD and antidumping statutes, addressed in a rather lengthy Trade Act title labeled "Relief from *Unfair* Trade Practices" (emphasis added).

This was a natural, even inevitable, emphasis, for the Kennedy Round's success in reducing industrial tariff levels had focused attention on nontariff barriers (NTBs) and other trade-distorting governmental practices. Among those thought to require regulation or discipline, subsidies were

---

10. US Congress, Senate Committee on Finance, *Trade Reform Act of 1974*, 93rd Congress, 2nd session (26 November 1974), Staff Report 93-1208, 25.

11. In *Immigration and Naturalization Service v. Chadha*, the US Supreme Court declared a similar legislative veto provision unconstitutional, on grounds that it did not provide for "presentment to the President," as in the normal legislative process. Congress responded, in the Trade and Tariff Act of 1984, by providing for a joint resolution congressional veto for presidential decisions under Section 201. Such a resolution is presented to the chief executive for his signature; should the president veto it, a two-thirds majority of both houses would be required to override.

at the top of the list for American trade specialists. To some, in Gary Clyde Hufbauer's metaphor, subsidies were a "rising reef," increasingly granted in order to buttress favored industries and influence trade flows. Others concluded, more modestly, that it was the "falling water level" of reduced tariffs that had made the NTB reef more important, and certainly more visible.[12]

Joined with increased complaints about foreign subsidies was the sense that the United States was not doing much to combat them. The Senate Finance Committee expressed unhappiness "that the Treasury Department has used the absence of time limits to stretch out or even shelve countervailing duty investigations for reasons which have nothing to do with the clear and mandatory nature of the countervailing duty law."[13] This charge was not ungrounded, for at Treasury there was a fairly widespread view that the law was archaic, with its old-fashioned language ("bounty or grant") and 19th century origins.

The increased attention to nontariff trade distortions, and above all to subsidies, reinforced the widespread Washington perception that other countries were taking advantage of the United States—that it was, in the words of Nixon White House aide Peter M. Flanigan, "more sinned against than sinning."[14] There was evidence to support this view.[15] Moreover, the opaqueness of governments' nontariff policies affecting trade—the difficulty in seeing and measuring them and determining their extent—made it hard to resist those who argued that such foreign practices were endemic and that the United States needed to respond forcefully.[16] The record on CVDs and dumping suggested that it had not been doing so.

One way Congress addressed this problem was by making clear that subsidies should be given priority in the upcoming Tokyo Round, in which nontariff trade distortions were to be the central focus. The other way was to tighten the remedy procedures. On countervailing duties, the

---

12. Gary Clyde Hufbauer and Joanna Shelton Erb, *Subsidies in International Trade* (Washington, DC: Institute for International Economics, 1984), 2.

13. US Congress, Senate Committee on Finance, *Trade Reform Act of 1974*, 93rd Congress, 2nd session (26 November 1974), 183.

14. Quoted in *National Journal*, 13 January 1973, 45.

15. One study of overall Organization for Economic Cooperation and Development (OECD) data concludes that, among the seven major advanced industrial countries, "the United States has persistently exhibited the lowest ratio of subsidies to GDP and, unlike [that of] other countries, the US ratio has declined since the late 1960s." Hufbauer and Shelton Erb, *Subsidies in International Trade*, 2.

16. For a perceptive discussion of how the opaqueness of nontax trade policy nourishes perceptions of foreign "unfairness," see J. David Richardson, *Currents and Cross-Currents in the Flow of U.S. Trade Policy*, NBER Conference Report (Cambridge, MA: National Bureau of Economic Research, 1984), 2–3.

1974 act added a requirement that final action be taken within a year of receipt of a petition and made provision for judicial review of decisions that denied relief. Such review was also provided for negative antidumping decisions. One technical provision required the Treasury Department to disregard certain low-cost home-market sales in determining the price against which export sales were compared to ascertain whether dumping existed. This had the effect of favoring petitioners and could even lead to findings of dumping in cases in which the average home and export prices were the same!

The Result: Slightly More Relief

The immediate result of the changing of the rules in 1974 was that firms filed many more cases and the government moved more expeditiously in handling them. Petitions for escape clause relief, for example, rose from two in 1973 (and none in 1974) to 13 in 1975. The number of CVD investigations initiated shot up from one in 1973 (and five in 1974) to 38 in 1975, both because new claims were being submitted and because the Treasury was moving faster on old ones under the new timetable.[17]

But in terms of actual relief granted, industry petitioners were again to be disappointed.

The new escape clause criteria established by Section 201 were affecting the US International Trade Commission, which was now finding regularly in petitioners' favor. Between 1975 and 1990, the commission conducted 62 investigations, which resulted in 30 affirmative determinations. This 48 percent success rate at the USITC for those who sought relief contrasted sharply with the 13 percent rate (4 of 30) under the previous law. And the escape clause cases included important import-affected industries: carbon and specialty steel, shoes, color television sets, and, grandest of all, automobiles.

In the 1974 act, however, Congress had reluctantly retained the president's discretion to modify or reject a USITC relief recommendation, provided he determined that "provision of such relief is not in the national economic interest of the United States." This was a broader criterion than the industry-specific rules that governed the decisions of the commission. Applying this more comprehensive standard, presidents repeatedly rejected or modified the commission's escape clause recommendations.

In the 30 cases in which the USITC recommended import relief between 1975 and 1990, the president ordered tariffs or quotas in only 10 and denied all relief in 12. In five cases, he provided only adjustment assistance, and in the remaining three he initiated negotiations leading to orderly

---

17. *International Economic Report of the President* (Washington, DC: Government Printing Office, March 1976), 45.

marketing agreements (OMAs) with the exporting nations to limit their sales. Congress complained that the law was not being implemented, but it never actually voted to override the president.

As it did prior to the 1974 Trade Act, this situation again yielded present gains for the liberal trade order.[18] But it piled up future costs, for the effect was to discredit the process, perhaps more than previously. Before, almost nobody got relief, but at least the rules were being followed. Now, industries were playing by the rules and winning in the USITC, only to have those decisions reversed by the president, who asserted his prerogative in an opaque White House decision-making process in which they had no established role. The footwear case of 1976 was a good example. The Ford administration's trade representative had promised favorable consideration of such a case when the Trade Act was before the Senate.[19] But it reached the president for decision one month after he had granted relief to the specialty steel industry, and Ford was worried about the international repercussions of restricting trade twice in a row. So he rejected import relief, granting only adjustment assistance.[20]

The shoe case was in fact reconsidered, and the Carter administration negotiated export restraint agreements with Korea and Taiwan a year later. Nor was this unique. The producers of "bolts, nuts, and large screws," to cite another example from the latter 1970s, were denied relief by President Carter in 1978, only to be granted it the next year after strong congressional pressure led to reconsideration of their case.

By easing the criteria but retaining presidential discretion, Congress had turned the political process on its head. The aim had been to take trade "out of politics." But once the USITC began regularly finding in petitioners' favor, product cases were thrown squarely into the political arena and resolved in a process governed by different "rules" entirely. The president had to weigh the demands of an injured industry, of trade politics, and sometimes of electoral support against the interests of the larger economy, the need to combat inflation, the demands of international economic leadership, etc. Industries had reason to fear that their legitimate cases would get lost in this larger shuffle.

The escape clause received a further blow in the automobile case of 1980, the most important and visible import issue ever addressed under the procedure. The American auto industry and its workers were suffering a severe drop in their production and sales, which was clearly exacer-

---

18. For a detailed analysis welcoming this result, see Walter Adams and Joel B. Dirlam, "Import Competition and the Trade Act of 1974: A Case Study of Section 201 and its Interpretation by the International Trade Commission," *Indiana Law Journal* 52, no. 3 (Spring 1977): 535–99.

19. STR William D. Eberle to Senator Thomas J. McIntyre, *Congressional Record*, 13 December 1974, 39813.

20. See Roger Porter, *Presidential Decision Making: The Economic Policy Board* (Cambridge, MA: Cambridge University Press, 1980), chapter 6.

bated by record Japanese imports. Yet a three-to-two majority of USITC members found that the industry failed to meet the "substantial cause" criterion: factors other than imports were more important causes of the industry's plight—above all, the shift in market demand toward smaller cars brought about by the oil price increase of 1979. Thus, the USITC was unable to recommend relief.

The decision was defensible in terms of the law. Nonetheless, the result was to further discredit Section 201. The US political system found the negative outcome impossible to live with. House Trade Subcommittee Chairman Charles A. Vanik (D-OH) had argued repeatedly for running trade according to the rules, "depoliticizing" it. Yet when the "economic law" produced a negative outcome on autos, he was quick to call hearings to explore the need for alternative trade action.

In response to congressional pressure, and to a Reagan campaign commitment, the new administration ended up pressing—successfully—for Japanese voluntary restraint on auto exports. As a result, the escape clause procedure was further discredited. In the three years after 1980, the USITC received only four escape clause petitions.

On countervailing duties—unlike the escape clause—there is no general presidential authority to override the procedure in the name of broader American interests. The basic law is mandatory: If a subsidy is found, a duty "shall be imposed." However, a special waiver authority was added for the Tokyo Round multilateral trade negotiations (MTN) of the 1970s, in which a primary US negotiating goal was to discipline trade-distorting subsidies.

The US government had something to give on this issue. Contrary to GATT rules, as Europeans had long complained, US law did not require that injury be found from imports before a CVD was imposed. Europeans were not about to negotiate if the United States simultaneously began enforcing a tough antisubsidy statute. So Congress reluctantly granted the secretary of the Treasury the authority to waive imposition of CVDs for four years if the foreign government was taking steps to reduce a subsidy's effect, and if the secretary found that imposition of a duty would "seriously jeopardize" completion of the MTN, including the desired subsidies code.

In practice, this waiver authority took away from affected industries much of the gain that the 1974 act provided. From 1976 through 1978, for example, the Treasury made a total of 35 affirmative CVD decisions, a marked increase from previous years. But the secretary then exercised the waiver in 19 of the cases. More than half of the time, then, "successful" petitioners were denied the full remedy that the law, in principle, provided.[21]

---

21. US Department of the Treasury, *Annual Report*, Washington, DC, various issues; US Congress, House Committee on Ways and Means, *Temporary Extension of Countervailing Duty Waiver Authority*, 96th Congress, 1st session (22 February 1979), HR 96-15. The latter describes the 19 waivers and their status as of the report date.

In contrast, the number of antidumping cases during this period remained at about the level of previous years. However, the filing of a large number of such cases by the steel industry in 1977 led the Carter administration to establish a price floor on imports with the trigger-price mechanism, which was enforced under the antidumping law.[22]

In summary, in the years after 1974, industries were getting only slightly more relief from administrative procedures than they had before—Trade Act changes notwithstanding. So unhappiness built up again about the remedy procedures. The House Ways and Means Committee reflected this in 1979, declaring that "both the countervailing duty and antidumping duty laws have been inadequately enforced in the past, including the lack of resources devoted to this important area of law."[23]

The Trade Agreements Act of 1979

The required approval of the Tokyo Round/MTN in 1979 gave Congress a new opportunity to act. The minimum need was legislation to implement the nontariff barrier codes completed early that year. Since the principal countries were unable to resolve their differences on escape clause issues, the intended safeguards code was not completed. So Section 201, the US law governing escape clause relief, was left unchanged.

The codes on subsidies and countervailing measures and on antidumping, however, were the MTN's centerpieces. The negotiation of the former had been fueled by a widely shared conviction, in the words of one leading authority, that "the current rules on subsidies and countervailing duties" were "woefully inadequate to cope with the pressures put upon importing economies by a myriad of subtle (and sometimes not so subtle) governmental aids to exports."[24] Now that the code was completed, legislation was necessary to make US law conform. The United States had to incorporate in its statutes the requirement that "material injury" be proven before countervailing duties were imposed on imports from coun-

---

22. See Hideo Sato and Michael W. Hodin, "The U.S.-Japanese Steel Issue of 1977," in I. M. Destler and Hideo Sato, eds., *Coping With U.S.-Japanese Trade Conflicts* (Lexington, MA: Lexington Books, 1982), 27–72.

23. US Congress, House Committee on Ways and Means, *Trade Agreements Act of 1979*, 96th Congress, 1st session (3 July 1979), HR 96-317.

24. John H. Jackson, "The Crumbling Institutions of the Liberal Trade System," *Journal of World Trade Law* 12, no. 2 (March–April 1978): 95.

tries adhering to the code. But nothing barred more extensive statutory changes as long as they were consistent with the codes and other US international obligations. So revision of these statutes became part of the bargaining process for MTN ratification.

In the 1974 act, Congress had committed itself to an expeditious, up-or-down vote on whatever implementing legislation the president submitted. To maximize congressional support, Special Trade Representative Robert S. Strauss, who led the Carter administration's negotiating enterprise at home as well as abroad, accepted the proposal of the Senate Finance Committee to have the bill designed and drafted on Capitol Hill, as a collaborative effort of the two branches (see chapter 4). Key industries like steel, and concerned senators like John Heinz (R-PA), made it clear that their priority was the trade remedy laws. They wanted to ensure, this time, that they would provide petitioners effective and timely relief. And Strauss saw this as a tolerable price for their support.

The most visible change—a "material injury" test for all CVDs on products of countries adhering to the new code—had the formal effect of tightening the criteria relief-seeking firms had to meet. Here, the administration and the House Ways and Means Committee prevailed over a Senate Finance Committee proposal to soften the requirement to the single word "injury." Lobbyists for the European Community actively supported the tougher standard. Still, "material injury" was defined as "harm which is not inconsequential, immaterial or unimportant"; this is significantly less demanding than the escape clause test that imports be "a substantial cause of serious injury." More important, perhaps, by bringing US law into conformity with GATT and international practice, the injury standard legitimized use of CVDs in future cases.

If the new injury test affected the criteria for obtaining relief, the Trade Agreements Act of 1979 employed a different means to aid petitioners—reforming the law's procedures and administration. Tighter time limits were mandated not just for CVD cases taken as a whole but for their specific stages; for example, an investigation had to be initiated within 20 days, and only "clearly frivolous" petitions, or those lacking key information reasonably available to petitioners, were to be dismissed without any formal investigation. The overall timetable from initiation to final determination was compressed, in normal cases, from a year to seven months. This tended to favor petitioners, since foreign governments and firms had less time to develop the complicated countercases that were needed to rebut the data of those seeking relief. Moreover, if there was a preliminary finding of subsidy (and injury), importers would now have to post a deposit just three months (instead of a year) after a petition was submitted. Thus effective trade restraint could be obtained much sooner.[25] Parallel steps were taken on antidumping procedures to shorten time limits, advance the time when exporting firms had to pay or advance penalty duties, and promote openness and judicial review.

But the most important single change was organizational, the shift of administrative responsibility for the unfair-trade remedies laws. This, although not an explicit provision of the Trade Agreements Act of 1979, was a not-so-subtle condition of its approval, as the Senate Finance Committee declined to bring that act to the floor until the president had submitted a comprehensive trade reorganization plan. In this plan, the power to enforce the rewritten CVD and antidumping laws was delegated not to the secretary of the Treasury—the responsible official since 1897—but to the secretary of Commerce. Members of both key congressional committees were convinced that his department would take the job more seriously and be more sympathetic to industry concerns. And they were right.

The Declining Use of the Escape Clause

How did the administrative trade remedies—"the rules" as amended—play out in practice after 1979? The most dramatic development was the contrast between the declining use of Section 201 and adjustment assistance and the upsurge in new petitions alleging unfair foreign trade practices. (See table 6.1.)

The escape clause was used above all during the Reagan reelection campaign. The USITC ruled on just one case in 1981, one case in 1982, and two cases in 1983. In January 1984, however, the carbon steel, shoe, copper, and table flatware industries all submitted petitions in order to pressure the Reagan White House for sympathetic action at a time of maximum political vulnerability.[26] By March, the USITC suddenly found itself investigating no fewer than five escape clause cases. Section 201 had been transformed from a means of diverting political pressure into a device for exerting it. In two prominent cases—steel and copper—the USITC recommended protection, forcing presidential decisions in September, within two months of the general election. The president denied relief to the copper industry but ordered negotiation of export restraint agreements for steel, as spelled out later in this chapter.

---

25. There were also a number of changes aimed at greater procedural openness. Administrative protective orders gave petitioners' counsel access to confidential business information supplied to the government by foreign exporters. Limits were imposed on private ex parte meetings between government officials and one party to a case; the substance of these meetings now had to be made public. Rights to public hearings and judicial review were also expanded. For example, labor unions and trade associations that had not initiated a case could now appeal.

26. In 1980, the United Auto Workers—in what was widely seen as a political blunder—did not submit its auto escape clause petition until June; as a result, the USITC did not reach its finding until after the November election.

Table 6.1   Antidumping, countervailing duty, and Section 201 investigations initiated from 1979 to 1994

Year	Antidumping cases	Countervailing duty cases	Section 201 cases
1979	26	40	4
1980	21	14	2
1981	15	22	1
1982	65	140	3
1983	46	22	0
1984	74	51	7
1985	66	43	4
1986	71	27	1
1987	15	8	0
1988	42	11	1
1989	23	7	0
1990	43	7	1
1991	51	8	0
1992	99	43	1
1993	42	5	0
1994	43	7	0
Total	742	455	25

Sources: Author's calculations, based on tallies from US International Trade Commission; ALLAD-Casis and ALLCVD-Casis databases, and the *Federal Register*, various issues.

The footwear industry was not so fortunate. In July 1984, the USITC made a unanimous negative finding on injury, because manufacturers' profits were high. At the initiative of Senator John C. Danforth (R-MO), Congress then changed the law so that profits could not be, by themselves, the decisive USITC criterion. The industry then resubmitted its case in December. Responding to the statutory change and a worsening of the industry's plight, the USITC now recommended stringent quotas. But now President Reagan said no, denying all import relief to the footwear industry in August 1985.

The rest of the decade saw only one more successful escape clause case—the petition of the wood shingles and shakes producers claiming injury from Canadian competition. Concerned about generating support for US-Canada free trade negotiations, President Reagan imposed in May 1986 a declining tariff with a peak of 35 percent. Only two escape clause petitions were submitted in 1987–90, neither of them successful.

The Decline of Trade Adjustment Assistance

Also in decline over this period was that pressure-diverting program that had once seemed most promising and constructive: trade adjustment assistance for workers.

When such a program was originally proposed, the most sophisticated postwar study of trade policymaking lauded it as an approach that "could destroy the political basis of protectionism by giving the injured an alternative way out."[27] But because the injury threshold was originally set so high, it yielded little trade relief in the decade after its enactment in 1962. In the late 1970s, however, following the 1974 act's expansion of benefits and easing of eligibility criteria, this program began at last to be seriously tested. The explosion of TAA claims (mainly from laid-off auto workers), combined with the very generous financial benefits provided, drove the cost to $1.6 billion in fiscal year 1980, six times the previous peak.[28]

Jimmy Carter pointed to this expansion as a humane response to the workers' plight and a constructive alternative to protection. But Ronald Reagan came to power looking for programs to cut and predisposed against the economic interventionism that TAA exemplified. Since analytic studies indicated that TAA was not in practice fulfilling the goal of adjustment—helping workers move to other, more competitive industries—it was a vulnerable target for Reagan's new budget director, David A. Stockman, who was opposed to entitlement programs available only to certain groups of workers. Nor did the Reagan administration make this program a chosen instrument when it shifted to trade activism in the fall of 1985.[29]

So beginning with the Omnibus Budget Reconciliation Act of 1981, the level and duration of benefits were cut and total program funds were slashed. Stipends were limited to the level of regular unemployment insurance, whereas previously they had supplemented such benefits. Moreover, they were now available only after a worker's eligibility for unemployment benefits had been exhausted, and they were generally limited—by a 1988 amendment—to workers undergoing retraining. Congressional champions managed, through persistent effort, to keep TAA alive in statute. And a modest additional trade adjustment program was inaugurated in 1994 for workers displaced by NAFTA. But as of 1994, the overall TAA budget (including NAFTA) totaled only about $200 million annually, with just 65,000 workers eligible for benefits.

---

27. Raymond A. Bauer, Ithiel de Sola Pool, and Lewis Anthony Dexter, *American Business and Public Policy: The Politics of Foreign Trade* (Chicago: Aldine-Atherton, 2d ed., 1972), 43.

28. C. Michael Aho and Thomas O. Bayard, "Costs and Benefits of Trade Adjustment Assistance," in Robert E. Baldwin and Anne O. Krueger, eds., *The Structure and Evolution of Recent US Trade Policy* (Chicago: University of Chicago Press, 1984), 184. For a comprehensive assessment of trade adjustment programs in the 1970s and 1980s, see Gary Clyde Hufbauer and Howard F. Rosen, *Trade Policy for Troubled Industries*, POLICY ANALYSES IN INTERNATIONAL ECONOMICS 15 (Washington, DC: Institute for International Economics, 1986).

29. Howard Rosen, "US Assistance for Trade-Related Workers: A Need for Better Coordination and Reform," statement before US Congress, House Committee on Ways and Means, Subcommittee on Trade (1 August 1991), processed, 8–12.

The Upsurge in "Unfair Trade" Cases

But if use of the escape clause had waned, and if TAA barely survived, there was a sharp increase in petitions under the unfair-trade practices statutes. Many more cases were submitted, covering a much greater volume of trade. And many more were decided in petitioners' favor. For the first time, the process was a serious one, with the responsible bureaucracy (the Commerce Department) making a strong effort to administer it according to its intended purposes.[30]

In response to industry petitions, Commerce initiated 249 CVD investigations over 1980–84, and 96 more in 1985–89. (This compares with one investigation initiated in 1973 and five in 1974.) Parallel antidumping investigation numbers were 221 for 1980–84 and 217 for 1985–89.[31] Gary Horlick and Geoffrey Oliver observed in 1989 that "AD [antidumping]/CVD laws have become the usual first choice for industries seeking protection from imports into the U.S."[32]

Moreover, when petitioners sought relief under these statutes, they more often than not obtained it. Of 258 CVD petitions in 1980–89 carried through the full statutory process, 135, or 52 percent, won either imposition of duties or suspension of the offending foreign practice. The remaining 87 were withdrawn by petitioners, almost always because the source nation had promised to limit exports. On antidumping, the numbers over the same period were similar—out of 327 petitions carried to term, 173 (53 percent) resulted in duties or suspension agreements, and 111 more petitions were withdrawn, largely after agreement on voluntary export restraints.

Unlike relief under the escape clause—which is limited to a specified term—CVD and antidumping relief continue indefinitely, unless and until

---

30. See Shannon Stock Shuman and Charles Owen Verrill, Jr., *Recent Developments in Countervailing Duty Law and Practice*, NBER Conference Report (Cambridge, MA: National Bureau of Economic Research, 1984). See also the candid testimony of former Deputy Assistant Secretary of Commerce Gary Horlick in US Congress, House Committee on Ways and Means, *Options to Improve the Trade Remedy Laws*, 98th Congress, 1st session (16 March 1983), part 2, 535–87.

31. The numbers that follow are a compilation based on analysis and cross-checking of data from a range of documents, including Commerce Department reports submitted semiannually to the GATT; USTR Trade Action Monitoring System reports; USITC annual reports; congressional hearings; other Commerce, USTR, and USITC reports; and the *Federal Register*. These have been supplemented by direct communication with responsible officials to fill gaps and resolve contradictions. I am grateful to Diane T. Berliner for her persistent and painstaking work in putting these numbers together for the original edition, and to Paul W. Baker, Steven Schoeny, Tomoyuki Sho, and Andrew Mosley for their equally thorough and professional efforts in reviewing and updating these data. The underlying case information is posted at www.iie.com.

32. Gary N. Horlick and Geoffrey D. Oliver, "Antidumping and Countervailing Duty Law Provisions of the Omnibus Trade and Competitiveness Act of 1988," *Journal of World Trade* 23, no. 3 (June 1989): 5.

a Commerce Department review determined that circumstances no longer justify it. Thus, at the end of 1990 there were 72 countervailing duties still in effect, and 202 antidumping duties. This compares with 56 and 137, respectively, in effect in mid-1983.

The "unfair trade" statutes were now a real alternative to statutory trade restrictions. So if the original political logic remained valid, both the petitioning industries and the supporters of liberal trade should have been more or less satisfied: the former because their cases were at last being taken seriously, the latter because they were being handled by apolitical, quasi-judicial procedures that considered each case in isolation, protecting Congress and minimizing the risk of protectionist contagion.

In the real world, alas, discontent remained. Affected industries continued to protest the laws' inadequacy and seek their further elaboration and complication to cover imports that still escaped their reach. But the same lack of executive branch discretion that kept executive officials from denying or diluting relief also prevented them from tailoring it to an industry's needs, whether the goal be protection or adjustment.

Foreign interests were dismayed because the trade remedy procedures seemed arbitrary and unfair (and expensive) to them. They were also unhappy because the US legal tradition clashes with their more discretionary ways of handling such issues. US laws are, for the most part, GATT-consistent, proper under the international trade rules that Americans have done so much to create. Indeed, elaborating these rules was one of the prime accomplishments of the Tokyo Round. But other peoples— Europeans, Japanese, Koreans, and Brazilians—see "due process" for American domestic interests as a threat to their interests. They (the Europeans above all) are typically anxious about the real trade effects of US legal decisions: their overall magnitude and how the pain will be distributed among foreign suppliers. They are unwilling to let their fates be determined by procedures that might seem objective and fair and nonpolitical to Americans, but which to foreign eyes appear both unpredictable and skewed in favor of the import-affected petitioner. And these cases inevitably involve "a host of arbitrary determinations":[33] calculating fair value, the full cost of production, the effect of different government programs on export prices, etc.

So it is not surprising that foreign firms and governments are receptive to alternatives. If US processes are going to end up restricting their trade, they want to have a voice in how the pain is allocated.

Actually, the 1979 law did create one new procedure for negotiating an end to a trade remedy case. In a major departure from previous trade laws, it authorized "suspension of investigations" through agreements

---

33. Robert W. Crandall, "The EEC-US Steel Trade Crisis," paper prepared for Symposium on Euro-American Relations and Global Economic Interdependence, College of Europe (Bruges, Belgium, 13 September 1984). Quoted with permission.

with foreign governments, or with "exporters representing substantially all of the imports of the merchandise"[34] covered by a case. But Congress sought to ensure that the purposes of the laws would not be subverted by conditioning such suspension on one of two forms of remedial action: elimination of subsidies or dumping (directly, or through imposition of an offset like an export tax), or elimination of their injurious effect. In other words, the point was to remove the subsidy, or at least its trade impact, not to bargain about market share.[35]

Typically, foreign firms and governments want more leeway than this. They may not agree with US legal determination of subsidy or "less-than-fair-value" (dumped) sales, and even if they do, they may have their own political or legal problems in complying. US firms have recognized and exploited this foreign vulnerability. Beginning with the steel antidumping petitions of 1977, they submitted cases aimed less at achieving the specific relief provided by statute than at creating an intolerable situation for foreign competitors, forcing them to come to the bargaining table and cut deals. Once a satisfactory arrangement was reached, the constraints of the law on suspension of investigations were circumvented by a simple device: the complaining industry withdrew its petition, and Commerce then terminated the investigation, as the law explicitly allows.

Forcing Political Solutions

A dramatic illustration came in the steel cases of 1982. There was little doubt that some foreigners were subsidizing steel that was being shipped to the US market; within Europe, the French and British were especially guilty.[36] So when on 11 January 1982, seven US steelmakers jointly delivered 494 boxes

---

34. House Committee on Ways and Means, *Trade Agreements Act of 1979*, 54.

35. For a description and defense of Commerce Department administration of this provision through mid-1984, see Alan F. Holmer and Judith H. Bello, "U.S. Import Law and Policy Series: Suspension and Settlement Agreements in Unfair Trade Cases," *International Lawyer* 18, no. 3 (Summer 1984): 683–97.

36. For one comprehensive effort to catalog such subsidies, see Bethlehem Steel Corporation and United States Steel Corporation, "Government Aid to the Steel Industry of the European Communities: Market Distortion in Europe and Its Impact on the U.S. Steel Industry," report prepared by Verner, Liipfert, Bernhard, McPherson, and Hand (Washington, DC, 1984).
    It does not follow, however, that foreign subsidies are the primary cause of US industry woes, or that their removal would bring substantial market relief. Robert W. Crandall argues, in fact, that while in an entirely private (nonsubsidized) European steel industry the worth of plants might be very much lower, "no one has presented any convincing evidence that capacity and output would be much lower under such a regime." And even if European output and exports did fall, "Brazil, Taiwan, Korea, and even Canada and Japan have the ability to expand their output and even their capacity substantially in response to any upward movement in export prices." See Crandall, "The EEC-US Steel Trade Crisis," 26.

containing 3 million pages of documentation for 132 countervailing and antidumping petitions against foreign (mainly European Community) suppliers, this flood of litigation had real-world justification. And the remedy sought was the proper one provided under American law. Further petitions followed, bringing the total for 1982 to about 150.[37]

But there was little doubt also that pursuing these cases to their legal conclusion would be highly disruptive to the steel industries of individual European Community countries and to the network of political understandings among them. Inevitably, the Europeans sought to bargain. And US Secretary of Commerce Malcolm Baldrige was pushed into the position of brokering between foreign governments and domestic steel makers for a trade-restricting arrangement entirely outside established procedures. Under this arrangement the EC "voluntarily" restricted carbon steel exports to the United States to 5.44 percent of the US market. And while this overall limit corresponded roughly to what the outcome of enforcing US law would have been, the Europeans distributed the pain among themselves so that the efficient Germans ended up worse off than they would have been, and the inefficient British and French better off.[38]

In the fall of 1983 came another example, involving China and textiles. Unhappy with the terms of a bilateral quota agreement concluded in August, the US textile industry retaliated with an innovative suit, alleging that China's dual exchange rate system constituted a subsidy under the CVD law.

This put US authorities in another bind. They had just reached a deal with China, but its substance was being threatened by a procedure over which they had little control in the short run. They feared that, to Beijing, the administration would appear either two-faced or impotent at a time when the president was preparing for a major state visit the following spring. And the Chinese government, choosing to treat the matter as an internal US problem, resisted supplying information to contest the suit.

---

37. US International Trade Commission, Annual Report, 1982, Washington, DC, x; Office of the United States Trade Representative, *Twenty-sixth Annual Report of the President of the United States on the Trade Agreements Program, 1981–82*, Washington, DC, November 1982, 114; Timothy B. Clark, "When Demand Is Down, Competition Up, That Spells Trouble for American Steel," *National Journal*, 7 January 1984, 9.

38. It was primarily the Europeans who administered the restraint. However, to be on the safe side, the Commerce Department—with the aid of Senator Heinz and over the procedural protests of House Trade Subcommittee leaders—slipped through Congress an amendment to the Tariff Act of 1930 providing that "steel mill products" under arrangements entered into "prior to January 1, 1983" would be denied entry into the United States if they lacked proper foreign government documentation. (*Congressional Record*, 29 September 1982, S12474–75; *Congressional Record*, 1 October 1982, H8368–71, H8388–89.) With these "arrangements" completed, the industry petitioners withdrew their suits.

The administration might have ridden the storm out internationally and domestically.[39] But senators from key textile states—Strom Thurmond (R-SC) and Jesse Helms (R-NC)—were up for reelection in 1984. They pressed the White House to do something for the industry. President Reagan, also up for reelection, saw personal political advantage in responding; moreover, in the 1980 campaign, he had made a general commitment to moderate the growth of textile imports. So in December 1983, against the overwhelming advice of his cabinet, he ordered a deal that gave the US textile industry tighter enforcement of existing quota arrangements, not particularly vis-à-vis mainland China but on East Asian imports generally. The industry then withdrew its suit at the last possible moment. Reagan had appeased the textile people without alienating Beijing, but at the cost of further compromise of both trade process and trade policy.

As 1984 began, the steel industry inaugurated a new round with the same old tactics. With European sales fixed at about 5 percent of US consumption and the Japanese informally limiting themselves to about the same amount, the remaining threat was the newly industrialized countries: Brazil, Mexico, and Korea in particular. Again, there was a blizzard of paper, with multiple submissions of CVD and antidumping cases. This time no one tried very hard to conceal the political rationale. As David M. Roderick of United States Steel told a press breakfast in early February, US firms planned to file "a tremendous number" of unfair trade complaints, aiming to make the total impact so "burdensome" that the administration, and "all players of substance in the import game . . . would be very pleased to enter into quotas in a negotiated manner."[40]

The steel industry had been the prime force behind the legislative changes of 1979 and the prime user of the rules on unfair trade practices since then. Now its explicit goal was "temporary" steel import quotas, however they might be achieved or implemented. The results would demonstrate that for trade as well, in Justice Holmes's words, "great cases make bad law."[41]

Steel Wins Comprehensive Protection

What ended up forcing a decision was an action by United States Steel's principal rival, Bethlehem Steel, and their union, the United Steelworkers. Citing an increase in the market share taken by imports from 15 percent

---

39. In May 1984, in fact, the Commerce Department would rule that the CVD law did not apply to imports from nonmarket-economy countries, and this position was later upheld in the Federal Circuit Court of Appeals. (Without a competitive market as a reference point, the word "subsidy" loses its meaning.)

40. *Washington Post*, 9 February 1984.

41. Oliver Wendell Holmes, Jr., *Northern Securities Company v. United States*, 193 US 197, 400 (1904).

in 1979 to 25 percent in early 1984, at a time of decline in domestic production and a 200,000-person drop in steel employment, they submitted an escape clause petition in January 1984, seeking protection so that domestic firms could generate the cash flow to remain in business and finance modernization.

The following July, the USITC found by a three-to-two vote that imports had been a substantial cause of serious injury in five of the nine major steel import categories. For relief it recommended a mixture of tariffs, quotas, and tariff-rate quotas for five years on products in those five categories. This recommendation came in late July, and under the law the president had just 60 days to implement, modify, or reject it.

Ronald Reagan's response, in the midst of the general election campaign, was, in the words of one administration insider, "a masterpiece of blue smoke and mirrors."[42] He had his trade representative, William E. Brock, announce that the president was rejecting the USITC recommendation: "The President has clearly determined that protectionism is not in the national interest. It costs jobs, raises prices and undermines our ability to compete here and abroad."[43] But having hoisted the banner of free trade in the first paragraph, Brock's announcement then "noted," in the second paragraph, that American steel firms and workers faced an "unprecedented and unacceptable" surge of imported steel due both to "massive unfair trade practices" and "diversion of steel imports into the US markets due to quotas and import restraints in other nations."[44] Brock would therefore "consult with those nations responsible . . . with a view toward the elimination of such practices." Meanwhile, the government was "to vigorously enforce US fair trade laws."

So far, so good, perhaps. But after further bows to the need "to liberalize world trade" and not "put at risk the exports of our farmers and other workers in export industries," the statement reached the crux of the matter on its third page:

> The president's decision assumes the continuation of the US/European Community's arrangement on steel as well as voluntary agreements announced earlier by Mexico and South Africa. . . . In some instances the US Trade Representative could be instructed to negotiate voluntary restraint agreements with other

---

42. The announcement had both protectionists and antiprotectionists cheering—for a day! Then the latter figured out its real content. The insider was William A. Niskanen, then a member of Reagan's Council of Economic Advisers. See Niskanen, *Reaganomics: An Insider's Account of the Policies and the People* (New York: Oxford University Press, 1988), 143.

43. Office of the United States Trade Representative, press release, 18 September 1984, 1.

44. Such quotas and import restraints were indeed rife abroad, but the case linking them to diversion of steel here was weak. Were that the case, prices in the US market would have been below those in, say, Japan. In fact, they were higher. The prime cause of increased imports was, rather, the growing competitive disadvantage of US firms in many product lines, which was exacerbated by the strong dollar.

countries. . . . Such restraint could cover products on which there was no injury determination. . . .

The statement concluded with an expression of "hope" that "this combination of actions, taken without protectionist intention or effect," would cause the market to "return to a more normal level of steel imports, or approximately 18 percent, excluding semi-finished steel."[45]

Brock insisted initially that this market share figure was a target, not a binding commitment, but steel officials who had just met with the president clearly felt otherwise, and they expressed their gratification with the decision. And little wonder: the events of the remainder of 1984 made it clear that the president's "national policy for the steel industry," as it came to be labeled, was a lot more protectionist than the USITC program he rejected. Asked to provide backup enforcement authority for foreign export restraints, Congress did this and more. It put into statute a target for fair import share: 17 percent to 20.2 percent of the US market, declaring further that in the absence of "satisfactory results within a reasonable period of time, the Congress will consider taking further legislative action."[46]

In the months that followed, agreements were negotiated or reaffirmed with every major foreign seller, whether or not the seller in question subsidized sales, and whether or not the USITC had found injury from imports of the seller's products. What all this amounted to was systematic circumvention of the rules for enforcing fair trade, for creating a level playing field, to which the administration, and Congress, claimed to give highest priority!

Ronald Reagan's successor, George H. W. Bush, initially followed a similar course. The Reagan VERs lasted five years, through 30 September 1989. Having committed himself to extending them during the 1988 election campaign, Bush now needed to decide how. The circumstances clearly favored some relaxation of the system: over the original quota period, the dollar had plummeted and the US steel industry had undergone major restructuring. As a result, according to the USITC, "nearly all of the VRA countries exported less steel to the United States in 1988 than they were allowed."[47] After an intense debate among competing interests,

---

45. This translated into an import share figure of 20.2 percent when semifinished products were added.

46. Quotations taken from the Trade and Tariff Act of 1984, section 803, and US Congress, House, "Joint Explanatory Statement of the Committee of Conference," *Trade and Tariff Act of 1984*, 98th Congress, 2nd session (5 October 1984), HR 98-1156, 197–98.

47. US International Trade Commission, *The Effects of the Steel Voluntary Restraint Agreements on U.S. Steel-Consuming Industries*, Report to the Subcommittee on Trade of the House Committee on Ways and Means on Investigation No. 332-270 Under Section 332 of the Tariff Act of 1930, USITC Publication 2182, Washington, DC, May 1989.

Bush announced on 23 July a "Steel Trade Liberalization Program," with the declared objective "to phase out in a responsible and orderly manner the voluntary restraint arrangements . . . and to negotiate an international consensus to remove unfair trade practices."[48] In the short run, Bush basically kept the quotas in place, though country ceiling levels were raised slightly. But he rather bravely set the phaseout period for two and a half years, so quotas would come off early in the election year of 1992, and he delivered on his pledge and ended them then. The industry responded with 36 new CVD and 48 new antidumping cases.

In the United States, this tendency to exploit unfair-trade laws to gain favorable trade-restricting deals left liberal traders and procedural purists isolated and vulnerable. It also put executive officials in a bind. It was hard for them to resist cutting a deal when producing interests on both sides of the border wanted one—foreign exporters seeking market stability (and quota rents) and home firms pressing for import constraint.

New Legislative Initiatives

Even as steel and other industries were exploiting existing laws to force negotiated protection, other parties were seeking further amendment of these laws. Foremost among these were industries pointing to alleged abuses the laws did not cover, but also seeking change were persons who opposed political fixes and wanted to make it harder for industries to use the laws to this end. An early leader in this movement was a man with a foot in both camps, Chairman of the House Ways and Means Subcommittee on Trade Sam M. Gibbons.

The Florida Democrat opposed quotas and trade restrictions generally, but supported those designed to counter unfair foreign trade practices. Gibbons did not think it proper, however, that the trade remedy laws be circumvented through negotiation of quota arrangements.

Gibbons also had problems that were specific to his personal situation in the House. As a labeled free trader, he was vulnerable to the charge that he no longer reflected the prevailing view of House Democrats. This charge threatened the leverage of his subcommittee, and of Ways and Means as a whole, at a time of fierce jurisdictional conflict with Energy and Commerce under the aggressive leadership of John D. Dingell (D-MI) (see chapter 4). Gibbons therefore needed to show that he too could be tough about trade, but in a way consistent with the liberal system.

So he held comprehensive hearings on the trade remedy laws in the spring of 1983, and his subcommittee proposed a "Trade Remedies Reform

---

48. Letter from USTR Carla A. Hills to Anne Brunsdale, chairman, USITC, in *Steel Industry Annual Report*, Report to the President on Investigation No. 332-289 Under Section 332 of the Tariff Act of 1930, USITC Publication 2316, Washington, DC, September 1990, A-2.

Act" in early 1984 that would have extended the CVD law to two previously uncovered foreign practices. One of these was *export targeting*, defined broadly as "any government plan or scheme . . . the effect of which is to assist the beneficiary to become more competitive in the export of any class or kind of merchandise."[49] The second of these practices was *natural resource subsidies*: A government such as Mexico would keep the domestic price of, say, oil or natural gas below international market levels, conveying a cost advantage to producers of an energy-intensive product like fertilizer. So US ammonia producers sought relief.[50]

The bill balanced these potentially trade-restrictive steps with an effort to protect the integrity of the rules. It required that the president, not the secretary of Commerce, make all decisions to suspend or terminate CVD or antidumping investigations, and it provided that any resulting export restraint agreement could not "have an effect on US consumers more adverse" than the imposition of penalty duties through normal operation of the law.[51]

These proposals met serious resistance as the proposal reached the full committee and the House floor, and none of them were included in the 1984 Trade and Tariff Act. But trade remedy reform became a central issue in the omnibus trade legislation that began in the House in 1986 and became law in 1988. In HR 4800, the omnibus measure approved by

---

49. US Congress, House Committee on Ways and Means, *Trade Remedies Reform Act of 1984*, 98th Congress, 2nd session (1 May 1984), HR 98-725, 26. The object of concern was Japan. The semiconductor case had brought to prominence the claim that "industrial targeting," or the singling out of specific industrial sectors for government favor to enhance their future export prospects, had been a prime cause of Japanese economic success. See Semiconductor Industry Association, *The Effect of Government Targeting on World Semiconductor Competition: A Case History of Japanese Industrial Strategy and Its Costs for America*, report prepared by Verner, Liipfert, Bernhard, and McPherson under the direction of Alan Wm. Wolff (Washington, DC, 1983). More idiosyncratic was the Houdaille machine-tool case. An enterprising Washington attorney, Richard Copaken, developed an ingenious argument for a once-obscure Florida machine-tool firm, alleging that Japanese subsidies of its competing industry derived (in part) from proceeds of community bicycle races. This case was, in the end, rejected by the Reagan White House in the spring of 1983, but in the meantime Copaken made the "Houdaille case" a household word among trade cognoscenti and a preoccupation within the executive branch for the better part of a year.

50. Such subsidies had not been countervailable under US and international practice because they did not meet the specificity test: they were not provided selectively to particular firms or industries, but were available on an economywide basis. For detailed treatment of these issues by two lawyers who addressed them in the Department of Commerce, see Alan F. Holmer and Judith Hippler Bello, "The Trade and Tariff Act of 1984: The Road to Enactment," *International Lawyer* 19, no. 1 (Winter 1985): 287–320; and Bello and Holmer, "Subsidies and Natural Resources: Congress Rejects a Lateral Attack on the Specificity Test," *George Washington Journal of International Law and Economics* 18, no. 2 (1984): 297–329.

51. US Congress, House Committee on Ways and Means, Subcommittee on Trade, "Description of HR 4784, the Trade Remedies Reform Act, as Ordered Reported" (29 February 1984), processed, 2.

a 295 to 115 House vote in May 1986, "resource input subsidies" were made actionable under the CVD law and "export targeting" was listed as an "unreasonable or unjustifiable" foreign practice under Section 301. The escape clause was amended to allow emergency relief for producers of perishable products, and to transfer final decision-making authority from the president to the US trade representative.[52]

The 1986 bill died in the Senate, as chronicled in chapter 4. But such provisions were dusted off and included in the legislation of 1987 and 1988. The House bill contained "several amendments sought by coalitions of import-competing U.S. industry seeking more restrictive AD/CVD laws." These were "greatly changed in the Senate, following sustained lobbying by the Administration and by export-oriented large U.S. businesses," but that body added several additional antidumping/CVD amendments, "none of which were in the House bill."[53] Most prominent, once again, was the natural resources provision. Others featured such lawyerish labels as "diversionary input dumping," or addressed thorny technical problems like "non-market-economy dumping."

These problem provisions were split between the two bills, and the administration (and some export-oriented businesses) fought hard against them. With leaders in both houses wanting a bill the president would sign, the conference negotiations "led to the rejection or dilution of nearly all the 'restrictive' antidumping/CVD amendments."[54]

The experience of the 1980s underscored the impossibility of managing volatile trade issues primarily through the elaboration of quasi-judicial procedures. One could not make the laws reach potential, borderline subsidies without extending them into uncertain and controversial new areas supported by neither domestic nor international consensus. It was hard to avoid seeing the trade remedy reform movement as a new pursuit of an old illusion—that the really "hot" major trade cases could somehow be diverted from the political arena, and that the United States could, in the words of Gibbons's predecessor, "run trade on economic law." There was to be one more rewriting of the laws in the 1971–94 period, however, and this time the initiative came from those who would limit their reach.

---

52. See US Congress, House Committee on Ways and Means, *Comprehensive Trade Policy Reform Act of 1986*, 99th Congress, 2nd session (6 May 1986), HR 99-581, part 1.

53. Horlick and Oliver, "Antidumping and CVD Law Provisions," 6.

54. Ibid. There was a modest clarification of the "specificity test" for subsidies—Commerce was to consider not just whether a subsidy was de jure available to all producers within a country, but whether it was de facto widely used. If it was not widely used, then it would meet the specificity test and be countervailable under US law. In fact, Commerce had been applying the test in this way for several years, but the statutory language cleared up the confusion created by several Court of International Trade decisions.

The Uruguay Round Antidumping Agreement

Antidumping law was among the major agenda items in the Uruguay Round. One might have thought that US officials, at a disadvantage in fighting the protectionist tilt domestically, would have seized on international negotiations as an antiprotectionist counterweight, just as their counterparts did with the tariff beginning in the 1930s. But neither the Bush nor the Clinton administration was so inclined. Using international agreement to constrain protectionist use of this mechanism does seem to have been in the mind of GATT Secretary General Arthur Dunkel, however, whose text—put forward in December 1991 to break a stalemate in the overall negotiations—contained provisions for antidumping law reform. In the climactic weeks of November–December 1993, US negotiators gave top priority to watering down these provisions, with some success, but substantial changes nonetheless remained in the final text—changes aimed at curbing practices that had tilted the process in favor of domestic protection seekers. Among the new requirements were the following:

- **Sunset**. An antidumping duty "shall be terminated on a date not later than five years from its imposition," unless a review establishes its continued justification. (US law had provided for antidumping duties to continue indefinitely unless a party requested and was granted a review.)

- **Start-up**. Production costs were to be adjusted for nonrecurring items that occur in the start-up period. (US law had not deducted for start-up.)

- **Price averaging**. "The existence of margins of dumping shall normally be established" by comparing a weighted average of export prices with a weighted average of the exporter's home-country prices. (US practice had been to compare average home-country prices with individual export sales, increasing the chances that substantial dumping will be found.)

- **Standing**. Producers submitting a case must account for at least 25 percent of the domestic output of the product. (US law did not have such a minimum requirement.)

- **De minimis**. An investigation must be terminated if the dumping margin is less than 2 percent or (in most cases) if dumped imports from the exporting country represent less than 3 percent of total imports. (US law included a 0.5 percent de minimis requirement for the dumping margin.)

None of these changes were as substantial as antidumping reformers had sought. But in the view of US experts on both sides of the issue, they would—if implemented in a straightforward manner—have made it significantly more difficult for domestic petitioners to obtain protection under the antidumping statute.

Industries prone to employ the antidumping law fought back, steel in particular. They sought language in the US implementing legislation that would limit the impact of the Uruguay Round changes. In this effort they had the sympathy and cooperation of the Clinton administration. USTR Mickey Kantor made no bones about where he stood: he was convinced that the administration's (and his own) reputation for toughness, and hence its credibility in pushing trade expansion, depended on defense of the antidumping laws. Commerce, which administered the law, agreed.

Representatives Sander Levin (D-MI) and Amo Houghton (R-NY) were active on the petitioners' side. Also unchanged from earlier periods was the relative weakness of internationalist firms and import users. Each of them had interests in changing the laws to bring treatment of import pricing closer to treatment of pricing of domestically produced goods. But in the main, CEOs of internationalist firms were preoccupied with other issues. So ambiguities in the Geneva agreement were resolved in favor of the petitioning industry in drafting the implementing bill and the related "statement of administrative action." Users of the law also won certain changes in their favor on matters not covered by the Geneva agreement at all,[55] including the following:

- **Sunset**. The legislation pushed the time for reviews as far back as possible within the five-year period. And capitalizing on ambiguities in the agreement, it specified that mandated reforms on price averaging would be applied only to new cases, not to reviews.

- **Start-up**. The administration's statement of administrative action explicitly limited the adjustment to fixed costs, excluding such things as advertising and other sales expenses.

- **Price averaging**. The bill mandated the agreed-upon "average-to-average" comparison rule for new cases (but not for reviews, which the agreement did not explicitly require). It also, however, established "a new fair comparison methodology that deducts an amount for the importer's profit from the US price,"[56] which has the effect of increasing the amount of dumping that is found.

---

55. For details on this process, see Robert E. Cumby and Theodore H. Moran, "Testing Models of the Trade Policy Process: Antidumping and the 'New Issues,'" chapter 6 in *The Effects of U.S. Trade Promotion and Protection Policies* (cf. p. 209, footnote 33) (Chicago: University of Chicago Press for the National Bureau of Economic Research, 1997), Robert C. Feenstra, ed.

56. *Uruguay Round Agreements Act*, Joint Report (No. 103-412) of the Committee on Finance, Committee on Agriculture, Nutrition, and Forestry, and Committee on Governmental Affairs of the United States Senate, to accompany S 2467, 22 November 1994, 7.

- **Standing** and **de minimis**. The bill included straightforward language implementing these provisions but limited the latter to new investigations.

The bill also included changes, beyond the Uruguay Round agreement, that benefited users of the law. These included toughened language on anticircumvention and a provision to exclude "captive production" (inputs manufactured by a firm for its own use) from the total US market for a product on which injury determinations are based. Critics of the antidumping laws, moreover, failed in their effort to win agreement on a provision to limit imposition of duties in "short supply" situations. Though a firm conclusion is difficult to reach, supporters of antidumping laws appear to have won back in Washington most, but probably not all, of the ground they lost in Geneva. If so, this was not—as some have alleged—a protectionist takeover of US policy via the antidumping laws. It was a lost opportunity to make them significantly less restrictive.[57]

In the end, the movement to change trade remedy legislation had only modest net impact in the 1980s and early 1990s. What did have effect, however, were the changes enacted in the 1970s. In addition to facilitating the political fixes treated at some length above, they led to many more specific impositions of countervailing and antidumping duties. And the threat of their imposition had an additional trade-deterring effect.

Administrative Remedies: A Balance Sheet on 1980–94

In the 1980–94 period, there were 424 countervailing duty and 718 antidumping investigations initiated in response to specific petitions. Table 6.1 (p. 149) shows their distribution by year. And it shows clearly contrasting patterns.

Countervailing duty cases surged in the early years, peaking in 1982 and 1984 and dropping precipitously after 1986. This reflects the fact that a very large share were steel cases, intended to force political settlements. These fell to a fraction of their former level once this goal had been achieved (and spiked temporarily in 1992, when the quotas were phased out). Outside of steel, government subsidies were harder to prove—and their use probably declined through this period as more and more countries adopted market-oriented economic strategies.

---

57. My effort to sort through the complexity of these issues was aided immensely by my research assistant, Steven Schoeny; by the summation in Jeffrey J. Schott (assisted by Johanna W. Buurman), *The Uruguay Round: An Assessment* (Washington, DC: Institute for International Economics, 1994); by the Senate Report, *Uruguay Round Agreements Act*; and by several conversations with experts on these issues. This does not mean that any of them will be satisfied with the balance struck here.

In contrast, antidumping cases persisted. They peaked in 1984 and 1986, to be sure, and fell thereafter with the decline of the dollar, which cut into the growth of imports and made it harder for firms to prove injury. Nonetheless, they averaged 45 per year in 1987–94 (compared with 12.5 per year for CVD cases).

There was one piece of "good news" for liberal traders and procedural purists: resolution through negotiated VERs dropped sharply. As shown in table 6.2, 1980–85 featured many occasions when plaintiffs withdrew their petitions, predominantly because they had forced political solutions. The number fell off sharply in the years thereafter.

The other side of the coin, however, was a rising success rate of petitioners in winning relief under the antidumping statute itself. In 1980–84, 38 percent (53 of 138) of petitions carried to completion led to either antidumping duties or suspension agreements. In 1985–94, 55 percent (246 of 444) were successful.

When petitioners were unsuccessful, moreover, it was rarely because they were unable to meet the statutory criterion for dumping. Only 35 of 582 petitions (6 percent) failed for this reason, and only 19 of 444 (4 percent) in 1985–94. In contrast, 43 percent (248 of 582) failed because the USITC did not find "material injury" to the producer from the imports alleged to be dumped.[58]

Clearly, by the late 1980s petitioners were finding relief. Indeed, the numbers suggest that unfair trade must have been rampant, since the Department of Commerce had been finding dumping on the overwhelming majority of petitions submitted. There is substantial evidence, however, that the enforcement of the unfair-trade laws had become sharply skewed in favor of petitioners and against their foreign competitors. The basic premise of the law is consistent with GATT Article VI: that US producers should not be undercut by foreign competitors who sell at lower prices in the US market than in theirs.[59] However, the way US law was written and implemented tilted the playing field in favor of the petitioner—and thus against the foreign producer *and* the US users of its products, through

---

58. For a comprehensive account of 1980–88 cases that reaches similar conclusions, see J. Michael Finger and Tracy Murray, *Policing Unfair Imports: The U.S. Example*, Working Paper 401 (Washington, DC: World Bank, Country Economics Department, March 1990). Finger and Murray also offer interesting information on which countries are most likely to be targeted with unfair-trade petitions. For a broader analysis treating specific cases in detail, see Finger and Nellie T. Artis, *How Antidumping Works and Who Gets Hurt* (Ann Arbor: University of Michigan Press, 1993).

59. Even this principle does not go uncontested. Carried to extremes, "dumping" amounts to the predatory pricing for which remedy is available against competing *domestic* firms. But as typically carried out, it is similar to market discrimination, setting different prices for different customers or in different economic circumstances, which is common and indeed necessary business practice *within* national boundaries.

Table 6.2 Antidumping cases and results, 1980–94

Year	Total	Cases withdrawn	Cases completed	Cases affirmed Number	Cases affirmed Percent	No dumping Number	No dumping Percent	No injury Number	No injury Percent
1980	21	9	12	4	33.3	1	8.3	7	58.3
1981	15	4	11	7	63.6	1	9.1	3	27.3
1982	65	24	41	14	34.1	3	7.3	24	58.5
1983	46	5	41	19	46.3	5	12.2	17	41.5
1984	74	41	33	9	27.3	6	18.2	18	54.5
1985	66	16	50	29	58.0	2	4.0	19	38.0
1986	71	7	64	44	68.8	3	4.7	17	26.6
1987	15	1	14	9	64.3	0	0.0	5	35.7
1988	42	0	42	22	52.4	3	7.1	17	40.5
1989	23	3	20	14	70.0	0	0.0	6	30.0
1990	43	2	41	19	46.3	5	12.2	17	41.5
1991	53	4	49	24	49.0	2	4.1	23	46.9
1992	99	11	88	45	51.1	1	1.1	42	47.7
1993	42	6	36	19	52.8	2	5.6	15	41.7
1994	43	3	40	21	52.5	1	2.5	18	45.0
Total	**718**	**136**	**582**	**299**	**51.3**	**35**	**6.4**	**248**	**42.2**

Sources: US International Trade Commission, annual *The Year in Review* reports; Bruce Blonigen, *US Antidumping Case-Specific Data*, 1980–95; and the *Federal Register.*

"practices and procedures which tend to systematically favor higher rather than lower dumping and CVD margins."[60]

Specifically, the law encouraged the Commerce Department to exclude from the calculation of the "foreign market value" of a product (the foreign producer's home-market average price) any sales that were below his average costs and to ignore in the calculation of the average price at which he sold in the United States any sales that were above the foreign market value. And when data on the accused producer's production costs were judged insufficient, Commerce substituted a "constructed value" based on estimated average cost of production plus overhead plus profit. Since it is standard business practice to sell below average total cost of production on a variety of occasions—and by definition profitable, at the margin, to sell at any price above marginal costs—this meant that the only way a producer could avoid being found guilty of dumping was to sell in the US market at prices well above those at home![61]

It is no wonder that escape clause cases had virtually disappeared by the late 1980s, for if a finding of dumping was quasi-automatic, the antidumping procedure had the advantage of a lower injury threshold, no

---

60. Richard Boltuck and Robert E. Litan, *Down in the Dumps: Administration of the Unfair Trade Laws* (Washington, DC: Brookings Institution, 1991), 13. The remainder of this section draws upon their analysis.

61. For a thoroughgoing critique, see Brink Lindsey and Dan Ikenson, *Antidumping 101: The Devilish Details of "Unfair Trade" Law* (Cato Institute, Center for Trade Policy Studies, Trade Policy Analysis 20, November 21, 2002).

presidential power to overturn an affirmative decision, and (until the Uruguay Round changes) indefinite duration for any import relief imposed—unless the foreign producer won revocation of the duty by raising prices, which has the same net benefit for the US producer.

The Limits of Administrative Remedies

"The rules" had come full circle. For decades they had been a sideshow on an obscure bureaucratic stage; now they were prominently affecting—and impeding—trade flows. For years they were properly denounced as ineffective; by the 1990s they were, with equal accuracy, attacked as tilted in favor of US producers. And the debate continues.

To ignore the trade sins these laws were designed to counter would be inconsistent with GATT rules and politically counterproductive. To be obsessed with them, however, exaggerates their marginal contribution to overall American trade woes, fueling the growing, rather self-indulgent conviction among businesspeople and politicians that the international trade game is systematically rigged against the United States. And the moral cast of this ongoing debate not only favors domestic plaintiffs over foreign producer interests, but it also disadvantages the domestic users of the products subject to trade sanctions. Their interests have no special standing in the litigation over unfair-trade laws, but they suffer if prices of steel, for example, are increased as a result of the outcomes of unfair-trade cases.[62]

Still, the unfair-trade laws affect only a rather modest slice of American trade (over the years, steel producers accounted for close to 50 percent of total cases). Even when one adds the deterrent effect of such laws on some export sales, it has been hard for critics to show that their trade costs are large in relation to overall US international transactions. Thus some ex-

---

62. For evidence that this moral disadvantage dampens political reaction by those interests hurt by import restrictions imposed under the "unfair trade" statutes, see I. M. Destler and John S. Odell with Kimberly Ann Elliott, *Anti-Protection: Changing Forces in United States Trade Politics* (Washington, DC: Institute for International Economics, POLICY ANALYSES IN INTERNATIONAL ECONOMICS 21, September 1987), especially 73–74.

Occasionally, import users have mobilized in response. When the price understandings in the US-Japan semiconductor agreement of 1986, reached pursuant to antidumping petitions, led to a doubling of the price of chips in the US market, IBM and other computer makers protested and forced a modification of the antidumping provisions in the follow-on agreement reached in 1991. A similar reaction followed antidumping duties imposed on ball bearings, an important input to many manufacturers, in 1989. And in the summer of 1991, users rose up in arms when a small American producer of flat-panel display screens for laptop computers succeeded in winning huge antidumping duties against the Japanese imports that dominate the US market. Such a determination, Apple and Compaq and IBM declared, would render it uneconomic to produce their next-generation laptops in the United States and would force a transfer of production to overseas plants.

perts of liberal trade persuasion argue that it is better to live with the quasi-judicial trade remedy system. One of America's foremost trade law authorities, John H. Jackson, reviewed the trade cases of several decades through the early 1980s and concluded with a cautious affirmative: The system is better than likely alternatives "if we can believe . . . that the US legalistic system—cumbersome, rigid, and costly as it is—in fact provides for an economy more open to imports than virtually any other major industrial economy in the world."[63] This argument remains credible, notwithstanding the substantial broadening of antidumping protection since its publication.

The unfair-trade statutes do impose substantial costs on particular US producers: for example, foreign governments are increasingly invoking similar dumping laws against US exporters. And this book will argue for amending them in its concluding chapter. But changing them is an uphill political struggle, ever vulnerable to the charge of "weakening the unfair-trade laws" or aligning with foreign adversaries. For unfair-trade laws remain politically popular, and they have become—at long last—economically successful for their users. They have become, to repeat a phrase quoted earlier, "the usual first choice for industries seeking protection from imports into the U.S."[64] And for members of Congress pressed by trade-affected constituents, predisposed to see unfairness in foreign competition, and reluctant to take action directly, they seem to offer the best of all worlds: a chance to occupy the moral high ground of backing "free but fair trade."

---

63. John H. Jackson, "Perspectives on the Jurisprudence of International Trade: Costs and Benefits of Legal Procedures in the United States," *Michigan Law Review* 82, no. 6 (April–May 1984): 1579–80, 1582. Jackson recognizes, however, that as discussed in earlier pages, for "very big cases . . . the system breaks down and in fact returns, by one subterfuge or another, to a 'non-rule system' of extensive executive discretion and 'back-room bargaining.'" Ibid., 1580–81.

64. Horlick and Oliver, "Antidumping and CVD Law Provisions," 5.

7

The National Arena:
New Dimensions of Conflict

Through much of the postwar period, the American trade policymaking system operated within a national political environment that was unusually conducive to liberal policies. There were four basic reasons.

First and foremost, foreign trade was not a major partisan issue. There was competition between Democrats and Republicans for the favor of specific interest groups, but neither party used trade policy as a major means of defining its differences with the other. This both reflected and reinforced a second condition: There was an overwhelming elite consensus in favor of market openness and trade expansion. Given limited interest among the relatively protectionist mass public, this bolstered governmental leaders in their liberal inclinations.

Third, the issue posed by interests seeking import relief was typically a straightforward one—whether to insulate a particular industry's firms and workers from international competition or to make them take their market medicine. This made it easy to label these interests "protectionist," placing them very much on the defensive in the postwar policy environment. Fourth and finally, interest group initiative was limited and usually followed a simple pattern. A relatively small number of industries sought protection, each on its own track—textiles, shoes, steel, and smaller ones like watchmakers. Other manufacturing and labor interests were typically inactive on trade issues, but many were on call to be mobilized for major liberalizing initiatives.

All four of these conditions made trade policy relatively manageable, facilitating the liberal policies that government leaders wished to pursue. And all four conditions changed markedly in the 1970s and 1980s.

Trade politics grew more partisan, as a number of prominent Democrats began to see electoral opportunities in assuming a trade-restrictive posture, and as some Republicans reacted by toughening their trade stances. Elite leaders, particularly those in business, grew weaker and more qualified in their commitment to liberal trade. New trade-related issues entered the policy debate—industrial and "competitiveness" policy, misaligned exchange rates. These issues weakened the notion that, on international economic matters, government was best when it intervened least. And they offered broad national-interest rationales for certain trade-restrictive proposals. Finally, interest group politics became more complex. The AFL-CIO became an across-the-board backer of trade restrictions, and a much larger range of interests sought government trade action, including segments of frontier, high-technology industries like semiconductors. But the protectionist forces were being countered by a new antiprotectionist activism among certain exporters, importers, and industrial consumers. And there seemed to be some erosion in the effectiveness of the mainstays of traditional protectionism, the textile-apparel coalition in particular.

On balance, however, these changes tended to make the maintenance of open trade policies more difficult. Together with the developments addressed in previous chapters, they undercut time-tested methods of managing trade issues without substituting reliable new ones.

■ ■ ■

In 1962, in the key House vote on John F. Kennedy's Trade Expansion Act, Democrats voted 210 to 44 in support; Republicans lined up 127 to 43 behind a motion to "recommit" (kill) the bill. This was consistent with the basic political alignment of the three prior decades, beginning with Smoot-Hawley in 1930 and the Reciprocal Trade Agreements Act of 1934. Democrats backed liberal trade and lower tariffs; Republicans sought to maintain or increase protection for domestic industry.

But little more than a decade after President Kennedy's landmark legislative victory, a new alignment seemed to be developing. When authorizing legislation for a new major trade round came before the House in 1973, it was the Democrats who voted 121 to 112 against, while Republicans were almost unanimous, 160 to 19, in favor. For northern Democrats, the turnabout was even greater: 141 to 7 "yea" in 1962; 101 to 52 "nay" in 1973.

An "Amazing Political Reversal"?

At the time, this shift attracted little attention. Trade had not been a prominent source of partisan contention since the 1930s. There was, of course, tactical competition for the support of specific constituencies. President Kennedy, for example, promised comprehensive protection for cotton textiles in 1960, strengthening his position in New England and the southern coastal states. Richard M. Nixon, not to be twice outdone, made an even stronger textile promise eight years later. But although these pledges (Nixon's in particular) did have important policy consequences, neither was rooted in a broader trade stance that distinguished one party from its rival. And neither was directed at the national electorate. Similarly, Republicans who voted "protectionist" in 1962 (and Democrats who did so in 1973) were not inclined to advertise that fact. Advocacy of trade restrictions might win plaudits from trade-affected interests, but the mass public was indifferent and opinion leaders were hostile.

Some of the difference between 1962 and 1973, moreover, could be explained by the fact that members were voting on the program of a Democratic President (Kennedy) in the first instance and a Republican (Nixon) in the second. On almost any issue, partisan loyalties pull members toward support of an administration initiative when the White House is occupied by one of their own.

But deeper forces were at work, forces that had been percolating for many years. Most important was the shift in the geographic bases of the two political parties. In the first half of the 20th century, the Republican heartland was the industrial Northeast and Midwest: Herbert C. Hoover carried Pennsylvania in 1932, but not a single state farther west (and no state south of Delaware). Indeed, from the first Lincoln election until the reign of Franklin D. Roosevelt, not a single Democratic presidential candidate carried either Pennsylvania or Michigan. This general pattern persisted as late as 1948: Harry S. Truman scored his upset reelection victory even though his favored Republican rival, Thomas E. Dewey, carried those two states, and New York and New Jersey as well. But the Kennedy-Nixon election of 1960 reversed the pattern. JFK won 303 electoral votes, exactly the same number as Truman. But unlike Truman, he lost badly in the West but won Michigan, Pennsylvania, New York, and New Jersey. Since that time, the Northeast has become the Democratic heartland, while the GOP has flourished in the sunbelt—the West and, increasingly, the South.

This shift reduced Republican dependence on historically protectionist northeastern and midwestern industrialists. In contrast, the Democrats' new heartland was where organized labor was the strongest. It was therefore natural to expect some adjustment of the parties' dominant positions on trade, and in fact Raymond A. Bauer and his colleagues detected signs of an "amazing political reversal" as early as 1953. Closely analyzing a Roper poll taken that year, and looking particularly at respondents with the most polar views, they found that "ultrafree-traders" were "strongly Republican," whereas "ultraprotectionists" tended to be Democrats. And important among the group most committed to trade restrictions were "industrial workers who see a threat to their jobs."[1]

---

1. Raymond A. Bauer, Ithiel de Sola Pool, and Lewis Anthony Dexter, *American Business and Public Policy: The Politics of Foreign Trade* (Chicago: Aldine-Atherton, 1972), 91–92.

Through the 1950s and 1960s, the major national labor organizations still held to a free trade position, although the textile unions were an important exception. The AFL-CIO endorsed the Trade Expansion Act of 1962, in part because of its new provisions for trade adjustment assistance to workers. A decade later, however, labor leaders were deriding that program as "burial insurance," and AFL-CIO President George Meany was singing a decidedly different trade tune. Urban Democrats followed him from support to opposition of liberal trade, particularly in the House of Representatives. But with a few iconoclastic exceptions, like Senator Vance Hartke (D-IN) of Burke-Hartke fame, they did so quietly. In the Senate, in fact, liberal activists like Walter F. Mondale (D-MN) fought the House-passed quota bill of 1970 and backed the Nixon-Ford trade act when it came before them four years later.

It was a Republican, John B. Connally, who was the first postwar presidential aspirant to make trade a prominent issue in the quest for his party's nomination. He won cheers on the campaign circuit in 1979 with his threat to leave Japanese Toyotas rusting on the docks. But his bottom line—exactly one convention delegate in 1980—did not inspire emulation.

By 1982, however, Democrats began to sniff major political opportunity. They were again outsiders in the White House and newly a minority in the Senate as well. The economy was suffering its deepest and longest recession in more than 40 years. The rust belt, industrial heartland states like Pennsylvania, Ohio, and Michigan were particularly hard hit, as were their key industries like autos and steel. And US trade was moving deeper into deficit. Mondale was now seeking the Democratic presidential nomination, and the AFL-CIO had decided, for the first time, to endorse a candidate before the primaries. Mondale needed that endorsement; he also needed an issue on which he could take a "tougher" stand than the president. He fastened upon trade. He did not neglect the broader macroeconomic causes of America's distress. But to labor audiences in particular, he went after the Japanese and unfair-trade practices, and denounced the Reagan regime for failing to combat them. The United States needed to get tough on trade, he argued, lest job opportunities for its youth be limited to working at McDonald's or sweeping up around Japanese computers.

For the most part, Mondale avoided concrete commitments to trade protection; he remained at heart an internationalist, who would rather open foreign markets than close American ones. Nevertheless, the United Auto Workers had made its highly restrictive domestic-content bill a litmus test for labor Democrats, and Mondale endorsed it. So did the Democratic-controlled House of Representatives in 1982, and again in 1983. In the latter year, only two Democrats from the Northeast and industrial Midwest voted "no" on final passage. Thus, as the nation approached the 50th anniversary of the Reciprocal Trade Agreements Act of 1934, it seemed to be witnessing the reemergence of trade as a highly visible partisan issue, but with the two major parties having switched positions. Senator John H. Chafee (R-RI) remarked, seemingly with some relief, that here was one issue on which the Republicans were wearing "the white hats."

The new advocacy of trade restrictions by certain Democrats was not without its logic. Ever since the New Deal, theirs had been the party favoring an active government to redress the imbalances and inequities of the marketplace. Republicans, by contrast, had been critics of government intrusion in business. On trade, however, these positions had been reversed. Would not a new trade realignment make more intellectual sense, then, with the domestic interventionists becoming international interventionists as well?

For all of these reasons, it seemed very possible in the 1980s that trade would become, as in the years before 1930, one of the prime issues dividing and defining the two major political parties. But this did not happen: The "realignment" remained incomplete. Democrats hedged their bets; Republicans did also.

Mondale found that the "protectionist" label retained its sting, as editorial writers and internationalist Democrats reacted with dismay.[2] So the Democratic challenger backpedaled adroitly. He did not change any specific stand, but from early 1983 onward he deemphasized trade restrictions and highlighted the macroeconomic causes of the trade imbalance.[3]

Meanwhile, Ronald Reagan was looking more protectionist. The president remained a free trader in principle, but as noted in chapter 5, he was protecting his political flanks in practice, approving new restraints on heavyweight motorcycles, textiles, and specialty steel; a fourth year of Japanese auto export limits; and—in the middle of the election campaign—a network of voluntary restraint agreements on carbon steel aimed at limiting imports to 20.2 percent of domestic production.[4] So, contrary to widespread expectations, trade did not become a major issue in the 1984 general election.

But trade reemerged as a partisan issue in 1985 and 1986. Democrats, staggering from Reagan's 49-state electoral sweep, needed to counter the

---

2. Moreover, once Senator Edward M. Kennedy (D-MA) withdrew from the contest, Mondale no longer had serious competition for the labor endorsement.

3. The Democratic party platform negotiated by Mondale's aides actually attacked the Reagan administration from the internationalist side, citing as the administration's "most fundamental" mistake its acting "as if the United States were an economic island unto itself." The platform's only specific reference to trade relief employed the modifier "temporary," and called for a quid pro quo in the form of industry commitment to "a realistic, hardheaded modernization plan which will restore competitiveness." Reprinted in *Congressional Quarterly*, 21 July 1984: 1748, 1760.

4. Reagan's stand was less restrictive than that of Mondale, who called for a 17 percent import share, but the Democrat conditioned his proposal on the industry's commitments to adjust. Not to be outdone, Congress incorporated elements of both candidates' positions—and a modified industry adjustment requirement—into the Trade and Tariff Act of 1984.

administration in its two areas of electoral strength—economic recovery at home and "standing tall" in the world. To Representative Tony Coelho of California, chairman of the House Democratic Campaign Committee, trade met both needs perfectly: it was the "Democratic macho issue."[5] By targeting the unparalleled trade deficit, Democrats could spotlight the underside of Reaganomics and attack White House softness toward trade competitors.

Thus, partisan interest was one force driving the congressional upsurge chronicled in chapter 4: the Bentsen-Rostenkowski-Gephardt bill taxing imports from countries running large trade surpluses; House Speaker Thomas P. "Tip" O'Neill's declaration about trade having become the "number one" issue on Capitol Hill;[6] and the omnibus trade bill with a decidedly protectionist tilt that O'Neill and other Democratic leaders pushed through the House the following spring. When Democrats regained control of the Senate in the mid-term election of 1986, trade was the issue they chose to show that their party could legislate. When Richard A. Gephardt (D-MO) decided to run for president in 1988, an aggressive trade posture helped him win the Iowa caucuses.[7] When the Bush administration initiated negotiations toward a North American Free Trade Agreement (NAFTA), a majority of Democrats voted against extending fast-track authority in 1991, driven importantly by the AFL-CIO campaign against it. And though they lost the vote on Capitol Hill, they won one that fall in Pennsylvania, with NAFTA reasonably prominent among the issues in Democratic Senator Harris Wofford's surprise special election victory over former Bush administration Attorney General Richard Thornburgh.

Yet trade remained, for Democrats, a two-edged sword. Mondale and Gephardt found their "protectionism" attacked by editorialists and by Democratic primary competitors. Other Democrats, like Ways and Means Chairman Dan Rostenkowski (D-IL) in the House and Bill Bradley (D-NJ) in the Senate, were unwilling to abandon the legacy of Cordell Hull, however much they might criticize the administration's passivity on trade and related issues. Rostenkowski and Finance Chairman Lloyd Bentsen (D-TX) both supported fast track for NAFTA, as did the House and Senate democratic leadership. As long as Democrats were deeply divided on whether to move in a protectionist direction, the issue could not be a good one for mobilizing and unifying the party against the opposition. Their ambivalence was underscored when Gephardt, in his new role of House majority

---

5. Quoted in Pietro Nivola, "Trade Policy: Refereeing the Playing Field," in Thomas E. Mann, ed., *A Question of Balance: The President, Congress and Foreign Policy* (Washington, DC: Brookings Institution, 1990), 235.

6. "President Reagan," he intoned, "seems willing to preside over the de-industrialization of America. We in Congress are not." Quoted in the *Washington Post*, 20 September 1985.

7. Important in Gephardt's narrow plurality, by most accounts, was a television spot attacking the unfairness of Korean import restrictions against American-made automobiles.

leader, voted in favor of fast track for NAFTA in the spring of 1991, and then rebalanced his position by introducing a new Gephardt amendment targeting Japan in the fall.

Nor were Republicans prepared to stand still while Democrats decided whether to attack. Just as Reagan had made protectionist concessions in 1984, Senate Finance Republicans led the campaign against Japanese trade practices in 1985. Fifty-nine House Republicans joined 236 House Democrats in supporting the omnibus legislation in 1986, and *their* need to balance their positions pushed the Reagan administration toward trade compromise in 1988. Patrick Buchanan took a blatantly protectionist stance in his "conservative" challenge to President George Bush's renomination in 1992.

Still, there had developed in the 1970s and 1980s the potential for sharp interparty division on trade in the years to come. And if a future Democratic president were to come to power on a truly protectionist platform, this would remove from the American trade policymaking system the most crucial pillar of support for open policies—the liberal-leaning leadership of the executive branch.[8]

A Newly Ambivalent Elite

A related development was the weakening of support for liberal trade policies within the American leadership community. As spelled out in chapter 2, open trade policies had never won overwhelming backing from the mass public. Rather, they were sustainable because of mass indifference, combined with strong support from leadership groups. These conditions helped keep trade issues out of the larger public arena, so that specific pressures could be diverted or accommodated by special deals.

Between the 1930s and the 1960s, elite support of liberal trade increased. Postwar prosperity served to confirm the rightness of open trade policy just as the Great Depression had discredited the Smoot-Hawley alternative. Thus, as Judith L. Goldstein has written, liberalism became the dominant ideology because it was associated with the unparalleled prosperity of the years after 1945.[9]

But just as the Munich lesson for security policy was supplanted by Vietnam, the connection between Smoot-Hawley, global depression, and World War II also faded. One reason was time. Another was the afflictions chronicled in chapter 3: increased trade exposure, the American

---

8. In the 1995–2004 period, general partisan polarization would spill over into the trade arena. See chapter 11.

9. Judith L. Goldstein, "Ideas, Institutions, and American Trade Policy," *International Organization* 42, no. 1 (Winter 1988): especially 187–88.

"decline," the rise of new competitors, the erosion of the General Agreement on Tariffs and Trade (GATT), stagflation, and the misaligned dollar. Substantial—if not entirely conclusive—evidence from opinion polls tends to confirm what the tone of the American trade debate suggested: that leadership backing for liberal trade weakened significantly. At the same time, the mass public, always somewhat inclined toward protection, may have grown stronger in this inclination.

Analysis of public opinion on trade is impeded by the lack of any staple questions that were posed consistently by pollsters throughout the postwar period. Gallup asked regularly, during the 1940s and 1950s, whether people favored higher or lower tariffs, and got consistent pluralities for the latter. It also got a consistently positive response to questions about whether people supported continuation of the reciprocal trade agreements program. But these questions are no longer put to the public.

When questions have been posed in terms of jobs or the desirability of imports per se, mass opinion has shown a consistently protectionist tilt. In 1953, Roper asked, "Would you rather see this country import more goods from foreign countries than we do now, or put more restrictions on goods imported into this country from abroad?" Of those willing to take a position, 37 percent favored restrictions, and 26 percent favored imports.[10]

Later surveys suggested a stronger leaning in the restrictive direction. When, between 1977 and 1983, Gallup asked virtually the same question as Roper in 1953—posing a choice between more imports and more restrictions—imports won just 12 to 15 percent support, as against 68 to 75 percent for restrictions.[11] And most Americans saw a direct connection between imports and the loss of jobs. A 10 March 1983 Harris survey found that a 75 to 21 percent majority of respondents were convinced that import competition from abroad was harmful to American labor. There was also evidence that public sentiment was moved by both the trade balance and the state of the US economy. The percentage of Americans saying that "restrictions" were necessary to protect domestic industries fell from 56 percent in 1988 to 51 percent in 1990, then jumped to 63 percent in the recession year of 1991. Conversely, those willing to "allow free trade even if domestic industries are hurt" rose from 34 to 39 percent, and then dropped to 27 percent.[12]

---

10. Bauer, Pool, and Dexter, *American Business and Public Policy*, 85.

11. Gallup Report International, October 1983. Roper asked, from 1973 to 1984: "Generally speaking, do you think the government should or should not place restrictions on imports of goods from other countries that are priced lower than American-made goods of the same kind?" Responses fluctuated narrowly, with 61 to 68 percent prorestriction and 21 to 31 percent against. The 68 percent pro came in late 1979 and early 1983; the 31 percent against in late 1981. See William Schneider, "Protectionist Push is Coming from the Top," *National Journal*, 27 April 1985, 932.

12. *New York Times*/CBS News Poll, June Survey, 3–6 June 1991, processed, 4.

Yet ambivalence remained, together with relative lack of interest. Presented in 1983 with the proposition that "we have to produce better products with more efficiency to compete in the world rather than depend on artificial trade barriers, such as tariffs," Americans agreed by 90 to 7 percent![13] One expert writing during the congressional trade storm in the spring of 1985 found "not much evidence" of "surging public resentment over our imbalance of trade."[14] A *New York Times*/CBS News poll three months later found "foreign trade" dead last in importance among five listed issues "that people are concerned about,"[15] even though the subject had been in the news more prominently than at any time in postwar memory.[16]

There was, however, increasing public concern about Japan. In the 1990 Chicago Council on Foreign Relations poll, Japan tied for third place (and tied for first among the leadership sample) among countries Americans considered most important to the United States, but 60 percent of the public saw "the economic power of Japan" as "a critical threat . . . to the vital interest of the United States in the next 10 years." An overwhelming 71 percent of Americans agreed with the general statement that Japan practiced "unfair trade with the United States," compared with 40 percent believing the European Community was unfair. And on the Chicago Council's "feeling thermometer" charting Americans' attitudes toward specific countries, Japan dropped from an exceptionally high level of 61 percent in 1986 to 52 percent in 1990.[17]

With the modest changes in mass opinion came evidence of emerging divisions within leadership groups. The Chicago Council polls found that "top figures in business, labor, government, the media, religion and education" were 75 percent in favor of eliminating tariffs in 1978 but only 64 percent in favor in 1990. "Among labor leaders, the change was quite sharp," from 53 percent favoring tariffs in 1978 to 75 percent in 1990. Earlier indicators of such trends led William Schneider, a leading public

---

13. "The Harris Survey," 14 March 1983.

14. Schneider, "Protectionist Push," 932.

15. "Here are five things that people are concerned about—arms control, foreign trade problems, tax reform, the budget deficit and war in Central America. Which of these is most important right now. . .?" Answers: arms control (19 percent); foreign trade (9 percent); tax reform (19 percent); budget deficit (29 percent); war in Central America (19 percent). July 1985 Survey, 3.

16. However, the 1990 poll of the Chicago Council on Foreign Relations found "Protecting the jobs of American workers" and "Protecting the interests of American business abroad" ranked no. 1 and no. 2 by the general public (though not by its leadership sample) among "a list of possible foreign policy goals that the United States should have." John E. Rielly, ed., *American Public Opinion and U.S. Foreign Policy 1991* (Chicago Council on Foreign Relations, 1991), 15.

17. Ibid., 20–22, 28. By comparison, the "temperature" was 58 in 1986 and 56 in 1990 for France, 53 and 45 for China, and 62 in both years for Germany.

opinion analyst, to conclude in 1983 that "trade protectionism is growing from the top down."[18] Lending further credence to Schneider's view was a 1983 survey of "opinion leaders" by the Opinion Research Corporation (ORC). It found 75 percent in favor of versus 20 percent against "industrial modernization agreements," which might include short-term relief from imports in exchange for management and labor commitments to improve efficiency.[19]

Doubtless the recession of 1982 and the strong dollar of 1980–85 influenced these polls. Conversely, business support for eliminating tariffs rose from 71 to 78 percent between 1986 and 1990, reflecting—presumably—the late 1980s export boom. Still, it was clear that elite support for liberal trade had eroded, though it remained substantial.

Challenges to Laissez-Faire Trade Doctrine

Both reflecting and contributing to elite ambivalence was the increased questioning of liberal trade ideology, not just in the Washington policy community but at leading intellectual centers. Just as the Great Depression and postwar prosperity had discredited "protectionism," the relative decline of the United States weakened support for "free trade." The audience was growing for perspectives that held free trade ideology to be flawed or incomplete. The new challenges were of two basic sorts. The first, focusing on specific firms and industries, argued that the free trade–protectionist distinction was obsolete in a world characterized by pervasive government intervention in the marketplace. The second, which rose and fell with the trade imbalances, questioned the compatibility of open market policies with exchange rate misalignments that saddled producers with enormous competitive burdens not of their own making.

At the broadest level, proponents of the first school argued that the actual world economy was not at all like that posited by Adam Smith. The United States did not face autonomous foreign firms jousting for business on their own, with rewards to the most efficient. Rather, other governments rigged the game through a range of actions—subsidies, product standards, procurement regulations—that favored their national producers at the expense of foreign competitors. American firms thus operated not on a level playing field, but on one tilted against them.

For some critics, the challenge was economywide. The Labor-Industry Coalition for International Trade (LICIT), comprising eight firms and 11

---

18. Schneider, "Trade Protectionism is Growing from the Top Down," *National Journal*, 29 January 1983, 240–41. Figures earlier in this paragraph come from Schneider and from Rielly, *American Public Opinion 1991*, 26–27.

19. LTV Corporation, "The Future of America's Basic Industries: A Survey of Opinion Leaders," conducted by Opinion Research Corporation, 1983.

labor organizations, found in 1983 that "our nation's industrial base has been weakened across a spectrum ranging from basic industries to the most technologically advanced." It placed much of the blame on "the widening gap between specific industry support efforts in other countries and the absence of such policies and programs in the United States." It argued that the "resulting 'industrial policy gap' has put American industry at a systematic disadvantage." To close the gap, LICIT recommended a range of policy changes aimed at both offsetting the effects of foreign industrial subsidies and providing broader government support to American industrial enterprise.[20]

In essence, the argument was that because other nations subsidized and protected their industries, the United States must do so, lest it fall behind. But the very comprehensiveness that made the LICIT line attractive for coalition-building purposes made it relatively easy for trade traditionalists to refute. For what made products move in international commerce was *comparative* advantage. No country could gain an across-the-board trade supremacy, since one had to import in order to export, and vice versa. A foreign government that subsidized its industries in general would not help any particular one and would probably contribute to overall inefficiency. Or if it subsidized a particular industry, like steel, costs would be borne by other sectors of its economy, and benefits would accrue to consumers of its steel, importers included. For the United States, the choice was then a simple one: accept the foreign subsidy in the form of cheaper steel (which would harm US steel makers but help steel users), or offset it with a countervailing duty. In this case also, no comprehensive policy response was required.

But what if a nation could prepare the way for market success tomorrow by helping an industry today? Many critics correctly argued that trade theory rested on "static comparative advantage." Trade flowed according to current prices, reflecting current production costs. But the process by which producers achieved international competitiveness was a dynamic one, subject to influence by national policies.[21] Governments might, by targeting growth sectors, create comparative advantage: they could aid and protect industries that would one day become strong enough to conquer world markets. Japan had done so persistently and

---

20. Labor-Industry Coalition for International Trade, *International Trade, Industrial Policies, and the Future of American Industry* (Washington, DC: Labor-Industry Coalition for International Trade, 1983), iii, iv, 57–66.

21. Classical trade theory did focus on static comparative advantage, but it does not necessarily follow that a longer-term perspective undercuts the liberal trade case. Indeed, a central theme in Mancur Olson's analysis is the opposite: that the "gains from trade" are much larger than traditional models specify because of the pressure that competition generates for technological innovation and ongoing resource reallocation. See Olson, *The Rise and Decline of Nations* (New Haven, CT: Yale University Press, 1982).

successfully, argued scholars such as Ezra Vogel of Harvard and Chalmers Johnson of the University of California, Berkeley, creating what Johnson labeled the "developmental state."[22]

This raised the question of whether, for certain products in certain types of markets, industry-specific trade policy intervention might promote broader national interests, not just those of the specific workers and firms involved. The National Bureau of Economic Research (NBER) inaugurated a major project examining possible economic rationales for interventionist trade policies, export subsidies as well as import barriers, drawing upon oligopoly models of "imperfect" interfirm competition. In a world with a limited number of firms, some drawing support from home governments, the NBER analysts hypothesized, laissez-faire might not always be the best policy. In certain oligopolistic industries with increasing returns to scale, timely government intervention could enable American firms to gain a greater share of "supernormal profits," bringing gains to the nation greater than the cost of the subsidy provided.[23]

The conclusions of the NBER-sponsored analyses were tentative and cautious, recognizing the real-world difficulty of determining, in advance, when to intervene, in which industries, and through what instruments. Centers of political analysis like the Berkeley Roundtable on the Interna-

---

22. Ezra Vogel, *Japan as Number One: Lessons for Americans* (Cambridge, MA: Harvard University Press, 1979); Chalmers Johnson, *MITI and the Japanese Miracle: The Growth of Industrial Policy, 1925–1975* (Stanford, CA: Stanford University Press, 1982). On the critical side, Philip H. Trezise countered that such "models of Japan's postwar economic development are subject to so substantial a discount as to make them largely valueless as guides to understanding. . . . To suppose . . . that politicians and officials in league with businessmen were able to plan and guide Japan's explosive economic growth in detail is neither credible in the abstract nor (as will be seen) supported by the realities." See Trezise, "Politics, Government, and Economic Growth in Japan," in Hugh Patrick and Henry Rosovsky, eds., *Asia's New Giant: How the Japanese Economy Works* (Washington, DC: Brookings Institution, 1976), 753–811. Marcus Noland found that "while in some cases Japanese industrial policy may have successfully targeted industries, welfare-enhancing interventions have been the exception, not the rule." See Noland, "The Impact of Industrial Policy on Japan's Trade Specialization," *Review of Economics and Statistics* 75, no. 2 (May 1993): 241–48.

23. See Paul R. Krugman, ed., *Strategic Trade Policy and the New International Economics* (Cambridge, MA: MIT Press, 1986), especially the articles by advocates James A. Brander and Barbara J. Spencer and by critic Gene M. Grossman. For a comprehensive critique of this literature, see J. David Richardson, "The Political Economy of Strategic Trade Policy," *International Organization* 44, no. 1 (Winter 1990): 107–35.

Of course, oligopoly has multiple effects, and in another essay Richardson cited empirical work showing "that the gains from trade were *larger* under imperfect competition than they would have been with perfectly competitive markets" (emphasis added). The quote is a paraphrase by Anne O. Krueger in Robert Z. Lawrence and Charles L. Schultze, eds., *An American Trade Strategy: Options for the 1990s* (Washington, DC: Brookings Institution, 1990), 84n. The Richardson work is "Empirical Research on Trade Liberalization with Imperfect Competition: A Survey," *OECD Economic Studies*, no. 12 (Washington, DC: Organization for Economic Cooperation and Development, Spring 1989): 8–44.

tional Economy (BRIE) at the University of California, led by John Zysman and Stephen S. Cohen, were less hesitant in setting forth conceptual rationales for government intervention, which they viewed as essential to meet the Japanese challenge and guide the United States toward a competitive future industrial structure.[24] Meanwhile, at the Harvard Business School, Bruce R. Scott and George C. Lodge were making a case for activist government industrial policy.[25] And before the end of the Reagan administration, one of its battle-scarred trade negotiators, Clyde V. Prestowitz, Jr., had resigned and written a book entitled *Changing Places: How We Allowed Japan to Take the Lead*. In it he documented, relentlessly, his argument that the divided, disorganized, multipurpose US government was no match for centrally orchestrated Japanese industrial policies. Hence we were "losing the chips,"[26] and many other industries besides.

Prescriptions varied as to how Americans should respond to government-created comparative advantage. Indeed, even critics like Prestowitz were not immune from the tendency to follow sweeping critiques with proposals for marginal policy change. No one in this school called for protection per se; in fact, all warned that a simple defensive response would only make things worse for the United States. But most were inclined toward some form of selective intervention, although their purposes varied. One formulation was that of Robert B. Reich, who saw a need for the United States to move "beyond free trade." He argued that trade-related US policy should not be laissez-faire but proadjustment. The US goal should be one of "promoting the rapid transformation of all nations' industrial bases [especially that of the United States] toward higher-value production." Existing US trade policies had, in Reich's view, "just the opposite effect."[27]

The case for activist industrial policy rested on the conviction that the United States faced a deep and pervasive industrial competitiveness problem. As summarized by a trenchant skeptic, Charles L. Schultze, the cases of most proponents in the early 1980s were built on four premises: first, the United States had been "deindustrializing" and was suffering substantial losses (absolute or relative) in its manufacturing capacity; second, without assistance, US management and labor might not be capable of

---

24. Stephen S. Cohen and John Zysman, *Manufacturing Matters: The Myth of the Post-Industrial Economy* (New York: Basic Books for the Council on Foreign Relations, 1987).

25. See Bruce R. Scott and George C. Lodge, eds., *U.S. Competitiveness in the World Economy* (Boston: Harvard Business School Press, 1985).

26. This was the title of Prestowitz's second chapter, on the semiconductor industry. See Prestowitz, *Changing Places* (New York: Basic Books, 1988). For a comprehensive look at how Americans defined and waged the trade competition with Japan over this period, see John Kunkel, *America's Trade Policy Towards Japan: Demanding Results* (London and New York: Routledge, 2003).

27. Robert B. Reich, "Beyond Free Trade," *Foreign Affairs* 61, no. 4 (Spring 1983): 790.

making the transition from old heavy industries to new high-technology industries; third, the United States was losing its edge in world export markets, with a consequent threat to its global leadership position; and fourth, other countries, and Japan in particular, had been successful in pursuing industrial policies, "selecting potential winners in the technological race" and nurturing them through a range of policy devices.[28]

If these four premises were correct, the conclusion followed clearly: the United States needed an aggressive industrial policy to manage the transition to a new industrial era, to move resources from declining industries into growth industries, and to defend itself in a mercantilist world. Otherwise, this school suggested, the US economy might end up a sort of residual composed of those industries that were left after more purposive nations had chosen theirs.

Schultze found this case unpersuasive: the evolution of international trade in the 1970s did not, on balance, support any of the four premises of the "industrial policy" critique. In fact, the US balance of trade in manufactured goods improved markedly during this period.[29] In addition, advocates of activist, industry-specific policy intervention carried a political burden. Such policy was far easier to prescribe than to pursue. Was the United States capable of selective mercantilism? Could its political system tilt in favor of industries with future potential and allocate resources to them? Or would political pressure from those currently feeling trade pain inevitably channel public resources to the entrenched, embattled industrial "losers"? Alternatively, if economywide industrial policy were attempted along LICIT-recommended lines, would not this build up, within the US government, strong bureaucratic interests in the welfare of specific industrial sectors, interests that would impede economywide adjustment and slow down growth for the nation as a whole?[30]

Industrial policy proposals flourished particularly in 1981–82, when the US economy suffered a severe cyclical downturn. They withered in the years thereafter, as the economy recovered and domestic laissez-faire gained backing inside and outside the administration. But if "industrial policy" became a label for policy packagers to avoid, the same was not true of "critical technologies," or "high-tech industries."[31] These phrases evoked a response both from many in the business community worried

---

28. Charles L. Schultze, "Industrial Policy: A Solution in Search of a Problem," *California Management Review* 24, no. 4 (Summer 1983): 5–6.

29. See Robert Z. Lawrence, *Can America Compete?* (Washington, DC: Brookings Institution, 1984).

30. For a comprehensive argument linking the rise of "distributional coalitions" seeking maximum income for their members to slowdowns in national economic growth, see Olson, *The Rise and Decline of Nations*.

31. For an analysis by a "cautious activist," see Laura D'Andrea Tyson, *Who's Bashing Whom? Trade Conflicts in High-Technology Industries* (Washington, DC: Institute for International Economics, 1992).

about future economic competitiveness, and from many in the defense community who saw loss of technological leadership as a threat to military preparedness.[32] There was particular anxiety about dependence on Japanese suppliers, and lively debate over whether and how the United States should respond. Congress enacted the Exon-Florio amendment to the 1988 Trade Act authorizing the president to block foreign takeovers of US firms on national security grounds, and a prominent 1991 proposal—the Collins-Gephardt bill—aimed to broaden the Exon-Florio review process to encompass threats to US technology.[33]

As these examples illustrate, Capitol Hill was a ready market for such ideas. Especially receptive were those who would challenge existing centers of trade leadership. This was part of the broader flowering of "issue politics." With decentralization in the Congress and electoral entrepreneurship in individual districts, members sought press attention by espousing "new ideas" that differentiated them from their political rivals. Both the internationalization of the US economy and the new forms of (fair and unfair) foreign competition provided ample sources of such ideas, particularly among activist Democrats. And the ideas of Cordell Hull were no longer at the intellectual cutting edge.

And even as the industrial-policy school was losing its audience, the American industrial trade balance was turning enormously negative. The prime cause was another phenomenon that highlighted the limits of laissez-faire trade doctrine—the incredible, unanticipated surge of the dollar (see chapter 3). By early 1985, the massive international capital inflows that were needed to finance record US budget deficits and rising private borrowing had driven the dollar to roughly 40 percent above the level that would have brought balance to the US international current (trade and services) account. This meant that in competition with foreign producers, American firms faced the equivalent of a 40 percent tax on their exports and a 40 percent subsidy on competing imports.[34]

As the French economist Albert Bressand put it, the United States seemed afflicted with " 'good things' that do not go together," a free market currency regime that wreaked havoc on the free market in trade.[35] And, as C. Fred

---

32. See Defense Science Board, *Defense Semiconductor Dependency* (Washington, DC: Defense Science Board Task Force, Department of Defense, Office of the Under Secretary for Acquisition, February 1987).

33. See Edward M. Graham and Paul R. Krugman, *Foreign Direct Investment in the United States* (Washington, DC: Institute for International Economics, 2d ed., 1991), 121–28.

34. John Williamson, *The Exchange Rate System*, POLICY ANALYSES IN INTERNATIONAL ECONOMICS 5 (Washington, DC: Institute for International Economics, second edition, 1985); Stephen Marris, *Deficits and the Dollar: The World Economy at Risk*, POLICY ANALYSES IN INTERNATIONAL ECONOMICS 14 (Washington, DC: Institute for International Economics, second edition, 1987).

35. Albert Bressand, "Mastering the 'World Economy,' " *Foreign Affairs* 61, no. 4 (Spring 1983): 762.

Bergsten noted as early as 1981, the trade imbalance produced by a strong dollar was bound to generate enormous pressure for trade restrictions as it expanded the ranks of the "trade losers" in the American industrial economy.[36] At the urging of such international economic policy analysts, organizations like the Business Roundtable began to make the overvalued dollar (and the undervalued yen) one of their chief "trade" policy priorities.

As in the case of industrial malaise, a focus on the exchange rate did not yield a persuasive, broadly supported, general-interest alternative for US trade policy. On the contrary, its message was that the required measures lay outside the trade sphere—such as the Group of Five initiative of September 1985, which helped move the dollar down, and the continuing need to reduce the federal budget deficit. Explicators of macroeconomic causes and cures, in fact, performed a singular service to American trade politics in the mid-1980s, muting protectionist responses by exposing their irrelevance to the trade imbalance.[37] But then, after the dollar went down, the trade deficit continued to rise—for a year longer than most experts had expected.[38] A new skepticism emerged, built upon the seeming limits of exchange rate adjustment—especially vis-à-vis Japan—or on its costs in making US assets cheap to foreign investors.

In due course, the trade balance did improve, with manufactured products sharing disproportionately in the gains. Rust belt areas devastated by the 1981–82 recession were less affected by the recession of 1990–91. Still, US manufacturing employment remained below its spring 1979 record of 21.1 million workers. When it reached another prerecession peak a decade later, the total was just 19.6 million.

Still, years of misaligned exchange rates, together with intensified industrial competition, had spawned an intellectual challenge that put free market purists on the ideological defensive. Liberal values continued to be widely held, of course; no competing doctrine for trade policy won comparable acceptance. Still, these challenges muted the liberal-protectionist dichotomy that served as an enormous political advantage to trade expanders throughout the postwar period. Intellectually as well

---

36. C. Fred Bergsten, "The Costs of Reaganomics," *Foreign Policy*, no. 44 (Fall 1981): 24–36.

37. Thus one contemporary analysis of the 1988 trade legislation noted that "the economic sophistication of Congress" had "improved greatly." "Most members of Congress recognize that foreign protection is not the cause of the trade deficit." Raymond J. Ahearn and Alfred Reifman, "Trade Legislation in 1987: Congress Takes Charge," in Robert E. Baldwin and J. David Richardson, eds., *Issues in the Uruguay Round* (Cambridge, MA: National Bureau of Economic Research, 1988), 80.

38. The common prognosis, reflected in the first edition of this book, was that dollar decline beginning in 1985 would lead to decline in the annual trade deficit by 1987. In fact, this did not arrive until 1988.

as politically and procedurally, the trade policy game had become more open, and this added to the unpredictability of policy outcomes.[39]

New Patterns of Interest Group Politics

Finally, there were significant shifts from the pattern of trade politics that had predominated in the early postwar period. During that time, a modest number of industries typically sought protection, each more or less on its own. Executive and congressional leaders encouraged each to go it alone in order to avert logrolling of the Smoot-Hawley variety. They pointed the smaller industries toward the Tariff Commission (now the US International Trade Commission) and the quasi-judicial trade remedy procedures. Larger industries, mainly textiles, cut separate deals for themselves, part of which involved promises not to obstruct broader trade-liberalizing initiatives like the Kennedy and Tokyo Rounds. No important groups took across-the-board protectionist stances.

Nor was there much self-initiated interest group activism on the liberal trade side. National business and labor organizations were generally on call to endorse major new trade-expanding initiatives; yet once particular legislative battles were fought and won, the coalitions supporting them faded away. Nor were those who benefited specifically from open trade—importers, industrial consumers, and retail consumers—inclined to enter the political fray.[40]

The 1970s and 1980s brought four significant changes in this pattern. First and most important, the number and range of industries seeking governmental trade action increased. Substantial (if oft-temporary) protection was won not just by the textile-apparel coalition, but by other mature industries such as steel and automobiles. Nor was pressure on trade policy any longer limited to those who were clearly current trade losers: the low-technology sectors whose manufacturing processes could be widely replicated around the world. The old rule was that losers enter

---

39. For a historical analysis of intellectual challenges to free trade, see Douglas Irwin, *Against the Tide* (Princeton, NJ: Princeton University Press, 1996).

40. Those whose overall interests tilted toward open trade but who might at some point want protection for certain products were influenced by the long-established practice of "reciprocal noninterference," which induced them, in the words of E. E. Schattschneider, "to accept the incidental burdens" of others' protection without protest. See Schattschneider, *Politics, Pressures and the Tariff* (New York: Prentice-Hall, 1935), 284. Those actively involved in the import business felt disadvantaged in the political arena, since they could be charged with helping foreign interests take away American jobs. In both cases, abstention from politics therefore seemed the wisest course.

trade politics while winners stick to business. But beginning in the late 1970s, producers of high-technology products like semiconductors, telecommunications, and machine tools were pressing for governmental action.

The Semiconductor Industry Association (SIA) went to Capitol Hill with its concerns about Japanese competition. Executives of Corning, a leader in fiber optics, expressed concern that Japanese industrial targeting was making international trade a losing proposition for them. An important electronics firm, Motorola, began in 1982 to place a series of 20 full-page advertisements in the *Wall Street Journal* under the heading, "Meeting Japan's Challenge." And in early 1985, even David Packard, chairman of the board of the successful high-tech Hewlett-Packard Co. and cochair of a binational US-Japan Advisory Commission, suggested that the United States consider imposing temporary quotas to "decrease the growth of Japan's exports to the U.S."[41]

What moved Motorola and other firms in technology-intensive industries was a new mix of export-market interest and import-market anxiety. As a group, they had done very well in the international marketplace; as noted in chapter 3, they were disproportionately responsible for the explosion of US exports in the 1970s. But they had suffered trade losses also, particularly in 1982–86, and they worried about competing, as solitary private actors, against what they feared was a government-industry combine headquartered in Tokyo. They contrasted the inroads Japanese producers were making in American markets with their own problems in selling across the Pacific. Their call was seldom for out-and-out protection (although the machine-tool industry did win import limits in 1986 on national security grounds). Rather, they became advocates of what trade specialists call "sectoral reciprocity."[42] If, by hard negotiations, the US government could not persuade other nations—above all Japan—to open up their markets to US products and establish a level playing field for trade, then the United States should take protective action in return.[43]

By and large, trade-afflicted firms still pursued their campaigns separately, on behalf of their particular industry groupings, though (as noted in chapter 6) they did join in coalitions seeking revision of the general trade remedy laws. A textile-shoe alliance was formed in 1970—and again

---

41. Letter from Packard to Stephen R. Levy, chairman, International Committee, American Electronics Association (AEA), 5 March 1985, released by the AEA, Washington, DC.

42. For an academic defense of this position, see Stephen D. Krasner, *Asymmetries in Japanese-American Trade: The Case for Specific Reciprocity*, Policy Papers in International Affairs 32 (Berkeley: University of California, Institute of International Studies, 1987).

43. For a sophisticated comparative analysis of the extent to which high-technology industries embraced the new "strategic trade" gospel, see Helen V. Milner and David B. Yoffie, "Between Free Trade and Protectionism: Strategic Trade Policy and a Theory of Corporate Trade Demands," *International Organization* 43, no. 2 (Spring 1989): 239–72.

in 1985—to win statutory import quotas, but it faded as soon as the textile firms won new protection by traditional (executive-negotiated) means. At the same time, there did emerge in the 1970s and 1980s a major national, cross-industry organization—a coalition, more accurately—that took a general trade-restrictive stance. That was, of course, organized labor, whose shift from early postwar trade liberalism was the second major development in interest group politics.

In its direct impact on trade legislation, labor's new protectionism was limited. After two decades, it had virtually nothing in statute to show for its major trade stands: for the Burke-Hartke quota bill of 1971, against the Nixon-Ford trade bill in 1973–74, for domestic-content legislation for autos in 1981–84, and against extension of trade preferences to advanced developing countries in 1974 and 1984. An older labor priority, trade adjustment assistance for workers, was inaugurated in 1962 and expanded in 1974, but was gutted in 1981. Steel unions were able to obtain in the trade bill of 1984 a provision requiring firms to reinvest net cash flow in steel facilities and worker training. But as discussed in chapter 4, labor failed to exploit the vulnerability of that bill to extract concessions on any of a number of its long-standing concerns. In 1988, labor did better. It won inclusion of "worker rights" as the fourteenth of sixteen "principal trade negotiating objections" for the Uruguay Round. And unions scored a major symbolic victory in the legislative endgame of 1988: first, attaching to the omnibus legislation a requirement that workers be prenotified of plant closings; and then, after the president vetoed the bill because of this measure, forcing Reagan to swallow a separate bill with the identical requirement. Labor was, moreover, fast off the mark in 1991 in mobilizing opposition to granting fast-track authority for a free trade agreement with Mexico. But labor ended up losing this one, as it had more often than not on major trade issues.[44]

What labor did achieve was indirect: It neutralized important potential supporters of liberal trade. The hearts and minds of many Democrats who voted for the domestic-content bills were elsewhere, but House members who were unwilling to buck the United Auto Workers (UAW) on a proposal that had so little other support were not going to be spear carriers for trade liberalization more generally. Instead, they would either look for issues on which they could take a trade-restrictive stance or confine their activism to other policy areas. Similarly, organizations like the Consumer Federation of America (CFA), an umbrella group that counted the UAW among its members, found the union "calling in some old debts" to extract an endorsement of domestic content. "On the surface, this might appear to go against consumer interests" in lower prices and in variety

---

44. For a detailed analysis of labor's impact on trade issues through 1995, see I. M. Destler, "Trade Politics and Labor Issues, 1953–1995," in Susan M. Collins, ed., *Imports, Exports, and the American Worker* (Washington, DC: Brookings Institution, 1998), 389–422.

and quality of products, admitted the CFA's executive director to the *Wall Street Journal*. But "we appreciate all the work for consumer issues that the UAW has done over the years."[45]

More generally, consumers did not fulfill the hopes of liberal traders who saw them as a natural domestic constituency for international openness. Consumers Union did file a suit that contributed to temporary abandonment of US-EC-Japanese steel export restraint in the early 1970s. But the more politically activist consumer advocates like Ralph Nader did not play, lest labor be offended. (A symptom of this difficulty is the fact that Consumers for World Trade, a dedicated antiprotectionist lobbying group in Washington, had a board of directors that was impressive in its international economics and business expertise but limited in its connections to the domestic US consumer movement.)

There did emerge, however, an activist group on the trade-expanding side: the Emergency Committee for American Trade (ECAT), created in 1967. Unlike labor, this organization representing major multinational firms kept a relatively low profile but cultivated congressional power centers skillfully, supplying needed analysis and argumentation and staying alert to the timing of trade action (as labor often did not). Also active were general-purpose industry organizations like the Business Roundtable, the Chamber of Commerce, and the National Association of Manufacturers. In the mid-1980s, such general business groups became subject to cross-pressures within their memberships as a result of increased US trade exposure and the record trade deficit.[46] But they recovered some of their unity and energy in the final stages of the omnibus legislation battle in 1988, and put forward a strong, unified effort to win extension of fast-track authority in 1991.

The third new development in interest group politics was the emergence of "special interests" who benefited from exports or imports and were driven, by the prospect of economic losses, to do direct battle against seekers of protection.[47]

One example came in mid-1983. The Reagan administration, unable to win Chinese adherence to stringent textile restraints, imposed quotas unilaterally. The government in Beijing, urged on by Washington-based liberal trade advocates, retaliated by withholding purchases of American grain. This brought farm organizations—and Senate Finance Committee Chairman Robert J. Dole (R-KS)—into the fray in a campaign to soften the administration's stance.

---

45. *Wall Street Journal*, 3 September 1982.

46. See I. M. Destler and John S. Odell with Kimberly Ann Elliott, *Anti-Protection: Changing Forces in United States Trade Politics*, POLICY ANALYSES IN INTERNATIONAL ECONOMICS 21 (Washington, DC: Institute for International Economics, 1987), chapter 6.

47. Ibid.

In mid-1984, again under industry pressure, the administration moved to tighten enforcement of country-of-origin rules under the textile quota regime. Importers and retailers charged that this would "steal Christmas" by making them unable to fill their orders for the holiday season. The Retail Trade Action Coalition (RTAC), representing major chain stores and trade associations, raised such a howl that the administration first deferred implementation of the new rules and then adjusted them to ease their impact.

In that same summer, after the USITC found that imports had injured the US copper industry, fabricators of wire and other copper products protested that this would simply lead to increased import competition for them without giving the copper producers more than temporary relief. They made it clear to the White House, facing a decision in the midst of the election campaign, that they had more workers than did the copper mines, and that their workers were more strategically placed insofar as electoral college votes were concerned. Their argument was a factor in the president's decision not to grant protection to the copper producers. A year later, shoe retailers mobilized against a USITC recommendation for footwear import quotas, getting 19 Republican senators to sign a letter in opposition. Reagan said no to shoe protection as well.

The new activism of apparel retailers was visible in resistance to textile quota bills of 1985, 1988, and 1990. Users of steel worked against the renewal of negotiated quotas in 1989 and may have influenced President Bush's commitment to phase out protection in two and a half years. And when the Semiconductor Industry Association sought renewal, in 1991, of the trade agreement with Japan, it had to deal with chip users burned by the sharp price rises that the agreement had precipitated in 1987 and 1988.[48] They insisted that the renewal pact include softer constraints on pricing in the US market. SIA acceded, since it needed the users' backing in order to persuade the lukewarm Bush administration to back a renewal.

Such antiprotectionist groups often worked in parallel with foreign interests: auto retailers worked with Japan-based companies; on copper, the National Electrical Manufacturers Association played an up-front role, with the government of Chile (the principal copper exporter) very active in the background. And while Toshiba spent millions to block a statutory embargo on its products—an initiative provoked when a Toshiba subsidiary sold sensitive equipment to the Soviet Union—the decisive pressure came, by several accounts, from US firms that feared the disruptive costs of being cut off from Toshiba inputs.[49] Taken together, the activity of

---

48. Laura D'Andrea Tyson, *Who's Bashing Whom?*, chapter 4.

49. For a sweeping and thoroughly unconvincing picture of omnipresent, ever-winning lobbyists for Japanese interests, see Pat Choate, *Agents of Influence: How Japan's Lobbyists in the United States Manipulate America's Political and Economic System* (New York: Alfred A. Knopf, 1990).

domestic and foreign antiprotection interests provided a welcome—if hardly equal—balance to the activity of protection seekers. It communicated one important political point. As firms seeking trade relief escalated their demands, they could no longer be assured that adversely affected business interests would stay on the sidelines. Politicians were likely to feel pressure from more than one direction.

And if some saw the foreign element in this lobbying as nefarious, others viewed it as a normal consequence of internationalization. In a world of multinational firms, Kenichi Ohmae preached the pervasiveness of interdependence,[50] and Robert Reich asked the gut question, "Who Is Us?"[51] If, in certain industries, it was the foreign-owned firms that were producing high-value-added products on American soil, should not US policy be supporting them rather than the Asia-based production of American-owned electronics firms?

The fourth interesting development in interest group politics was the apparent erosion in the strength and political astuteness of the oldest supporters of protection. The steel industry was one apparent case. More significant, at least potentially, was the textile-apparel coalition.

Throughout the postwar era, textile industry leaders had dealt effectively with both branches of government. They would win action commitments from presidential candidates of both political parties: John F. Kennedy in 1960, Richard M. Nixon and Hubert H. Humphrey in 1968, Ronald Reagan in 1980. They would show, on Capitol Hill, a capacity to block or threaten trade-liberalizing legislation—from the Eisenhower administration in the late 1950s to the Carter administration in the late 1970s. They seemed to understand that Congress would not, in the end, enact a bill restricting textile imports: That was outside the rules of the postwar policy game. But by working both ends of Pennsylvania Avenue, the textile executives repeatedly won new increments in *negotiated* textile protection.

In the mid-1980s, the industry began by employing a similar strategy. Imports were now a really serious problem: after slow growth in the 1960s and 1970s, the import-consumption ratio for textiles and apparel rose from 12.1 percent in 1980 to 22 percent in 1986, and from 18.4 percent to 31.1 percent for apparel alone.[52] In response, the industry put forward a bill, proposed by Ed Jenkins (D-GA), whose formal aim was to impose statutory quotas on textile imports but whose effect was to toughen the US position in negotiations for renewal of the Multi-Fiber Arrangement (MFA). After favorable House and Senate action and the expected Reagan

50. Kenichi Ohmae, *Triad Power: The Coming Shape of Global Competition* (New York: Free Press, 1985).

51. This was the title of a widely read article in the January–February 1990 *Harvard Business Review*, 53–64.

52. William R. Cline, *The Future of World Trade in Textiles and Apparel* (Washington, DC: Institute for International Economics, revised edition, 1990), 49.

veto in December 1985, the industry's House backers developed a new twist. Rather than following the standard practice of going for an override vote as soon as possible after the bill was returned, they arranged for such a vote to be scheduled eight months later, when the MFA talks were to be concluded. This kept the heat on negotiators from the Office of the US Trade Representative (USTR) and achieved at least a marginal stiffening of the US position.

But in the years thereafter the industry overreached, abandoning its hitherto winning formula. Intoxicated perhaps by coming so close to enacting a quota bill—the House override vote in 1986 was eight votes shy of the two-thirds required—textile executives overrode the cautions of their Washington representatives and made enactment of stiff quota legislation their overarching political goal. Previously they might have held an omnibus bill hostage; now they allowed the legislation of 1987–88 to move forward, in exchange for the promise of smooth procedural sailing for their separate bill.[53] Both the House Ways and Means and Senate Finance committees kept the promise, reporting the industry bill for floor action without recommendation, but the Senate did not pass it until September 1988. Reagan promptly vetoed it, and the House override failed by 11 votes. In 1990, the ritual was repeated, with George Bush casting the veto this time and the industry losing the override by 10 votes.

Neither vote yielded anything discernible for the industry, though both allowed strong majorities in both chambers to go on record for textile protection, secure in the expectation that the bill would fail. In the meantime, textile representatives reportedly alienated USTR Carla Hills with both the style and substance of their uncompromising position on the Uruguay Round textile talks. This increased the risk of a negotiated phaseout of the MFA, which developing countries were demanding.

At a minimum, the industry seemed guilty of serious tactical miscalculation. Its failure also reinforced a growing feeling that its trade policy power had peaked, an impression reinforced by evidence of strains in the coalition between cloth and apparel makers.[54] The industry remained one, of course, that no trade policy leader could ignore. But in contrast to previous decades, the industry was now presenting to executive and congressional leaders both the incentive and the opportunity to confront and beat it politically, rather than join in negotiating trade-restrictive compromises.

---

53. In the House they had no choice: Speaker Jim Wright (D-TX) insisted on keeping product-specific measures out of the omnibus trade bill. In the Senate, however, industry leaders could have exploited the chamber's more open rules by seeking to attach their bill as a rider to the omnibus legislation.

54. Beginning in the 1990s, US textile makers separated from their apparel brethren (many of whom had become major importers) and encouraged trade agreements whereby apparel made abroad from US fiber and cloth could enter the American market tariff- and quota-free. See chapters 8 and 9.

Conclusions

In the 1970s and 1980s, trade politics became more partisan. The elite became less committed to liberal trade. Intellectual challenges to open-market policies grew. Patterns of trade politics became more complex. All these changes weakened the 1934 system for diverting and managing trade policy pressures, and many increased the political weight of those backing trade restrictions.

The greatest risk, at least potentially, was that posed by the threat of new interparty competition on trade policy. If the Democrats were in fact to become an out-and-out protectionist party, this would risk for trade policy the fate that befell policy toward the Soviet Union and arms control in the late 1970s and early 1980s. A new president would represent not continuity but drastic change. And this would remove the strongest anchor of the old trade management system—the liberal-leaning executive branch.

Most of the other changes pointed not toward protectionism in the traditional sense, but toward greater negotiating activism, more confrontation with trading partners, stronger emphasis on unfair-trade statutes, and increased readiness to brandish the threat of protection at home to pry open markets abroad. Super 301 was a natural response to these pressures.

At a minimum, over the 1970s and 1980s, these changes in the national arena combined with changes in the congressional, executive, and regulatory domains to make trade politics a much more open, unpredictable game. Yet what followed in the early 1990s was not policy stalemate, but unprecedented new trade liberalization.

8

Triumph! NAFTA and the WTO

The early 1990s were big years for American trade policy. Two landmark agreements were completed and then implemented by Congress. One of them—the North American Free Trade Agreement (NAFTA)—set off the most prominent and contentious domestic debate on trade since the Smoot-Hawley Tariff Act of 1930. The second—the Uruguay Round under the General Agreement on Tariffs and Trade (GATT)—broke new ground in three major ways: the comprehensiveness of its coverage; the number of countries signing onto its main obligations; and the creation, at long last, of a World Trade Organization (WTO) with strengthened dispute settlement procedures.

The same years featured other important trade action. There were contentious talks with China: over human rights improvements as a condition for extending most favored nation (MFN) status and over Chinese violations of international norms of intellectual property. The Clinton administration, which entered office in 1993, also took an aggressive new tack on economic issues with Japan, generating new conflict and modest results. However, it balanced this bilateral aggressiveness with an active consensus-building role in the Asia Pacific Economic Cooperation (APEC) forum, whose 18 members committed themselves to achieving free trade by the second decade of the 21st century. Western Hemisphere nations followed by establishing 2005 as their target date for completing a NAFTA-type arrangement among themselves.

The evolution of trade policy was not entirely in the liberal direction. Antidumping laws, for example, survived a major international reform effort without significant change in their net impact. But taken as a whole, the period was one of major policy and political victories for advocates of trade expansion. Protectionists were unusually vocal and visible, but they ended up losers.

Back from the Precipice

Before its triumphs of the early 1990s, of course, US trade policy had to get through the 1980s. Fortunately, in the middle of that decade, even as the trade politics steamroller seemed to gather speed, the economics were changing direction. The dollar peaked in late February 1985, and dollar depreciation became the declared objective of the advanced industrial countries in the Plaza Agreement the following September. By the last quarter of 1986, the *constant-dollar* US trade deficit (reflecting all-important volumes of goods) began to decline. A year later, the *nominal* deficit followed. American exports surged—doubling between 1986 and 1992. Not until 1991 would the total merchandise deficit fall below the magic number of $100 billion, to $74.1 billion, but the ratio of imports to exports dropped over this period from 1.65 in 1986 to 1.18 in 1991.

During 1980–85, the trend had been quite the opposite. The trade deficit shot up from $26 billion to $122 billion, dwarfing the previous peak deficits of $6.5 billion in 1972 and $34 billion in 1978. Some of this reflected inflation and increased trade volume, but what was alarming was that the US imbalance was proportionately greater with each cycle. US merchandise imports were 113 percent of exports in 1972, 124 percent in 1978, and 157 percent in 1985.[1]

Moreover, these record current-dollar trade imbalances understated the real changes in product flows, and hence the impact of trade on US producers, because the super-strong currency depressed the dollar prices of imports. Measured on a price-deflated basis, total merchandise imports rose from 18.9 percent to 25.8 percent of US goods production between 1980 and 1986. And between 1980 and 1984, exports plunged as a share of goods production from 18 percent to 14.8 percent,[2] a drop nearly as great as that precipitated 50 years earlier by the Great Depression and the Smoot-Hawley Act.[3]

---

1. Imports would reach 182 percent of exports in 2004.

2. These percentages are based on production and trade in 1982 dollars, as reported by the Bureau of Economic Analysis, Department of Commerce. See *Economic Report of the President*, February 1991, tables B-7 and B-21. The careful reader may notice that these figures differ from those in the first edition, which were calculated using the 1972 dollar data then available. The pattern between 1970 and 1980, by contrast, was of a significant increase in the proportion of both imports and exports: the former rose from 14.7 percent to 18.9 percent of US goods production, and the latter surged from 11.7 percent to 18 percent. This growth was part of an enormous expansion in the volume of trade worldwide.

3. Between 1929 and 1933, price-deflated merchandise exports dropped from roughly 9.6 percent to 7.6 percent, or by 21 percent, as a share of US goods production. Between 1980 and

Thus, American producer interests that normally had the strongest stakes in trade expansion found themselves at a serious disadvantage in overseas markets, even as foreign products surged into US markets. Consequently, even as many more industries hurt by imports sought trade protection, the political counterweight weakened as exporters lost market share and grew demoralized.

And trade restrictions grew, particularly in the form of "special deals" for "special cases," arranged by the executive branch. Automobiles, the largest and long the proudest of US manufacturing industries, sought and won voluntary export restraints (VERs) enforced by Japan in 1981. Sugar import quotas were reimposed in 1982. Carbon steel restraints were negotiated with the European Community in 1982 and with other major exporters two years later. Meanwhile, producers of motorcycles, specialty steel, and wood shingles gained temporary protection through escape clause proceedings, machine-tool makers won a presidential import relief decision on national security grounds, and the textile industry won several tightenings of quota restrictions.

Taken together, these cases meant a substantial expansion of the proportion of the US market governed by "managed trade."[4] It seemed to vindicate the conclusion of many contemporary observers that, in the words of a 1985 *New York Times* editorial, "industry by industry, the battle to maintain open markets is being lost."[5] But quantitative estimates showing substantially increased overall US protection rested overwhelmingly on the automobile restraints. And while these remained technically in

---

1984 they dropped by 18 percent. Percentages are computed from data in 1982 dollars. See *Economic Report of the President*, February 1991, tables B-7 and B-21.

4. Bela and Carol Balassa found just 6.2 percent of US manufactured imports subject to visible quantitative restrictions in 1980; in 1981–83, an additional 6.52 percent of US imports came under such restraints. Bela and Carol Balassa, "Industrial Protection in the Developed Countries," *World Economy* (June 1984): 187. For the product breakdown, see their "Levels of Protection on Manufactured Goods: The U.S., EC, Canada, Japan," 1984, processed.

Gary Clyde Hufbauer and his colleagues calculated that "US imports covered by special protection," including high tariffs as well as quantitative restraints, rose from 12 percent of total imports in 1980 to 21 percent in 1984. Gary Clyde Hufbauer, Diane T. Berliner, and Kimberly Ann Elliott, *Trade Protection in the United States: 31 Case Studies* (Washington, DC: Institute for International Economics, 1986), 21.

5. "Even Out the Free Trade Pain," *New York Times*, 14 January 1985. Even then, of course, the increased imposition of legal impediments to imports represented in part a rear-guard, defensive reaction to the ongoing internationalization of the US economy. In this sense, it was perhaps a testimony to the success of liberal policies rather than a harbinger of their failure. A related interpretation is that of Charles Lipson, who asked in 1982 why "world trade has continued to grow while trade restraints have been tightened." He concluded that the new barriers were in mature, basic industries, while trade expansion had come mainly in growth sectors where industries have differentiated products and high R&D expenditure. See Lipson, "The Transformation of Trade: The Sources and Effects of Regime Change," *International Organization* 36, no. 2 (Spring 1982): 417–55.

force into the early 1990s, the quotas were enlarged by 24 percent in 1985, and by the end of the 1980s they had lost their bite.

Restraints on textiles retained *their* bite, of course, notwithstanding the failure of the industry to win statutory protection. And the number of products subject to countervailing or antidumping duties rose 42 percent between mid-1983 and the end of 1990. There was also, as discussed in chapters 5 and 7, a new precedent for managed trade in semiconductors under the US-Japan agreement reached in 1986 and renewed in 1991. In summary, however, the most reasonable conclusion is that American trade protection increased sharply in the early 1980s but receded somewhat thereafter. The Reagan administration, which had granted much import relief in its first term, gave surprisingly little in its second.

A major reason was that, by late 1986 the trade numbers had begun to improve: The constant-dollar ratio of exports to goods production rebounded to 15.2 percent in 1986, 19.4 percent in 1988, and 23.2 percent in 1990.[6] And as the trade balance improved, the political balance did likewise. American exporters reentered the political fray to support liberalization and fight proposed laws that might impede open trade. Their boom was beginning, and they wanted it to continue.

Even at the peak of their activism, congressional leaders were reluctant to reclaim direct, product-specific authority over trade policy. They failed to override a presidential veto of textile quotas in 1986, as well as in 1988 and in 1990. They did initiate, and push to fruition, the Omnibus Trade and Competitiveness Act of 1988, the first major trade bill *not* originating with the executive since the days before Smoot-Hawley. But Congress excluded product-specific measures from that law, and watered down measures aimed at further tilting the trade remedy laws. The act's main theme was not protectionism on imports but aggressiveness on exports. And though the prime vehicle of this approach, Section 301, has been widely and bitterly denounced abroad, it appears to have had a net liberalizing effect on world trade, and to have been tolerated by America's trading partners.[7]

The latter 1980s also saw a reassertion of executive branch trade leadership. This began on 23 September 1985, the day after the Plaza Agreement, with President Ronald Reagan's White House speech calling for "fair trade" and announcing that the administration would, for the first time, initiate unfair-trade cases against foreign firms and governments. And if, under the circumstances, US Trade Representative (USTR) Clayton Yeutter was inevitably in a defensive posture, his successor—Carla Hills—was

---

6. The parallel imports/production ratio also kept rising, albeit at a slower pace, from 25.8 percent in 1986 to 28.2 percent in 1990.

7. Thomas O. Bayard and Kimberly Ann Elliott, *Reciprocity and Retaliation in U.S. Trade Policy* (Washington, DC: Institute for International Economics, 1994).

able to take the offensive. Turning statutory mandates into opportunities, she pressed specific trade cases with Japan and other nations, even as she softened the hard edges of "Super 301." Consulting assiduously with Congress in general, and the trade committees in particular, she could declare the Uruguay Round her "top trade liberalization priority" and subsequently win plaudits on Capitol Hill for her willingness to walk away from the negotiating table when the requisite deal did not materialize.

Hills's enhanced credibility helped make possible the extension of fast-track authority in the spring of 1991, as Congress renewed one more time its delegation of negotiating power. Thus was continued the notable, inter-branch political innovation of the 1970s, which made it possible for the United States to negotiate and implement nontariff trade agreements. Extension of fast-track authority renewed the possibility of constructive US leadership in the Uruguay Round, just as the procedure had made possible the completion of the Tokyo Round. The vote of confidence was all the more impressive given the stalemate at Geneva and the new issues raised by the proposal by President Bush and Mexican President Carlos Salinas de Gortari for what became the North American Free Trade Agreement (NAFTA).

So the system held. Congress pressed its priorities—its predisposition toward toughness—but refrained from reclaiming, directly, the primary trade power granted by the Constitution.[8] Protrade interests rose to counter the forces for restriction. The USTR, armed with new statutory powers, had once again vindicated its anomalous, but critical, brokering role. Just as in the 1970s it had secured legislative authority for the Tokyo Round and brought that round to completion, so it had in the 1980s resisted trade protection, launched the Uruguay Round, turned congressionally forced unilateralism to domestic and international advantage, and won continued delegation of congressional trade authority.

The USTR entered the 1990s with a continuing—and in some ways strengthened—central role. As set forth in chapter 5, Hills was unable to complete the Uruguay Round talks before President George H. W. Bush's term expired. But she did complete NAFTA, and this presented the first major trade-political challenge to Bush's successor, William Jefferson Clinton.

From Candidate to President

Republicans were overwhelmingly positive about the NAFTA negotiations; Clinton's party was divided but leaning against, as reflected in

---

8. For an extended discussion of why such restraint may serve legislators' political interests, see I. M. Destler, "Constituencies, Congress, and US Trade Policy," in Alan V. Deardorff and Robert M. Stern, *Constituent Interests and U.S. Trade Policies* (Ann Arbor: University of Michigan Press, 1998), 93–108.

House Democrats' 170–91 vote against fast-track renewal in May 1991. Thus, once agreement was reached, Bush pushed candidate Bill Clinton to take a stand one way or the other (and thereby alienate part of his party). In October 1992, Clinton responded with a major speech endorsing NAFTA, rejecting the idea of renegotiating the text but declaring it insufficient in dealing with three issues: the environment, worker standards, and the threat of sudden import surges. He called for negotiation of side agreements for each of these three. Through this politically adroit response, which gave something to both sides, Clinton solved his campaign problem. But the cost would prove dear once he entered office, for the speech encouraged NAFTA opponents to believe that he might reconsider his support, since he could always declare that satisfactory side agreements were proving unattainable.

In any case, Clinton entered office with two major pieces of unfinished trade business: to implement NAFTA, assuming suitable agreements could be reached on labor and the environment, and to complete the Uruguay Round. He had not, in his campaign, given special attention to trade policy, but he had given top billing to the economy, hammering away at the weak recovery from the Bush recession, and to the longer-term problem of stagnation in middle-class incomes. He had signaled, moreover, that he intended to elevate the weight given to economic interests in US international relationships.

Charged with the task of bringing NAFTA and GATT to fruition was Clinton's national campaign chairman (and Democratic party activist) Mickey Kantor. Kantor was smart, experienced as a bargainer in his legal and political careers, and a tabula rasa on trade. In choosing such a person for US trade representative, Clinton was emulating his three predecessors. None of their initial designees—Robert Strauss, William Brock, and Carla Hills—had been identified with trade policy before being chosen for the post. And in so acting, Clinton passed over trade policy veterans clearly associated with the free trade and protectionist camps. Both continuity and trade expertise, however, were provided by the designation of Rufus Yerxa as deputy USTR with prime Washington responsibility for the Uruguay Round. Yerxa had served as the Geneva deputy during the Bush administration and prior to that as senior staff aide to the House Ways and Means Committee.

In its initial months, the Clinton administration sent off mixed signals, both substantive and organizational. The president gave a free trade speech in February but appeared to be supporting in March a steep rise in tariffs on minivans[9] and became identified—beginning in April—with a

---

9. Technically, the question was whether minivans should be classified for tariff purposes as passenger cars or light trucks. Established practice was to treat them as cars, since they had, in practice, replaced station wagons in the US market. This meant a tariff of 2.5 percent. If

"managed trade" stance in negotiations with Japan. He gave Kantor the principal mandate for trade policy implementation but created a National Economic Council (NEC), parallel to the National Security Council (NSC), to raise the priority to overall economic policy, international as well as domestic. The NEC's trade role was distinct from USTR's in theory—coordination and oversight, not negotiations—but it overlapped in practice. Clinton appointed a "cautious trade activist," Laura Tyson, as chair of his Council of Economic Advisers (CEA), a move widely interpreted as a break with the normal practice of placing a vintage free trader in that position.[10] He did seek, and win, legislation extending to 15 December 1993 the deadline for concluding the Uruguay Round.[11] But on NAFTA there was mostly silence, as Kantor moved to negotiate the labor and environment side agreements.

The NAFTA Debate: Critics Rush to Fill the Vacuum

This silence made some tactical sense. If the president was to deliver on his campaign promise, he needed to withhold final endorsement of NAFTA until the side agreements were completed and he could declare the overall package improved and worthy of his endorsement. Moreover, the president was centering his attention on his budget and tax package, a serious (and politically courageous) attack on the federal deficit. Winning its enactment (in modified form) took until early August, and the margins were razor-thin: 218-216 in the House and 51-50 (with Vice President Albert Gore's tiebreaker) in the Senate.

But the president not only withheld the final go-ahead on NAFTA, he allowed White House aides to fight one another more or less publicly over it through the spring and into the summer. Nor did the White House press congressional Democrats to remain neutral until the side agreements

---

reclassified as trucks, they would be subject to the 25 percent duty established in the 1960s in retaliation for new European Community trade restrictions. In the 1990s, of course, this tariff bore principally on Japanese light trucks, and Japan was the principal source of imported minivans as well. The import share of the minivan market was modest, however. In the end, the administration did *not* take this step, which would certainly have been challenged as a violation of US commitments in prior trade negotiations.

10. The quotation is from the title of chapter 1 of her book, *Who's Bashing Whom?* (Washington, DC: Institute for International Economics, 1992), published just before her designation as CEA chair. In fact, Tyson generally supported liberal trade—spiced with some aggressive export bargaining—and she proved a "free trade" stalwart within the Clinton administration.

11. Technically, the deadline was 16 April 1994, but the president had to notify Congress of his intent to enter the agreement no later than 15 December, and this notification had to contain details on the expected substance of the agreement. Advisory committee reports were due 30 days thereafter. If these target dates were not met, the fast-track procedures would not apply to the Uruguay Round implementing legislation.

were negotiated.[12] All this had the effect of fueling doubts as to whether Clinton would *really* support NAFTA in the end, much less make the all-out push that congressional approval would require. These doubts extended to NAFTA supporters inside the administration: Secretary of the Treasury Lloyd Bentsen, by Bob Woodward's account, "felt that the odds were that Clinton would abandon NAFTA because the labor groups in the party opposed it,"[13] and Mickey Kantor reportedly offered as late as midsummer to "blow up" the negotiations over the side agreements if the president so wished.[14] With the administration divided and ineffective for a full half year, NAFTA opponents had a field day. They won the ear of the public and votes on Capitol Hill.

Most visible among these opponents was Ross Perot. In his self-financed independent campaign for president in 1992, Perot had attacked NAFTA (though he gave much more prominence to the fiscal deficit). But in 1993, he made NAFTA his central issue—with frequent speeches, with a widely circulated book entitled *Save Your Job, Save Our Country: Why NAFTA Must be Stopped—Now!* He wrote (and spoke) "of a giant sucking sound": NAFTA would mean "the loss of millions of jobs" pulled southward by low Mexican wages, with no less than one-third of US manufacturing jobs (6 million out of 18 million) "at risk."[15]

These arguments had real resonance in a nation where middle-class incomes had been stagnant for 20 years and whose industrial heartland had faced fierce foreign competition. They established "jobs" indelibly as the central NAFTA issue, with the public disposed to see the agreement as a job loser.[16] And if Perot supplied the most visible opposition, organized

---

12. Carter administration officials had done this on the Panama Canal treaties in 1977, persuading a number of senators not to cosponsor an opposition resolution but hold off until negotiations were completed. Pro-NAFTA Congressman Robert Matsui (D-CA) had asked that at least the freshmen be brought to the White House so the president could suggest to them that they remain neutral, but this proposal fell victim to the internal White House fight.

13. *The Agenda: Inside the Clinton White House* (New York: Simon and Schuster, 1994), 317–18.

14. Elizabeth Drew, *On the Edge: The Clinton Presidency* (New York: Simon and Schuster, 1994), 288–89. Kantor argued at the same time, however, "that if Clinton fought for congressional approval of the treaty and won despite the opposition of labor and some of the House leadership, it would be a big win and a big plus for him. He would have stood up to the unions and fought a bipartisan fight . . . " (289).

15. Ross Perot (with Pat Choate), *Save Your Job, Save Our Country: Why NAFTA Must Be Stopped—Now!* (New York: Hyperion [for United We Stand America], 1993), especially 41–57.

16. A Yankelovich poll published in *Time* on 7 June asked, "Do you agree with Clinton's view that the free trade agreement will create US jobs, or with Perot's view that it will cost US jobs?" Twenty-five percent sided with Clinton, 63 percent with Perot! (Some polls conducted in the fall showed less lopsided results.)

labor provided the muscle. With membership declining and wages being squeezed, its rank-and-file members saw competition from low-wage Mexican workers as a serious threat. So the AFL-CIO and its member unions went to their many Democratic friends in Congress, making it clear that labor considered NAFTA to be *the* test of fidelity to the workers' cause. Their hope, of course, was to confront the president with such overwhelming opposition within his own party that he would decide not to press ahead. Many members signed up—enough so that Clinton's budget director, former Congressman Leon Panetta, declared NAFTA "dead in the water" that spring.

Not only was labor aroused; environmental groups were upset as well. They had at least three concerns. First, they saw trade as spurring industrial development, which produced environmental degradation—unless it was carefully regulated. Terrible conditions on the US-Mexico border made this more than a theoretical concern. Second, they saw lower developing-country environmental standards as an incentive for industries to leave the United States, thus putting pressure on the United States to ease its standards in order to prevent the flight of US manufacturing. Last but not least, in some circumstances environmentalists wished to employ trade sanctions in support of environmental goals: The Marine Mammal Protection Act of 1972, for example, provided that tuna harvested by foreign fleets be barred from the United States if the methods used killed too large a number of dolphins. When this resulted in blocking imports of tuna from Mexico, the Mexicans appealed to the GATT. USTR lawyers defended the US position in Geneva, but a GATT panel ruled in the Mexicans' favor. Environmentalists hit the roof.

It was assumed throughout that the main NAFTA battle would be in the House, just as had been the case with fast-track extension in 1991. And the Democratic leadership was divided: Speaker Tom Foley (D-WA) was supportive, but Majority Leader Dick Gephardt (D-MO) was leaning against, and the number three Democrat, David Bonior (D-MI), was leading the opposition. To lead the pro-NAFTA forces, the White House initially looked to Bill Richardson (D-NM), a Hispanic-American (surname notwithstanding) who would later serve as Clinton's UN Ambassador and Secretary of Energy. But Ways and Means Chairman Dan Rostenkowski demurred. He felt he and his committee should be calling the shots, and he insisted on a senior Ways and Means colleague, Robert Matsui (D-CA), a focused, effective legislator (who happened to be a Japanese-American). The presumption was that NAFTA would need overwhelming Republican support. But unless Democrats could deliver a substantial number of their own, it was not clear that Minority Whip Newt Gingrich (R-GA) would play ball. And Gingrich was *the* rising force on the Republican side of the aisle.

Clinton Recovers, and Wins Big

In August, the labor and environmental side agreements were completed. Clinton approved them, had more than one "last" meeting among his advisers, and came down strongly, at last, in NAFTA's favor.[17] The side agreements did nothing to soften labor opposition, but the results were much better on the environment: NAFTA now won support from most of the mainstream environmental organizations.[18] Environmental issues, very prominent during the NAFTA negotiations, now receded to the periphery in the congressional battle, particularly after the administration won its appeal of a 30 June decision in Washington, DC District Court that NAFTA required submission of a comprehensive "environmental impact statement."[19]

Progress with environmentalists notwithstanding, NAFTA still faced an uphill struggle. The White House congressional relations chief, Howard Paster, feared that the votes were not there and that the administration had spent all its political chips in the budget fight. But once the decision was made, the administration knew it had to go all out. The president recruited William Daley of Chicago (brother of the mayor) to coordinate the pro-NAFTA congressional campaign. Republicans asked for their own representative on the White House team, and after consulting with them Clinton named William Frenzel, a Minnesotan recently retired from 20 years of congressional service. Frenzel took the job after asking for, and receiving, face-to-face assurance from the president that "you're going to work your head off on this." Frenzel then set out to "sell Republicans," stationing himself in the minority staff office of the House Ways and Means Committee.[20]

---

17. Drew, *On the Edge*, 290. As Drew notes, Clinton was so open to discussing and rediscussing issues that his staff didn't always treat matters as decided even when the president thought he had decided them.

18. NAFTA was endorsed on 14 September 1993 by six major groups, including the National Wildlife Federation, the Environmental Defense Fund, and the Natural Resources Defense Council. They called it "an unprecedented tool for reconciling ecological and economic objectives." Grassroots-oriented organizations like Friends of the Earth and the Sierra Club opposed the pact, aligning with the Citizens Trade Campaign to denounce it as "ravaging" the North American environment. For a more detailed discussion, see Daniel C. Esty, *Greening the GATT: Trade, Environment, and the Future* (Washington, DC: Institute for International Economics, 1994), especially 27ff, and John J. Audley, *Green Politics and Global Trade: NAFTA and the Future of Environmental Politics* (Washington: Georgetown University Press, 1997).

19. The case was filed by Public Citizen, the Sierra Club, and Friends of the Earth. The requirement was routinely applied to domestic legislation but had never been imposed on an international agreement.

20. For a fascinating, detailed treatment of the politics of NAFTA negotiation and ratification, see Frederick W. Mayer, *Interpreting NAFTA: The Science and Art of Political Analysis* (New York: Columbia University Press, 1998).

With Daley as overall coordinator and Kantor handling the substance, the campaign began in earnest after Labor Day, in the expectation of a vote before Congress adjourned for the year. President Clinton invited three former presidents to the East Room of the White House on 14 September to dramatize their united, bipartisan support. In a stirring speech, he pointed to the global changes that were revolutionizing the US marketplace— NAFTA or no NAFTA—and defined "the debate about NAFTA" as centering on "whether we will embrace these changes and create the jobs of tomorrow, or try to resist these changes, hoping we can preserve the economic structures of yesterday."[21] His governmental team worked in tandem with USA-NAFTA, the corporate support coalition. With a widely circulated survey finding the sentiment in the House still moving the wrong way, the first need was to stop further erosion in support.[22] Fence-sitting Democrats were feeling heat from labor; Republicans were worried about Ross Perot, with whose local organizations many of them had allied in the budget fight.

One immediate need was to firm up support in the elite media—the editorial writers traditionally disposed toward free trade. This was done expeditiously: Administration officials pulled together the economic case, stressing that NAFTA would create US jobs and buttress global US competitiveness. This campaign was aided by careful outside analyses.[23] It was also aided unwittingly by Ross Perot. A number of statements in his book were illogical, extreme, and easy to refute, and they drew attention away from more moderate anti-NAFTA arguments.

When the campaign began, members' mail was running overwhelmingly against NAFTA. USA-NAFTA set out to turn it around, and by November "the mail bags were balanced," in the words of one active participant. And while this involved mainly working with pro-NAFTA business interests, the fall also brought a significant rise in public support: from 42 percent in September to 53 percent in November.[24] Republicans were reluctant to commit unless Democrats did their share; they insisted on a minimum of 100 votes. (Ninety-one Democrats had backed fast-track

---

21. Transcript released by White House Press Office, 14 September 1994. Speaking after the president, George Bush declared graciously that after hearing Clinton's "very eloquent statement . . . now I understand why he's inside looking out and I'm outside looking in."

22. A USA-NAFTA poll found that, as of 20 September, 47 Democrats and 114 Republicans were in favor (strongly or leaning), with 159 Democrats and 31 Republicans against. The remainder were undecided or their views were unknown. (*Inside US Trade*, Special Report, 1 October 1994) This was a decline in support from a survey taken in August.

23. See Gary Clyde Hufbauer and Jeffrey J. Schott, *NAFTA: An Assessment* (Institute for International Economics, revised edition, October 1993).

24. NBC News/*Wall Street Journal* polls of September and November 1993, cited in Eric M. Uslaner, "Trade Winds: NAFTA, the Rational Public, and the Responsive Congress," draft paper, 1994.

extension in 1991.) So targets were agreed to: 100 Democrats, 120 Republicans. The president was phoning Democrats and finding the going hard—the price of his earlier neglect. Members expressed sympathy substantively and politically but declared they were committed. At one point, this drove Clinton to frank, public criticism of labor, and this helped with Republicans by showing he was really serious. Also, of course, Republicans took satisfaction in the strains that NAFTA was imposing on the Democrats' support coalition.

Early in the year, NAFTA supporters saw Majority Leader Gephardt as key: He had backed fast track in 1991 after extracting commitments on labor and the environment. But he was increasingly critical of NAFTA, and soon came out in opposition. White House Chief of Staff Mac McLarty stayed in touch, but it was increasingly clear that the battle would need to be won without Gephardt's help. And the number three Democrat, David Bonior of Michigan, was leading the fight against. So neither supporters nor opponents could use the regular House organization to line up votes. Matsui played a central role among the Democrats in mobilizing support, and Richardson proved important as well. The most energetic and effective Republicans included two members not on Ways and Means: Jim Kolbe of Arizona and David Dreier of California. In the end, however, the single most effective Republican was Minority Whip Gingrich, who was particularly helpful in negotiating agreement on how to replace the tariff revenues that NAFTA would cost the US Treasury.[25]

The battle remained uphill through October and into November, driving the administration into policy bargaining as well. An October promise to create a North American Development Bank, aimed at Hispanic legislators, netted at first only the idea's originator, Rep. Esteban Torres (D-CA). "One bank, one vote," concluded skeptics. But attention soon moved to product areas directly affected by the agreement. Two key industries, automobiles and textiles, had done their policy bargaining during the negotiations. The Big Three automakers won a 62.5 percent "North American content" requirement, making it harder for Japanese firms to produce in Mexico and export tariff-free to the United States. Textiles won a "triple transformation test": to benefit from NAFTA's provisions, apparel would have to be made in North America from North American cloth that was produced from North American fiber.[26] The

---

25. The budget law required that any measure that reduced revenues must contain provisions to offset this loss.

26. Kenneth Oye has argued that regional free trade agreements that produce trade diversion are particularly capable of gaining domestic support because of the particularized benefits they convey. See his *Economic Discrimination and Political Exchange: World Political Economy in the 1930s and 1980s* (Princeton, NJ: Princeton University Press, 1992).

American Textile Manufacturers Institute responded with a strong endorsement of NAFTA.[27]

The House vote was set for 17 November, and with each side looking to win, neither used parliamentary powers to delay it, even though the president did not actually submit the implementing bill until 4 November. Submission had been preceded by "nonmarkups" in the key committees, where members helped draft implementing bill language, but this was subordinate to the larger public fight. In the final struggle for votes, attention focused particularly on members with sugar and citrus constituencies. On the former, USTR Kantor extracted from a very reluctant Mexican government a new commitment that would effectively limit sugar exports to the United States. On citrus, several concessions of lesser importance were made.

This policy bargaining provoked press and opposition cries that the administration was "buying votes." This characterization was accurate but oversimplified, for the people being "bought" were, by and large, members who wanted to support NAFTA but needed a reason to justify doing so. By the time of the vote, it was widely recognized that a secret House vote would have endorsed NAFTA decisively; extracting concessions therefore cleared the way for on-the-fence members to vote their consciences! And while the sugar deal did change, significantly, how the agreement would affect that politically sensitive commodity, the total impact of the concessions on NAFTA's substance was modest.[28]

As the day of reckoning approached, with their "NAFTA creates jobs" case established, supporters began adding more traditional arguments: about how US-Mexican relations and US global leadership would be devastated by NAFTA's rejection and about the need to send the president off a winner to the upcoming summit of the Asia Pacific Economic Cooperation (APEC) forum in Seattle. And with the tide in Clinton's favor but the outcome not yet assured, the president took a giant gamble. He authorized his vice president, Albert Gore, to accept an invitation to debate Ross Perot on the national talk show "Larry King Live." A Perot "win" might conceivably have turned things around, but in fact the vice president dominated the encounter. He was relentless in challenging Perot, even presenting him with a joint portrait of Smoot and Hawley. The practical effect was to liberate some of the Republicans still on the fence.

---

27. Congressmen from the most important single textile state, North Carolina, would shift from a 9-2 margin against fast-track extension in 1991 to 8-4 *support* of the agreement itself.

28. Some NAFTA promises concerned US positions in the Uruguay Round, raising concern that the global negotiation would be mortgaged to pay for the regional one. In practice, the impact proved limited here also. A promise to the textile industry that the administration would seek an extension of the MFA phaseout period to 12 or 15 years (from 10) meant just that: the administration sought the extension, but other countries rejected it!

Once a NAFTA victory appeared likely, a common assumption was that it would win just enough votes for passage—a frequent occurrence when marginal members favor a measure on its merits but see it as unpopular. Congressional action on Clinton's budget package followed this pattern. The final NAFTA vote of 234-200 was thus a surprise: 102 Democrats and 132 Republicans came down in favor. The margin was remarkably similar to the 233-194 vote in favor of fast-track extension two and a half years before. Comparing the two votes, 11 more Democrats supported NAFTA, and 10 fewer Republicans. The shift among the Democrats was virtually all within the southern delegations, which had opposed fast track by 41-43 but backed NAFTA by 53-32. They were less affected by labor and more influenced by the textile provisions—and the deals of November.

For Clinton, the NAFTA vote was a big win—the biggest of his presidency. The budget vote was arguably more important, but it was eked out in a way that made the chief executive look weak. On NAFTA, by contrast, he was strong and persistent once he made his final commitment. In the spring and summer, he had dug himself one deep hole, but he and his team dug themselves out in the fall, turning the public debate around and winning the House of Representatives going away. The Senate followed as expected, clearing the way for the agreement to take effect in January 1994. Finally, and particularly important in the image-conscious 1990s, Bill Clinton had confounded press expectations that he would lose, and he had won by confronting major figures and interests within his party. His victory thus launched the most successful-seeming period of his incumbency.

Winning approval of NAFTA inaugurated what became a Clinton administration "triple play" on trade in November–December 1993. A day after the key House vote, the president flew to Seattle to host the first-ever summit meeting of Asia-Pacific states under the auspices of the APEC forum. And Mickey Kantor entered down-to-the-wire negotiations to win Uruguay Round agreement by the new deadline of 15 December.

Japan, China, and APEC

The APEC summit in December 1993 was the president's second major Asia policy venture of the year—the first was his trip to Tokyo in July,[29] during which the president sought to further his earlier commitment to "the rebalancing of our relationship" through "an elevated attention to our economic relations."[30] Administration officials declared repeatedly

---

29. The impetus for this trip was the seven-nation economic summit, but the administration also used the trip for important bilateral trade negotiations with Japan.

30. Clinton spoke these words to Japanese Prime Minister Kiichi Miyazawa during their joint White House news conference of 16 April 1993.

(and inaccurately) that previous negotiations to open Japan's markets had been uniformly unsuccessful. One important reason for failure, they insisted, was the lack of agreed-upon ways to measure success: "specific results," in Clinton's words, for "specific sectors of the economy." Therefore, such measures should be included in future agreements. Two previous agreements had done so: the semiconductor arrangement of 1986 and the auto parts agreement of 1992. Both contained quantitative targets for import expansion—labeled voluntary import expansion (VIE) targets, or temporary quantitative indicators (TQIs)—and Clinton mentioned these two agreements explicitly in his April 1993 press conference as examples that "gave some hope that this approach could work."[31]

Japanese bureaucrats seized upon the evident US interest in VIEs and launched a successful national and international campaign against such "numerical targets," accusing the United States of seeking a new form of "managed trade." They thus united, against the US position, both those Japanese who had always resisted market opening and those who had frequently supported it. The two nations reached a compromise at the July summit, a "framework" agreement to negotiate on market opening and deregulation in specific market sectors that made no mention of targets, calling rather for development of agreed "qualitative and quantitative indicators" of import progress in each sector. But through the fall, Americans continued to advance proposals that could reasonably be construed as quantitative targets, and Japanese gave far more energy to resisting these than to devising alternative measures.

Within the administration, Japan policy became a prime preoccupation, and the NEC Deputies Group met to address it as often as two or three times a week. At USTR, the lead actor was Deputy US Trade Representative Charlene Barshefsky, a purposive, knowledgeable trade negotiator. At the National Economic Council, Deputy Assistant to the President Bowman Cutter played a major Japan policy role, not just in development of strategy but in negotiations as well. Commerce was visibly engaged, as was State, and the Council of Economic Advisers was active in internal debates. And Secretary of the Treasury Lloyd Bentsen was always a force to be reckoned with. There was exceptional agreement on basic policy, at least by comparison with past administrations. But the Japanese were atypically united in their resistance.[32]

US trade relations were also strained with Asia's other economic giant, the People's Republic of China. As a communist country (and a nonmember of GATT), China was subject to general provisions of US law

---

31. Ibid.

32. For details, see I. M. Destler, *The National Economic Council: A Work in Progress* (Washington, DC: Institute for International Economics, POLICY ANALYSES IN INTERNATIONAL ECONOMICS 46, November 1996), 21–22 and 27–39.

denying MFN status to its exports. Under the provisions of the Trade Act of 1974, however, China had received, since 1980, MFN treatment through a presidential waiver, which had to be renewed annually. This was done without controversy until the brutal suppression of Chinese dissidents at Tiananmen Square in June 1989. In its wake, human rights advocates (among them congressional Democrats, including Senate Majority Leader George Mitchell) demanded that President Bush revoke MFN status or condition it explicitly on human rights improvements. Bush resisted but had to wage annual campaigns to prevent Congress from overriding his annual decisions extending China's MFN status.

Clinton had attacked Bush's softness on the matter during the presidential campaign, and thus entered office committed to linking China MFN and human rights. On 28 May 1993, he granted another one-year waiver but also issued an executive order setting forth human rights criteria for his decision the following year. This order provided that the secretary of State "shall not recommend extension" in 1994 unless he determined that it would "promote freedom of emigration," that China was complying with a bilateral agreement concerning prison labor, and that the People's Republic had "made overall, significant progress" on such specifics as "releasing and . . . accounting for Chinese citizens imprisoned or detained" in the 1989 democracy campaign, "ensuring humane treatment of prisoners," "protecting Tibet's distinctive religious and cultural heritage," and "permitting international radio and television broadcasts into China."

With serious ongoing disputes with Japan and China, and facing a broader East Asian reaction to US trade aggressiveness, Clinton came to the APEC summit in Seattle bearing real burdens. But he was politically reinforced by his NAFTA success, which many pundits had labeled unlikely. Moreover, East Asians worried that NAFTA signaled a US shift from a strategy of global trade liberalization to one stressing regional blocs. By assuaging such fears, by committing the United States to open trade relations within the world's fastest-growing region, by winning agreement on the goal of building a regional "community," and simply by hosting the first Asia-Pacific summit meeting ever, the president scored another triumph. And as the administration intended, movement in APEC raised alarms among Europeans, who feared the United States was turning away from its traditional Atlantic-first orientation.

Brussels and Geneva: Completing the Uruguay Round

Thus when Mickey Kantor flew to Brussels for the penultimate Uruguay Round talks, he did so with somewhat enhanced leverage. The European Union, pressed forward by its determined lead negotiator Sir Leon Brittan, was clearly committed to reaching agreement this time, and APEC was a force against backsliding. The basis remained the "Dunkel text," submitted by GATT Director General Arthur Dunkel in December 1991. And pressing the talks toward completion was Dunkel's aggressive Irish successor in Geneva, Peter Sutherland.

Agreement required further concessions to the French position on agriculture: in the end, the United States and the "Cairns Group" of farm product exporters settled for modest limits on European subsidies and a slight opening of the Japanese and Korean rice markets in exchange for bringing agriculture as a whole under GATT discipline for the first time and for the requirement that agricultural quotas be converted to tariffs. Unable to budge the Europeans (again the French!) on treatment of cultural properties, but unwilling to risk the wrath of the US motion picture industry and its advocate, Jack Valenti, Kantor agreed to set the issue aside. Kantor won—from Japan, the Asian newly industrializing countries, and Canada—some modification of the Dunkel text on antidumping to ease its impact on petitioning US industries.[33]

Other major deals were firmed up: tariff cuts averaging nearly 40 percent; a 10-year phaseout of the Multi-Fiber Arrangement (MFA) on textile and apparel trade; a comprehensive agreement on trade safeguards, including an outlawing of VERs; language restraining domestic subsidies, but with a green light for certain government support of research and development; a new General Agreement on Trade in Services (GATS), coupled with modest liberalization commitments in specific services sectors; a substantial new agreement on Trade-Related Aspects of Intellectual Property Rights (TRIPS); a major strengthening of dispute settlement procedures, which removed the ability of the party found "guilty" to block a decision; and the formal establishment of a new, umbrella institution—the World Trade Organization (WTO)—to succeed the GATT (which had evolved into an international organization despite its original establishment as a temporary device).

The United States had placed high priority on establishing "a more effective system of international trading disciplines and procedures,"[34] so

---

33. According to GATT Director General Sutherland, "It was the United States versus the rest of the world" on the 11 antidumping changes it proposed. "But it had been made abundantly clear politically by Mickey Kantor from the very beginning that this was a crunch issue as far as the US was concerned." (Interview in *Inside US Trade*, Special Report, 24 December 1993, 4.) Nor should this have been a surprise, for Kantor was simply delivering on promises made to win approval of an unencumbered Senate extension of fast-track authority the previous summer. For details on this issue, see Robert E. Cumby and Theodore H. Moran, "Testing Models of the Trade Policy Process: Antidumping and the 'New Issues,'" chapter 6 in Robert C. Feenstra, ed., *The Effects of U.S. Trade Protection and Promotion Policies* (Chicago: University of Chicago Press for the National Bureau of Economic Research, 1997).

34. This was one of three "overall US trade negotiating objectives" set forth in Section 1101 of the Omnibus Trade and Competitiveness Act of 1988, which authorized the round. A "more effective and expeditious dispute settlement process" was the first of the 16 more detailed goals spelled out in the same section.

the dispute settlement provisions constituted a major victory. The WTO, by contrast, was something to which the United States agreed only at the very end. Its most prominent advocate was an American, trade law authority John H. Jackson, but the proposal was in fact initiated by the Canadians and embraced by the Europeans as a means to constrain US unilateralism. US resistance was more tactical than strategic, however. After procedural improvements, the administration supported the WTO as consistent with its aim of a truly global, enforceable trade regime.[35] But because it emerged at the end of the negotiations, the WTO idea had received little attention in Congress, or in the broader public. This would cause problems during the implementation phase.

Perhaps most important was the sheer sweep of the Uruguay Round agreement. It was, for the most part, a "single undertaking" subscribed to by no fewer than 125 countries as of 15 September 1994. This meant that agreements on dispute settlement, intellectual property, and so on were universal in their coverage and the discipline they imposed. By contrast, the Tokyo Round codes on issues such as subsidies applied only to nations specifically adhering to them. The substantive coverage was also comprehensive. Agriculture was brought into GATT rules effectively for the first time; the special MFA regime for textiles was to be phased out. And important new issues were incorporated in the regime: trade-related investment and intellectual property rights, and trade in services.[36]

The Uruguay Round agreement completed Clinton's "triple play" on trade in 1993. And the president's persistence paid political dividends. The NAFTA victory had shown him willing to take a stand and fight for what he believed; the follow-on achievements suggested a broader trade liberalization strategy. The press began treating the president with new respect. His public approval rating, below 40 percent through most of the summer, topped 50 percent in December.[37]

Unlike NAFTA, the Uruguay Round agreement generated little controversy in the United States when it was signed. House Majority Leader Gephardt, who had opposed NAFTA, endorsed it within a week. Organized labor did not take up arms and would remain largely on the sidelines throughout the next year. The administration entered 1994 determined to move expeditiously and avoid giving opponents the sort of

---

35. See John H. Jackson, "The World Trade Organization, Dispute Settlement, and Codes of Conduct," together with comments by Julius L. Katz, in Susan M. Collins and Barry P. Bosworth, eds., *The New GATT: Implications for the United States* (Washington, DC: The Brookings Institution, 1994), 63–78.

36. For a comprehensive analysis of the round, see Jeffrey J. Schott (assisted by Johanna W. Buurman), *The Uruguay Round: An Assessment* (Washington, DC: Institute for International Economics, 1994).

37. The figures are for positive responses to the *New York Times*/CBS News poll question: "Do you approve or disapprove of the way Bill Clinton is handling his job as President?"

open political field they had enjoyed during the NAFTA side agreement negotiations of 1993. USTR began working with congressional staff on implementing legislation in January, even as they were pinning down the details for the final Uruguay Round text to be signed in April.

But progress on the implementing legislation was slow. One reason was the complexity of certain issues, particularly the antidumping law revisions. Another was that the Clinton administration was giving top priority to the president's health care initiative. And this dominated the agenda of the key trade committees—Senate Finance and House Ways and Means—through the spring and into the summer. A third reason was the relative weakness of trade policy leadership in both House and Senate. A fourth was the lack of supportive pressure from business.

Business leaders were cool because of Mickey Kantor's pursuit of a labor and environmental trade agenda not to their liking. More important was the priority that multinational firms were giving in early 1994 to another trade issue: MFN status for China.

US Business, Human Rights, and the China Market

Business had been concerned about Clinton's potential China policy well before the 1992 election.[38] Reacting to his criticism of Bush's refusal to link China's MFN status to its human rights performance, the National Association of Manufacturers (NAM) released a statement calling MFN "the minimum requirement of meaningful economic exchanges between two countries. It is the sine qua non of the US-China commercial relationship. As such, it cannot be the basis for the exercise of US leverage within that relationship."[39] After Clinton's victory, the NAM joined with other business organizations in the Business Coalition for US-China Trade. In May 1993, the coalition sent Clinton a letter signed by 298 companies and 37 trade associations opposing any conditioning or compromising of MFN status. Prominent were firms such as Boeing and General Electric, which feared loss of current and future export markets. Also active were wheat growers and footwear retailers; the latter "flooded the White House with letters from thousands of shoe store managers."[40]

There were many previous occasions when broad business coalitions had been formed to support the president on a critical trade-expanding vote. Typically, however, these were orchestrated by executive branch leaders. The 1992–94 China campaign was different, for here a broad

---

38. This section draws upon the research assistance of Ning Shao.

39. "NAM Statement on US-China Commercial Relations," 24 October 1992.

40. *New York Times*, 14 June 1993.

range of commercial interests united for a major, trade-expanding purpose. One reason was the fear of big losses in current business, something that often drives businesspeople to political action. But there was a strong, forward-looking element to the campaign as well. China loomed large— for exports, for investment—in almost all major multinationals' corporate plans. It was the most rapidly growing large economy in the world and potentially the dominant economy of the 21st century. Being shut out of that market could prove devastating for firms' broader competitiveness— in East Asia and throughout the world. This mix of hopes and fears produced what became known as "the new China lobby,"[41] perhaps the most formidable, protrade coalition ever sustained by US business on its own initiative.

As earlier recounted, Clinton responded in 1993 by extending MFN and establishing relatively moderate human rights criteria for his decision due in June 1994. This was widely perceived as a victory for commercial interests. But China's human rights performance on the specified criteria continued to be, at best, mixed, and Secretary of State Warren Christopher went to Beijing in early March 1994 to press the linkage policy. He was publicly rebuffed by Chinese officials. He was then rebuffed at home a day after his return, when the Council on Foreign Relations sponsored an unprecedented public forum in Washington in which three former secretaries of state and numerous other notables attacked the linkage policy.

With Chinese human rights cooperation at best partial, grudging, and hard to square with the criteria in Clinton's executive order, business criticism of the policy intensified. During the president's trip to California to attend Richard M. Nixon's funeral, the Business Coalition presented a petition signed by nearly 450 California-based companies saying MFN revocation would be "an additional devastating blow" to the state's economy.[42] The coalition also worked with supportive legislators to counter advocates of the human rights linkage led by Nancy Pelosi (D-CA); Jim McDermott (D-WA), who counted thousands of Boeing workers among his constituents, helped mobilize 106 representatives to sign a May letter to Clinton calling for MFN renewal.[43] Visibly aligned with business (and against the State Department's tough human rights position) were the economic agencies—Treasury, Commerce, USTR, and the NEC. Together they reinforced expectations that Clinton would not, could not, revoke

---

41. The original "China lobby," much feared in the 1950s and early 1960s, supported the "Republic of China" on Taiwan and opposed recognition of Beijing.

42. *Far Eastern Economic Review*, 12 May 1994, 16.

43. Congressman Matsui's office provided another sort of balance by sponsoring a May press conference for some Chinese students who had gathered more than 1,000 student signatures on a pro-MFN petition for the president and Congress.

MFN, effectively undercutting whatever leverage the threat might have had on Chinese human rights behavior.

Also influential in Washington was the argument that, over the longer term, trade and human rights were not competing but mutually reinforcing values. Market freedom and economic development and international engagement were more likely over time to promote democracy and basic freedoms in China, many believed, than heavy-handed US pressure. By this logic, it was important not only that the president continue MFN in 1994 but that the United States abandon the practice of linking its extension to annual human rights reviews.

As the early June deadline approached, therefore, Clinton faced a tough political choice. Even a selective denial of MFN—the choice of some human rights advocates—would have serious economic consequences, but an unconditional extension would violate the spirit, and perhaps the letter, of his own executive order. He opted for the latter, and played it straight. The Secretary of State had concluded "that the Chinese did not achieve overall significant progress in all the areas outlined in the executive order. . . . " Clinton agreed with this assessment. Given this fact, he asked, "how can we best advance the cause of human rights and other profound interests the United States has in our relationship with China?" The answer he had reached was to "renew Most Favored Nation trading status," which "will permit us to engage the Chinese with not only economic contacts but with cultural, educational and other contacts, and with a continuing aggressive effort in human rights. . . . I am moving, therefore, to delink human rights from the annual extension of Most Favored Nation trading status for China . . . we have reached the end of the usefulness of that policy."[44]

There was some negative reaction from Democratic liberals, including Senate Majority Leader George Mitchell (D-ME), a champion of the linkage policy. But it proved short-lived and ended with the decisive defeat of a House disapproval resolution. Clinton's decision commanded the political center, as Bush's similar decisions had not. And one major reason was the fierce business campaign that the possibility of MFN denial had brought forth. For liberal traders, this campaign suggested a new capacity for internationalist business to mobilize on a trade expansion issue when the administration was not leading the charge. In the context of early 1994, however, the campaign had a price. For it diverted business energy from support of the Uruguay Round and from specific struggles on implementing language.

---

44. News conference of May 26, 1994, *Weekly Compilation of Presidential Documents*, 30, no. 21 (May 30, 1994): 1166–67.

Japan: Failure and Modest Success

As the China issue was moving toward resolution, fractious economic talks continued with Japan. The administration was united in its determination to press for major Japanese market-opening measures, as well as macroeconomic policy change (in the form of an income tax cut) to stimulate demand.[45] Offering hope—but also frustration—was the reform government of Prime Minister Morihiro Hosokawa, whose eight-party coalition had ended 38 years of Liberal-Democratic Party rule in the summer of 1993.

Hosokawa was committed, in principle, to economic deregulation and to the weakening of the special-interest influence that had made Japanese import liberalization so difficult to attain. But his government was also weak and inexperienced. This meant even greater power for Japan's traditionally strong bureaucracy. As discussed earlier, the way the administration had developed and described its proposal provoked a strong Japanese reaction, uniting that bureaucracy with Japanese business and liberal academics in opposing what they labeled a US campaign for "quantitative targets" for imports. US officials called this a misrepresentation of their goal; they just wanted agreements with meaningful "qualitative and quantitative indicators" of progress in specific sectors, as the Japanese government had agreed to seek in the "framework talks" launched in July 1993. It was Japan that "managed trade," Americans asserted.[46] But other nations joined Japan in denouncing the US position.

Matters came to a head at the Clinton-Hosokawa summit of February 1994. The sectoral negotiations were deadlocked, and the Japanese government was divided over economic policy—hence its macroeconomic package was weak. So in a joint news conference, Clinton and Hosokawa announced that the framework talks had failed, and they would not paper over the failure. Instead, the US administration indicated its readiness to consider unilateral action, including trade sanctions. Luckily, there was a particularly ripe issue: Japanese regulatory authorities had prevented Motorola from competing effectively for market share in the lucrative Tokyo cellular telephone market, despite a previous official agreement.

---

45. Japan's prolonged recession, in reaction to the "bubble economy" of the late 1980s, had produced new records in Japan's trade surpluses as demand for imports stagnated. The bilateral imbalance with the United States, which had shown significant reduction between 1987 and 1990, reached a new record of $59.4 billion in 1993.

46. Independent evidence in support of this argument can be found in C. Fred Bergsten and Marcus Noland, *Reconcilable Differences?* (Washington, DC: Institute for International Economics, 1993), and Yoko Sazanami, Shujiro Urata, and Hiroki Kawai, *Measuring the Costs of Protection in Japan* (Washington, DC: Institute for International Economics, 1995).

The Clinton administration threatened sanctions, and the Japanese regulators backed down.[47]

In the weeks after the February summit, the Clinton administration refused to reopen the talks unless the Japanese made significant movement toward reaching an agreement. But as weeks became months, the benefits of this posture receded. Hosokawa resigned on 8 April over charges of shady financial practices in financing his governorship campaign 12 years before. A successor "reform government" under Tsutomu Hata took power. On 23 May the two nations reached a written understanding clarifying the framework and relaunching specific sectoral talks. The Japanese accepted new language on goals "to deal with structural and sectoral issues in order substantially to increase access and sales of competitive foreign goods and services." The US side accepted an explicit statement that the "qualitative and quantitative criteria" to be developed "do not constitute numerical targets, but rather are to be used for the purpose of evaluating progress. . . . "[48] Four months later, after an all-night session, Kantor announced agreement the morning of 1 October 1994 on government procurement of medical technology and telecommunications equipment and on government deregulation of insurance. By this time, Japan had its fourth government in a year, under Socialist Prime Minister Tomiichi Murayama in coalition with the LDP.

Disagreement remained on the long-festering issue of trade in automobiles and auto parts. And in the spring of 1995, with the arrival of the Section 301 deadline, this dispute moved to the brink of what the press labeled "trade war," with the United States initiating multibillion dollar sanctions against imports of Japanese luxury automobiles, and both sides preparing cases to take to the newly established WTO. In June, the two sides reached a singular agreement: the United States proclaimed specific goals for Japanese purchases of imported autos and parts (based on Japanese private industry targets) and Japan's Minister of International Trade and Industry, Ryutaro Hashimoto, formally disassociated his government from these numbers. Both sides declared victory, and the US-Japan trade conflict receded rapidly.[49]

---

47. Clinton also responded to the breakdown of the framework talks by issuing, in early March, what he labeled a "Super 301 executive order"—presumably meant to be a basis for pressing product issues with Japan. While the original "Super 301" had provided that the USTR name "priority foreign countries," Clinton's version referred instead to naming "priority foreign country *practices*" (emphasis added). This made it diplomatically more acceptable but less distinguishable from actions taken under the regular section 301. (Bayard and Elliott, *Reciprocity and Retaliation*, 48–49.) "Not-so-Super 301" seemed a more appropriate label. It was nonetheless popular on Capitol Hill as another "shot across the bow" vis-à-vis Japan.

48. "US-Japan Agreement on Framework," published in *Inside US Trade*, 27 May 1994, 2.

49. For details and analysis, see Leonard Schoppa, *Bargaining with Japan: What American Pressure Can and Cannot Do* (New York: Columbia University Press, 1997) chapter 9, and Edward J. Lincoln, *Troubled Times: US-Japan Trade Relations in the 1990s* (Washington: Brookings Institution Press, 1999), chapter 4.

Implementing the Uruguay Round: A Slow Start

Approval and implementation of the Uruguay Round were, nonetheless, the major trade-political action of 1994 in the United States. As noted earlier, the action began with staff-level discussions in January, as Mickey Kantor and his deputy, Rufus Yerxa, pursued the now established "nonmarkup" process to get bipartisan consensus on the provisions of the nonamendable bill that the president would submit under the fast-track procedures. There was talk of rapid movement at both ends of Pennsylvania Avenue: agreement on the substance of a bill by April, and final congressional action before the August recess.

The reality proved very different. On the House side, the first formal Trade Subcommittee session on the agreement was a 26 May review of its agricultural provisions. Specific administration proposals on key issues were not available until mid-June. The full Ways and Means Committee did not hold its comprehensive "walk-through" session with Mickey Kantor until 14 July. Senate Finance began its nonmarkups on 19 July.[50] It was not until 27 September that the president submitted his implementing bill for congressional action.

The most important cause of this delay was Washington's preoccupation with health care, which was the administration's absolute top priority until the failure of the Clinton-backed legislation in August, and which dominated the attention of the House and Senate leadership and the members of Ways and Means and Finance. Hence USTR had to carry the trade issue pretty much alone for most of 1994.

Another problem was the weakness of congressional trade leadership, at least when compared with 1988, the year of the last major trade legislation. In May 1994, Congressman Dan Rostenkowski was indicted on long-pending charges of abusing his office for personal gain, forcing him (under Democratic caucus rules) to yield the Ways and Means chairmanship. The Illinois Democrat had achieved formidable effectiveness in this role: One senior colleague found his performance even more impressive than that of Wilbur Mills, if one factored in the reduced formal powers of chairs in the postreform era. Replacing him (on an "acting" basis) was longtime Trade Subcommittee Chair Sam Gibbons (D-FL), a committed and knowledgeable liberal trader who lacked Rostenkowski's bent for moving legislation. Succeeding Gibbons in the post of acting Trade Subcommittee chairman was Matsui, who was emerging as the most effective trade Democrat. Ranking Republican Bill Archer played an increasingly important role as the nonmarkup proceeded, but his capacity to speak for his party colleagues was not always clear. Most of all, the administration

---

50. This stands in contrast with the Tokyo Round agreement, finalized in April of 1979—on that occasion, nonmarkups began in March, the "nonconference" was held in May, the bill was sent down in June, and the House and Senate votes came in July.

sorely missed having, at the top of the committee, a leader who could cut policy deals and make them stick.

On the Senate side, the change had been of Clinton's making: His appointment of Lloyd Bentsen as Secretary of the Treasury brought Daniel Patrick Moynihan into the chairmanship of Senate Finance. The New Yorker was an erudite policy thinker of vast experience. He had voted against NAFTA, as had most Democrats with similar labor constituents, but his commitment to the liberal, multilateral trading system was deep and genuine. He knew trade history, including the failure of the International Trade Organization during the Truman administration, and he was generous enough to share this knowledge more than once with his colleagues. He lacked, however, Bentsen's power and focused approach, and his meandering reflections on substance and process entertained his audiences without instilling confidence. On the Republican side, ranking member Bob Packwood of Oregon was hobbled by charges of recurrent sexual harassment, though he would increasingly use the trade issue as a means to reestablish himself as a consequential and substantive player in the Senate.

Another source of delay was the vexing matter of how to pay for the Uruguay Round. The financing problem arose because cutting tariffs reduced revenues, by roughly $12 billion over five years. Under congressional rules designed to hold down the fiscal deficit, any reduction in revenues had to be offset by other measures (e.g., spending cuts, tax increases). Thus, the administration had to find $12 billion in fiscal offsets or ask Congress to waive the budget rule.

The budget issue was tailor-made for posturing, with the administration squirming to find acceptable revenue increases and antitax Republicans quick to denounce them. Determined to maintain a strong posture on deficit reduction, President Clinton did not seriously consider seeking an overall waiver of the budget rules. So USTR excluded certain matters from the bill to limit the cost—the expiring system of trade preferences, for example, was extended for just one year, and a proposal to offset the negative impact of NAFTA on Caribbean nations had to be postponed. In any case, the specifics of the budgetary package were bound to generate controversy and some delay.

All these matters were outside the control of USTR Mickey Kantor. But he made his own contribution to GATT's slow legislative progress by his handling of two key matters: the revision of US antidumping law to comply with the Uruguay Round accord and the issue of providing fast-track authority for future trade negotiations.

Antidumping: Reversing the Round

As spelled out in chapter 6, the antidumping laws had become the best recourse for US industries seeking protection, with the rules so tilted that few petitioners failed to win dumping findings from the Department of Commerce. If they could also persuade the US International Trade Commission that imports had caused them "material injury," imposition of an antidumping duty was automatic.[51] As noted in chapter 6, the Uruguay Round featured a major effort, facilitated by GATT Director General Arthur Dunkel, to constrain the use of such laws for protectionist purposes. This precipitated, in turn, a strong reaction by the champions of the "fair trade" statutes.

Robert E. Cumby and Theodore H. Moran have chronicled the struggle within the Clinton administration, where Moran was among an unsuccessful group of officials seeking to push US policy toward support of antidumping law reform.[52] The policy struggle continued during the drafting of implementing legislation. Here, as in the final Geneva talks, Kantor and his USTR colleagues sided with those who worked to dilute, or offset, the changes agreed to at Geneva. The technical details are laid out in chapter 6 and will not be repeated here. The net result, in this author's analysis, was not—as Cumby and Moran argue—an increase in trade protection. But it did represent a lost opportunity to bring greater balance to the US antidumping procedures.

Tilting this way was a political choice made by the Clinton administration. The congressional committees were not especially protectionist, though Gibbons had shifted his position somewhat in this direction, and Representatives Sander Levin (D-MI) and Amo Houghton (R-NY) were active on the petitioners' side. Also unchanged from earlier periods was the relative weakness of internationalist firms and import users, each of which had interests in changing the laws to bring treatment of import pricing closer to treatment of pricing of domestically produced goods. There had been dramatic cases showing the costs of high dumping duties to certain US firms—those on ball bearings and flat-panel displays were particularly telling. But in the main, CEOs of internationalist firms were preoccupied with other issues—especially China MFN. And some of them, companies such as Boeing, Kodak, and Motorola, had found the antidumping laws useful for their own purposes.

The decision to limit or offset the impact of the Uruguay Round changes on antidumping petitioners complicated the rewriting of the dumping laws and increased the time required. Four months is normal for such a comprehensive effort, according to one experienced official. But the administration's approach did apparently buttress overall congres-

---

51. Douglas Nelson has argued, in a cogent essay, that the politics of antidumping resemble the pre-Smoot-Hawley politics of tariffs, with a built-in protectionist bias in the law arising from the asymmetrical activism of interests that were hurt by "dumped" imports. See his "Domestic Political Preconditions of US Trade Policy: Liberal Structure and Protectionist Dynamics," *Journal of Public Policy* 9, no. 1 (1989): 83–108.

52. "Testing Models of the Trade Policy Process" (footnote 33).

sional support. Gephardt and Levin, two respected "tough on trade" Democrats, were solid supporters of the GATT bill.

The Loss of Future Fast Track

The second issue where the administration's approach cost precious time concerned future trade negotiations: whether fast-track authority for them would be included in the Uruguay Round bill. In this case, it cost USTR the substance as well. Mickey Kantor and his colleagues needed congressional authority to pursue their regional and global negotiating agenda. They did not get it.

Authority to employ fast-track procedures for the results of future trade negotiations had been included, almost unnoticed, in the 1979 legislation implementing the Tokyo Round. But the 1991 renewal debate had made fast track a visible and controversial issue, particularly for members of Congress not on the principal trade committees. Kantor made the matter more controversial by delaying his specific renewal proposal until mid-June, springing it on the trade community without full consultation, and including in it two provisions bound to provoke opposition. One was the duration of the proposal: It would cover essentially all trade negotiations completed by December 2001, seven years into the future. This seemed to many legislators an excessively long and broad request, particularly since the post–Uruguay Round trade agenda was only beginning to be developed. The second was a proposal to include trade-related labor and environmental issues among the specific negotiating priorities set forth in the fast-track extension. This got the business community up in arms.

In its post–Uruguay Round planning, USTR had placed very high priority on initiatives to reconcile trade liberalization and environmental protection and to bring internationally recognized labor standards into the trade dialogue. Politically, the latter was a peace offering to labor and its congressional allies, who had opposed NAFTA. Early in 1994, therefore, USTR launched an aggressive international campaign to include labor standards on the agenda of the new World Trade Organization. Specifically, Kantor pressed for agreement to be announced on this matter at the Marrakesh meeting on 15 April, where final Uruguay Round agreements would be signed. He faced "overwhelming international opposition,"[53] particularly from developing countries, and in the end had to settle for agreement that the issue would be discussed by the Preparatory Committee, which was being established to help manage the transition from GATT to WTO. But Vice President Gore highlighted the issue in the address he delivered at Marrakesh.

---

53. *Inside US Trade*, 1 April 1994, 1.

Business interests had acquiesced only reluctantly in NAFTA labor and environmental side agreements, fearing they would increase regulation. They reacted very negatively to the administration's spring labor-standards campaign. Then USTR, with only limited consultation, unveiled its fast-track proposal in June, which made "labor standards" and "trade and the environment" the fifth and sixth of seven "principal trade negotiating objectives" for which the new authority was to be employed.[54] The business community reacted strongly. Before long, many Republicans were saying that they would approve new fast track only if labor and environmental issues were explicitly *excluded*, a stance heartily endorsed by small and medium-sized businesses. Multinational firms in the Business Roundtable accepted the idea that some treatment of labor and environment issues might be appropriate in trade talks. But they felt frustrated. The administration, they believed, was undercutting its own cause by not working closely with the business allies upon whose support extension of fast track would depend. With Moynihan and Packwood already skeptical about fast track's inclusion in the implementing bill, the best hope was for the administration to win agreement in the House and then work hand-in-glove with business in persuading the Senate. But from the business standpoint, there was a lack of the close consultation and confidence that would make this possible.

The labor-environment issue, and the way Kantor was handling it, divided Congress along partisan lines—just the thing that he needed to avoid. The financing issue had a similar effect. Moreover, while Republicans remained generally supportive of free trade in general and the agreement in particular, their sights were increasingly set on the upcoming November elections, where they saw a chance for major gains. They feared that a Clinton "victory" on a major piece of legislation—or, worse yet, several major victories—would give him and the Democrats a political countermomentum like that which he had gained from the NAFTA vote. Their immediate target was health care, the predominant business of the second session of the 103rd Congress. But as Clinton's prospects on this issue receded, Republicans began thinking of denying him a trade victory as well, or at least of making sure that the victory came on their terms. Thus, although the core Uruguay Round debate was never substantively partisan (like the budget in 1993 or health care in 1994), the issue became tactically partisan, and remained so through the November elections.

The WTO and US "Sovereignty"

The most prominent public issue was the creation of the new World Trade Organization. As noted earlier, US officials had initially resisted it, partly

---

54. For the full text, see *Inside US Trade* Special Report, 21 June 1994, S-26.

out of concern over its domestic reception. And once the WTO was agreed to, it became the target and mobilizing issue for an odd anti-GATT alliance, bringing together Ralph Nader, Pat Buchanan, and Ross Perot. The buzzword was "sovereignty," and whether the WTO would take it away from the United States. Newt Gingrich pressed the issue in the spring, partly because a Georgia primary opponent was raising it. He won a special hearing in House Ways and Means and won also a provision, in the implementing legislation, whereby the Congress could vote every five years on withdrawal from the WTO.

For the Buchanan-led hard right, the WTO was a new manifestation of the threat of a "world government." For the left, the WTO raised concerns that the new trade institutions and procedures would override US laws on such matters as environmental protection and product safety. For Senate Minority Leader Robert Dole, it was a rationale for withholding support until the politically opportune moment. Claiming he had had more phone calls to his Wichita office on WTO than on NAFTA, he asked why Congress could not wait until the issue was clarified and why there was the need to rush to a vote in 1994.[55] Supporters brought in conservative jurist Robert Bork to quash the sovereignty question, and Bork declared that the WTO took away no authority from US institutions and could not force any changes in US law. The Heritage Foundation weighed in with a similar analysis. Together with the strengthened dispute settlement procedures, however, the WTO could produce legitimate decisions that US laws violated US trade commitments. And while it could not force changes in these laws, it could sanction retaliation by other nations if the laws were not changed. A specific aspect of this issue receiving prominence was the impact on laws below the federal level. State attorneys general mobilized and won a provision to protect their participation in any changes of state laws required to conform to Uruguay Round agreements, or as a result of adverse WTO decisions.

Other issues also brought complications. The textile industry, whose quotas the agreement would phase out in 10 years, sought (and would win) short-term gains through promised changes in the "rules of origin" used to enforce those quotas. Senator John Danforth (R-MO) led an early Republican protest against rules governing subsidies, which gave a green light to those aimed at enhancing research and development. Curiously absent from the debate, however, was the issue of trade adjustment measures. One reason was that, with the AFL-CIO on the sidelines, the issue of "jobs" was as marginal to the Uruguay Round debate in 1994 as it had been central to the NAFTA debate in 1993.

---

55. See Keith Bradsher, "Dole Urges Postponement for Approval of Trade Pact," *New York Times*, 31 August 1994. Kansas was a particular target of GATT opponents, who apparently orchestrated the phone calls. Dole presumably knew this at the time, and he admitted it later.

Delaying the Process: Dole, Hollings, and Gingrich

Thus, despite its determination to move fast on Uruguay Round implementation, USTR found itself bogged down on a variety of issues as spring became summer and summer approached fall. And the process seemed to maximize the leverage of those who stood in the way. If the head start of opponents of NAFTA was the result of a Clinton political strategy, on GATT a somewhat similar political pattern was rooted in the fast-track procedures themselves. The way in which policy bargaining was centered on the drafting of legislation gave business interests an incentive to delay or condition their support in order to extract the last bit of gain—in the wording of the antidumping laws, for example, or in rules of origin for textiles. Once the package was finally put together, time was short, the opposition was mobilized, and business could not simply turn on a dime to all-out support. Thus the internationalist interests that had come together so strongly on NAFTA and on China MFN were not a powerful counterweight when Republicans subordinated GATT approval to their determination to deny all victories to Clinton.

The original administration goal was to get final action—or at least a House vote—before the August congressional recess. But while health care dominated members' attention, negotiations on the implementing bill ran on endlessly—in particular on the budget, future fast track, and antidumping. The first "nonconference" between Senate Finance and House Ways and Means was not held until 19 August, and the final one was on 20 September. Kantor struggled repeatedly to formulate a follow-on fast-track proposal acceptable to both Gephardt Democrats and Archer Republicans. He thought he had one in August, but by then Senate Finance was adamantly against including any such language. Under strong White House pressure, he continued to press the matter after its prospects had evaporated, delaying the process further. The administration finally gave up on future fast track in September.[56]

More important, the bill now faced a time bind that threatened its very enactment. The law allowed up to 90 legislative days for Congress to consider trade-implementing legislation after its submission, and there were nowhere near 90 days between late September and the anticipated October adjournment. Of course, no previous fast-track bill had taken all of the 90 days, as steps had been skipped or statutory times truncated through leadership power (in the House) or unanimous consent agreements (in the Senate). The NAFTA bill was not even introduced until 4 November 1993, just 16 days before the final Senate vote, and the Senate skipped

---

56. At a meeting of the National Economic Council, Treasury Secretary Lloyd Bentsen declared that the votes were not there for fast-track extension. Deputy National Security Assistant Sandy Berger reportedly responded, "We shouldn't yield on this matter until the last minute." Bentsen's Texas drawl was heard once more: "This is the last minute."

over the statutory requirement that the bill, after House passage, "shall be referred to the appropriate committee or committees" in that body. But that required acquiescence of key committee chairs, and support from the minority. For the Uruguay Round, neither was automatic. Dole was not helping at all, seeing political advantage in delay. Patrick Leahy (D-VT), chairman of the Senate Agriculture Committee, had threatened to use the 45 days the law allowed his committee if he did not win satisfaction on certain provisions. And after Leahy's agreement was won, there remained the chair of the Commerce Committee and one of the Senate's few out-and-out protectionists, Ernest Hollings of South Carolina.

Moreover, the predominant interpretation was that the administration could submit a fast-track implementing bill only once for each agreement. If the Uruguay Round legislation was stalled and never came to final vote in the 103rd Congress, approval would have to be sought by regular legislative procedures in the 104th—with the bill open for amendments and filibusters. And even if procedural cooperation could be attained, the key committees would all have new members, who were unlikely to acquiesce in all of the balances struck by the old.

Understanding Hollings' blocking power, USTR was solicitous and accommodating to him throughout—on antidumping laws, on textile rules of origin—although his committee's actual jurisdiction covered only a modest number of Uruguay Round provisions. Thus, in the frenetic late-September days prior to submitting the president's bill, USTR officials sought a commitment from the senator not to use his delaying power and explored at the same time the possibility of stripping from the bill the provisions under Commerce jurisdiction. They failed to win the first, and received overwhelming advice from friendly senators not to pursue the second, as it would alienate other senators now on the fence. They could, of course, have held off the bill until 1995, but that would have meant, in all probability, starting the nonmarkup process from scratch with a mix of old and new committee members. So they sent the bill down, and hoped for the best. Hollings was considered a friend of the president. Would he play into Republicans' political hands by preventing a vote before the election?

The answer turned out to be yes. The implementing bill was sent to Congress on 27 September. After meeting with President Clinton, Hollings announced on 28 September that he would not waive his committee's prerogative; he would insist on his 45 days.

On trade policy, Hollings was best known as an advocate of textile protection: As described in chapter 4, he had been proposing textile quota legislation as far back as 1968. And he numbered among his constituents Roger Milliken, the most politically prominent of mill executives and a fierce opponent of liberal trade. But while Hollings' move was widely interpreted as doing textiles' bidding, the larger industry did not back him. The American Textile Manufacturers Institute was officially neutral on the agreement, and a number of firms were actually supportive—because of concessions they had won on textile tariffs and the details of the MFA phaseout, and because they, in some cases, had decided to go with the internationalist flow. Hollings, in turn, insisted he was fighting not just for textiles but for broader protectionist reasons, contending that free trade had been ravaging American firms and workers for decades. He would use his 45 days for hearings to make this case to the American people.

The South Carolinian's action killed the chances of a Senate vote before October adjournment, but the administration had a procedural fallback: to call a "lame duck" session after the election. Clinton had made it clear that he would do so if necessary, perhaps hoping that the inconvenience caused to Hollings' colleagues might deter him from delaying the vote. It didn't. But Hollings did not press his procedural rights as far as he could have; the White House and Senate leader Mitchell were able to work with him on the details.

On 30 September, standing with Hollings on the Senate floor, Mitchell sought and received unanimous consent "that the time for committee consideration of S 2467, the GATT implementing legislation, continue to be counted regardless of whether or not the Senate is in session." Hollings thus made a decisive procedural concession he did not have to make: that the 45-day clock would run while the Senate was in recess for the November elections! All he insisted on, at least in public, was "that I be recognized and have the floor and I can explain to my colleagues my position on this." With this key unanimous consent agreement, Mitchell was free to follow with a schedule consistent with giving Commerce its 45 days: the Senate would reconvene on 30 November for 12 hours of debate on GATT, and continue on 1 December with the remaining eight hours that fast track allowed—voting "at approximately 6 p.m." that day.[57] These arrangements minimized the inconvenience that the delay caused to senators, and they prevented further procedural maneuvers on Hollings' (and others') part.[58]

House committees had no comparable power to delay if the leadership wished to proceed. So the administration pressed the House to proceed with its scheduled vote on 5 October, with GATT supporters and editorialists joining in the call. But while the Uruguay Round never became as hot an issue as NAFTA, it had become more than controversial enough to make members reluctant to take a preelection vote that could be avoided, especially when their Senate counterparts were avoiding *their* vote.

---

57. Quotations are from *Congressional Record*, 30 September 1994, S13765.

58. For example, once the House delayed its vote to 29 November, the language of the fast-track authority indicates that Senate committees would have had a right to hold the House bill for an additional 15 legislative days. Had someone exercised this right, the earliest date for Senate action would have moved perilously close to Christmas. But the unanimous consent agreement, reached before the House deferred action, rendered this option moot.

The politics became further heated when it was revealed that the *Washington Post* Company had a private interest in enactment of the legislation, one that had not been acknowledged in its editorials calling for GATT's enactment. At issue was a Federal Communications Commission (FCC) license being granted to a *Post* subsidiary, American Personal Communications, Inc. (APC) to provide wireless telephone service. Originally, it had been promised free, as a reward for "pioneering" communications work, but in 1993 Congress established a policy that such licenses should be auctioned, and the FCC moved to charge APC and other "pioneers" the amount that it estimated an auction would bring. APC filed suit, claiming the government had no right to charge it anything. A compromise was negotiated, requiring APC and others to pay a total of $1.5 billion over five years.

The Clinton administration, needing revenue to offset GATT tariff losses and wishing to preempt possible court action denying the Treasury any payment, consulted with House Commerce Committee Chairman John Dingell and then included the agreed payment in the implementing bill sent to Congress. It was a substantial contribution to the $12 billion total required. A rival company, Pacific Telesis, was outraged—insisting that the license was worth more than the *Post* and the other pioneers were paying. So in early October, shortly after a *Post* editorial endorsed the implementing bill without mentioning the deal, PacTel published full-page ads in the *Post* and the *Washington Times* denouncing the arrangement. The day after, the Nader-backed, anti-GATT Citizens' Trade Campaign took out ads denouncing the "multi-million dollar giveaway to the *Washington Post*." Talk radio picked up the issue, reinforcing the idea—pressed by Nader, Perot, and their allies—that the GATT legislation was the very sort of secret, inside deal, and back scratching among narrow interests in Washington that so incensed the public.[59]

The *Post* affair gave House politicians yet another reason to step aside until the issue could be resolved or had spent its course. And last but not least, Republicans were increasingly bullish on the fall election and increasingly caught up in their strategy of denying Clinton legislative victories, even partial ones. So House Minority Whip Newt Gingrich began talking of having Republicans oppose the *rule* that had to be passed to allow the House to vote on the legislation. If Republicans united with anti-GATT Democrats, they could block the vote. The administration and the House leadership kept calling for that vote up to its scheduled day, but they knew the political logic working against them, and ultimately they had to yield.

This additional setback unleashed a torrent of criticism. Carla Hills, USTR under Bush, who had been working with Clinton to win the House

---

59. This paragraph draws particularly on Mike Mills, "How an Editorial and an Ad Changed the GATT Debate," *Washington Post*, 25 November 1994.

vote, accused the administration of a "major, major miscalculation in introducing the bill so late in the session," when it had been "ready to be acted on since the spring. I'm a lawyer and this borders on malpractice. If I were involved," she concluded, "I think I would have fired myself."[60] The 7 October *Journal of Commerce*, on the other hand, saved its main fire for Gingrich. In an editorial entitled "Gutless on GATT," it attacked the speaker-to-be as "too obsessed with pandering to Mr. Perot and bashing Bill Clinton to uphold his party's historical commitment to free trade. If this is the kind of leadership Mr. Gingrich intends to provide in the future, Republicans, Congress and the country are in trouble."

From Partisan Wrangle to Bipartisan Victory

Even as partisanship scuttled the vote, however, bipartisanship was paving the way for postelection action. In exchange for the postponement, Gingrich agreed to back a rule calling for a vote on 29 November, and this passed by a bipartisan margin of 293-123. He underscored his support in a letter to the president promising to work for approval of the legislation on that date.

Everyone agreed, however, that the harder test would be in the Senate because a 60-vote supermajority would be required for a necessary procedural vote,[61] and because minority leader Robert Dole remained on the fence.[62] Hoping to sway him was a curious left-right alliance signified by three prominent personalities—Ralph Nader, Ross Perot, and Pat Buchanan. Particularly energetic were Nader and the consumer advocacy organization, Public Citizen. Even more curious was the thinness of visible opposition within Congress. Hollings was actively and vociferously opposed, but his position was familiar and therefore discounted. Jesse Helms would urge, after the election, that the legislation be held over until 1995, and Robert Byrd opposed it on grounds of budget process. But it was hard to find prominent names beyond these three.

The business community was late getting organized and never really waged an all-out campaign, as they had on NAFTA. Business leaders did play an important role in October and November, however. Since Congress was not in session, they had to work through companies in the appropriate states and districts. They followed a two-stage strategy. Aware that the populist, antiestablishment tenor of the campaign did not tilt

---

60. Quoted in *Journal of Commerce*, 7 October 1994.

61. The administration was seeking waiver of a Senate rule that budget offsets needed to be provided for 10 years out—it had only been able to do so for five years.

62. "If the Uruguay Round legislation fails," remarked one key administration trade official to the author around that time, "Bob Dole will bear a heavy share of the blame."

things in their favor on trade, the umbrella business organization Alliance for GATT Now asked members to withhold commitment until after the election. This effort was generally successful; trade was not a front-rank issue in the campaign, despite Buchanan-Perot-Nader efforts to make it so. The second round, pushing for commitments, was also effective if judged by results. But "the business effort on GATT was not as vigorous, not as broadly based, and not as sustained as the effort on NAFTA a year earlier," according to one trade veteran deeply involved in both. And it was considerably less critical to the outcome than the administration's dialogue with key Republican leaders.

Bipartisan support is generally necessary in trade policy. It was overridingly necessary for Bill Clinton after 8 November 1994. The result of that day's election—the remarkable Republican capture of both House and Senate—was a devastating repudiation of his leadership. Moreover, the vote was bound to raise questions as to the legitimacy of the rejected, Democrat-controlled 103rd Congress taking final action on the Uruguay Round in a lame-duck session. The only people who could give this process legitimacy were the Republican victors, and especially those with the new mandate: Newt Gingrich and Robert Dole.

Gingrich had, as earlier noted, signed on unambiguously in October, in exchange for the agreement to postpone the vote. He would deliver on this commitment, just as he had delivered on NAFTA the year before. Dole, by contrast, had promised nothing before the election—indeed, he had been nothing but trouble to the administration. So the spotlight was on him—what would he do? In postelection press conferences he expressed a hope that he could support GATT. He wanted some safeguard against adverse, arbitrary decisions against the United States in the WTO. In addition, he wanted some way to reopen the *Washington Post* deal embedded in the nonamendable implementing legislation. When the administration suggested willingness to address these issues, the senator upped the ante and asked for a procedural concession on reduction in the capital gains tax rate! In the spirit of bipartisan comity, wouldn't Clinton support that?

On this last item, the administration drew the line. It would not yield on an extraneous tax issue marked by strong partisan differences. With the boundaries of bargaining thus set, the deal quickly followed. On the Wednesday before Thanksgiving, Dole announced, from a White House podium, that he had won concessions that "fixed this as much as we can." On the WTO, he won an administration commitment to support legislation to establish a "WTO Dispute Settlement Review Commission." This would be composed of "five Federal appellate judges, appointed by the president in consultation with [congressional] leadership." This commission would "review all final dispute settlement reports . . . adverse to the United States." If it found, within any five-year period, three such decisions in which a WTO panel "demonstrably exceeded its authority" or "acted arbitrarily or capriciously," then any member of Congress could introduce and force a vote on a joint resolution mandating US withdrawal from the organization.[63] On the *Washington Post* controversy, Dole won a promise of a review that could lead to a higher price being paid for the license.

The deal was vintage Washington politics: the "good" kind, because it brought adversaries together behind a larger objective, but, ironically, the sort of practice that November voters had resoundingly repudiated. The deal had enough substance to address real concerns about a runaway international entity wreaking havoc with US policy, and some liberal traders felt that such a commission could in fact play a constructive role: in providing legal discipline for the new procedures in Geneva and in discrediting groundless attacks on WTO decisions. In any case, by settling with the key fence-sitting Republican, Clinton and Kantor had secured the necessary votes and won legitimacy for the lame-duck proceeding. And Dole achieved what was presumably *his* broader purpose—to signal, on the first available issue, his central role as power broker in the new Washington.

After the Dole deal, victory in the Senate was assured. Both opponents and supporters concealed this: the former for obvious reasons, the latter because they wanted to keep the pressure on and win the largest possible margin. There were therefore the last-minute White House meetings with undecided congressmen and senators, and a few minor policy deals.[64] These reinforced the strong pro-GATT momentum of the final week, and when the House voted the Tuesday after Thanksgiving, both parties supported the bill by margins of two-to-one, and the bill received at least 64 percent support from every region of the country.[65] GATT did even better in the Senate: the waiver passed with eight votes beyond the 60 required, and the count on final passage was 76-24, a happy surprise to the Clinton White House. In the Senate, the bipartisanship was mathematically perfect—as noted by Dole, each party voted 76 percent in favor: Democrats 41-13, Republicans 35-11. There were some unexpected defections, most notably that of outgoing Trade Subcommittee Chair Max Baucus.

---

63. Quotations are from Kantor's 23 November letter to Dole, reprinted in *Inside US Trade*, 25 November 1994, 23–24. It was too late for Dole's resolution to be considered in the 103rd Congress, which would adjourn shortly after the GATT vote. And in fact, the proposal was never enacted.

64. Because success was not riding on them, they were generally of minor consequence. For example, Senator Larry Pressler (R-SD) reportedly won an administration promise to push China to ease its import restrictions on soybeans (*Journal of Commerce*, 2 December 1994).

65. The House split 288-146, with Democrats 167-89 and Republicans 121-56. Regional percentages in favor were: Northeast, 70 percent; South, 64 percent; Midwest, 66 percent; and West, 67 percent. (Calculations are from the *New York Times*, 30 November 1994.)

Getting more national notice, however, was the decision of labor Democrat Barbara Mikulski of Maryland to "vote for GATT."

> I am a blue-collar Senator. My heart and soul lies with blue-collar America. . . . And in the last decade, working people have faced the loss of jobs, lower wages and a reduced standard of living, and a shrinking manufacturing base, everything that the critics say. But voting against GATT will not save those jobs or bring those jobs back. . . . The Uruguay Round [will] cut tariffs and reduce trade barriers for many of Maryland's top export industries. . . . So I am voting for GATT to generate more exports, to create more jobs in my own State of Maryland and in the United States of America.[66]

In November, before his GATT victory, Clinton had flown to Indonesia to sign an APEC summit declaration committing member states to achieving free trade by 2020 (by 2010 for the most advanced among them). In December the trade venue was Miami and the Summit for the Americas. The result there was a commitment to conclude a free trade arrangement for the hemisphere by 2005.[67]

As 1994 came to a close, President Clinton was still absorbing his crushing mid-term election setback. But he was also, in the words of one commentator, "compiling a more ambitious record of trade liberalization than any President since at least Harry S. Truman."[68] The road had been anything but smooth, and some of its obstacles had been of the administration's own making. One important battle was lost—that for fast-track extension. But in the end, with bipartisan support, the administration came through. Mickey Kantor in particular had proved an adept "closer" of deals: with Mexicans on NAFTA issues, with the European Union on GATT, and with senators and representatives on both. Carla Hills and others had moved both enterprises very far along, completing the NAFTA pact and winning the key US-EC breakthrough at Blair House. Kantor had pushed them over the top. He was the first US trade representative called upon to deliver major results in his first two years. And he did.

End of an Era?

Once again, the US trade policymaking system had worked. Congress played an active role but allowed the administration to lead. On NAFTA, members came around because they were substantively persuaded, but also because they were unwilling to take the responsibility for its rejection.

---

66. *Congressional Record*, 30 November 1994, S15102.

67. This was the target date for agreement, not for the actual removal of barriers. This left ambiguous the question of which goal—APEC or Western Hemisphere—was more ambitious.

68. Ronald Brownstein, "Clinton Drawing Visionary Blueprint of Global Economy," *Los Angeles Times*, 5 December 1994.

On GATT, direct rejection always seemed unlikely, but the limited enthusiasm of its backers made the agreement constantly vulnerable to other agendas. In the end, it received resounding bipartisan support. The trade policy process had once more overcome both partisan conflict and the separation of powers.

Kantor's USTR was less dependably antiprotectionist than the USTR of Carla Hills, reflecting the broader forces at play within Clinton's Democratic administration. It was responsive to a range of restriction-seeking industries: to steel on antidumping, to textiles on Uruguay Round and implementing-bill details, and to autos in seeking quantitative export targets vis-à-vis Japan. Its unrequited courtship of labor also fueled doubts over where Kantor and USTR stood. But these departures from free trade purity were well within the postwar trade-brokering tradition. The more important truth was that yet another administration had mastered the formula: firm commitment to negotiate and implement trade-liberalizing agreements and flexibility in accommodating key producer constituencies on the details. And trade continued to expand.

With NAFTA and GATT ratified, the biggest items had been removed from the US trade agenda. A new global trade organization had been launched, with robust dispute settlement rules. Protectionism was very much on the defensive. There were also, on the horizon, hemispheric negotiations toward free trade and the APEC liberalization process as well. All this suggested a bright future for liberal trade.

But 1994 would prove to be a high point, and the failure of fast track that year an omen. Thereafter, comparable trade policy achievements would elude the Clinton administration. Not only did it fail in subsequent efforts to gain fast-track renewal, but its effort to launch a new global trade round at the 1999 WTO Ministerial Conference in Seattle ended in disaster. Claiming credit were new antiglobalization forces that rose from the ashes of the losing campaign against NAFTA.

American trade politics would enter a new era. The chapters that follow tell that story, and assess its meaning for the United States in the 21st century.

POLARIZATION: 1995–

9

The Decline of Traditional Protectionism

The decade following completion of the North American Free Trade Agreement (NAFTA) and the Uruguay Round brought no comparable breakthroughs in American trade policy. During this period, the United States reestablished itself as the world's leading economic power, with rejuvenated productivity and growth. But there were no major new multilateral trade deals, though several sectoral agreements were concluded. A narrow group of industries, mainly steel, continued to exploit antidumping laws. The new World Trade Organization (WTO) established a credible dispute settlement process, and its membership grew to 148 countries by the end of 2004. Particularly notable was the entry in 2001 of the People's Republic of China after that nation had concluded a broad market-opening deal with the United States two years earlier.

World trade continued to grow—and US trade continued to expand as a share of national production. After receding in the early 1990s, the US trade deficit rose to heights that dwarfed those of the 1980s, both in absolute terms and as a proportion of total trade and GDP. Yet the new import surge did not trigger the sort of broad protectionist response that dominated the earlier high-deficit period of the mid-1980s. Only steel mounted a strong campaign for new trade relief, winning a number of antidumping cases and securing significant—albeit temporary—escape clause protection from President George W. Bush in 2002. Other industries pursued mixed strategies. Even textiles, faced with the phaseout of quotas under the Multi-Fiber Arrangement (MFA), emphasized free trade agreements that encouraged processing of US fiber and cloth in partner nations. Concerns did mount sharply in early 2005 about the US-China trade imbalance and the low fixed exchange rate of China's currency, the renminbi. They were voiced particularly by members of Congress and by Americans worried about the financial risks posed by global imbalance.[1] The mainstream business community was significantly less engaged in the issue, however, than it had been about the overvalued dollar 20 years before.

The weakness of traditional business protectionism was the product of the broader globalization process—major US firms overwhelmingly saw their futures as intertwined with global markets. But if capital was internationally mobile, labor was not. US production workers continued to suffer losses from trade competition, and the AFL-CIO remained a foe of new trade liberalization. Its resistance helped limit further reduction of US trade barriers, notwithstanding structural shifts within the business community. But the major new challenges to trade liberalization were the rising concerns over the impact of trade on labor and the environment, and the deepening of partisanship in Washington.

■ ■ ■

From the Nixon presidency through the early years of the Clinton administration, a pervasive sense of national decline burdened US trade policy. US growth performance was inferior to that of major trading partners. As a result, other nations—and Japan in particular—were seen as overtaking the United States. President George H. W. Bush's trip to Tokyo seeking trade concessions in January 1992 came to symbolize the perceived US plight. East Asia expert Chalmers Johnson spoke for many with his pithy aphorism, "The Cold War is over; Japan won."

Initially the Clinton administration accepted this view and gave, in the new president's words, "heightened" attention to the US-Japan economic relationship.[2] Enormous senior-level negotiating energy yielded modest results, epitomized by the resolution of a particularly fractious dispute over auto trade in June 1995 in which both sides claimed victory.[3] But even as the trade negotiators were climbing down from confrontation, their nations' economic fortunes were reversing themselves. Japan, beset

1. C. Fred Bergsten, "An Action Plan to Stop the Market Manipulators Now," *Financial Times*, 14 March 2005.

2. I. M. Destler, *The National Economic Council: A Work in Progress* (Washington, DC: Institute for International Economics, POLICY ANALYSES IN INTERNATIONAL ECONOMICS 46, November 1996), especially 37–38.

3. Leonard Schoppa, *Bargaining with Japan: What American Pressure Can and Cannot Do* (New York: Columbia University Press, 1997), chapter 9; I. M. Destler, "Has Conflict Passed Its Prime? Japanese and American Approaches to Trade and Economic Policy," *Maryland/Tsukuba Papers on U.S.-Japan Relations*, I. M. Destler and Hideo Sato, eds., Center for International and Security Studies at Maryland (March 1977), 21.

by the bursting of bubbles in land and stock prices, and resulting weakness in its banking system, suffered its worst economic decade since World War II and its aftermath. The United States, by contrast, was reaping the benefits of the revolution in information technology to a degree few had anticipated.[4]

Economic Resurgence

For the United States, the economic numbers were of a sort undreamed of since the stagflation of the 1970s. The annual unemployment rate dropped below 5 percent for five consecutive years (1997–2001); the last time it had been that low for even a single year was 1973. Yet prices remained stable—increases in the Consumer Price Index averaged 2.6 percent and never reached 3.5 percent over 1991–2002. And growth in GDP averaged 4.1 percent in 1996–2000, even though unemployment was low at the beginning of this period.[5] Over 1994–2003, growth in the United States substantially exceeded that of Europe and Japan for the first time since the 1940s.[6]

With the growth of the economy came an even more rapid rise in international commerce. From 1992 to 2000, total US merchandise trade (exports plus imports, measured in current dollars) more than doubled. The increase was greater than any since the 1970s and early 1980s, when inflation ballooned all trade statistics.

How could the US economy do so well? Inflation was certainly dampened by global competition—producers faced severe losses in market share if they increased their prices. But the underlying cause was a surge in business productivity. Just as the productivity slowdown starting in 1973 had been a source of economic woe thereafter, a surge in output per hour now brought unexpected gains. Driven by the application of computer technology, business productivity began in 1996 to post regular annual gains in the neighborhood of 2 percent plus. From 1997 to 2002, productivity jumped by 16.3 percent, the greatest five-year gain since the 1960s. As this indicates, the productivity surge continued unabated into the 21st century, even though overall US economic performance fell off beginning in late 2000.[7] (In 2001–02, both exports and imports were below 2000 levels.)

All Americans have not gained from this overall resurgence, of course. For more than a quarter century, US income distribution has been growing

---

4. For a comprehensive comparison of the two economies during the 1990s, see C. Fred Bergsten, Takatoshi Ito, and Marcus Noland, *No More Bashing: Building a New Japan–United States Economic Relationship* (Washington, DC: Institute for International Economics, 2001), chapters 1–3.

5. *Economic Report of the President*, February 2005, tables B-42, B-64, and B-4.

6. US GDP growth averaged 3.3 percent a year. For the European Union, that figure was 2.3 percent and for Japan, 1.2 percent (*Economic Report of the President*, February 2005, table B-112, and, 2003, table B-112.)

7. *Economic Report of the President*, February 2005, tables B-49 and B-50.

less equal. In particular, globalization has favored those with education and skills, while the incomes of males with just a high school education have suffered an absolute decline.[8] Indeed, the very flexibility and market orientation that has enabled Americans to exploit the computer age more effectively than have Europeans and Japanese has also generated greater income inequality. Drawing on "globalization balance sheet" studies at the Institute for International Economics and a broader survey of relevant economic literature, J. David Richardson finds that "Americans with average skills, women, blue-collar union members, and insular communities . . . seem to be on the periphery of globalization's gains."[9] They suffer from both competitive pressure on wage levels and a greater possibility of job displacement. However, as the productivity surge continues, it generates overall national gains sufficient to cushion such losses—a matter that will be addressed in chapter 12.

The resurgence of the US economy assuaged American fears of being supplanted by other advanced industrial nations. It did not, however, have a major positive impact on US trade politics or policy. In fact, the decade that followed the Uruguay Round proved one of modest accomplishment. It would take seven years to launch a new global trade round, and eight years to renew fast-track negotiating authority. And neither of these steps would be accomplished under Bill Clinton.

Clinton and Barshefsky: Business (Mostly) As Usual

In early 1996, Secretary of Commerce Ron Brown died in a plane crash during an official mission to Croatia. US Trade Representative (USTR) Mickey Kantor was named to succeed him, and his deputy, Charlene Barshefsky, assumed the USTR position—for a year in an acting capacity, thereafter with Senate confirmation and the full authority of the office. She held the post until the end of the Clinton administration. Like most USTRs, she lacked a strong relationship with the president of the sort that Kantor had enjoyed. She was regarded as more trade centered and less partisan, however, which made it easier for her to work with the Republican majorities in Congress.

There was unfinished business from the Uruguay Round, and US negotiators completed much of it. An Information Technology Agreement was negotiated in 1996 and went into effect the following year. It provided for reciprocal elimination of tariffs on information technology prod-

8. See, for example, Frank Levy and Richard J. Murnane, "Got a Routine Job? Not for Long," *Washington Post*, Outlook Section, 4 July 2004, 3.

9. J. David Richardson, *Global Forces, American Faces: US Economic Globalization at the Grass Roots* (Washington, DC: Institute for International Economics, January 2005 draft), 6.

ucts by countries constituting at least 90 percent of global trade in these products. This was followed in February 1997 by an Agreement on Basic Telecommunications Services, under which 69 nations constituting over 90 percent of global telecommunications revenues made commitments to liberalize regulation and improve market access in a sector long characterized by heavy-handed governmental restrictions. An Agreement on Financial Services, completed in December 1997, opened the major world markets in such areas as banking, securities, insurance, and financial data.

Barshefsky's USTR was effective in negotiating these accords, and her personal persistence was critical to the greatest trade policy achievement of her tenure—completion in 1999 of a comprehensive, market-opening agreement with the People's Republic of China that was a prerequisite to that country's entry into the WTO.[10] But there was little progress toward fulfillment of the two broad US regional commitments of 1994—free trade within the Asia Pacific Economic Cooperation (APEC) forum, and the projected Free Trade Area of the Americas (FTAA). NAFTA was implemented on schedule, with some fractious exceptions involving Mexican tomatoes and trucks, and US-Mexican trade grew enormously. But the treaty remained controversial, particularly after the peso crisis of 1994–95 turned the bilateral trade balance from a projected modest surplus to a substantial and persistent deficit.

The USTR under Barshefsky completed a free trade agreement with Jordan in October 2000, and launched talks on a free trade agreement with Singapore and Chile during its final year. Overall, however, with the important exception of the China deal, the Clinton administration proved more effective in completing the work of its predecessors than in carrying out major new initiatives.

Trade Remedies, Especially Antidumping

Continuity was also the rule in the use of trade remedy procedures. As shown in table 9.1, resort to the standard escape clause (Section 201) remained minimal—no more than two cases in any year. There was a slight rise in countervailing duty (CVD) petitions in 1998–2001,[11] but the numbers were a fraction of those in the early 1980s. The main action remained in the venerable sphere of antidumping.[12]

---

10. See chapter 10 for details. That chapter also discusses the two prominent Clinton administration failures: its campaign to renew fast-track trade authority and its effort to launch a new global trade round.

11. Typically, two-thirds of them (36 of 54) involved steel products.

12. The case data underlying the numbers presented here are posted on the Web site of the Institute for International Economics, www.iie.com.

Table 9.1 Antidumping, countervailing duty, and Section 201 investigations initiated from 1979 to 2004

Year	Antidumping cases	Countervailing duty cases	Section 201 cases
1979	26	40	4
1980	21	14	2
1981	15	22	1
1982	65	140	3
1983	46	22	0
1984	74	51	7
1985	66	43	4
1986	71	27	1
1987	15	8	0
1988	42	11	1
1989	23	7	0
1990	43	7	1
1991	51	8	0
1992	99	43	1
1993	42	5	0
1994	43	7	0
1995	14	2	1
1996	20	1	2
1997	16	6	1
1998	36	12	1
1999	61	16	2
2000	51	12	2
2001	69	13	1
2002	37	5	0
2003	45	6	0
2004	22	4	0
Total	**1,113**	**532**	**35**

Sources: Author's calculations, based on tallies from the US International Trade Commission (especially its annual *The Year in Review* reports); ALLAD-Casis and ALLCVD databases; Bruce Blonigen, US Antidumping Case-Specific Data, 1980–85; and the *Federal Register.*

As analyzed in chapter 6, US officials resisted—and largely offset—a major international effort during the Uruguay Round to constrain the use of the antidumping remedy. The details of this effort, within the executive branch and in "nonmarkup" drafting sessions with Congress, are set forth admirably and persuasively by Robert E. Cumby and Theodore H. Moran.[13] But at the time, the net effect did not appear to this author to make relief easier to obtain, and experience since then supports this assessment. The number of new antidumping cases dropped sharply in 1995–97, then rose sharply in the next four years. A simple statistical "t-test" indicates no

---

13. See Cumby and Moran, "Testing Models of the Trade Policy Process: Antidumping and the 'New Issues,'" chapter 6 in Robert Feenstra, ed., *The Effects of U.S. Trade Protection and Promotion Policies* (Chicago: University of Chicago Press for the National Bureau of Economic Research, 1997).

Figure 9.1 Total antidumping cases, 1980–2004

number

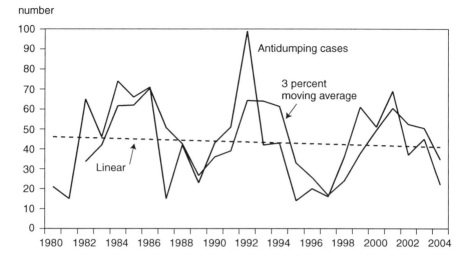

trend (upward or downward) in the numbers of cases submitted over the 1980–2002 period and no significant change either way under the new rules enacted in 1994 (figure 9.1). This stands in contrast to the general increase following the legislative changes of 1974 and 1979 and the transfer of administrative authority to the Department of Commerce in 1980.

The pattern of disposition of the cases was essentially unchanged as well (table 9.2). Department of Commerce findings of "no dumping" became even rarer (5 percent over 1980–2003, and 3 percent over 1995–2003); findings by the US International Trade Commission of "no injury" rose slightly (to 44.3 percent for 1995–2003, compared with 43.2 percent for the entire period). The net effect was basically a wash—51.8 percent of all antidumping cases carried to completion led to imposition of antidumping duties over the full period, and 52.6 percent after 1994.[14]

More than ever, the primary US user of the antidumping remedy was now the steel industry (498 of 1,067 cases since 1980, 186 of 349 after 1994). And the disposition was similar, though a large percentage of no-injury

---

14. Using a slightly different database for numbers of antidumping cases, Douglas Irwin has reached conclusions that go beyond the above but are not inconsistent with this analysis. He finds that "the number of imported products involved [in antidumping cases] has actually fallen since the mid-1980s," and that one important cause of "the increased number of cases in recent decades" is the rise of "petitions that target multiple source countries." He finds that "the annual number of antidumping cases is influenced by the unemployment rate, the exchange rate, import penetration . . . and changes in the antidumping law and its enforcement in the early 1980s." See *The Rise of U.S. Antidumping Actions in Historical Perspective*, National Bureau of Economic Research Working Paper 10582, June 2004.

Table 9.2   Antidumping cases and results, 1980–2003

Year	Total	Cases withdrawn	Cases completed	Cases affirmed Number	Cases affirmed Percent	No dumping Number	No dumping Percent	No injury Number	No injury Percent
1980	21	9	12	4	33.3	1	8.3	7	58.3
1981	15	4	11	7	63.6	1	9.1	3	27.3
1982	65	24	41	14	34.1	3	7.3	24	58.5
1983	46	5	41	19	46.3	5	12.2	17	41.5
1984	74	41	33	9	27.3	6	18.2	18	54.5
1985	66	16	50	29	58.0	2	4.0	19	38.0
1986	71	7	64	44	68.8	3	4.7	17	26.6
1987	15	1	14	9	64.3	0	0.0	5	35.7
1988	42	0	42	22	52.4	3	7.1	17	40.5
1989	23	3	20	14	70.0	0	0.0	6	30.0
1990	43	2	41	19	46.3	5	12.2	17	41.5
1991	53	4	49	24	49.0	2	4.1	23	46.9
1992	99	11	88	45	51.1	1	1.1	42	47.7
1993	42	6	36	19	52.8	2	5.6	15	41.7
1994	43	3	40	21	52.5	1	2.5	18	45.0
1995	14	1	13	8	61.5	0	0.0	5	38.5
1996	20	0	20	17	85.0	1	5.0	2	10.0
1997	16	1	15	8	53.3	0	0.0	7	46.7
1998	36	0	36	22	61.1	0	0.0	14	38.9
1999	61	4	57	24	42.1	1	1.8	32	56.1
2000	51	0	51	34	66.7	5	9.8	12	23.5
2001	69	6	63	23	36.5	1	1.6	39	61.9
2002	37	4	33	13	39.4	0	0.0	20	60.6
2003	45	10	35	21	60.0	2	5.7	12	34.3
Total	1,067	162	905	469	51.8	45	5.0	391	43.2

Sources: US International Trade Commission, annual *The Year in Review* reports; Bruce Blonigen, US Antidumping Case-Specific Data, 1980–85; and the *Federal Register*.

findings in 2001 and 2002 drove the overall steel success rate down below 50 percent (table 9.3). Steel also continued to be the principal source of year-to-year variation in cases submitted.

One product of the Uruguay Round agreements was a "sunset" requirement—antidumping orders could no longer remain in place indefinitely, but had to be reviewed every five years. Typically, the Clinton administration leaned against this reform by delaying sunset reviews to the last feasible time period allowed, but the result was still a sharp drop in antidumping orders in effect between 1998 and 2000. At the end of 2003, there were 291 operative antidumping orders (including eight suspension agreements), down from the 1998 peak of 313 (figure 9.2).

In summary, the US antidumping process continued to be biased against defendants, as discussed in chapter 6. But it also continued to be marginal insofar as overall US trade was concerned.[15]

---

15. In "Testing Models of the Trade Policy Process," Cumby and Moran assert that the Clinton administration's action under congressional pressure to reinforce the antidumping laws

Table 9.3   Steel antidumping cases and results, 1980–2003

Year	Total	Cases withdrawn	Cases completed	Cases affirmed Number	Percent	No dumping Number	Percent	No injury Number	Percent
1980	9	8	1	0	0.0	1	100.0	0	0.0
1981	6	2	4	3	75.0	0	0.0	1	25.0
1982	49	24	25	7	28.0	1	4.0	17	68.0
1983	15	3	12	8	66.7	1	8.3	3	25.0
1984	52	38	14	2	14.3	2	14.3	10	71.4
1985	40	14	26	16	61.5	1	3.8	9	34.6
1986	12	3	9	8	88.9	0	0.0	1	11.1
1987	2	0	2	1	50.0	0	0.0	1	50.0
1988	5	0	5	3	60.0	1	20.0	1	20.0
1989	1	0	1	0	0.0	0	0.0	1	100.0
1990	7	0	7	0	0.0	3	42.9	4	57.1
1991	11	0	11	9	81.8	0	0.0	2	18.2
1992	66	0	66	34	51.5	0	0.0	32	48.5
1993	13	2	11	6	54.5	1	9.1	4	36.4
1994	24	1	23	10	43.5	1	4.3	12	52.2
1995	4	0	4	1	25.0	0	0.0	3	75.0
1996	6	0	6	5	83.3	0	0.0	1	16.7
1997	11	0	11	6	54.5	0	0.0	5	45.5
1998	24	0	24	17	70.8	0	0.0	7	29.2
1999	35	0	35	17	48.6	0	0.0	18	51.4
2000	36	0	36	28	73.3	1	3.3	7	23.3
2001	46	3	43	9	20.0	1	0.0	33	80.0
2002	17	1	16	3	18.8	0	0.0	13	81.3
2003	7	0	7	5	71.4	0	0.0	2	28.6
Total	**498**	**99**	**399**	**198**	**49.6**	**14**	**3.5**	**187**	**46.9**

Note: All suspended cases are counted as completed and affirmative.

Sources: US International Trade Commission, annual *The Year in Review* reports; Bruce Blonigen, US Antidumping Case-Specific Data, 1980–95; and the *Federal Register.*

goes against the "model" of "protection for Congress," developed in chapter 2 of this book, that features congressional deference to executive branch decisions, and executive branch exploitation of this deference to move trade policy in a liberal direction through negotiated reductions in US trade barriers. They are right in the sense that Congress was not deferential and that the Kantor USTR Office did not tilt in the liberal direction on antidumping. However, the model developed in chapter 2 explicitly includes administrative remedies (see "the rules," pp. 21–24 and subsequent sections) as an important element of the system, a counterbalance to its generally liberal tilt, allowing for protection in exceptional cases for producers following procedures defined in trade statutes. And as set forth in chapter 6, Congress has regularly made trade protection easier to obtain under these statutes—in particular in the 1974 law authorizing the Tokyo Round agreements and the 1979 law implementing them. Thus, antidumping has always been part of the broader US trade policymaking system, and it has never (since the Kennedy Round, at least) been a sphere where Congress granted leeway to the leadership of the executive branch.

There is another reason, however, to believe that the model set forth in chapter 2 is of diminishing utility in explaining US trade policymaking. This is the decline of traditional, business-based protectionism as the overriding political problem that policy must address. Chapter 12 considers the implications.

Figure 9.2 Number of antidumping orders and suspension agreements in effect, 1986–2003

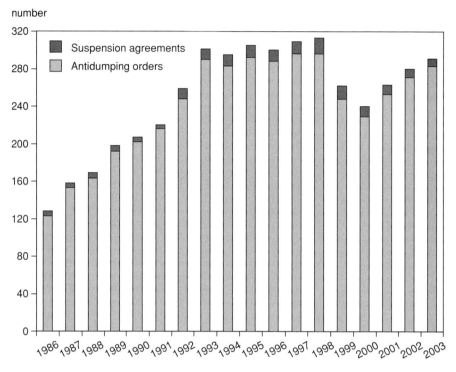

Source: US International Trade Commission, annual *The Year in Review* reports, 1987–2003.

The most visible change in US antidumping law since 1995 has been the "Byrd amendment," which provides that the proceeds of antidumping duties be passed on to the petitioners. This was neither proposed nor reviewed by the trade policy committees but rather was slipped into a 2000 appropriations bill by the crafty senior senator from West Virginia, Robert Byrd. Once enacted, it proved difficult to remove. But it also highlighted the increasing challenge to US trade remedy laws powered by a new force in the global trade regime: the WTO's dispute settlement procedures that came into existence in 1995. Within months of its enactment, the Byrd amendment was challenged by 11 nations as inconsistent with the Uruguay Round antidumping agreement. In January 2003, it was ruled a violation of US trade commitments under that agreement.

The World Trade Organization

When the Reagan administration was dissatisfied with Japanese implementation of the bilateral semiconductor agreement in the spring of 1987, it imposed sanctions (100 percent tariffs on selected electronic products) under Section 301 of the Trade Act of 1974. These sanctions survived, in modified form, for the life of the agreement. When the Clinton administration was dissatisfied with what it saw as Japanese intransigence on market access for autos and auto parts in the spring of 1995, it also imposed sanctions under Section 301—100 percent tariffs on imports of luxury automobiles. This time, however, the government of Japan launched a WTO case charging the United States with breach of its trade obligations. Within weeks, the United States settled for far less than it had sought, the sanctions were lifted, and the WTO case became moot.

Why the difference? In both situations, the US sanction was inconsistent with a binding international tariff commitment. But in the former case the Japanese had no recourse, as the dispute settlement process operative through 1994 under the General Agreement on Tariffs and Trade (GATT) gave the defendant nation the power to block a decision. The WTO's dispute settlement mechanism removed this power, as the United States in fact had sought. The Japanese case against US auto sanctions was only the sixth filed with the fledgling organization, but the parameters were clear to both parties. The United States could no longer retaliate, unilaterally, without the risk of being "taken to court" and losing.

Thus the dispute settlement mechanism took the bite out of Section 301. The United States no longer had the leeway to retaliate against foreign impediments to US exports that it deemed "unreasonable." Beginning in 1995, Section 301 cases against WTO members were overwhelmingly channeled through the WTO process.[16] And such cases were frequent: From 1995 to the end of the Clinton administration, the United States submitted 68 complaints to the WTO, an average of 11 per year. During the first Bush term, by contrast, the United States filed just 12 cases, or three per year.

The new dispute settlement mechanism proved popular with other nations as well. A total of 324 cases were filed as of 31 December 2004, an average of 32 per year. Over half (168) involved the United States, 80 as plaintiff and 88 as defendant. And the frequency of other nations' cases against the United States has been increasing. During the six Clinton years, 50 complaints (8.3 per year, on average) were filed against the United States by other countries. This rose to 9.5 per year (38 in all) in President Bush's first term.

When the USTR took other nations to court, the new organization proved an effective instrument of US trade policy. Of the 22 cases the USTR brought before the WTO as of 31 December 2004 that were litigated

---

16. Of the 25 Section 301 investigations launched from 1995 through 2001, 17, or 68 percent, were brought to the WTO.

to completion, 18 were decided in favor of the United States.[17] This added up to an impressive 82 percent overall success rate. Among the more prominent were early challenges to the European Union on its ban on imports of beef grown with hormones, and its system for the importation of bananas. A more recent case involved Japanese restrictions on the import of apples.

But when the tables were turned, and other nations brought cases against the United States, US law or practice was usually found wanting. The United States was found in violation of its trade obligations in 74 percent (25 of 34) of WTO panel or appellate body decisions reached by January 2005.[18] Prominent among these were a European challenge to the US system of subsidizing exports through a favorable tax treatment regime (the foreign sales corporation, or FSC), a US law banning imports of shrimp not caught with turtle-excluder devices, and President George W. Bush's decision in 2002 to impose Section 201 (escape clause) safeguards on certain imports of steel.[19]

A nation that loses a WTO case is obligated to change its law or practice to bring it into line. But in contrast to, say, a US Supreme Court decision invalidating a specific US statute, compliance does not flow directly from a WTO decision. Rather, the ball passes back to the national government, which may or may not act. If it does not, the plaintiff is entitled to retaliate, and a separate WTO process is available to determine the damage done by the barrier and hence the damage the plaintiff can do in return. Overall, compliance has been the norm: "In a majority of cases over the last seven years where the complaining country won a WTO dispute, the losing state removed or revised the offending trade barriers."[20] High-profile cases can be harder, however. In the beef hormones case, the European Union has failed to comply, accepting instead imposition of equivalent trade barriers by the United States (and Canada). Since July 1999, the

---

17. This counts as single cases those submitted separately but reviewed together (e.g., three linked cases against the EU's import regime for bananas). If such cases are counted individually, the United States won 22 and lost six, a success rate of 79 percent. This excludes 25 (27) that were negotiated, nine that are pending , and 14 (16) that are inactive. The case data upon which these summary statistics are based are posted at www.iie.com.

18. If cases are counted individually (e.g., the eight separate country filings in 2002 against US steel safeguards), the United States won nine and lost 37, or 80 percent of WTO cases that were litigated to completion. Excluded are 14 (16) cases that were negotiated, 17 that are pending, and nine that are inactive.

19. The Bush administration reported, in mid-2004, an overall WTO won-lost record of 13–10 (56 percent) during its tenure, and 18–15 (54 percent) during the Clinton years. See "Real Results: Leveling the Playing Field for American Workers and Farmers," Trade Facts Press Release, Office of the US Trade Representative, 8 July 2004.

20. Susan Esserman and Robert Howse, "The WTO on Trial," *Foreign Affairs*, January/February 2003, 132–33.

United States has imposed 100 percent duties on imports of selected products of EU countries, adding up to $116.8 million in value. On the banana case, the first European response was judged inadequate by the WTO; thereafter the United States and the European Union resolved the matter in bilateral negotiations.

The US compliance record is likewise mixed, even allowing for the delays needed to enact legislation. Action was prompt when the WTO ruled that President Bush's steel tariffs were improperly imposed and the European Union threatened sanctions—Bush simply ended his tariffs, declaring that they had accomplished their purpose (and mentioning neither the WTO nor the European Union in his short statement). Compliance was dragged out on eliminating the FSC—members of Congress agreed on the goal but differed on the means—and the European Union began imposing escalating retaliatory tariffs in early 2004 to spur US action. The United States has complied by changing standards for reformulated gasoline found to discriminate against imports and changing the law requiring turtle-excluder devices for shrimp harvesting so that it did not favor certain countries over others. More elusive has been action to repeal the Byrd amendment. Overall, looking at decisions more than two years old, the United States has complied in 16 of 21 cases.[21]

Has the cumulation of decisions against the United States provoked a broad reaction against the WTO? To date, the answer is no—opinion surveys show no decline in general public support.[22] Advocates of US trade remedy laws—antidumping in particular—have expressed concern from the outset: When Senator Bob Dole (R-KS) won President Clinton's endorsement of his proposal for a "WTO Dispute Settlement Review Commission"[23] in late 1994, he had defense of US "unfair trade" laws in mind. But when the House first voted in 2000 on whether to withdraw from the organization, as required by the Gingrich amendment (described in chapter 8), only 56 members voted in favor (33 Republicans, 21 Democrats, two independents). Since that vote, however, US losses in WTO cases have continued to mount, and the preponderance of them have involved antidumping, countervailing duties, or safeguard actions. Moreover, of the 17

---

21. These are cases that the United States lost on core issues, which ended before 31 December 2002. The United States has been noncompliant in three cases (WT/DS176–United States–Section 211 Omnibus Appropriations Act; WT/DS184–United States–Antidumping measures on certain hot-rolled steel products from Japan; and WT/DS217 & DS234–United States–Continued Dumping and Subsidy Offset Act of 2000 [Byrd Amendment]), and has complied partly in two cases.

22. When asked in 2003–04 whether "the US should comply" if "the World Trade Organization . . . rules against the US," 67 percent of respondents said yes, up slightly from 65 percent in 1999. See Program on International Policy Attitudes (PIPA), *Americans on Globalization: A Study of US Attitudes on Globalization*, 22 January 2004, 8.

23. The proposal was never enacted. See pages 227–28, chapter 8 for details.

cases pending against the United States as of the end of 2004, all but three involved those same three areas. So it is plausible to expect a somewhat larger anti-WTO vote when the issue comes up automatically again in 2005.

Like the US Supreme Court, at times, the WTO and its appellate body have been charged with "judicial activism"—a tendency to overinterpret the trade agreements it is enforcing rather than defer to national authorities in ambiguous cases. This charge has focused particularly on national procedures enforcing trade remedies: For example, there is nothing in the Uruguay Round agreements that explicitly outlaws channeling anti-dumping proceeds to successful plaintiffs, however opprobrious critics may find the practice.

The larger WTO problem, however, is structural imbalance: The efficient and binding dispute settlement problem is married to a highly cumbersome and inefficient "legislative" process.[24] The WTO capacity to make new rules or amend old ones is constrained by the norm of consensus decision making among its 148 members. In practice, trade rules are rarely amended except as the outcome of global trade rounds, with more than a decade from one to the next.[25] And the path to such agreements is not straight, as reflected in the failures of key GATT and WTO Ministerial Meetings in 1982, 1990, 1999, and 2003. Hence the WTO lacks the capacity to rein in its judges if they do not show restraint.

Adverse WTO decisions also pose a challenge to the trade policy process in the United States when they find US statutes inconsistent with trade obligations. In such cases, the president and the USTR must seek direct legislative action, and Congress must therefore take the heat for changes. Nor is it usually possible to subsume such changes within broad trade legislation, since major trade bills are years apart. It is therefore no surprise that all three cases of clear US noncompliance call for legislative action.

Reemergence of the Trade Deficit—and Its Lesser Political Impact

Driven by a strong dollar, the US merchandise trade deficit soared in the 1980s to unprecedented, 12-digit dimensions. Industry after industry was

---

24. Highlighting this imbalance from different perspectives are Claude Barfield, *Free Trade, Sovereignty, Democracy: The Future of the World Trade Organization* (Washington, DC: American Enterprise Institute Press, 2001), and Theodore R. Posner and Timothy M. Reif, "Homage to a Bull Moose: Applying Lessons of History to Meet the Challenges of Globalization," *Fordham International Law Journal* 24, November–December 2000. See also John H. Jackson, "The Role and Effectiveness of the WTO Dispute Settlement Mechanism," *Brookings Trade Forum 2000* (Washington, DC: Brookings Institution, 2001), 179–220.

25. The Kennedy Round was concluded in 1967, the Tokyo Round in 1979, the Uruguay Round in 1994. The Doha Round will not be wrapped up before 2006 at the earliest.

hit, and demanded trade protection: textiles, steel, autos, shoes, machine tools, semiconductors, etc. The Reagan administration resisted to some degree, but also granted some form of trade relief to most of them.

The trade deficit receded late in that decade, facilitating compromises in (and enactment of) trade legislation in 1988. The deficit dropped below $100 billion in 1991 and 1992 and grew only modestly through 1997. Thereafter it skyrocketed—from $198.1 billion in 1997 to $452.4 billion in 2000, $549.4 billion in 2003, and $665 billion in 2004.[26] In that year, the United States imported $1.473 trillion in goods and exported just $808 billion.

In absolute terms, this deficit dwarfed the $159.6 billion that had triggered so much anxiety in 1987. But total US trade had soared also, roughly tripling between 1987 and 2000. As a proportion of trade, the deficit was comparable in those years—24 percent in 1987 and 23 percent in 2000. But it reached a new peak of 29 percent in 2004, meaning that the country imported more than $9 in goods for every $5 that it exported, a truly remarkable ratio. As a proportion of GDP, the deficits of the early 21st century came to exceed their 1980s counterparts, reaching a record 5.7 percent in 2004.

The deficits were and are a macroeconomic phenomenon, and the proximate causes varied.[27] Throughout, they reflected an unpleasant reality: Americans were saving too little, and consuming more than they were producing. But such lofty explanations were no consolation to US-based goods producers who felt the heat. And for them, the new deficits were at least comparable to the 1980s. Looking directly at the goods with which domestic producers competed, the value of imports rose 83 percent from 1994 to 2000, compared to 81 percent from 1982 to 1988.

And just as in the early 1980s, the rising dollar meant that the dollar statistics understated the increase in import volume, because they came in at lower prices. If we look at a better measure of quantity—price-deflated import data—we find greater impact. From 1982 to 1986, the value of US imports rose by 48 percent, but the quantity went up 65 percent. From 1996 to 2000, the value of US imports rose by 52 percent, but the quantity (measured in chained 2000 dollars) went up 63 percent.

Finally, if we use quantity measures again and look at the ratio of imports to US goods production—a good proxy for overall market pressure

---

26. See table 3.1 in chapter 3. Here and throughout, this book focuses on the trade balance in goods, not the overall balance in goods and services now highlighted by the Department of Commerce, nor the still broader balance on the current account. The reason is that trade policy is still mostly about goods (though services have undeniably grown in importance), and the products and producers in farms and factories have dominated the trade policy process.

27. In the late 1990s, a strong dollar, a surge in investment that precipitated capital inflows, and the Asian financial crisis dampened exports. By 2003, the new Bush budget deficit was an important contributor, as was Reagan's before.

on domestic producers—we find that this ratio rose from 27.5 to 36.1 between 1996 and 2000 before leveling off at 36.5 in 2003.[28]

Thus, in terms of increases in import pressure, the late Clinton years look very much like the middle Reagan years. Yet the political response was very different. In the first period, multiple industries sought protection, Congress seized the initiative in trade policy, and many experts trembled over whether open US policies could survive. In the second period, only one dog barked—steel. It had won comprehensive (if temporary) protection under Reagan from 1985 onward in the form of a number of export restraint agreements with key producers. But steel won no such protection under Clinton (aside from a number of antidumping cases), and just 21 months of relief from George W. Bush, who imposed tariffs on a range of steel products in March 2002 but removed them in December 2003 after a WTO finding that they were illegal.

Why weren't more injured claimants demanding import relief post-1995? One reason was certainly the overall strength of the US economy as compared with the mid-1980s: With a happier economic mood, campaigns for trade relief were harder to sustain. Together with this was the fading of the prime trade "adversary," Japan (though China seemed poised to take its place). But there was also precious little new business protectionism after the stock market bubble burst in 2000 and the economy entered recession and slow growth in the early George W. Bush years.

Textiles? Its leaders were certainly concerned about trade, and sought to shape trade rules to their advantage. But as they lost the MFA, and failed to get its phaseout period extended beyond 2004, they were crafting a very sweet deal for themselves in NAFTA by focusing on a relatively arcane matter: its "rules of origin."[29] Since the member nations were eliminating tariffs among themselves but maintaining different tariff levels vis-à-vis the outside world, they needed criteria to determine whether a good crossing an intra-NAFTA border came from inside or outside the NAFTA region. The question is complicated by the globalization of manufacturing: A product may draw its main raw material from country A, be assembled in country B with inputs from countries C and D, etc. For autos, NAFTA used a percentage rule: A car was North American in origin if 62.5 percent of its value was added within the region.[30]

---

28. This was parallel to the rise (using 1982 as a base year) from 18.9 to 25.8 between 1980 and 1986, as reported in chapter 8. The quantity measures and ratios are calculated from data in tables B-9 and B-25 of the *Economic Report of the President*, various years.

29. For a broader discussion, see Destler, "Rules of Origin and US Trade Policy," in Olivier Cadot, Antoni Estevadeordal, Akiko Suwa, and Thierry Verdier, eds., *The Origin of Goods: Rules of Origin in Preferential Trade Agreements* (Oxford and London: Oxford University Press and Center for Economic Policy Research, forthcoming).

30. See Frederick W. Mayer, *Interpreting NAFTA: The Science and Art of Political Analysis* (New York: Columbia University Press, 1998), especially 157–62.

For textiles, the rule was even more restrictive. As set forth in chapter 8, NAFTA provides that for apparel to be deemed North American, three processes must all take place within the region: the making of the fiber, its conversion into fabric, and then the crafting of the garment. This "triple transformation test" (also known as the "yarn forward rule") is anything but free trade: A recent broad analysis that examines rules of origin for 20 product sectors in five separate free trade agreements finds the NAFTA textile-apparel rules the most restrictive of all.[31] But it represents a separation of US mills from their long-standing domestic apparel allies—to whom they long expected to sell most of their cloth—in favor of a strategy that sees expanding international trade as inevitable and potentially profitable.

Of course, there was no guarantee that this particular strategy would continue to be effective: By the early 2000s, textile officials were having second thoughts as, with the lifting of some MFA quotas, Chinese apparel began displacing Mexican apparel in the US market, notwithstanding the latter's NAFTA advantages. The final phaseout of the MFA at the end of 2004 could only bring further changes. But their realistic options fell well short of the comprehensive trade protection they had long championed.

No other industries rose up to claim the protectionist banner. There were flare-ups over China in late 2003 and thereafter, as congressional critics linked a sharp post-2000 drop in US manufacturing employment to the rise of the bilateral trade deficit with China and that country's fixed (arguably undervalued) dollar exchange rate. And in early 2004, Democratic presidential contenders vied with one another to show toughness on trade, with the "outsourcing" of jobs by US corporations the latest dragon to be decried if not cleaved. But while the winner of the Democratic nomination, Senator John F. Kerry (D-MA), denounced "Benedict Arnold corporations," all he could promise as a remedy was to amend US tax law to make it neutral as regards whether those firms produced at home or abroad.

And the fact that US business was the target of such criticism was itself very telling. Through much of US history, it was manufacturers who led the charge for high tariffs. In the decades following 1934, it was protection-seeking firms and sectors whose efforts needed to be resisted or deflected in order for trade liberalization to proceed. By the dawn of the 21st century, business was clearly identified with trade expansion, by critics and advocates alike.

The Globalization of US Business

US markets have steadily become more internationalized during recent decades. Goods production has in fact declined as a share of the total

---

31. Antoni Estevadeordal and Kati Suominen, "Rules of Origin in FTAs: A World Map," table 7. www.iadb.org/intal/foros/LAestevadeordal.pdf (accessed 15 April 2005).

economy, from 43 percent in 1970 to 35 percent in 2000. But over the same period, *trade in goods* has grown from 4 to 10 percent of GDP.[32] Thus the ratio of trade (average of imports and exports) to goods production has risen even faster, from .09 to .29. Producers export a larger share of their output. They also import a larger share of their products' final value. And those that lag in exploiting the gains from international specialization face uphill competition from those that do exploit them.

In the context of a globalizing economy, a pure protectionist position becomes harder and harder to sustain, while support for maintaining open markets is easier to find. When, in late 2003, President Bush weighed how to respond to the adverse WTO ruling on steel, press reports highlighted the concerns of steel-*user* industries in Pennsylvania, West Virginia, and Ohio as much as they stressed the steel-*producing* interests in those key electoral states. White House political adviser Karl Rove was reported to be taking the steel users' interests fully into account.

There remained entrenched redoubts of protection, of course, most of them agricultural. The 2002 farm bill flew in the face of long-standing US trade-negotiating goals by increasing producer subsidies. Sugar survived under an import quota system that made US prices a multiple of those in the global market, and opened up economic opportunity for producers of corn sweetener as well. US rigidity on sugar was evident in early 2004: Central America was granted little increased sugar access in the Central American Free Trade Agreement (CAFTA),[33] and Australia was granted none at all in its free trade agreement. Orange juice was another well-protected market, which Brazil clamored to enter. Sugar and oranges both stood in the way of a comprehensive Free Trade Area of the Americas, and US cotton subsidies undercut the livelihoods of African farmers and helped trigger the breakup of the Cancún Ministerial of the Doha Round. In the spring of 2004, a WTO panel held that US cotton subsidies were in excess of those allowed under the Uruguay Round agreements (a finding later affirmed by the appellate body).

These still-restricted US markets remained barriers both to trade and to progress in trade negotiations. But they were now exceptions, not the rule. As recently as the 1980s, it was plausible to argue that the threat of a type of Smoot-Hawley protection was real, that concessions to one or two new industries could put the United States on a "slippery slope," and that the

---

32. Trade here is the average of exports and imports, $(X + M)/2$. Properly speaking, trade/GDP and trade/goods production should be seen as ratios, not percentages, since trade statistics represent the final value of goods bought and sold, and GDP and goods production represent just value added in the United States. All statistics are calculated from the *2004 Economic Report of the President*, tables B-1, B-8, and B-13.

33. USTR calculated this as "about one and a half teaspoons per week per American." Nonetheless, domestic sugar producers launched a fierce campaign to defeat CAFTA in 2005.

trade bicycle would fall down if the country did not move forward. It is much harder to make this argument today.

There remains one strong institutional opponent to further trade liberalization as currently practiced, and that is organized labor. Decades ago, unions' trade stances tended to be aligned with their industries—apparel workers were antitrade, while Walter Reuther's United Auto Workers backed the Kennedy Round. Now capital is increasingly mobile but labor is generally not. Thus workers find their trade interests less and less in line with those of their employers. The growing divergence is reflected in employers' readiness to suggest they might move to Mexico if unions do not make wage concessions, and workers' tendency to take the threat seriously whether or not it is real. Workers tend to see trade as a threat; union leaders see it as an issue for mobilizing support. Partly for this reason, when faced with comprehensive trade bills like fast track and trade promotion authority (as well as NAFTA and CAFTA), labor has sought to defeat the legislation rather than to bargain and shape its details.

Two Questions

The globalization of business in general raises two large questions. One involves the "model" or "system" of trade policymaking described and endorsed in earlier chapters and editions of this book. Are institutions and practices built to counter and limit producer protectionism still appropriate? Or are they obsolete? If the opponents such as sugar producers cannot be bought off by modest protectionist concessions, should proponents shift their tactics? Should they abandon their preference for "inside politics" and rely more on open substantive debate? Should they embrace the "dirty little secret" that imports are good for the economy (albeit not good, of course, for everyone within the economy)? These basic questions will be addressed in this book's concluding chapter.

The second question is in the nature of a puzzle. If business protectionism—long the primary impediment to trade liberalization—is only a shadow of its former self, why doesn't trade legislation sail through the Congress? Why couldn't President Clinton win approval of fast-track legislation when he pressed it in 1997? Why did Bush win it by only one vote in 2001–02, and only through concessions to the very protectionist interests here alleged to be so weakened?

Part of the answer lies in a hard political truth: Producer interests may no longer be protectionist, but this does not necessarily make them proactive forces for additional reductions in trade barriers. For one thing, they may already have won, in prior negotiations, most of the gains that trade liberalization can offer them. There has also been a trend within the corporate community toward relentless pursuit of the "bottom line" of profits and share value. In the past, company executives pushed goals like trade liberalization because of potential future gains, and they joined with like-minded colleagues toward this end. Now they are more likely to focus their energies on just one or two key targets—and trade policy seldom ranks that high.

Beyond this, the explanation for limited trade policy progress is a complex one. As always, personalities have played a key role. But above all, two new dimensions of policy conflict arose to complicate trade policy in the 1995–2004 period. The first was the rise of concerns about trade's social impact, particularly on labor and the environment. The second was the exacerbation of partisanship in Washington, impeding cooperation and compromise across party lines.

During the Clinton administration, the main impediment was increasing concerns over labor and environmental standards. As chapter 10 will show, these concerns divided liberals from conservatives and fractured the long-standing, centrist consensus in favor of open trade.

Then, just as the trade community was grappling with this issue, policy succumbed to increasingly bitter partisanship and ideological divisions—in Washington generally, but particularly on Capitol Hill, and above all in the House of Representatives. This polarization emerged full-blown during the first administration of George W. Bush. That story is told in chapter 11.

10

New Issues, New Stalemate

An important feature of American trade politics over the decade beginning in 1995 was the rise of issues involving the relationship between trade and other prominent policy concerns. Driven by the same globalization process that made producers less protectionist, the "trade and . . . " issues involved not the balance to be struck among economic interests and goals, but rather the proper balance between economic concerns and other societal values. Chief among these "new" issues were those concerning labor standards and the environment.

The new issues posed a challenge that long-standing trade policy institutions were ill-equipped to meet, or even to understand. And they undercut the bipartisan consensus upon which prior trade-liberalizing legislation had been based. Their impact was highlighted by President Bill Clinton's failure to win renewal in 1997 for fast-track trade negotiations and by the dramatic and well-publicized failure of the World Trade Organization's (WTO) Seattle Ministerial Conference in 1999 to reach agreement on a new global trade round. The president was able to revive the bipartisan consensus in 2000 to win approval of permanent normal trade relations with China. But the "trade and . . . " issues continued to pose a challenge in the new millennium.

■ ■ ■

From the days of the early American republic through the 1980s, US trade politics was dominated by economic interests in general and producer interests in particular. This gave policy a distinctly protectionist tilt up to the 1930s. But it also provided the foundations for the "system" of antiprotectionist counterweights, which turned that policy around from the Roosevelt administration onward. Reciprocal trade negotiations energized export interests that would gain from reducing overseas barriers. This balanced the power of import-threatened industries, which were also bought off in part by trade remedy procedures and special deals for the strongest sectors, particularly textiles.

The success of the new, liberal policies could be seen in the reduction of most US tariffs to minuscule levels by the start of the 21st century. This reduction, in turn, helped fuel an ongoing internationalization of the US economy that gave increasing trade-political weight to firms with global interests, as described in chapter 9. Even the textile industry was forced to accept the phaseout of its long-institutionalized quota protection, and to include offshore production in its survival strategy.

But for trade politics, globalization proved to be a double-edged sword. Even as it weakened traditional, business-based resistance to trade, it fueled broader social concerns. This was natural—as trade grew, to paraphrase Georges Clemenceau, trade policy became too important to be left to the trade specialists. Advocates of other values saw trade and trade negotiations increasingly impinging on these values. Sometimes they saw trade negotiations as providing leverage to advance these values. In any case, they saw no reason why trade talks should be limited to their traditional agenda or goals.

The expansion of the agenda was foreshadowed by the Tokyo Round of 1973–79, the first negotiation of the General Agreement on Tariffs and Trade (GATT), whose priority was nontariff impediments to trade. This brought negotiators into laws that had other social purposes, such as subsidies or regulation of product standards. Thereafter, producers looked to other areas where foreign practices impeded their overseas sales. One cause that gained substantial steam in the 1980s was intellectual property protection. Makers of pharmaceuticals and recordings saw their sales cut by overseas operators who copied and "stole" their patented and copyrighted products. A broad coalition of technology-dependent industries—gaining visibility with the extension of trade preferences in 1984 and then with the Uruguay Round authorization of 1988—made the tightening of developing nations' intellectual property laws a priority goal of US negotiators. And in the Uruguay Round agreements of 1994, they won much of what they had sought.[1]

Reaching likewise beyond the movement of goods across national boundaries were advocates of a very different cause—international human rights. In 1973–74, the plight of Soviet Jews seeking to emigrate to Israel had brought Congress to condition the granting of most favored nation status (MFN) to any nonmarket-economy nation on presidential

---

1. They were in turn subject to counterattack by anti-AIDS advocates, who saw these intellectual property rights as pricing life-saving drugs out of reach for tens of millions of Africans, and who made the rollback of those rights a priority goal in the Doha Round.

certification, subject to congressional override, that such nation respected the rights of its citizens to emigrate.[2] After the Tiananmen Square massacre of student demonstrators in 1989, Congress used the annual vote extending MFN to China to highlight that nation's broader abuses of its citizens and the need for reform. And as spelled out later in this chapter, the House of Representatives passed legislation granting permanent normal trading relations (PNTR) to China in 2000 only after adopting an amendment cosponsored by Representatives Douglas Bereuter (R-NE) and Sander Levin (D-MI) establishing a commission to monitor that nation's human rights performance.

Trade negotiations even entered the area of US immigration policy. To the chagrin of the House Judiciary Committee, free trade agreements signed with Chile and Singapore in 2003 promised the annual issuance of US visas to workers from these countries, up to specified numerical limits.[3]

But by far the most prominent linkages to other policy spheres were those addressing the interplay of trade with national labor and environmental laws and practices. From the North American Free Trade Agreement (NAFTA) onward, these connections were central to the US trade policy debate. By 2004, insistence on strong labor-environmental provisions in future trade agreements had become the minimum that a viable Democratic presidential contender could demand.

Threat to the Social Contract?

Throughout the 20th century, liberals and reformers in the United States fought to regulate capitalism in the name of important societal values. The labor movement sought to protect workers from exploitation and increase their share of the growing economic pie, and it achieved particular success in the mid-1900s. Environmentalism's major achievements came a bit later, cresting in the 1970s with key legislation to protect air and water quality. For both, an emerging "social contract" reflected a policy and political balance: private enterprise was the best formula for economic growth, but it needed to be constrained lest it maldistribute income, brutalize working conditions, and despoil the natural landscape.

This contract now seemed threatened by globalization.[4] Just as the nationalization of the US economy had undercut state regulation in the late

---

2. See Paula Stern, *Water's Edge: Domestic Politics and the Making of American Foreign Policy* (Westport, CT: Greenwood Press, 1979).

3. Committee Chairman James Sensenbrenner (R-WI) warned the Bush administration that henceforth "changes in immigration law are off the table as far as this committee is concerned in future free-trade agreements" (*Inside US Trade*, 11 July 2003, 1).

4. See, for example, Dani Rodrik, *Has Globalization Gone Too Far?* (Washington, DC: Institute for International Economics, 1997).

1800s, so the increasing international exposure of US workers and firms seemed to be undermining domestic norms. Trade put growing pressure on the wages of unskilled American workers, just as economic theory suggested it would.[5] And to a substantially lesser degree, it placed US factories in competition with those in countries with less stringent environmental regulation, encouraging them to shift operations overseas or lobby for relaxation of laws at home. It was reasonable, therefore, for advocates of these causes to seek international agreements that might mitigate globalization's domestic effects. Raising labor and environmental standards abroad was surely preferable to seeing them erode at home.

Labor

From its earliest days, the campaign for labor rights was international in scope, as reflected in the famous Marx-Engels summation: "Workers of the world, unite! You have nothing to lose but your chains!"[6] Even after it became clear that reforms would come primarily at the national level, organized labor movements in advanced countries devoted energy to raising standards beyond their borders. There was an idealistic motivation, but also a self-interested one, both of which were reflected in the creation of the International Labor Organization (ILO) in 1919. After citing humanitarian and political reasons for its founding, the ILO's official history notes:

> The third motivation was economic. Because of its inevitable effect on the cost of production, any industry or country adopting social reform would find itself at a disadvantage vis-à-vis its competitors. The Preamble states that "the failure of any nation to adopt humane conditions of labour is an obstacle in the way of other nations which desire to improve the conditions in their own countries."[7]

Hence, it was hardly surprising that the AFL-CIO would promote unions abroad as an essential ingredient of democratic capitalism during the Cold War, nor that it would seek to use trade legislation to advance this goal. Even during its generally unsuccessful effort over the 1970s and

---

5. The classic Heckscher-Ohlin and Stolper-Samuelson models posit that trade expansion will reduce wages in a country where labor is relatively scarce, like the United States. A particularly comprehensive effort to measure the impact of trade on wages is William Cline's *Trade and Income Distribution* (Washington, DC: Institute for International Economics, 1997). Cline concludes that trade and immigration have made real but modest contributions to the increased wage gap between skilled and unskilled workers in the United States.

6. The following pages draw upon the more extensive discussion in I. M. Destler and Peter J. Balint, *The New Politics of American Trade: Trade, Labor, and the Environment* (Washington, DC: Institute for International Economics, POLICY ANALYSES IN INTERNATIONAL ECONOMICS 58, 1999), especially chapters 2 and 3.

7. "ILO History." www.ilo.org/public/english/about/history.htm (accessed 23 March 2005).

1980s to block new trade-liberalizing legislation, organized labor won some modest victories. Though it opposed trade preferences for poor countries, its advocates nevertheless succeeded, in 1984, in getting them conditioned on adherence to internationally recognized labor standards. And when fast track was renewed for the Uruguay Round negotiations in 1988, "worker rights" was enshrined as a "principal trade negotiating objective" (no. 14). Nonetheless, American labor increasingly saw itself as the victim of foreign competition that threatened both jobs and wages, with union locals often exceeding the national federation in their militancy.[8]

Objectively, of course, workers' actual trade interests varied by occupation—while autoworkers were hard-hit by trade, machinists at the Boeing Corporation were major beneficiaries, and members of the Association of Federal, State, County, and Municipal Employees (AFSCME)—the largest US union—have very little direct trade interest either way. Workers also benefit as consumers from low prices.[9] And they gain from the economic growth to which trade contributes. In practice, however, none of these interests have significantly affected labor's overall trade stance in recent decades.

From the late 1960s through the early 1990s, that stance centered on measures that would directly limit imports or slow their increase and on measures to limit foreign direct investment by US-based firms. Overseas labor standards were a subordinate concern. Then, in the 1990s, the presentation, at least, seemed to reverse itself. Front and center in labor's critique of NAFTA, or fast track, was the lack of strong provisions in trade agreements to improve partner nations' labor standards. Union representatives argued, moreover, that provisions promising such improvements needed to be enforceable by sanctions (just as nations' commitments on trade typically were). Critics suggested, with some plausibility, that this was at most new packaging, simply an attractive new cover for the old protectionism. Labor spokespeople denied this: they could not stop globalization, they argued, but they could seek to shape its terms. In any case, the focus on worker rights had a political appeal greater than a simple anti-import stance, particularly among Democrats.[10]

---

8. For more on this history, see I. M. Destler, "Trade Politics and Labor Issues, 1953–1995," in Susan M. Collins, ed., *Imports, Exports, and the American Worker* (Washington, DC: Brookings Institution, 1998), 389–408.

9. This is one apparent reason why, in the interwar period (1919–39), labor-supported governments of the left generally supported free trade. See Beth A. Simmons, *Who Adjusts?* (Princeton, NJ: Princeton University Press, 1994).

10. Alan Krueger found that House cosponsors of a proposed "Child Labor Deterrence Act" that would ban imports made with child labor were more likely to come from districts with high average education and income than from districts with the most workers competing with such labor ("Observations on International Labor Standards and Trade," Working Paper 362, Industrial Relations Section, Princeton University, 13 April 1996).

The Environment

Compared with organized labor, the environmental movement was late coming to the trade policy table. Its initial focus was overwhelmingly domestic. The 1988 trade legislation did not include environmental issues among its negotiating objectives. By the early 1990s, however, the movement was deep into the trade policy debate. NAFTA was the catalyst, but broader concerns—some supporting trade, others fueling resistance—also came to the fore.

One way that trade can support environmental goals is by rewarding efficiency: Open markets go to those who use the least inputs per unit of output, hence reducing the overall drain on resources. Europe's Common Agricultural Policy, for example, encourages intensive, high-cost cropping, some of which would not be viable if farmers faced world prices for their output.

A second way that trade can enhance environmental protection is through its contribution to economic growth. Studies have shown that, as per capita incomes rise, citizens place higher value on environmental improvement. Governments enact more environmental legislation and enforce it better, and, in turn, air and water quality improves and deforestation slows.

Finally, environmental policy shares a characteristic that long dominated trade policy—the need to overcome concentrated economic interests in the name of a more diffusely held broader interest. The company accustomed to trade protection finds its parallel in one accustomed to discharging its waste without concern about the "external diseconomies" thus exhibited. And the trade policy institutions built to counter such interests may offer lessons for environmentalists as well.[11]

More prominent in the recent trade debate, however, have been images of trade's negative impact on the environment. The image of "GATTzilla" put forward by the nongovernmental organization (NGO) Public Citizen posits that relentless trade and investment by multinationals lay waste to the world we hold dear.

Some environmentalists challenge trade at the most fundamental level, by questioning the broader ethos of ongoing economic growth. The ecosystem is threatened by untrammeled economic activity, which trade reinforces. Over the not-too-long run, growth is unsustainable, argue adherents of this view, and in the meantime growth is defiling the natural world. Hence trade should be constrained as part of a broader regime of limiting overall economic activity.[12]

---

11. Daniel C. Esty highlights these and related interests in *Greening the GATT: Trade, Environment, and the Future* (Washington, DC: Institute for International Economics, 1994). He also proposes creation of a Global Environmental Organization to play the role that GATT/WTO has played in providing international institutional support to trade liberalization.

12. See, for example, Herman E. Daly, *Beyond Growth: The Economics of Sustainable Development* (Boston: Beacon Press, 1996).

This view has a broad following among the most committed environmentalists. Many who would not go this far, however, still see trade as damaging to the environment under current circumstances. They argue that prices do not reflect full production costs because they typically ignore or undervalue impacts on the natural world, and while in theory this flaw could be addressed by enforcing a "polluter pays" principle, in practice this is seldom done.

To the degree that this "external diseconomy" is addressed by domestic environmental regulation, there is fear that global competition will undercut it. In the "race to the bottom" scenario, producers in nations free of regulation drive out those elsewhere who must pay regulatory costs (or cause the latter to win from their home governments an easing of environmental rules).

There is further concern that in enforcing global trade agreements, the WTO will invalidate national environmental measures, that have trade-restrictive effects. In 1991, GATT ruled against a US law that kept Mexican-harvested tuna from US markets because Mexican fishermen used nets that killed many dolphins. In a broadly similar 1998 case, the WTO found illegal a US law that required shrimp sold in the United States to be harvested with nets that had turtle-excluding devices (though the WTO's appellate body endorsed the principle of such domestic restraints provided they were nondiscriminatory).

Finally, virtually all environmentalists see a need for a worldwide attack on environmental problems that increasingly cross national boundaries. Hence they will, at minimum, want international agreements to strengthen environmental protection. In the absence of a global environmental organization or comprehensive ongoing environmental negotiations, some will see trade agreements as the best available means of advancing the environmental cause abroad. And if environmental agreements include trade sanctions as a means of enforcement, they do not want the WTO to rule that such actions are illegal.

In general, moderate organizations like the National Wildlife Federation and the Environmental Defense Fund have been inclined to see the positive side of trade and pursue prospects of trade-environmental policy collaboration (though they have often been disappointed with the results). More radical groups—such as the Sierra Club and Friends of the Earth—have been more negative and confrontational.

Impact of NAFTA

Labor and environmental issues first became prominent in the US trade debate during the initial consideration of NAFTA.[13] As discussed in chapter 4,

---

13. They and related measures had a much longer history. See Susan Aaronson, *Taking Trade to the Streets: The Lost History of Public Efforts to Shape Globalization* (Ann Arbor: University of Michigan Press, 2001).

the 1988 trade law had granted fast-track authority only until mid-1991, with a two-year extension if neither house disapproved. The Uruguay Round talks needed the extra time, and the negotiations on NAFTA, the more controversial of the two, were just getting started. Labor and environmental concerns were raised prominently by early NAFTA critics; in response, the chairs of the committees of jurisdiction—Senator Lloyd Bentsen (D-TX) and Congressman Dan Rostenkowski (D-IL), both NAFTA supporters—asked the Bush administration what it would do about these issues in the NAFTA talks. The administration responded positively: It would provide adjustment aid for displaced US workers, support Mexican efforts to enforce labor standards, and promote both US and Mexican measures to safeguard the environment. The legislators declared themselves satisfied, at least for the time being, and the administration won the fast-track extension vote by a healthy (39-vote) margin in the House.

This sufficed until the election campaign of 1992, when Bill Clinton—balancing the concerns of advocates and opponents—endorsed the now-completed NAFTA accord in general but found its labor and environmental provisions inadequate. He therefore pledged that he would not send NAFTA to Congress for approval until his administration negotiated side agreements with Mexico and Canada remedying this defect. Delay in accomplishing this in 1993 gave valuable time to NAFTA opponents, as spelled out in chapter 8. But the successful negotiation of the side agreements won NAFTA important support within the mainstream environmental movement (though not the labor movement), and proved crucial in gaining House approval.

Things became dicier on the labor-environment front in 1994. Republican and business supporters of NAFTA had viewed the side agreements with some alarm, but they were trapped: they needed support from both Clinton and on-the-fence Democrats, and this was the main means to garner that support. So they limited themselves to loud protests—shots across the bow—when US Trade Representative (USTR) Mickey Kantor toyed with side agreement language that they felt went too far.[14] But they clearly wanted to limit such measures in future trade agreements.

Kantor, however, was moving in the other direction. Happy with the NAFTA victory but unhappy about the resulting frayed relations between the White House and key Democratic constituencies, particularly organized labor, he sought means to repair the damage. He and Vice President Albert Gore highlighted these issues (in a manner critics saw as heavy-handed) at the Marrakesh GATT Ministerial Meeting where the Uruguay Round accords were formally adopted. In USTR's forward planning, Kan-

---

14. A "coalition of every major business organization in the United States" sent Kantor a strong letter on 4 June that denounced, in particular, provisions allowing "unnecessary [and] counterproductive" trade sanctions. See Frederick W. Mayer, *Interpreting NAFTA* (New York: Columbia University Press, 1998), 192–93.

tor made trade-related labor and environmental issues the administration's new priorities—along with competition policy—in future trade talks. When it came time to propose to Congress the language of the Uruguay Round implementing legislation, Kantor's draft language made them the fifth and sixth of seven "principal negotiating objectives" in future trade agreements for which he sought fast-track authority. Business hit the roof; compromise proved unattainable, so future fast track was dropped from 1994 law, as detailed in chapter 8.[15]

In the years that followed, positions hardened. Business, emboldened by the Republican sweep of the fall 1994 congressional elections, sought to exclude most trade-related labor and environmental issues from new trade-negotiating authority. Most Republicans agreed. They felt Kantor was pushing these causes for political more than substantive reasons, and that he hadn't really listened to their views while negotiating the side agreements. They worried also that trade agreements covering these issues could be used to impose new labor or environmental regulations in the United States. Moreover, Kantor was evasive when Ways and Means Republicans, led by Chairman Bill Archer, tried to reach agreement with the administration on a fast-track authorization bill in 1995.[16]

On the other side, the social issues energized a broad, disparate coalition loosely coordinated by Public Citizen that continued to attack NAFTA and insist, as an absolute minimum, that future trade pacts include labor and environmental standards, enforceable by trade sanctions, not as side agreements but in their core language. Most Democrats agreed. And in the aftermath of the 1994 election, they were increasingly dependent on labor for funding their reelection campaigns.[17]

Labor-environmental skepticism was reinforced by a poor administration job in implementing the NAFTA side agreements and other commitments made to NAFTA swing voters. Mainstream environmental groups became disillusioned and moved toward the opposition camp. Anxieties

15. Interestingly, Kantor's labor language tracked—and softened somewhat—that which appeared in the 1988 Trade Act. And though that law contained no parallel environmental language, Congress did legislate environmental goals for GATT negotiations in 1992. See Steve Charnovitz, "Labor and Environmental Issues," in Jeffrey J. Schott, ed., *Restarting Fast Track* (Washington, DC: Institute for International Economics, Special Report 11, April 1998), 58. The difference in 1994, perhaps, was that the administration in power gave every indication of giving such goals priority.

16. In turn, Democrats and the administration were unhappy that the Archer bill only allowed labor and environmental objectives that were "directly related" to trade, by which they meant labor and environmental measures that *impeded* trade. For details, see I. M. Destler, *Renewing Fast-Track Legislation* (Washington, DC: Institute for International Economics, POLICY ANALYSES IN INTERNATIONAL ECONOMICS 50, 1997), 20–22.

17. In prior decades, business had tended to divide its Capitol Hill contributions between those in power (generally Democrats) and those whose policy positions it preferred (mainly Republicans). After November 1994, however, these became one and the same.

were heightened by developments in the implementation of NAFTA Chapter 11, which was "unique in allowing private investors to enforce government obligations" under the agreement by bringing alleged violations of a NAFTA member government's guarantees of investor rights to an ad hoc tribunal, which reviews the case and can award monetary damages.[18] At a maximum, this posed the threat that a nation's environmental regulations might be deemed "regulatory takings" of private property—a controversial legal doctrine that, if widely adopted, could cripple environmental protection measures.[19]

The overall trade-political environment was further damaged by the Mexican peso crisis and the resulting swing of the bilateral trade balance from modest US surplus to large US deficit. All this made it easier for the critical coalition—Public Citizen, the Economic Policy Institute, the Sierra Club, etc.—to issue a highly negative report in June 1997 entitled *The Failed Experiment: NAFTA at Three Years*. The administration mainly ducked. It quietly published a more systematic assessment (mandated by Congress) concluding that NAFTA had been (modestly) beneficial. But mostly it avoided talking about NAFTA at all.

This stalemate had consequences—in particular, it undercut the credibility of US trade negotiators. As 1997 began, Clinton was completing his third year without fast-track authority—the longest previous gap since its initiation had been eight months in 1988. Now safely reelected, he would make a forceful if flawed effort to regain it. And he would fail.

Clinton's Fast-Track Fiasco

The initial signs were favorable. The president had a new, four-year mandate, having bounced back from the humiliation that saw Republicans capture both houses of Congress in 1994. Republican congressional leaders were both positive, particularly House Speaker Newt Gingrich (R-GA).

---

18. Gary Clyde Hufbauer, Jeffrey J. Schott, and Yee Wong, "NAFTA Dispute Settlement Systems," 7. www.iie.co/publications/papers/nafta-dispute.pdf (accessed 23 March 2005) .

19. Actual results were more modest. The initial case that galvanized opposition from NGOs, *Ethyl Co. vs. Canada*, was settled in the company's favor but outside the NAFTA tribunal. While the outcome of this and subsequent cases made "the alarms over NAFTA Chapter 11 seem overblown" (ibid., 43), Congress acted (properly, in this author's view) to clarify and limit the threat of overweening investor rights in the Trade Act of 2002. The investment provisions of US free trade agreements with Singapore and Chile contain more restrained language. On the broader issue, see Edward M. Graham, *Fighting the Wrong Enemy: Antiglobal Activists and Multinational Enterprises* (Washington, DC: Institute for International Economics, 2000); and Graham, "Regulatory Takings, Supranational Treatment, and the Multilateral Agreement on Investment: Issues Raised by Nongovernmental Organizations," *Cornell International Law Journal* 31, no. 3, 1998: 599–614.

Ways and Means chair Bill Archer (R-TX) was anxious to resume the effort he had begun in 1995.

Kantor had been replaced as USTR by his former deputy Charlene Barshefsky. She had good relations on Capitol Hill, and was less distrusted by the majority Republicans (though she would never duplicate Kantor's personal relationship with the president). And she was joined in pushing fast track by economic policy officials (led by Treasury Secretary Robert Rubin and his deputy, Lawrence Summers) and foreign policy officials, particularly the new national security assistant, Samuel Berger.

There was also reason to move quickly. Since the measure would inevitably divide Democrats, it would be best to have the vote as far as possible from the 1998 election. The president underscored the importance he attached to the issue by giving it four paragraphs in his February 1997 State of the Union Message. He called for "authority now to conclude new trade agreements," so that Americans could "prosper in the global economy" rather than "be left behind as these emerging economies forge new ties with other nations."

But the president's political advisers were hesitant, as was Vice President Al Gore. They were worried about labor. There had been some early hope that newly elected AFL-CIO President John J. Sweeney might be looking for a way to avoid a repeat of the NAFTA fight, and he or his aides apparently conveyed that view to the White House around the end of 1996. But no one in the White House was able to convert that to a concrete commitment, due, presumably, to the strength of Sweeney's industrial union constituency. Gore may have hoped for progress when he accepted an invitation to the AFL-CIO Executive Council meeting in Los Angeles in February, but his cool reception there stood in sharp contrast to the warm greeting given House Minority Leader Richard Gephardt, his putative rival for the Democratic presidential nomination in 2000 and a vociferous critic of NAFTA and fast track. After a reportedly contentious discussion, the labor confederation concluded its meeting with a clear statement opposing "any grant of fast-track authority . . . that does not include provisions and enforcement mechanisms for addressing worker rights, labor standards, and environmental protection [as] part of the core agreement."

A week later, Gephardt dispatched a 12-page "Dear Democratic Colleague" letter denouncing the "failure" of NAFTA and saying any new grant of trade authority should be limited mainly to repairing its flaws. He added that future trade agreements not only should address labor and the environment but also such issues as "capital flight and currency stability," "human rights–rule of law," "trade in narcotics," and "foreign corrupt practices." The Missouri Democrat had come late to his NAFTA opposition in 1993. By this sweeping statement, he made it clear that he would not repeat that pattern in 1997.

So the basic lines were drawn early—and most players recognized this. "We had many conversations with the White House and USTR and various other people, where they told us they were not going to address our concerns," recalled AFL-CIO economist Thea Lee. "That's why we were willing to go out early; we didn't have to wait to see the bill."[20]

It proved to be a substantial wait. One reason was the weakness of administration processes for forcing decision on such an issue. The new National Economic Council (NEC) had played this role admirably for the complex Clinton economic program of early 1993.[21] But in December 1996, Clinton had effectively split the NEC by appointing one former deputy, Gene Sperling, as council director and another, Daniel Tarullo, as assistant to the president for international economic policy. Perhaps for this reason, the NEC did not play the central coordinating role for fast track in 1997; White House Chief of Staff Erskine Bowles had to establish a special group for this purpose under his direct chairmanship.

But the fundamental reason for delay was Clinton himself, caught between his personal preference and that of his constituency for substantial labor and environmental provisions on one side, and the predominant views of the majority Republicans in Congress on the other. Within the administration, Barshefsky recalled, "Sandy Berger, Larry Summers, and I were . . . saying, 'Do it now. Don't wait. The longer you wait, the more it's going to be like NAFTA' " four years earlier, when opponents gathered enormous steam before the president finally moved in September.[22] On Capitol Hill, Archer "waited patiently" (to use his own words), then went public with a sharply worded letter denouncing the administration for its failure to bite the bullet.[23] But the president gave graphic evidence of his indecision in a comprehensive April foreign policy address, which devoted 18 full and eloquent paragraphs to the importance of trade and the need for fast-track legislation. His punch line: "I have asked the United States Trade Representative, Charlene Barshefsky, to work with members of Congress of both parties, with labor and business and environmental groups to try to reach consensus on these issues."[24]

---

20. Quoted in Charan Devereaux for Robert Lawrence, *Fast Track Derailed: The 1997 Attempt to Renew Fast Track Trade Legislation*, Kennedy School of Government Case Program (NR15–02–1660.0), 19.

21. See I. M. Destler, *The National Economic Council: A Work in Progress* (Washington, DC: Institute for International Economics, POLICY ANALYSES IN INTERNATIONAL ECONOMICS 46, 1996), 13–15, and Bob Woodward, *The Agenda: Inside the Clinton White House* (New York: Pocket Books, 1995), chapter 11.

22. Quoted in *Fast Track Derailed*, 26. See also the NAFTA account in chapter 8.

23. Bill Archer to Bill Clinton, 15 May 1997, reprinted in *Inside US Trade*, 23 May 1997. He had "repeatedly" urged an early administration proposal and Barshefsky had "done admirable work on Capitol Hill . . . to lay the groundwork," Archer said, "but there comes a time when the preparatory work must end."

24. Comprehensive foreign policy address of 11 April 1997 to the American Society of Newspaper Editors.

By that time, such a consensus was most unlikely, and labor knew it. Recognizing that Clinton would not be able to accommodate them, the unions mobilized. Fearful that Clinton might move in the labor-environmental direction, business held back—encouraged by House Republicans who shared this concern. And Ways and Means eschewed moving its own bill, seeing that as a mistake they had made two years earlier. By late May, the early opportunity had passed and the administration was facing a congressional calendar with key votes imminent on balanced-budget legislation and the extension of most favored nation status for China. So the president, in a meeting with his top advisers, decided in May to delay submission of an administration proposal for four more months, until September.

In the meantime, the White House and USTR made efforts to shore up support. They urged business to mobilize in anticipation of the bill; in July they brought in Jason Berman, a widely respected business executive from the recording industry, to coordinate the campaign—a role similar to that which William Daley, now Secretary of Commerce, had played on NAFTA. And the Business Roundtable established an umbrella organization, America Leads on Trade, to coordinate a pro-fast-track campaign once its members saw the fine print. Through this and other vehicles, business was ultimately able to mount a substantial effort, with reported spending more than double that of the labor opposition. But serious business action did not begin until well into September.

Clinton, caught in the middle and congenitally inclined toward compromise, seemed to hope that once he could really focus on the issue, he would find a magic, bridging answer (as the side agreements had proved to be in 1993). In the meantime, by coincidence, opponents were energized by a distantly related issue, a proposed Multilateral Agreement on Investment (MAI). From 1995 onward, advanced industrial nations had been quietly working on a draft agreement that would, to some extent, do for investment what the GATT/WTO had done for trade—establish a set of common rules, such as "national treatment" for foreign-owned firms. Progress had been slow, and the outcome most uncertain when, in early 1997, Public Citizen published the hitherto confidential draft text on its website, accompanied by a critical analysis. Soon a virulent, Internet-driven campaign was under way, joined in particular by environmental groups wary of globalization, conjuring up visions of a government-business plot to exploit poor nations and despoil the environment—a "license to loot," as a Friends of the Earth publication called it.[25] The MAI's drafters were dumbfounded by the criticism: they had been struggling over a draft that "did little more than codify the status quo."[26] They never mounted a serious response. By

---

25. Mark Vallianatos with Andrea Durbin, *License to Loot: The MAI and How to Stop It* (Washington, DC: Friends of the Earth, 1998).

26. Graham, *Fighting the Wrong Enemy*, 7.

fall, USTR was assuring all that if the MAI were ever completed and sent to the Hill for approval, it would *not* be covered by the proposed fast-track legislation! A year later, the MAI would be dead. In the meantime, the overlapping anti-fast-track coalition of NGOs was energized: they had mortally wounded one dragon, and were eager to slay another.

When Clinton finally sent down a fast-track legislative proposal on 16 September 1997, he included those labor and environmental measures he felt he could (such as a commitment to "secure a review of the relationship of labor rights to WTO rules").[27] But in an inevitable bow to the Republican-business coalition, the primary thrust was to limit fast-track coverage to a narrow subset of these issues. They had to be "trade-related," and this was defined as measures that either impeded trade or weakened domestic labor and environmental laws in order to gain competitive advantage. The House Ways and Means Committee took the president's restrictive proposal and tightened it further. Prior fast-track legislation had given the executive branch broad leeway in interpreting—and going beyond—the statutory "negotiating objectives." The Ways and Means bill limited the use of fast-track implementing legislation to "provisions directly related to the [narrowly drawn] 'principal trade negotiating objectives.'" And it relegated broader goals ("seeking to protect and preserve the environment," "promoting respect for worker rights," etc.) to a separate section labeled "international economic policy objectives," which concluded with the words: "Nothing in this subsection shall be construed to authorize the use of the trade authorities procedures described in section 103 to modify United States law."[28] This further energized labor and environmental opponents, and played badly with most Democrats on the fence, since it was (in their minds) a clear step backward from the 1988 law and NAFTA.

In other respects, the bill was standard. The scope was broad—global, regional, and bilateral trade agreements. The time period was generous: from the bill's enactment until 1 October 2001, with extension of four more years possible under the same trade-favoring procedure as had been employed for the Uruguay Round and NAFTA in 1991. It was reported out on 8 October by a solid numerical margin, 24-14, but this included just four Democrats—only one of whom, Bob Matsui (D-CA), was in the senior ranks.[29]

---

27. "Clinton Fast-Track Bill Limits Scope of Labor, Environment Rules," *Inside US Trade: Special Report*, 17 September 1997.

28. HR 2621, Section 103(B)(3)(B) and Section 102(C)(2), as reported by Committee on Ways and Means, 10 October 1997.

29. The Senate Finance Committee voted out a bill earlier by a wider margin, but constitutionally the House had to pass the bill first.

The problem now was to muster 218 votes on the floor. Speaker Gingrich was a strong advocate, and he knew that his Republican party would have to carry the primary burden. But roughly one-third of party members tended to be antitrade (56 of 177, or 32 percent, had opposed the Uruguay Round legislation in 1994). Now the Republicans were the majority, with 228 members to 206 Democrats. So it seemed reasonable to them that they should produce 150 "aye" votes, with Democrats coming up with the remaining 70. But the top two House Democrats—Gephardt and Minority Whip David Bonior (D-MI)—were strongly opposed: Bonior had led the opposition to NAFTA. And the specifics of this bill had been tailored to Republican specifications. Matsui, the leader of pro-fast-track Democrats, had thought earlier in the year that Democrats could produce at least 60 votes for fast track, possibly more. Now he was more pessimistic.

In such circumstances, the buck naturally passes to the White House. Clinton had (finally) made this a priority; he would have to find ways to win over wavering House members. He had worked NAFTA impressively in 1993, winning even Gingrich's temporary admiration. But he faced serious problems four years later. Despite his solid reelection, his centrist position, and his political skills, he had little personal credit on either side of the House aisle. Republicans deeply disliked him—for his personal morals and what they saw as a slippery personality, but also for his political effectiveness—he had blocked the "Gingrich revolution," and played off it to win reelection. Many (particularly those in the militant "class of 1994") were reluctant to delegate increased authority to that man. But Democrats didn't exactly love him either. Some were furious and many were frustrated about the summer deal Clinton had just struck with Gingrich and Senate Majority Leader Robert Dole (R-KS) on balanced-budget legislation that squeezed social programs. Representative Barney Frank (D-MA) would later declare that in rejecting fast track, House Democrats had "taken a hostage."[30] They were waiting, he said, for the White House to press serious programs to address domestic income inequality and the plight of the worker in a globalizing world.

The conventional wisdom in Washington in 1993 had been that NAFTA would fail. By contrast, inside-the-Beltway opinion in 1997 was that Clinton would win. There was nothing like the broad public opposition NAFTA had spawned. Newspaper editorialists were overwhelmingly in favor. And presidents almost always win the "big ones," especially when they involve international policy. No president had lost a high-profile trade policy vote in Congress since Franklin Roosevelt and Cordell Hull had initiated the reciprocal trade agreements program in 1934!

But as Washington moved toward November, and Congress toward its anticipated adjournment for the year, the votes were not breaking the right

---

30. He never delivered a "ransom note," however. See his comments reported in Schott, *Restarting Fast Track*, especially 12–14 and 24.

way—despite Clinton's now serious engagement and a range of induce-ments being offered on trade and nontrade issues. Labor produced a blizzard of worker communications to swing legislators. The broad anti-NAFTA, antiglobalization coalition was energized. And skeptical Republi-cans were not above using fast track as leverage for other issues. A group of conservatives led by James Talent (R-MO) pressed for reinstatement of an international aid policy—put in place by Reagan, reversed by Clinton—that forbade funds going to any international organization that offered or counseled on abortion services.[31]

The business community pressed for a deadline for a vote, believing that only this would force on-the-fence members to come around. Matsui agreed. So even though he felt fast-track proponents were about 50 votes short, Gingrich announced on 29 October that there would be a vote on 7 November, the projected adjournment day. The president and the speaker made some progress in the coming days, but not nearly enough. The vote was pushed back to Sunday, 9 November. Late that evening, Gingrich called the White House to say that they were still short—around 155 Re-publicans, a maximum of 45 Democrats, for a rough total of 200. Clin-ton faced the choice: go ahead with a vote in the long-shot hope that 20 or so more members would come on board rather than see the bill go down; or pull it from the floor, with the hope of resurrecting it later. He chose the latter.

Clinton declared the following afternoon that his administration and its allies would "regroup a little bit and find a way to succeed," since "there are a large number of House members who are interested in trying to find some constructive resolution of this matter." But for the president, 1988 would be dominated by another issue—the revelation of a sexual affair with White House intern Monica Lewinsky, leading to his impeachment (in one of the more bizarre episodes in House history). Before this had run its course, Gingrich the politician triumphed over Gingrich the statesman. Recognizing that the bill could not win, but seeing a way to put a political squeeze on Democrats in the run-up to the mid-term election, he brought the fast-track bill back to the floor for a vote in September 1998. Clinton refused to back it; Matsui denounced the move as blatantly political and voted against the measure he had fought so hard for 10 months earlier. The bill was ignominiously rejected, 243–180. Just 29 Democrats voted in favor, and no fewer than 71 Republicans joined the opposition. Thus ended action on fast track in the 20th century.

---

31. This was the so-called "Mexico City policy," so named for the international conference at which it was announced. Clinton later declared, "Had we been able to resolve that, I think we could have gotten enough votes on the Republican side," but that "it would have been wrong for me to mix the two issues." Statement by the president, on the South Lawn, 10 No-vember 1997. See also Devereaux, *Fast Track Derailed*, 39.

Dilemmas of Substance and Process

Fast track failed in the second Clinton administration not because of old-fashioned protectionism, and not from opposition to trade expansion per se, but above all due to deeply felt differences over bringing labor and environmental issues onto the trade agenda. Business and House Republicans were sufficiently wary of opening this door that they were willing to risk failure. They were right in concluding that Clinton would have to go along with them, but wrong in believing that they—plus the president—could prevail. For House Democrats who held the swing votes were willing to ensure failure unless the social issues were more seriously addressed.[32]

Other issues were involved as well—Representative Charles Rangel (D-NY), ranking member of Ways and Means, declared in the aftermath, "There is no question in my mind, if the president had thrown in fast track with a jobs bill, this could have passed."[33] But neither he nor the administration took the initiative to put such a package together.[34] This stood in sharp contrast to 2001–02, when Senate Democrats would tie their support of trade-negotiating authority to expansion and reform of trade adjustment assistance.

Still, social issues had suddenly become the "800-pound gorilla" of trade policy. The main players and institutions were ill-equipped to deal with them. Their pre-1990 exclusion from the central trade debate had helped facilitate bipartisan consensus. But now they had forced their way to the trade policy table, presumably to stay.

Trade specialists often argue that, on grounds of principle, such issues should be excluded from trade negotiations. But this argument is hard to sustain. As trade grows as a share of the economy, its effects spread more and more outside the narrow traditional sphere. Negotiations have recognized this from the Uruguay Round onward, when they began to tackle nontariff barriers that had been put in place to serve a range of policy objectives. Traditionalists consider it demagogic, and thinly disguised protectionism, for a Gephardt to declaim before an AFL-CIO audience that it is wrong to place intellectual property rights above worker rights and environmental standards. But the statement itself is hard to dispute on its normative merits. And as workers and environmentalists see their hard-fought gains threatened by globalization, it is reasonable that they will fight to shape its terms.

---

32. Greater tactical skill might have eked out a victory had Clinton pressed the matter early in 1997, for example, as advocates desired. And the president could have rolled the dice and insisted on a floor vote—it would certainly have been better than the vote Gingrich forced 10 months later. But it was the conflict over social issues that made his margin for error so narrow in the first place.

33. Quoted in *Inside US Trade*, 11 November 1997.

34. See Rangel's pessimistic comments in Schott, *Restarting Fast Track*, 24.

There are plenty of labor and environmental abuses abroad to target, and some of them do offer at least marginal trade advantage to competitors. Pressing these issues could lead partner nations to adopted stronger labor and environmental regulations sooner than if this were left to the longer-term process of economic growth. And the alternative negotiating channels are often weak—in the case of the International Labor Organization—or nonexistent, given the lack of any comprehensive global environmental organization.

Finally, as Steve Charnovitz noted in early 1998, if a bill cannot muster a majority, a normal response is to "rewrite it" to broaden its appeal. "Fast track—which is now in a coma—might get healthier if it is not viewed as a trade-only mechanism." Broadening the labor-environment agenda seemed the most plausible route to restoring a broader, more bipartisan protrade coalition.[35]

But there are problems with moving too far in this direction. One, of course, is getting conservative acquiescence. This was unavailable in 1997 (though as described in chapter 11, a bill that was more permissive in this sphere won overwhelming Republican support in 2001–02). One major fear of Republicans has been that trade agreements would have the effect of increasing regulation of the US economy, as partner nations enforced labor and environmental commitments on us. This was, to some degree, the mirror image of environmentalist concerns that NAFTA's Chapter 11, which protects foreign investors in the three nations, could be and was being employed to roll back environmental regulations.

A particular problem for the left is that the governments of developing countries, whose people would ostensibly be helped by higher labor and environmental standards, are overwhelmingly opposed. They see such provisions as protectionism in thin disguise: Once such standards are in place, they feel that their social policy deficiencies would be used as an excuse to block trade. When the United States presses these issues aggressively—as Gore did in 1994—their resistance only stiffens. This resistance has kept labor issues out of the WTO and limited its trade-environment agenda. And even in bilateral free trade agreements, where the United States has a potent bargaining advantage, labor and environmental standards are founded on the "Jordan standard," under which the parties commit themselves to enforcing their existing laws.[36] If the United States were to press for stronger rules—tied to ILO core labor standards, for example, as advocates call for—

---

35. Charnovitz, "Labor and Environmental Issues," in *Restarting Fast Track*, especially 66, 67.

36. So named because of its inclusion in the US-Jordan free trade agreement negotiated by the Clinton administration and approved by Congress in 2001. The Chile free trade agreement supplements this with new institutions and mechanisms for bilateral cooperation on these issues. The pending Central American Free Trade Agreement (CAFTA) has similar provisions.

it might fail to get them, and this could undercut the consensus, driving their advocates back into opposition. Or, if it succeeded, conservatives might rebel out of fear that they would be applied to the United States.

There are other practical concerns. Too much emphasis on these goals could reduce US leverage on more traditional trade issues—this is a prominent business concern, particularly during a Democratic administration. The actual direct impact of any conceivable labor and environmental provisions on US labor and environmental interests, moreover, is likely to be quite small—far less than direct measures targeted at the situation here at home, such as enhanced trade adjustment assistance. Yet the struggle over the inclusion of such provisions increases party polarization on trade, since these are issues that have long been fought out on a party-line basis. And in any case, there is broad agreement that the most reliable path to improved labor and environmental standards overseas is strong, continuing economic growth, which open trade can facilitate.[37]

For all of these reasons, embracing trade and environmental issues has not proved an effective means of broadening trade policy's constituency. Efforts to address these issues are at best a "work in progress," as nations struggle for both consensus and effectiveness. The trade debate might be improved if advocates recognized these practical limitations, and critics acknowledged the normative case for trying. What happened in the aftermath of November 1997, however, was the opposite—further polarization between proglobalization forces and their critics. And it resulted in an even greater public humiliation for the Clinton administration.

The Battles of Seattle

At least once every two years, the World Trade Organization convenes a Ministerial Conference, where well over 100 trade ministers from member nations gather to address their most urgent pending issues. This conference is "the topmost body of the WTO," in the organization's words. It operates mainly by consensus, though votes can be taken. A successful Ministerial Conference typically moves the organization and its substantive work forward—the one held in Singapore in December 1996, for example, brought new issues onto the WTO agenda.

The second WTO Ministerial Conference, held in May 1998, featured an address by President Bill Clinton. He took the occasion to invite "the trade ministers of the world to hold their next meeting in 1999 in the United States." By January of that year, Seattle had been designated as the host

---

37. For a sophisticated, balanced assessment of one of these issues, see Kimberly Ann Elliott and Richard B. Freeman, *Can Labor Standards Improve Under Globalization?* (Washington, DC: Institute for International Economics, 2003).

city, and the European Union, Japan, and the United States (in that order) had all endorsed the idea that the WTO should launch a new trade round. Details were to be developed and differences narrowed in a series of preparatory meetings. The final deals would be struck at the Seattle conclave beginning 30 November.

What the world saw on its TV screens was something quite different. To quote John S. Odell's spirited summary of press reporting:[38]

> American critics used the occasion to organize a large campaign to protest globalization and the WTO and to attack its core norm of trade liberalization. They and allies from other countries circulated pamphlets painting the WTO as an unaccountable tool of greedy corporations and blaming it for world social and environmental problems. On the first day, union members, environmentalists, consumer advocates, and students marching in three columns converged on downtown Seattle chanting "No new round, turn around." Police allowed protesters to penetrate the space between the convention center and the hotels and block the ministers from entering the hall for a day. In the chaos, the Colombian minister was knocked to the ground. Privately, one of his officials groused that if the same had happened to an American cabinet secretary in Bogotá, the State Department would have declared a travel advisory on Colombia for six months. The minister from Estonia sputtered as he walked away, "I'm a socialist! . . . You people are nuts." The president of the United Steelworkers thundered, "Either they fix the goddamn thing [the WTO] or we're going to get out." Dockworkers up and down the Pacific coast briefly shut down ports in sympathy. A few protesters shattered shop windows and burned trashcans. Police threw tear gas and concussion grenades and eventually called out the National Guard to restore order. Bloody faces and banners denouncing the WTO dominated the televised images.

At the end of the conference, the ministers adjourned without even issuing a communiqué. The protesters got much of the "credit," but in fact, as Jeffrey J. Schott put it, "The WTO meeting fell victim not to protests *outside* in the streets, but rather to serious substantive disagreements *inside* the convention center among both developed and developing countries."[39] As one member of the Secretariat put it, "We would have failed without any help."[40]

The organization itself bore some of the responsibility—or, more precisely, the leadership crisis forced on the WTO by members' inability to agree on a successor to Director General Renato Ruggiero, who retired on 30 April 1999. The result was a vacancy in the top post from May to September, at which time Michael Moore of New Zealand assumed the director

---

38. John S. Odell, "The Seattle Impasse and Its Implications for the World Trade Organization," 2001, 1. Paper presented at the Convention of the International Studies Association, Chicago, February.

39. Schott, *The WTO after Seattle* (Washington, DC: Institute for International Economics, 2000), 5.

40. Odell quote from interview, "The Seattle Impasse," 2.

general position with a weakened mandate for a truncated, nonextendable term of three years,[41] with the Seattle meeting less than three months off. He had little time to broker a consensus.

The host country might have taken up some of the slack by developing a broad, inclusive proposal. Instead, the USTR, weakened by the lack of fast-track authority, pressed a narrow, partisan agenda for the new talks. Nor was it alone, for, as Odell noted, "governments held firm in their one-sided opening positions for so long that time ran out."[42] So the Ministerial Conference opened with an exceptionally wide range of conflicting positions to resolve. The US priority to labor issues provoked broad concern, which Clinton managed to exacerbate in a press interview. After noting a plausibly acceptable US proposal to develop a WTO working group on labor, he declared that "ultimately" agreements on this and other issues should be enforceable by "sanctions."[43]

Last but perhaps not least, the US organizers failed to book hotel space for the contingency that the conference would run beyond its four-day schedule, as such meetings typically do. So the ministers and other delegates, having lost at least half a day to protest disruptions, had to vacate their rooms to make space for an annual convention of optometrists.

Following upon fast track, the failure at Seattle was a second major blow to Clinton's trade leadership. And it was, in its outcome and theatrics, a significantly greater triumph for the antiglobalist coalition than the MAI or fast track had been.

Fortunately for the chief executive, he was able to end his trade presidency on an upbeat note. He secured enactment, in May 2000, of the African Growth and Opportunity Act (AGOA), a measure granting a broad range of trade preference to nations of that continent. And in a tough legislative battle, he won House approval of new legislation granting permanent normal trading relations (PNTR) to China upon its forthcoming entry into the World Trade Organization. Unlike fast track, both of these featured bipartisan cooperation at the leadership level of Ways and Means.[44]

---

41. Country votes were closely divided between Moore and Supachai Panitchpakdi of Thailand. The chairman of the WTO General Council, Ali Mchumo, following what he saw as established WTO procedure, pressed to win consensus for Moore on the grounds that he had more votes, better distributed. He failed and was denounced vehemently for the effort. A compromise splitting the term was finally agreed to in July. Moore, with no prior Geneva experience, had exactly three months to play a constructive role. And Mchumo, another important figure, was compromised by his role in the leadership fiasco.

42. "The Seattle Impasse," 10.

43. Interview with *Seattle Post-Intelligencer*, 1 December 1999.

44. In July 1999, the House had approved AGOA by 234-163, with 98 Democrats joining 136 Republicans in favor.

Normalizing China

During the last two decades of the 20th century, the country with the most impressive story of trade and development was the People's Republic of China. Moving from a centralized to a market economy, and from autarchy to increasing openness internationally, the nation's economy grew two-and-a-half times in the 1980s and did so again in the 1990s. Trade rose even faster, tripling in the 1980s and quadrupling in the 1990s.[45]

China looked increasingly like the economic superpower of the future, and American business wanted the strongest possible foothold there. For the same reason, imports from China posed a greater potential threat to certain American firms and workers than those from Mexico ever had or could. The US trade deficit with China rose from $10.5 billion in 1990 to $83.8 billion in 2000 (and would reach $162 billion in 2004, an all-time record for any bilateral balance). Since a large share of the increase represented sales taken from other exporters rather than US domestic producers, the political response was not as strong as that to Japanese export expansion in the 1980s. But concern was rising.

Since the Nixon administration, US policy had been to "open up" to China. Since the Carter administration, the United States had welcomed Chinese trade by providing most favored nation (MFN) status for its exports. The authority employed, however, was that of the old Jackson-Vanik amendment to the Trade Act of 1974, whose original aim was to encourage emigration of Jews from the Soviet Union. The president had to make a positive determination every year that China was meeting the law's criteria, and Congress had the right to override it.

As discussed in chapter 8, this process was smooth and uncontroversial until the Tiananmen Square massacre of June 1989. Clinton had attacked his predecessor's policy of extending open trade thereafter without human rights conditions, and sought, unsuccessfully, to impose such conditions in his first two years. Thereafter, he made the required annual determinations, and the House rejected disapproval resolutions by comfortable margins. The yearly debate, however, gave critics of China's restrictions on democracy and human rights a forum to denounce such practices and threaten to revoke MFN. Their case was aided, marginally, by the fact that the "most favored nation" label suggested that China was getting something very special rather than the market access granted to just about every other US trading partner. To remove this problem, Senators William Roth (R-DE) and Daniel Patrick Moynihan (D-NY) won enactment of legislation changing the name from most favored nation status (MFN) to "normal trade relations," or NTR.

---

45. Calculations are from data on international transactions (exports, imports) and national accounts (GDP volume, 1995 prices) in International Monetary Fund, *International Financial Statistics Yearbook*, 2002, 356–57.

China had sought membership in the WTO since the inception of the organization. For a country of such current and potential market importance, this required negotiating market-opening agreements with every major trading partner. And the biggest negotiation was with the United States, which was demanding that Beijing commit to broad measures to free up trade and deregulate domestic markets for trade and investment. The talks ebbed and flowed, notwithstanding Barshefsky's yeoman efforts, until a new economic reformer, Zhu Rongji, assumed China's number-two leadership post, that of premier. Zhu was pressing to open up his country internally and cut subsidies to state-owned enterprises. Like Mexico's president a decade earlier, he saw trade liberalization as an effective way to put competitive pressure on domestic enterprises. And the requirements of WTO membership could help drive China toward the rules-based domestic economic order that a strong and stable market economy required.

So Zhu pressed his Beijing colleagues and developed a Chinese WTO accession offer that went well beyond any previous proposal. The offer was transmitted to Washington shortly before the premier's scheduled April 1999 visit. His aim was to nail down an agreement with President Clinton at his Oval Office meeting. Clinton was by now deeply committed to a strong overall China relationship—he had surmounted a military crisis involving Taiwan in 1996 and exchanged productive visits with the Chinese president thereafter. Now he sought the views of his advisers. Barshefsky argued for acceptance, as did senior foreign policy advisers. But political aides were wary—the time might not be right for Congress— and joining them in skepticism was Treasury Secretary Robert Rubin. So Clinton decided to defer action and to seek a still better deal. Zhu was wounded, and USTR promptly made matters worse by releasing the confidential text of the Chinese offer. Shortly thereafter, the Chinese Embassy in Yugoslavia fell victim to accidental bombing during the NATO campaign to free Kosovo from Serbian repression. US-China relations were on the rocks once again.

The US business community was unhappy as well. It had strongly supported US-Chinese trade, and disliked the annual extension process. Its members had, of course, pressed for major concessions from Beijing (the specific content depending on their specific interests, of course). But they were impressed with what Zhu had brought, and uncertain that the United States could get much more. They now saw a chance to lock in a solid trade relationship for the long term. So they urged resumption of talks, with an eye to agreement before the end of the year. Barshefsky went back to China, accompanied by National Economic Council Director Gene Sperling. What they brought back went a little further in some areas— enough to justify a presidential about-face. This time Clinton said "yes."

The agreement was, essentially, a long list of unilateral Chinese commitments. But there was one thing that required congressional action. China was unwilling, understandably, to go ahead unless granted what was quickly labeled "PNTR"—permanent normal trading relations. And this would require new legislation.

The vote on the annual NTR renewals had become a ritual. In July 1998, for example, the House had rejected the disapproval resolution by 264-166, with majorities in both parties on the winning side. But permanence was another matter—it meant giving up an annual opportunity to press China issues, and a source of potential leverage. And the measure would go to the House in early 2000, with memories of Seattle fresh in everyone's mind.

The battle proved to be tough, as expected. But China PNTR legislation had an advantage that fast track had lacked—there were clear and serious costs to rejection. Those who voted no on fast track could take comfort in the fact that failure would cause no concrete, immediate damage—there were no comprehensive global negotiations under way, and the target date of the Free Trade Area of the Americas was January 2005, then more than seven years distant. A negative vote on China PNTR, however, would deal a devastating blow to US-China relations, just as voting down NAFTA would have done to US-Mexico relations. Members of Congress were very much aware of this—and aware that they would be blamed for the damage. Moreover, PNTR was the only significant concession the United States was making to China, whereas the bilateral agreement to which it was linked brought major benefits to US exporters and investors.

This situation fostered a political environment in which swing members of the House looked not to defeat the measure but to find ways, consistent with their convictions, to have it pass. Representative Sander Levin of Michigan, who was becoming the lead Ways and Means Democrat on trade, had frequently expressed concern over competition from poor, low-wage countries, and he was a skeptic on Chinese human rights behavior as well. But he saw a need to move forward if a basis for doing so could be found.

One time-tested method of achieving this was to add "parallel" provisions to the pending legislation. Ways and Means chair Archer was initially cool toward such provisions in this case, as were chamber leaders. They thought China PNTR could win without them. But as April turned into May and backers still lacked the necessary votes, Archer expressed greater flexibility.[46] Levin put forward two provisions—one to limit "import surges" from China, and a second establishing a new commission to oversee bilateral relations on human rights. On the latter his position was strengthened by the cosponsorship of Representative Douglas Bereuter

---

46. Archer announced on 2 May 2000 that he would support such provisions because "there is more work to be done now [in building support] than I had anticipated we would have to do." In a 10 April letter to President Clinton, he had labeled such provisions "the wrong way to go." Quoted in *Inside US Trade*, 2 May and 14 April 2000.

(R-KS), vice chairman of the House International Relations Committee and a specialist on East Asia.

With these provisions on track, the Ways and Means Committee reported out PNTR legislation by the overwhelming margin of 34-4, with ranking Democrat Rangel joining in the majority. In the end, a total of 73 Democrats bucked opposition from labor and NGOs and voted in favor on the House floor. Garnering strong Republican support, PNTR prevailed on 24 May 2000 by a vote of 237 to 197, a relatively comfortable margin. After parallel Senate action, it became law.

More than a year would pass before China actually joined the WTO, and the House would have to reject, in the meantime, two more NTR disapproval resolutions. But the United States at last had a stable statutory base for trade relations with this enormously important nation. China trade would remain a prominent issue, of course. With the rise in the bilateral deficit, China's undervalued currency would come under increasing attack from 2003 onward, as noted in chapters 9 and 12. Chinese labor practices would be the target of a prominent Section 301 petition filed by the AFL-CIO in March 2004 (a petition rejected by the Bush administration). But there was a stronger framework for addressing such issues, since China was now further incorporated into the network of international institutions that had ameliorated interstate relations ever since the Second World War.

Clinton ended his second term on the upbeat in trade policy, just as he had begun his first term. The period in between had been frustrating, however. The president had been unable, after his first year, to secure fast-track negotiating authority. He had been unable to break the stalemate over labor and environmental standards that had precipitated this failure. And the WTO Ministerial Conference he had hosted had proved a disaster. So there was plenty of trade work waiting for George W. Bush when he entered the White House in January 2001 after a bitter and protracted electoral struggle.

11

Partisan Rancor and Trade Politics in the New Century

In recent decades, there has been steady—nay relentless—growth in party polarization and interparty rancor within the United States Congress, the House of Representatives in particular. This has been driven by broad national forces outside of trade policy. But it has undercut one of the enduring sources of support for trade liberalization: bipartisan leadership cooperation at the committee and chamber level.

In the 1970s and 1980s, trade expansion legislation was typically crafted through bipartisan cooperation inside the key trade committees—Senate Finance and House Ways and Means. And when they reached the floor, trade bills were enacted by a cross-party coalition of moderates. So when a prominent feature of Congress became what former Senator John Breaux (D-LA) has labeled "the incredible shrinking middle,"[1] trade legislating was bound to become harder. And it has, as polarization has undercut bipartisan cooperation at the committee and floor levels—particularly in the House. The George W. Bush administration and the Republican congressional leadership managed nonetheless to win renewal of fast-track negotiating authority—now renamed trade promotion authority (TPA)—by exploiting the shadow of the September 11, 2001, terrorist attacks and by exerting extraordinary pressure from the party leadership to win three excruciatingly close House votes. But the support base for the negotiations that have followed is narrower, and more partisan, than for any previous major trade round.

---

1. Quoted in Sarah A. Binder, *Stalemate: Causes and Consequences of Legislative Gridlock* (Washington, DC: Brookings Institution Press, 2003), 69.

Drawing on the renewed negotiating authority, US Trade Representative (USTR) Robert B. Zoellick concluded several bilateral and regional free trade agreements (FTAs), four of which won congressional approval by comfortable margins. He also achieved progress in the difficult Doha Round trade talks under the World Trade Organization (WTO). But the daunting task of completing these talks was in the hands of President Bush's second administration and his new USTR, former Congressman Rob Portman.

■ ■ ■

As the new Bush administration relaunched the drive for congressional renewal of fast-track negotiating authority in 2001, the battle lines were softening on the social issues that had done so much to doom the Clinton legislation. Antiglobalization forces, riding high after Seattle, had been brought back to earth by their failure to block the granting of permanent normal trading relations (PNTR) to China. Organized business, in turn, recognized that the hard Republican line it had encouraged on labor and environmental standards had proved counterproductive in the 1990s and would likely continue to keep Democrats on the other side. With a Republican now in the White House, moreover, business was less fearful that US negotiators would give these issues undue priority if they were included among the statutory negotiating objectives.

So compromise now seemed plausible. Responding to this opening, "new Democrat" Representative Cal Dooley of California put forward what became labeled the "Dooley principles," providing for parallel treatment of the key items on the social agenda. Trade-related labor and environmental standards would receive parity with traditional negotiating goals like market access, but without language requiring that such standards be part of all trade agreements.[2]

Meanwhile, on the Senate side, staff aides were developing a new, expanded approach to helping workers displaced by trade. Howard Rosen, outgoing staff director to the Joint Economic Committee under Senator Jeff Bingaman (D-NM), had long been concerned about this problem. He raised this issue and was encouraged to draft a proposal by Greg Mastel, the lead Democratic staff member on Senate Finance. It broadened the definition of trade-displaced workers and, in major innovations, added health care and wage insurance to the benefits provided.

Incorporating the social issues and enhancing worker adjustment programs was consistent with public attitudes toward trade liberalization.

---

2. By contrast, legislation considered in 1997 and 1998 was drafted so as to exclude most labor and environmental matters from agreements that would receive fast-track consideration.

3. Summary language from the "International Trade" section of the "Americans and the World" Web site maintained by the Program on International Policy Attitudes (PIPA), University of Maryland. http://www.americans-world.org/digest/global_issues/intertrade/onbalance.cfm (accessed 26 March 2005).

Surveys indicated that "while a strong majority of Americans have a favorable view of trade in principle, most have significant reservations [in] practice," so "the net feeling about trade is lukewarm at best."[3] However, in a June 2002 poll conducted by the Chicago Council on Foreign Relations (CFR), 93 percent of respondents agreed that countries that take part in international trade agreements should be "required to maintain minimum standards for working conditions," and 94 percent said that such countries should be "required to maintain minimum standards for protection of the environment." Even more impressive, the same survey found no less than 89 percent of Americans "favor free trade" if "the government ha[s] programs to help workers who lose their jobs."[4]

It was also true, of course, that by the late 1990s a clear majority of House Democrats stood against fast-track renewal, urged on by organized labor and by nongovernmental organizations (NGOs) that challenged globalization. On the specific question of fast-track legislation, the public was ambivalent: one 21st century survey showed a 49–42 percent plurality in opposition; a second, which stressed presidential consultation with Congress, came out 46–37 in favor.[5] Nonetheless, flexibility on social issues and expansiveness on adjustment assistance seemed a formula for bringing a healthy minority of House Democrats back into the protrade expansion camp—if not 102 (the number that had backed the North American Free Trade Agreement in 1993), then at least over 45 (the number counted ready to support the Clinton bill in 1997). The ranking Democrat on the House Trade Subcommittee, Sander Levin (D-MI), a fast-track opponent in 1997, had brokered a deal in 2000 that helped bring 73 Democrats on board the legislation granting PNTR to China, and he was indicating a readiness to try again on fast track. So was the ranking Democrat on the full committee, Charles Rangel (D-NY), who had likewise opposed fast track and backed China PNTR. Long-time free trader Robert Matsui (D-CA) was now deferring to these two, but he would certainly have lent his weight to any compromise that they were party to.

---

4. Chicago CFR poll data from Americans and the World at www.americans-world.org/digest/global_issues/intertrade/overwhelm.cfm (accessed March 24, 2005). The final question mentioned here asked workers to choose one of three statements (responses in parentheses): "I favor free trade, and I believe that it is necessary for the government to have programs to help workers who lose their jobs" (73 percent); "I favor free trade, and I believe that it is not necessary for the government to have programs to help workers who lose their jobs" (16 percent); "I do not favor free trade" (9 percent). When PIPA asked the same question at the beginning of 2004, the majority was smaller but still substantial: 60 percent for trade with programs, 13 percent for trade without them, and 22 percent against free trade. Support for "minimum" labor and environmental standards was essentially unchanged: 93 percent for each. Steven Kull et al., *Americans on Globalization, Trade, and Farm Subsidies*, Program on International Policy Attitudes (PIPA) and Knowledge Networks, 22 January 2004, 16, 17.

5. *Investors Business Daily*/TechnoMetrica Institute of Policy and Politics (TIPP) poll of May 2002; EPIC-MRA poll of October 2001. See the Americans for the World Web site: www.americans-world.org/digest/global_issues/intertrade/lowsupport.cfm (accessed 18 November 2003).

But events played out very differently. On the three critical House votes on what was ironically labeled "The Bipartisan Trade Promotion Authority Act," only 21, 11, and 25 Democrats, respectively, voted in favor, and the legislation prevailed by wafer-thin margins of 215-214, 216-215, and 215-212. President Bush and USTR Zoellick got their negotiating authority, but not the broad consensus and mandate that had been provided to their predecessors.[6] To understand why, we must look beyond the issue of trade to what has been happening in the US Congress over the past 30 years.

Polarization of Congressional Politics

Since 1981, the *National Journal*, a respected newsweekly focusing on government, has published sophisticated voter ratings placing every member of Congress somewhere on the ideological spectrum from liberal to conservative. The general pattern in the early years was for most Democrats to cluster on the left side, and most Republicans on the right. But there was considerable overlap in the middle. By 1999, however, "for the first time" in the Senate, "every Democrat had an average score that was to the left of the most liberal Republican." In the junior chamber, moreover, the *Journal* found that "only two Republicans . . . were in that chamber's more-liberal half on each of the three issue areas . . . and only two Democrats . . . ranked in the more-conservative half."[7] Since then, the pattern has stayed essentially the same: two House Republicans (and no Democrats) meeting that criterion in 2004; just one Republican senator more liberal than just one Democrat the same year.[8]

Parallel data developed by political scientists underscore the same trend. In 1969–70, as noted by Sarah Binder, there was "substantial overlap between Democrats' and Republicans' right- and left-most members. . . . A large ideological middle dominate[d] the House." But, she added, "Thirty years later, there is virtually no ideological common ground."[9] Figure 11.1 shows this stark contrast.[10]

---

6. For a more positive take on their trade achievements, see C. Fred Bergsten, "A Renaissance for United States Trade Policy?" *Foreign Affairs*, November-December 2002.

7. Richard E. Cohen, "Going to Extremes: Our Annual Vote Ratings," A Special Supplement to the *National Journal*, 26 February 2000, 4. One of the two Democratic outliers left the party in 2000; one of the two Republicans was defeated for reelection in 2002.

8. *National Journal*, 12 February 2005, 427 and 440–54.

9. Binder, *Stalemate: Causes and Consequences of Legislative Gridlock*, 23–24.

10. The scores in Binder's figures are based on a measure developed by Nolan M. McCarty, Keith T. Poole, and Howard Rosenthal, *Income Redistribution and the Realignment of American Politics* (Washington, DC: American Enterprise Institute Press, 1997).

Figure 11.1 Ideological distribution of the parties in the US House, 1969–70 and 1999–2000

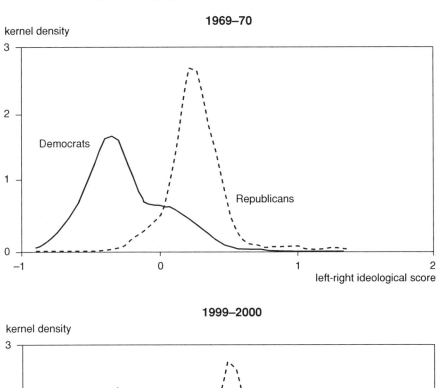

Notes: Ideological scores are first-dimension DW-NOMINATE scores. Graph shows density plot of House members' ideological score by party.

Source: Binder, Sarah A. 2003. *Stalemate: Causes and Consequences of Legislative Gridlock.* Washington, DC: Brookings Institution Press, 24–25.

Reprinted with permission of the Brookings Institution Press.

Why this huge shift? One possibility is that the American public has been growing far more polarized. There is, indeed, some recent evidence of this in the "50-50 (and 51-48) America" symbolized by the 2000 and 2004 presidential elections, and in the deepening partisan divisions on certain public issues during the Bush years.[11] There has also been what political scientists term an ideological "sorting out" between the two main political parties: Republicans have become more reliably conservative, and Democrats more likely to be on the liberal side. But the bulk of the evidence indicates that division within the broad public is far shallower than division between party activists, and between members of Congress.

Since the 1970s, Americans have become somewhat more conservative and significantly more Republican. But they remain clustered near the political center. In the 1972–76 period, an average of 77 percent of voters placed themselves in one of four center categories: middle of the road, slightly liberal, slightly conservative, or didn't know/hadn't thought about it. By 1990–94, that figure had dropped slightly to 75 percent.[12] But this was not the case with political leaders. As summarized by David C. King in the mid-1990s, "the parties are becoming more extreme . . . increasingly distant in their policies from what the average voter would like. . . . Strong Republicans have become more conservative, and . . . party activists are drawn almost entirely from their ranks. Likewise, strong Democrats have become more liberal, though the ideological shift has not been as steep."[13]

Has the public become more polarized since then, driven perhaps by the heat of partisan combat? Somewhat, according to the measure cited above. The portion of self-described centrists dropped to 62 percent in 2002, and averaged 68 percent over the 2000–04 period. But this indicator jumped back to 70 percent in 2004, notwithstanding a highly polarized presidential election campaign.

More generally, Morris Fiorina has demolished the "myth of a polarized America" in a brilliant short book that gives particular attention to the divisive issues of abortion and homosexuality. Most citizens in both

---

11. See Pew Research Center for the People and the Press, "The 2004 Political Landscape: Evenly Divided and Increasingly Polarized," survey released 5 November 2003. http://people-press.org/reports/display.php3?ReportID=196 (accessed 28 March 2005).

12. Calculations from National Election Studies, Center for Political Studies, University of Michigan (www.umich.edu/~nes), table 3.1. The specific question was, "When it comes to politics do you usually think of yourself as extremely liberal, liberal, slightly liberal, moderate or middle of the road, slightly conservative, conservative, extremely conservative, or haven't you thought much about this?"

13. David C. King, "The Polarization of American Parties and Distrust of Government," in Joseph S. Nye, Jr., Philip D. Zelikow, and David C. King, eds., Why People Don't Trust Government (Cambridge, MA: Harvard University Press, 1997), 165, 171.

"red" states (Republican) as well as "blue" states (Democrat) are ambivalent about these and other public issues. What the country has, Fiorina concludes, is "centrist voters and polarizing elites," and the latter have taken control of the political process in what he labels "the hijacking of American democracy."[14]

Why has Congress come to reflect the polarized activists rather than the centrist public? One reason for the ideological overlap in 1969–70 was the presence of many Southern Democrats from states where that party had dominated since the Civil War. They were typically more conservative than many Northeastern Republicans. But the enfranchisement of blacks through a movement in which national Democrats were particularly prominent drove conservative Southern Democrats (and their children) to the Republican side. By the turn of the century, members of Congress from that region had ideological positions similar to their party brethren from elsewhere in the nation.

This explains the increase in ideological cohesion within the parties. But why the movement of the leaders in both to relatively extreme positions? One powerful force also had its roots in the 1960s—regular congressional redistricting. Once the Supreme Court ruled that districts within a state had to have substantially equal populations, the lines had to be redrawn after each decennial census. Politicians had them redrawn with eyes to their own survival. This meant more "safe" districts with strong Republican or Democratic majorities and fewer "marginal" districts. This tendency was reinforced by pressure, under voting rights legislation, to create "majority-minority" districts where practicable, so blacks (or Hispanics) could elect their own to Congress.

In a competitive district, candidates will fight for the votes of the citizens in the center, so the representative is driven toward representing the median voter. In a one-party-dominant district, however, a member is virtually assured of reelection, provided he or she can win renomination. So priority shifts to maintaining the allegiance of the median party member (a substantial move from the center) or, in practice, the allegiance of the median activist party member most likely to vote in a primary (even further from the center).

Congressional movement toward the extremes has been further driven by the rise of activist "cause" groups on the left and right. In the words of Richard E. Neustadt (paraphrasing Hugh Heclo), a growing role in both elections and legislation has been played by movements—" . . . the civil rights movement . . . environmentalists and feminists—then, in reaction, right-to-lifers." This leads to "warfare among elites, waged since the 1960s in the name of causes, not compromises, fueled by technology, manned by

14. Morris P. Fiorina with Samuel J. Abrams and Jeremy C. Pope, *Culture War? The Myth of a Polarized America* (New York: Pearson Longman, 2005), 78, 99.

consultants, rousing supporters by damning opponents, while serving the separate interests of particular candidates and groups at given times."[15]

One other, technological factor deserves brief consideration—jet air travel. When travel back to the state or district was a time-consuming enterprise, members of Congress would live together in Washington through much of the year, weekends included, with their primary trips home during the heat of summer or after adjournment in the fall. They socialized with one another, and they frequently found persons in the other party whom they liked better than some of their own. But once jet planes made it possible for legislators to return to their states or districts for a short weekend, this became the natural way for them to consolidate political support, and it became the expectation of their constituents. So the norm in the House now is for real business to be conducted from Tuesday through Thursday. A member's Washington life has become a frenetic stopover, a rush from meeting to meeting with no time for rest and little time for cultivating personal relationships with colleagues.

These forces have affected both legislative chambers, but particularly the House of Representatives. House members' short, two-year terms reinforce their perceived need for constant contact with district voters. And by definition, theirs is the body that is subject to redistricting; Senators represent entire states. Finally, procedures in the House make it relatively easy for a cohesive majority to dominate, while the Senate's norm of unlimited debate forces cooperation among members—unanimous consent agreements, avoidance of filibusters (or overriding them by super-majorities)—if it is to legislate at all.

Binder has documented how polarization leads to "stalemate"—it has become harder and harder to enact legislation. She quotes Representative Barney Frank (D-MA) in 1999, in the wake of the Clinton impeachment battle: "Right now, the differences between the two parties are so great, it doesn't make sense for us to compromise. We'll show where we stand, and let the people decide."[16] This gridlock runs directly counter to the "responsible party" model, long in favor among political scientists, which argued that ideologically homogeneous parties would lead to more effective governance. (Scholars should be careful what they wish for.)

Within the House, partisan polarization has had a major impact on how business is conducted. Through most of the post–World War II period, committees dominated the process of developing and enacting legislation. They were run by the majority party, but they reached out for bipartisan majorities to improve the prospects for final passage. But as parties became

---

15. Neustadt, "The Politics of Mistrust," in Nye et al., *Why People Don't Trust Government*, 185, 187. On trade, the most visible manifestation has been the antiglobalist coalition under the Public Citizen umbrella, discussed at greater length in chapter 10.

16. See Binder, *Stalemate: Causes and Consequences of Legislative Gridlock*, 25.

more ideological, the pattern changed. Congressional party caucuses got more and more into the business of shaping legislation themselves.

As with many congressional trends, this began with the Democrats, whose caucus—in the 1970s and 1980s—came to take substantive positions and instruct committee leaders to adopt them. Committees retained substantial impact and often autonomy, but caucus influence was buttressed by members' readiness to evict committee chairs who were particularly unresponsive, and to select new chairs using criteria other than seniority. When Republicans under Representative Newt Gingrich (R-GA) swept to power in the 1994 mid-term election, this trend was accentuated. Party chairs were in fact selected by the new speaker, and the primary agenda—the "Contract with America"—was the party's 1994 campaign manifesto. And while the extreme centralization of 1995 could not be maintained indefinitely, a new power relationship was consolidated. On important issues, committee chairs served the party leadership rather than the other way around. Moreover, under the new rules imposed by the Gingrich revolution, committee chairs were now limited to three two-year terms, or six years in all.

This was bound to cause problems for trade policy, which was—as illustrated in prior chapters—particularly dependent on strong, broad-based, bipartisan support in Senate Finance and House Ways and Means. Bills authorizing and implementing major trade agreements had been worked out in subcommittee and full committee markups (or "nonmarkups"). Lopsided, bipartisan committee votes in favor paved the way for lesser, but solid, majorities in their parent chambers. And their strong role made these committees effective partners and interlocutors for successive US Trade Representatives.

Decline of House Bipartisanship on Trade

Cross-party, committee-based trade policy collaboration remained the congressional norm well after it was fading in other policy spheres. House Democrats did see partisan opportunity on the issue in 1987–88, of course, but the important provisions of the 1988 Trade Act were more the product of Chairman Dan Rostenkowski's (D-IL) bipartisan Ways and Means process, and that of his counterpart, Lloyd Bentsen (D-TX) in the Senate, than of Speaker Jim Wright's party-based initiatives. The battle over the North American Free Trade Agreement (NAFTA) was won through close collaboration between the Clinton White House and congressional leaders of both parties, with Republican Whip Gingrich and former senior Ways and Means member Bill Frenzel (R-MN) playing important roles. And after bipartisan "nonmarkup" drafting sessions in both chambers, the Uruguay Round/WTO legislation won 2-1 Republican *and* Democratic approval in the House, and 3-1 margins of each party in the Senate.

This is not to say that committee Democrats did not sometimes act in a partisan manner. Al Ullman of Oregon, who chaired Ways and Means from 1975 through 1980, sometimes had legislation shaped at Democrats-only meetings (responding to pressure from the Democratic caucus that had unseated his predecessor). His successor Rostenkowski "was by instinct and by practice a believer in bipartisan accommodation," but despite his personal strength he could not always operate in this manner.[17] When his indictment on corruption charges forced him to resign in early 1994, his successor reportedly went around the committee process in the drafting of certain antidumping language for the Uruguay Round bill, apparently with Clinton administration encouragement.

Trade bipartisanship broke down further, however, with the Republican takeover of Congress in 1995 and the concurrent rise of social issues on the trade agenda. Ways and Means Committee Republicans led by Chairman Bill Archer (R-TX) put together their own fast-track renewal proposal that year, though they were unable to win Clinton administration support. The bill was developed and voted out of committee along partisan lines, mainly because it excluded most labor and environmental concerns. The proposal died when Senate Majority Leader Robert Dole (R-KS) declared that "it would be a mistake to extend new fast-track authority at this time."[18]

Archer renewed his fast-track efforts in early 1997, and Clinton followed with the administration proposal in September. This time, as set forth at length in chapter 10, it was Clinton and the Republican leadership aligned against more than three-quarters of House Democrats—in part because the Republicans still insisted on restrictive labor-environment provisions. But after failure that fall, Gingrich resurrected the issue over White House objections in September 1998 with a clearly partisan purpose: he did not expect to pass the bill but wanted to squeeze House Democrats caught between labor and business constituents. This provoked enormous resentment among longtime protrade Democrats like Matsui, and drove the number of Democratic "yeas" down to 29 out of 200.[19]

Bipartisanship made a modest comeback in 2000 in the struggle over granting normal trade status to the People's Republic of China upon its entry into the World Trade Organization. This was Clinton's last major trade priority. It had enormous business support and won by a relatively comfortable margin of 237–197, with 73 Democrats in support, as earlier

---

17. Nelson W. Polsby, *How Congress Evolves: Social Bases of Institutional Change* (Oxford, UK: Oxford University Press, 2004), 116 and passim.

18. Statement on the Senate floor, 4 November 1995. For a fuller description of this initiative and the response of USTR Mickey Kantor, see I. M. Destler, *Renewing Fast-Track Legislation*, POLICY ANALYSES IN INTERNATIONAL ECONOMICS 50 (Washington, DC: Institute for International Economics, September 1997), 20–22.

19. Seventy-one Republicans also voted "nay," and the bill lost by 243–180.

noted.[20] Cooperation across party lines was also central to the enactment of trade preferences for African and Caribbean nations that year. And in June 2000, extreme trade *protectionism* showed bipartisan coloration when the House cast an obligatory vote on a resolution to withdraw from the WTO. Of the 56 members who voted to abandon the global trade organization, just 21 were Democrats and 33 were Republicans. (Two were independents.)

There are enduring factors in the structure of American business and politics, moreover, that limit party polarization on trade issues per se. While labor and business have pulled majorities of Democrats and Republicans, respectively, to opposite sides of the issue, and the emergence of trade-related labor and environmental issues has furthered this trend, subgroups within both parties have limited polarization. "New Democrats" in the Clinton-Gore mode continue to support trade expansion. And anti-internationalist "conservatives" have opposed it.[21] From 1994 through mid-2001, more than 50 Republicans voted "nay" on every major piece of trade legislation.[22]

The structure of contemporary American industry also seems to militate against full-blown party polarization on trade, in contrast to the situation in the early 20th century. According to research by Michael J. Hiscox, the fact that US labor is not currently mobile across manufacturing industries militates against the development of class-based trade politics.[23] Instead, trade policy divisions tend to pit industry against industry, and region against region.

---

20. As detailed in chapter 10, senior Ways and Means Democrat Levin brought some of them on board with a measure, cosponsored by Douglas Bereuter (R-NE), establishing a congressional commission to monitor Chinese performance on human rights.

21. After controlling for other variables, Robert E. Baldwin and Christopher S. Magee found that a higher rating given to a legislator by the American Conservative Union was associated with a greater likelihood of voting *against* NAFTA or the GATT-Uruguay Round Agreement. See Baldwin and Magee, *Congressional Trade Votes: From NAFTA Approval to Fast-Track Defeat*, POLICY ANALYSES IN INTERNATIONAL ECONOMICS 59 (Washington, DC: Institute for International Economics, February 2000), 30.

22. Fifty-six opposed the Uruguay Round in 1994; 71 voted against the fast-track bill pushed by Gingrich in 1998; and 57 stood against permanent normal trade relations with China in 2000. When the delay on China's WTO entry required President Bush to request one more temporary extension of normal trade relations in 2001, 62 Republicans voted "nay."

23. Michael J. Hiscox, *International Trade and Political Conflict: Commerce, Coalitions, and Mobility* (Princeton, NJ: Princeton University Press, 2002). Hiscox is joining the debate between trade policymaking scholars who stress industry groupings (e.g., Peter Gourevitch and, to some degree, this author) and those who emphasize class coalitions (e.g., Ronald Rogowski). His basic conclusion: "Concentrating on industry groups will yield more inferential power to a study of trade politics when levels of interindustry factor mobility are relatively low . . . for instance . . . in the United States and Britain since the 1960s" (162). And it is class-based trade politics that is associated with sharp ideological divisions between political parties.

Finally, there is no deep divergence of opinion on trade policy between rank-and-file members of the two political parties. A 2004 survey by the Program on International Policy Attitudes (PIPA) found that Republicans are more likely to be positive about international trade (46 percent of them versus 30 percent of Democrats), but Democrats are more likely to be positive about globalization (44 versus 40 percent). More Democrats believe that US trade policy gives too little consideration to the concerns of "working Americans" (83 versus 68 percent), but more also believe that the United States should comply with WTO decisions if "it rules against the US" (74 versus 60 percent). More Democrats also support specific free trade agreements, existing and potential.[24]

Hence, based on historical trade policy experience and the structure of interests and public opinion, one might have expected a continuation of the bipartisan tradition, albeit with substantially more Republicans than Democrats voting "aye." But the broader House trends, exacerbated by personalities, led to trade policy polarization in the House in the new century to an extent not seen since the 1930s.

The House Bill in 2001: Partisan Contention

With his six-year term as Ways and Means chairman expiring, Bill Archer retired at the end of 2000. Vying to succeed him were Trade Subcommittee Chairman Phil Crane (R-IL) and his somewhat younger, more junior colleague, Bill Thomas (R-CA). Crane was the better liked; Thomas was smarter and tougher. The Republican caucus chose the Californian. A former colleague and mentor who supported Thomas characterized him as very smart, policy-oriented, and purposive, but possessing "no interpersonal skills." Before the trade bill was enacted, the new chairman would vindicate all of these characterizations. He established himself as the strongest and most effective Ways and Means leader since Dan Rostenkowski. He also engendered greater suspicion and hostility than any of his predecessors in memory.

Taxes were the administration's number one priority that year, and the Bush tax cut proposal topped Thomas' list as well. But trade was not far behind. President Bush had signaled his interest in fast-track renewal in early January. His USTR, Robert Zoellick, was confirmed in early February. Zoellick made fast track (renamed "trade promotion authority," or TPA) a top priority, pressing for movement within the administration and

---

24. Additional questions asked if NAFTA has been "good for the United States" (52 percent of Democrats, 41 percent of Republicans); and if respondents "favor CAFTA" (53 versus 48) and "favor an FTAA" (60 versus 49). Data from Kull et al., *Americans on Globalization, Trade, and Farm Subsidies*. The party breakdowns, provided to the author by PIPA, are not in the published report.

floating the idea of a comprehensive trade bill, combining this with other, unfinished trade business, such as the recently completed FTA with Jordan and a trade agreement with Vietnam. House Democrats objected, as did some senior administration officials, and so Zoellick took a step back, awaiting congressional initiatives. House Democrats met through the spring to develop their approach. In June, Crane introduced a fast-track bill, with 62 largely Republican cosponsors, that took a hard line against labor and environmental standards.[25]

Zoellick did not endorse the Crane bill, declaring merely that "the formal legislative process has begun." Thomas was similarly cautious. Conservative but pragmatic, the Californian recognized that he would need Democratic support, and that this would require some flexibility on the social issues. So he embarked on negotiations with colleagues across the aisle in the summer. By late September, he released a summary of a "Bipartisan Compromise" that his committee would later report to the full House. Unlike the 1997 bill, it included "labor and the environment" among the principal negotiating objectives, and agreements reached pursuant to these objectives could clearly be part of a fast-track bill. Like the 1997 bill, it provided the president a broad but time-limited grant of authority.

Substantively, it was a real effort at compromise, representing one plausible middle ground. Conservatives had wanted to exclude these issues from the agenda. Supporters of organized labor had wanted to require their inclusion in any agreement. Making them full-fledged goals with flexibility in their pursuit gave something to each side. It was, in essence, the "no mandates/no new restrictions" formula advanced in vain by the Democratic Leadership Council in 1997.[26] The administration was not directly involved in the drafting, and held off any explicit endorsement. But Zoellick and Secretary of Commerce Don Evans released a positive statement: "This bill should allow the Congress to move forward quickly in a cooperative fashion to grant the President vitally needed trade negotiating authority."[27]

But the Democrats dealing with Thomas across the table were not Rangel and Levin, his senior Ways and Means counterparts. Rather, they were three more junior Democrats: William Jefferson (D-LA), John Tanner (D-TN), and their leader Cal Dooley (D-CA), author of the "Dooley principles" providing for parallel treatment of labor and environmental issues. All three were serious and committed protrade legislators, and Dooley— whose district bordered on that of the chairman—had taken the initiative in organizing the group and initiating dialogue. But the other two were junior Ways and Means members, and Dooley was not on the committee

---

25. Appendix A provides a more detailed account of the House process in 2001.

26. Testimony of Edith Wilson to the House Ways and Means Committee, 30 September 1997.

27. Statement of 3 October 2001, quoted in *Inside US Trade*, 5 October 2001.

at all. None of them could be expected to exert strong sway over their colleagues, either through position or informal influence.

Not surprisingly, the process infuriated the senior Ways and Means Democrats. A day after Thomas put out his summary, Rangel, Levin, and Matsui (numbers 1, 4, and 3 among Democrats, respectively, in Committee seniority) dispatched a "Dear Democratic Colleague" letter with the heading, "Thomas' 'Bipartisan Compromise' Is Neither." Declaring that "the Democratic leadership on the Committee has not been consulted in the development of Chairman Thomas' proposal," they expressed "significant concerns with the so-called compromise in three key areas": labor standards, environmental protection, and the role of Congress. Their specific criticisms in the letter were modest, however—for example, they stressed the need for "steps to reconcile Multilateral Environmental Agreements with trade agreements." And they urged colleagues to defer judgment until they could present their own proposal, which "holds the prospect for broad and true bipartisan support."[28]

Why then had Thomas gone around them? It was not because they were unwilling to talk. Rather, the chairman had apparently reached a conclusion, based on his reading of their policy statements, that no acceptable TPA deal could be struck with them. Since he believed negotiations would not be fruitful, he didn't try. During the Thomas-Dooley talks, when Levin reportedly raised the matter informally with Thomas with an eye to initiating a serious dialogue, the chair replied—no more than half in jest—"I consider you part of the enemy on this issue."

Was he right? The evidence is not all on one side.[29] What is clear is that serious negotiations within the committee between senior Ways and Means Republicans and Democrats never took place. On 3 October, Thomas and Dooley introduced HR 3005, their "Bipartisan Trade Promotion Act of 2001." On 4 October, the Democrats countered with HR 3019, the "Comprehensive Trade Promotion Act of 2001." Thomas had set his course and was determined to stick to it. The Democrats were responding in kind.

The partisan divide within Ways and Means was exacerbated by incompatibilities of style and personality. Conflict from other committee issues—taxes, social security—had spilled over to trade. Thomas and Rangel did not get on well, and their operating styles diverged markedly. Rangel believed in working an issue personally, feeling colleagues out,

---

28. Letter from Rangel, Levin, and Matsui to Democratic colleagues, 26 September 2001.

29. Appendix A probes this question in detail. If one judges by the contents of the Democrats' September letter, a deal was within reach—Thomas could easily have addressed most of the specifics therein, and it is hard to understand why he didn't try (if only for tactical reasons). If the standard is the bill (HR 3019) that the Democrats submitted a week later, compromise looks much harder, for that bill was both highly detailed in its negotiating objectives and required a level of success in meeting them that would have been difficult to achieve.

using committee procedures to move toward compromise if one were available, but keeping somewhat elusive on substance in the meantime. Thomas placed little if any value on formal procedures and was often contemptuous of "process" concerns. He was impatient to get to the substantive bottom line.

A graphic illustration of the personality-process gap came at a full committee markup on 5 October, at which Thomas had previously signaled (and committee members expected) that he would push his bill to a final vote with as little debate as possible. To everyone's surprise, he began the discussion by announcing that that issue would be postponed until the next week to allow members to compare his bill with the just introduced Democratic alternative. Rangel treated this as a concession with some promise of substantive flexibility, and said with gracious hyperbole that he was gratified to "have been relieved from having to read a very painful statement that . . . I have worked all night on."[30] But rather than responding in kind and taking credit for what seemed a conciliatory gesture, Thomas put down Rangel by saying that all he heard were complaints about "process, process." It was the substance that mattered.

And though the majority and minority staffs did meet over the weekend, they got nowhere. Neither side seemed willing to take a serious step toward the other. So when Ways and Means members reconvened on 9 October, the committee, led by Thomas, rejected the Democratic alternative by 26 to 12 and approved the Thomas bill by 26 to 13, a vote more partisan than the numbers make it seem (24 Republicans and just two Democrats, cosponsors Jefferson and Tanner, voted in favor). So, contrary to the standard practice in the postwar period, a major trade bill was not worked out substantially within the regular Ways and Means Committee process, with bipartisan participation. Instead, it was developed outside, brought formally to a full committee "markup," and passed there, essentially without change, and essentially along partisan lines.

Thomas' approach seemed extraordinarily risky in terms of his presumed goal of crafting a bill that the House would pass. The Republicans had just a 12-vote majority. And as noted earlier, no fewer than 50 Republicans had opposed every major trade bill since NAFTA. A Republican president would bring some of them along, and the post-9/11 environment would prove helpful as well. But until the afternoon of the vote, the Bush White House doubted that the Thomas bill could pass: in fact, at noon that day it urged the House leadership to pull the bill from the floor to avoid defeat.

So there were intermittent efforts toward compromise after the bill was reported. The most important began when President Bush met with Rangel on 1 November and seemed to endorse the idea of compromise

---

30. Statement of Charles B. Rangel, 5 October 2001, released by his office.

negotiations to bring more Democrats on board. Subsequent conversations involving Speaker Dennis Hastert and middle-ranking Committee Republican Rob Portman (R-OH)[31] led to the drafting of a one-page summary of the concerns of Rangel and his colleagues, which the senior Democrat sent to Hastert a week later. But neither Hastert nor Thomas responded. Rangel had been calling for "negotiation to see whether we can find some common ground that would allow Fast Track to pass the House with . . . broad, bipartisan support."[32] But notwithstanding Bush's encouragement, no such negotiation took place.

This rebuff could only deepen partisan rancor. The nonresponse gave wavering Democrats every excuse to oppose the bill, and vote counts had supporters from that party down in the 10 to 15 range until shortly before the actual tally. This placed an extraordinary burden on Republicans—it would be necessary for them to reduce their "nay" votes to around 20. This meant winning over members who had never voted for trade liberalization in their lives.[33] The White House put on a squeeze—so, even more, did Majority Whip Tom ("The Hammer") DeLay (R-TX). And because every conceivable vote was needed, the power of protectionist interests was inflated, since members responsive to those interests were in a position to put the bill over the top or sink it.

The situation also brought partisan motivations to the fore on both sides. DeLay was widely believed to like the idea of winning mainly with Republicans—he could then play hardball with business contributors, pointing out it was his party that delivered for them and they should allocate their political money accordingly. Democratic Whip Nancy Pelosi (D-CA), a backer of NAFTA and the Uruguay Round/WTO, reportedly urged on-the-fence party colleagues to vote no because each additional Democratic vote in the negative would require DeLay to put one more protectionist Republican at risk in his or her constituency.

In the end, Republicans won through a combination of procedural control and substantive concessions. They had already mollified Republican members of the House steel caucus by initiating a Section 201 case that would lead to temporary tariff protection for that industry. A farm bill increasing subsidies had passed the House in October, and administration friendliness toward this legislation also helped win TPA votes. Finally, it was an increase in textile protection that put the bill over the top.

---

31. Portman, a friend of the president, would become USTR in the second George W. Bush administration.

32. Statement of Charles B. Rangel, 9 October 2001, released by his office.

33. That fall, the author compiled a list of 20 hard-core, antitrade House Republicans who had voted to withdraw from the WTO in 2000 and against every important liberalizing initiative. The list did not include any freshmen, for whom little evidence was available. In the end, 11 of the 20 hard-core antitrade Republicans voted in favor of the bill. Two others managed to be among the five House members who did not cast ballots at all.

As time ran out, the nays outnumbered the ayes, but the vote was held open for about 20 additional minutes (a procedure made famous on the Medicare reform bill two years later) while Republican members were importuned to reverse themselves. In the end, a textile caucus member, Representative Jim DeMint (R-SC), "changed his vote from 'nay' to 'aye,'" as stated in *The Congressional Record*.[34] He did so in return for a promise of legislation to further restrict apparel eligible for favorable import treatment under the US trade agreement with Caribbean and Andean nations.[35] A second or so after his switch, the chair's gavel came down declaring the vote closed. The ayes had it, 215 to 214. Just 21 Democrats supported it; only 23 Republicans voted in the negative. The "Bipartisan Trade Promotion Authority Act" now moved to the Senate.[36]

Bipartisan Compromise in the Senate

In the senior chamber, cross-party relationships were better, particularly in the Committee on Finance. Senator Charles Grassley (R-IA) began the year as chair, yielding to Max Baucus (D-MT) after Jim Jeffords left the Republican camp in June and gave Democrats razor-thin control. Both Grassley and Baucus had something to prove, as neither was felt to measure up to the standard of prior chairs such as Lloyd Bentsen (D-TX), Bob Dole (R-KS), Bob Packwood (R-OR), or Pat Moynihan (D-NY). Baucus had long given priority to trade policy, but his record was mixed—he had voted against the Uruguay Round/WTO agreement, for example, for second-order constituency reasons. Moreover, with the Senate divided 50-49-1 and 60 votes needed to break a filibuster, a trade bill could pass only with significant support in both parties.

So Baucus and Grassley walked compatible paths. They looked for a workable compromise package, including on labor-environment issues, and found one that did not diverge sharply from the Thomas bill. Their committee reported out legislation on 12 December 2001, just six days after the House vote. And the 18-3 vote in favor was as bipartisan as its House counterpart's was not.

---

34. *Congressional Record*, 6 December 2001, H 9044. Representative Robin Hayes (R-NC), who some accounts credit with the final deciding vote, was rewarded with an immediate presidential statement endorsing his stand—and certain textile industry trade objectives.

35. Under the so-called "triple transformation test," apparel could enter the US market duty free only if the fiber, cloth, and clothing were all produced within the region covered by the agreement. The administration promised, in a letter signed by President Bush, to add the requirement that the cloth be dyed within the United States. Thomas strongly opposed this concession (as did Rangel).

36. The day after the vote, C. Fred Bergsten, director of the Institute for International Economics, asked this author to lead an IIE staff discussion. He opened by saying, "Mac, you've been telling us they couldn't win this way, now tell us how they did!" The reply: "They wanted to get fast track in the worst possible way, and they did it."

The full Senate did not take up the bill until 1 May 2002, however. The reason was the Democrats' determination to include in the bill a major expansion and reform of trade adjustment assistance (TAA). The House had passed a separate bill extending that assistance, but the issue had not been prominent in the TPA debate, in large part because House Democrats did not give it priority. Baucus, however, decided that major TAA reform was substantively desirable and a means to legitimize his support of the overall TPA measure. (He had alienated some of his party colleagues by supporting the Bush tax cut of 2001.) And before 2001 was out, Majority Leader Daschle (D-SD) had determined that TAA reform was the principal way to put his party's stamp on the legislation.

Republicans did not generally oppose trade adjustment assistance, but one element of the proposed reform did engender ideological conflict—the provision of health care benefits for trade-displaced workers. This moved the debate to a terrain characterized by strong partisan conflict, since Newt Gingrich targeted Clinton health care reform in 1993–94. The idea here was limited to workers laid off on account of trade, but liberals welcomed it as a foot in the door for a broader benefit, and conservatives feared it for the same reason. Senator Phil Gramm (R-TX) was particularly adamant in his opposition, saying he preferred no TPA at all to inclusion of the health benefit.

Once it was clear that Senate passage would not come without it, the issue was what percent of health care costs to cover (the Democrats' bottom line was any two-digit percentage beginning with a seven). The main negotiations were between Senate Democrats and the Bush administration, and they dragged on. But the TAA–health care deal was finally struck, as part of a broad expansion of the program that also

- broadened coverage to "secondary workers" (producers of inputs to trade-impacted final goods) and to certain workers who lost their jobs due to relocation of plants overseas;

- established a new, alternative program of "wage insurance" for trade-displaced workers taking lower-paying jobs;

- doubled the funds authorized for worker retraining;

- extended the maximum time period for assistance under the program; and

- increased support for job search and relocation.[37]

37. Lori G. Kletzer and Howard Rosen, "Easing the Adjustment Burden on US Workers," in C. Fred Bergsten and the Institute for International Economics, *The United States and the World Economy* (Washington, DC: Institute for International Economics, 2005), chapter 10. As noted earlier, Rosen played a key role in developing the legislation to expand trade adjustment assistance.

Regarding trade promotion authority, the provisions in the Senate bill were similar to what had passed the House and to the 1988 law: the negotiating authority ran until 2005, with an expedited procedure available for extending it two more years. But Senators Mark Dayton (D-MN) and Larry Craig (R-ID) raised another issue—the sanctity (in their eyes) of US antidumping laws. Despite considerable congressional opposition, Zoellick had agreed to the inclusion of antidumping laws in the Doha Development Agenda, using as his domestic rationale the need to attack unfairness in other nations' trade remedy laws. But there was broad congressional opposition to the United States making any changes in *its* laws (Baucus was among the hardliners on this point), and the Dayton-Craig amendment sought to block such changes through a procedural device—any agreement on these laws requiring US action would have to be implemented with a separate vote, in a separate bill. Zoellick and Commerce Secretary Evans declared that this would in fact torpedo the negotiations, but a proposal to table Dayton-Craig failed by 61-38. It was then approved by voice vote (administration supporters not wishing to lock it in further with an on-the-record tally). Thereafter, just before the Memorial Day recess, the full Senate approved the omnibus bill on a 66-30 vote. Bipartisanship prevailed, as did the Senate's general tendency to be more supportive of trade-liberalizing legislation. The bill would now go to conference.

But not for a while. In substance, the outlines of the deal seemed obvious. The Senate would yield on (or soften) Dayton-Craig—the administration had declared this unacceptable, and Daschle had already signaled his readiness to compromise. The House would buy into expanded TAA. This is in fact what occurred, but not before a bizarre endgame that served as a poster child for interparty and interchamber distrust.

First, the Senate delayed appointment of conferees and proposed working out matters informally (one reason being to limit the role of senior Republican Gramm). The House, and Thomas in particular, saw this as an attempt to limit its bargaining power. Then, after the Memorial Day recess, Thomas began to move toward conference on his own terms, through an extraordinary process the logic of which few of his colleagues understood: the drafting and enactment of a new House bill. The House, unlike the Senate, had passed not one but several trade measures. And the Ways and Means chairman believed that this put the House at a technical disadvantage. So he took the extraordinary step of attaching to the motion to appoint conferees a new, comprehensive 300-page bill that few if any of his colleagues had read or understood. This looked to many (not just Democrats) like an arbitrary move to impose his will on the conference. It drove even more Democrats into opposition, and delayed matters further as Republicans scurried for yet more votes from their ranks. Finally, five weeks after the Senate vote, the House rule to *start* the conference passed on 26 June by a 216-215 vote. Just 11 Democrats voted "aye"; just 14 Republicans voted "nay."

Then, before and after the July 4th recess, Senators battled over how many conferees to appoint, with Democrats pressing for a small number in order to exclude Gramm from the proceedings. The Democrats won that fight. It was followed by a week-long spat between Baucus and Thomas over whose turn it was to chair the conference—Thomas won this one. Finally, the conference met for the first time on 23 July, a full two months after the Senate vote, and just three days before the House was scheduled to go out for its August recess.

It was widely believed that enacting the trade bill would become harder the closer members came to the November mid-term election, so final action before the August recess seemed critical. In this context, the two months of procedural squabbling among the bill's supporters were weird indeed, especially given the basic compatibility of the two chambers' substantive enactments. But once the conferees got together they resolved matters in, literally, days. Thomas made a comprehensive, constructive compromise offer on 24 July; with this as a basis, agreement was reached on 25 July; the bill went to the House floor on 26 July; and it passed at 3:30 in the morning on 27 July by a relatively comfortable margin (for this bill) of 215-212. The trade adjustment assistance provisions brought the number of House Democrats voting in favor to 25, leaving room for 27 Republicans to vote no. The Senate followed on 1 August by 64-34. President Bush and USTR Zoellick had their negotiating authority, without major prohibitions or limitations. Trade-displaced workers had a program more commensurate with the scope of their needs.

Zoellick and "Competitive Liberalization"

USTR Robert Zoellick played a lesser role in lobbying for the bill than most of his predecessors would have. Congressional relations were not his forte; his capacity to reach out to Democrats was limited by the ferociously partisan House climate; and he sometimes acted to make things worse, as when he failed in December 2001 to respond to the Senate Finance Committee's request that he appear to explain concessions made a month earlier putting US antidumping laws on the international bargaining table.[38] However, he was more than holding his own on the

---

38. Zoellick was caught on this issue between the international demand to negotiate on these issues and widespread congressional opposition to "weakening" US trade remedy laws. He responded by emphasizing the need to combat arbitrary *foreign* procedures in this sphere, and two days before the Doha meeting began the House passed, by 410–4, a "sense of Congress" resolution aiming to "preserve the ability of the US to enforce its trade laws and . . . ensure that US exports are not subject to the abusive use of trade laws in other countries." Thus Zoellick gained formal cover for the deal he struck. But Finance Committee members were upset, particularly Baucus and Senator Jay Rockefeller (D-WV). The USTR's refusal to appear before them to explain (and absorb their flak) did nothing to improve matters.

international bargaining side. He was effective at Doha on both substance and tactics—making the US concession on trade remedy laws early, then joining with developing nations to strengthen the language on agriculture in the face of European Union resistance. This achievement gave the Bush TPA something Clinton's fast track had lacked—a prominent global negotiation for which the authority was needed. And just as the TPA bill conference was completing its work, Zoellick released—jointly with Secretary of Agriculture Ann M. Veneman—a comprehensive US proposal to slash farm subsidies and trade barriers (in exchange for parallel concessions by other leading agricultural nations). Thus he sought to offset the negative international message sent by the recently enacted 2002 farm bill that increased such subsidies. And with the timing of the release, he could claim to foreign trading partners that the proposal had congressional support, since it was public before the final TPA votes.

Zoellick's main immediate use of trade promotion authority, however, was for a series of bilateral and regional free trade agreements. His predecessors had also pursued such deals, beginning with the Israel and Canada FTAs of the 1980s—both for their own sake, and to generate pressure for concessions on global talks by signaling that the United States had an alternative route if global talks failed. The final Uruguay Round/WTO compromise of December 1993, in fact, owed something to House passage of NAFTA in November, followed quickly by Clinton's hosting the first summit meeting of leaders of the Asia Pacific Economic Cooperation (APEC) forum.

Bush's USTR expanded on this record, explicitly including political-strategic criteria in the choice of partner nations. The US-Jordan FTA, completed under Clinton, was approved before TPA's enactment, but two deals initiated by Clinton—with Singapore and Chile—were completed in early 2003 and brought up under the new authority. (Chile had been promised such a deal since the Miami Summit of 1994, but the lapse of fast track delayed the initiation of talks.) FTAs with Australia and Morocco were completed thereafter—and approved by Congress in July 2004. A Central American Free Trade Agreement (CAFTA) was completed in late 2003, and the Dominican Republic was added in 2004 (making it "CAFTA-DR)." Talks were also initiated or ongoing with a range of others, including Bahrain, the countries of southern Africa, Thailand, Panama, and the Andean countries of Colombia, Peru, Ecuador, and Bolivia. Finally, the Bush administration declared a long-term goal of creating a Middle East Free Trade Area (MEFTA).

Zoellick enveloped these initiatives in a broader strategy. By combining global, regional, and bilateral negotiations, he said, "the United States is creating a competition in liberalization, placing America at the heart of a network of initiatives to open markets." We would "proceed with countries that are ready" to open their markets, and success would create pressure on others."[39] Moreover, most FTAs were relatively popular with Congress, and hence useful for salving the wounds of the partisan TPA battle. Finally—though the USTR could not say this—his success in concluding free trade agreements buttressed his standing within the Bush administration. He was not close to the president; whatever credibility he achieved, therefore, had to come from visible results. With hemispheric talks flagging on the proposed Free Trade Area of the Americas (FTAA), and with the Doha Round proceeding by fits and starts, bilateral deals kept his trade vessel afloat.

Zoellick had long seen such agreements as having geopolitical as well as trade significance. And this view clearly found resonance in the Bush White House. New Zealand was excluded because of its long-standing refusal to welcome US vessels that might be carrying nuclear weapons. And the signing of the final agreement with Chile was delayed because that nation (unfortunate enough to be a member of the UN Security Council in early 2003) had failed to give clear support to a US-British resolution authorizing war with Iraq.[40]

Members of Congress did not warm to such punishment of Chile. They were, moreover, concerned that geopolitical goals led to a choice of free trade agreement partners of limited economic interest to the United States. And when they sought to generate pressure on potential partners, it was more likely to be because of their trade policy behavior. For example, Senator Grassley, once again chair of Senate Finance following the 2002 election, was outspoken in his criticism of Costa Rica and Guatemala for joining with the "Group of 21" nations that resisted the US-European agricultural proposal at the September 2003 WTO Ministerial Conference in Cancún, Mexico. Grassley argued that the United States should exclude the two nations from any Central American free trade agreement unless they "back out of their support" of the G-21 (they promptly declared that they did not see the G-21 as a unit with existence beyond the Cancún meeting).[41]

There was some skepticism about whether free trade agreements provided leverage for broader negotiations. Deals with Latin American nations might conceivably exert some leverage on Brazil, whose disagreements with the United States were the primary obstacle to progress on the FTAA. But it was implausible that CAFTA, for example, could generate

---

39. Address by Zoellick in Phoenix, Arizona, 30 April 2002, *Remarks by Ambassador Robert B. Zoellick* (Office of the US Trade Representative, 2002), 81.

40. In the end, the main damage Chile suffered was that, unlike Singapore, its leader was denied the photo opportunity of a White House signing ceremony. The Chile agreement won approval on 24 July 2003 by a vote of 270–156, virtually identical to the 272–155 margin the Singapore deal had garnered earlier in the day.

41. Grassley quoted in *Inside US Trade*, 19 September 2003, 1.

the pressure for liberalization in the 2000s that NAFTA and APEC had exerted on the European Union at the close of the Uruguay Round in 1993.[42] And while the domestic politics might be smooth with countries with which US trade was modest (Chile) or noncontroversial (Singapore), it was another matter for deals involving countries whose labor practices touched hot buttons in American trade politics. Hence CAFTA, completed before the Australia or Morocco deals, was not brought to Congress in the election year of 2004.

And the process of reviewing the easier deals was not entirely smooth. Thomas managed in the run-up to the votes on Singapore and Chile to rub salt in Democrats' wounds by indicating that he was planning to abandon the well-established, bipartisan "nonmarkup" process by which the Ways and Means Committee had reviewed draft implementing legislation for trade agreements to be considered under fast-track procedures.[43] Instead, *Inside US Trade* reported that the Ways and Means "majority" was "leaning toward . . . informal consultation with the Bush Administration, which would curtail the role of Democrats in shaping the implementing bill."[44]

Committee Democrats responded with a letter signed by all 17 minority members, including the two who had negotiated with Thomas in 2001. Without commenting directly on the report of Thomas' plans, they expressed "our hope that the Ways and Means Committee" would hold "an informal markup—sometimes called a 'nonmarkup' of the draft legislation," as Senate Finance had decided to do. "The informal markup reflects a broadly agreed-upon and well-established practice," they declared.

---

42. For a comprehensive review of the pros and cons, see Jeffrey J. Schott, ed., *Free Trade Agreements: US Strategies and Priorities* (Washington, DC: Institute for International Economics, 2004).

43. For the origin of this process and its employment in 1979 and 1988, see chapter 4. For its employment on NAFTA and Uruguay Round/WTO, see chapter 8. See also I. M. Destler, *Renewing Fast-Track Legislation*, POLICY ANALYSES IN INTERNATIONAL ECONOMICS 50 (Washington, DC: Institute for International Economics, September 1997), 9–13.

44. *Inside US Trade*, 13 June 2003, 23. As reported by veteran trade watcher Chris Nelson, 2003 had begun on a happier note when, at a 26 February session, Zoellick "was the soul of tact and discretion, frequently praising Rangel, Levin and other Democrats for various good deeds on behalf of free trade. Rangel responded in kind, and in classic form, at one point saying, 'If I'm elected President, I'll have you as my USTR!' to which Zoellick smoothly replied, 'If you are ever elected president, Mr. Rangel, I'll be pleased to serve with you!' Thomas also was on good behavior, clear from the outset, when he allowed Levin to read a long statement into the Record which amounted to a bill of particulars against Zoellick/Bush trade policy." Nelson described this as "in contrast to the bitter, partisan Thomas/Zoellick tactics of previous years." Now "from Chairman Bill Thomas and Ranking Democrat Charlie Rangel, to Zoellick himself, swords were sheathed, and barbs more humorous than pointed." (*The Nelson Report 2/26: Big Bush Iraq Speech; Zoellick/Trade*, distributed via e-mail.)

"Failure to proceed in this manner will only fuel suspicion about provisions in the legislation."[45]

In response to this protest, and to parallel concerns expressed by business representatives, Thomas changed his plans and agreed to hold non-markups. Thus the form of the traditional review process under fast track was preserved (although not entirely the practice, as Thomas "strongly discouraged" presentation of draft amendments, according to a Democratic aide).[46] The full committee voted the FTAs out overwhelmingly: 32–5 for Singapore and 33–5 for Chile. They passed with 75 Democratic "ayes" each—including Rangel, Levin, Matsui, and Pelosi (now elevated to the post of minority leader).

But 2003 also saw the perfecting of the DeLay process of one-vote House victories built almost entirely with Republican support. Increasingly, the time limit for members to vote would be ignored, until, under the aegis of Speaker Dennis Hastert, a House "vote stayed open . . . for two hours and 51 minutes, the longest roll call in modern House history . . . until Republicans were able to bludgeon two of their members to switch sides" and approve the controversial Bush proposal to add a prescription drug plan to Medicare.[47] Aficionados of the "Bipartisan Trade Promotion Authority Act" presumably were not surprised.

Cancún—and Geneva

Whatever the trade and political benefits of FTAs, Zoellick realized that the Doha Round was paramount. Only in global talks could US agriculture win major new market access, and only from its large trading partners could the US economy add to its already considerable gains from economic openness. And only a successful WTO deal offered the possibility of reenergizing the protrade business coalition.

But the WTO was an organization of 140-plus members, operating by consensus. And emerging economies were unwilling to defer to a US-EU duopoly, as they had, in the end, in prior trade rounds. They were disappointed, they said, with their gains from the Uruguay Round. They were also upset by the steel tariffs and farm bill of 2002, which went so directly against what the United States itself preached about trade.

The new, more fractious global trade politics became manifest when, in preparation for the Cancún Ministerial Conference of September 2003, Zoellick struck a deal with EU counterpart Pascal Lamy providing for modest reductions in farm subsidies on both sides of the Atlantic. Emerging

---

45. Rangel et al. to Thomas, 12 June 2003, reprinted in *Inside US Trade*, 13 June 2003, 24.

46. *Inside US Trade*, 27 June 2003, 1; and 18 July 2003, 16.

47. Norman Ornstein, ". . . And Mischief," *Washington Post*, 26 November 2003, A25.

economies refused to accept it as a basis for negotiation. Brazil joined with India and China in forming the "Group of 21" to demand a better deal.[48] Then, in the midst of the conference, a so-called Group of 90, driven by the concerns of African nations and egged on by activist NGOs, made more sweeping demands, including immediate removal of US cotton subsidies. Cancún was supposed to bring agreement—not on final Doha terms, but on the "modalities," the ground rules, under which they would be hammered out. Instead, it ended in disarray—the Mexican chairman and host, seeing no prospect of compromise, gaveled the meeting to a close.

Initial reactions were sharp. Zoellick denounced "can't do" nations (a label with some credibility because the G-21 and G-90 had shown little readiness to offer market concessions themselves). His EU counterpart, Pascal Lamy, labeled the WTO consensus process "medieval." By early 2004, however, tempers had cooled. Zoellick took steps to relaunch serious discussions, working with both developed and developing nations, and traveling to sub-Saharan Africa in July to facilitate compromise with (and among) the G-90. A new group made up of the United States, the European Union, Brazil, India, and Australia helped to shepherd the process.

On 1 August, following round-the-clock negotiations, WTO members reached agreement on the "July package," a document combining substantive and procedural accords on agriculture (and specifically cotton), nonagricultural market access, services, trade facilitation, and a range of development-related issues. The talks were back on track. But the destination remained a long way off. The original deadline had been December 2004. Now the target for substantial agreement was the Hong Kong WTO Ministerial in December 2005, with final details to be concluded within the year that followed.[49]

Into the Second Bush Administration

As he approached his reelection campaign, President Bush confronted a WTO decision declaring his steel tariffs inconsistent with US trade obligations. He responded, to the surprise of some, by lifting the tariffs in December 2003, declaring they had served their purpose. This choice was made easier by pressure from steel-using US industries, and by the fact that world steel prices had risen sharply in the 19 months since imposition of the tariffs. The decision cost the president little if anything politically, and he maintained a free trade posture throughout the election year.

---

48. The membership varied, so the group is sometimes referred to as the G-20 or the G-22.

49. For details, see Jeffrey J. Schott, "Confronting Current Challenges to US Trade Policy," in C. Fred Bergsten and the Institute for International Economics, *The United States and the World Economy*, chapter 8.

On the Democratic side, trade was—typically—a prominent issue during the primary campaign. Senator John F. Kerry (D-MA) took a relatively moderate stance, denouncing "Benedict Arnold corporations" for moving jobs overseas but admitting there was little a president could do about it (beyond denying them tax rewards for doing so). Once nominated, Kerry did not highlight trade issues, and they did not play a prominent role in the general election contest.

On the trade agreement front, 2004 was relatively quiet. A free trade agreement with Australia was signed and won overwhelming (314-109) approval in the House, although, in a concession to the sugar lobby, it included no increased market access whatever for that commodity.[50] An FTA with Morocco garnered an even larger margin, 323-99. The deal with Central America, however, faced stiff opposition, with labor vowing to mobilize and many Democrats unhappy with its labor provisions. No one was surprised when the administration deferred sending it to Congress for approval in 2004. And in early 2005, the sugar industry mounted a strong anti-CAFTA campaign because of its very modest increase of partner countries' access to the US market.

In the months after the election, trade policy seemed to disappear from the policy agenda. The USTR position went unaddressed, and unmentioned, as the president replaced (or reaffirmed) all other members of his Cabinet, and as he announced the nomination of Zoellick to be deputy to the new Secretary of State, Condoleezza Rice. Trade went unmentioned in the president's State of the Union address, which centered on his proposal to restructure the social security retirement system. Anxiety over this high-level neglect spread within the US trade policy community. Then, on 17 March 2005, Bush announced the appointment of a long-time political friend, Congressman Rob Portman (R-OH), to serve as US Trade Representative. "You couldn't have a person with a better relationship with Congress and the president," declared Benjamin L. Cardin (D-MD), a Ways and Means colleague who had just succeeded Levin as ranking Democrat on the Trade Subcommittee. A trade lawyer before his election to Congress in 1992, Portman won Senate confirmation on 29 April.[51]

The Trade Subcommittee also had a new chairman, Clay Shaw (R-FL), replacing Crane, who had lost his campaign for reelection. Both Shaw and Cardin were moderate in substance and collegial in style. Together with Portman, they offered the prospect of an easing of hostilities across the aisle. But the Hastert-DeLay leadership seemed to be moving in the other direction, buttressed by a modest increase in their House majority. And the first major issue Congress was likely to face was the contentious CAFTA-DR agreement.

---

50. This sent a terrible signal to Brazil and other potential FTAA partners.

51. However, in April one senator placed a "hold" on the nomination in order to force tougher administration action on trade with China.

Implications

Consensus on trade policy has become difficult to attain. Congress renewed presidential trade authority in 2001–02 and was expected to cooperate on a two-year extension in 2005.[52] Yet the path to initial enactment was tortuous, and the House victory margin razor-thin. A large part of the reason was the rise in partisan polarization, and the decline in the capacity of members to build centrist coalitions across party lines. More and more, issues are seen as weapons for combat with the other-party enemy. Less and less are they considered dispassionately, on their own substantive terms, with recognition that neither political side has a monopoly on truth and wisdom.

Of necessity, the Senate process was bipartisan—with expanded trade adjustment assistance at its center. But Democratic leverage was enormously facilitated by Majority Leader Daschle's control over Senate scheduling. He and his colleagues would have found it hard to bargain so effectively on TAA had Democrats been in the minority—as they became once again after the 2002 elections. After all, cross-aisle relationships have grown more fractious in the Senate as well. So trade bipartisanship there could well be harder to come by the next time around. Nevertheless, the 2002 combination of TPA and TAA epitomizes the sort of balanced approach that, sufficiently enhanced, could build stronger protrade coalitions in the future. How this might be done is addressed in Chapter 12.

Generally, polarization has strengthened chamber leaders at the expense of committee chairs. Thomas has managed to buck this trend— through his personal skills and assertiveness, but also by marginalizing the committee as a whole and playing the role of combative partisan leader. He has also exacerbated matters by his singular personality. Presumably, the personal dynamic will change when Thomas' six-year term runs out at the end of 2006. But differing institutional patterns tend to bring different types of leaders to the fore, and historians may find Thomas as fitted to his times as Wilbur Mills was to his, pre-1974.

Polarization also complicates the role of the USTR. Early incumbents made a point of cultivating relations with important members of the opposite party—interestingly, former party chairs Bob Strauss and Bill Brock were the best at doing so. And this made it easier for them to build and maintain trade's political base. By contrast, Mickey Kantor ended up distrusted by Republicans due to his unabashed partisanship, and Bob Zoellick was reportedly thwarted by House Republican leaders when he sought, early in his term, to reach out to Democrats. Rob Portman will have his work cut out for him if he seeks to reverse this trend and restore

---

52. The extension is automatic, assuming the president requests it by 1 April 2005, and neither house disapproves it by 1 July, and no disapproval resolution can be considered unless reported out by the Finance or Ways and Means Committees.

the sort of USTR–trade committee relationship that has done so much to keep policy on a relatively steady course.

Through exploitation of its partisan majority, the George W. Bush administration and its congressional allies won the trade-negotiating legislation that Clinton had failed to win. This was no small achievement. But unlike every prior postwar administration that had won such enactment—Kennedy, Nixon-Ford, Reagan-Bush—it did not emerge with a broad supporting consensus generated through the legislative process. And while enactment of free trade agreements bridged partisan differences in 2003 and 2004, the partisan gulf returned with consideration of CAFTA-DR in 2005.

This gulf renders the basic support margin narrow, making trade policy hostage to any protectionist interests that hold the decisive, marginal votes. Whether the product be steel, textiles, sugar, or orange juice, there is a bloc of House members ever ready to abandon ship if the administration seeks to negotiate, for example, a full-fledged Free Trade Area of the Americas, or thoroughgoing agricultural reforms in the Doha Round. The fierce sugar industry opposition to CAFTA-DR in early 2005 is a particularly sharp case in point. So stay tuned.

IV

CONCLUSION

12

Conclusion: Making America Fit for Globalization

As this book goes to press in the spring of 2005, trade temperatures are once again rising on Capitol Hill. With the global trade deficit for 2004 at a record $665 billion, and the bilateral imbalance with China at an astonishing $162 billion, 67 US senators have backed, on a procedural vote, a proposal by Charles Schumer (D-NY) and Lindsay Graham (R-SC) to impose a 27.5 percent temporary surcharge on imports from that country. The goal is to force revaluation of China's currency, the renminbi. Senator Evan Bayh (D-IN) placed a temporary hold on President Bush's nomination of Representative Rob Portman (R-OH) as United States Trade Representative (USTR), in an effort to force a vote on his China legislation; others decried the surge in Chinese textile sales brought by the ending of quotas under the Multi-Fiber Arrangement (MFA). Meanwhile, on the House side, Chairman Bill Thomas (R-CA) has chaired a Ways and Means Committee hearing where members of both parties denounced Chinese trade and exchange rate policies and the administration's weak response.

It sounds like the 1980s all over again: Congress bursting at the seams, protectionism about to explode, with China supplanting Japan as prime target. And certainly the economic imbalances of 2005 are, if anything, more worrisome than those that led to the Plaza Accord of two decades before. But in fact, things are not the same in American trade politics. For the decade beginning in 1995 has brought major changes.

First of all, traditional protectionism has clearly faded. Notwithstanding rising trade deficits throughout the period and minimal employment gains following the 2001 recession, there has been remarkably little pressure from business for new trade restrictions. This stands in stark contrast to the situation 20 years earlier, when a then record trade deficit of just over $100 billion triggered a broad range of protectionist demands.

But another source of resistance to trade expansion has burgeoned: concern over the social effects of trade. Legislation to renew presidential negotiating authority failed under Bill Clinton in 1997–98 and barely passed under George W. Bush in 2001–02: By far the most prominently stated reason for opposition was insufficient emphasis on enhancing labor and environmental standards in partner nations. Coupled with this has been broader anxiety over globalization's impact at home, especially on Americans with limited education and skills.

US capacity to address these issues has been weakened by the rise of partisan rancor on Capitol Hill, particularly in the House of Representatives. In past decades, cross-party internationalist coalitions centered in the Ways and Means Committee proved adroit at fashioning compromises on such issues. In 1973, for example, broadening worker eligibility for trade adjustment assistance (TAA) kept many Democrats in the trade-expanding camp. In 2002, a further reform and expansion of that program brought consensus in the Senate—but yielded just four additional Democratic votes in the House, including none of that party's trade leadership. The resulting one- and three-vote House victory margins diluted the Bush administration's mandate for negotiating further trade liberalization and inflated the power of the remaining, entrenched protectionist redoubts like sugar and citrus producers.

Taken together, these striking changes in circumstances call for rethinking core analyses and prescriptions. If business protectionism is a shadow of its former self, then diverting, channeling, and partially accommodating its demands may no longer be as necessary. If a major source of policy contention are matters over which legislators are typically divided along party lines, broad trade policy consensus may no longer be as attainable. If the key House trade committee no longer functions on a bipartisan basis, then a cornerstone of the 1934 system may not be as effective. At the very least, some reconsideration is in order.

Bringing the Benefits of Imports Out of the Closet

For decades, trade policy practitioners have rested their case for liberalization on a half-truth. The goal of trade talks is to secure new export opportunities; reductions of one's own barriers are "concessions" made reluctantly in exchange for export gains. This domestically critical half-truth is replicated in the international arena: The process in the succession of global trade-negotiating "rounds" has been one of benign mercantilism, where exports are good and imports a necessary evil. As recounted throughout this book, this story line has "worked," bringing large cuts in tariffs and nontariff barriers and enormous expansion in the volume of trade. A careful recent analysis estimates that Americans are a trillion dollars better off, every year, due to the gains from international trade.[1]

A policy management system central to this accomplishment should not be lightly abandoned. But what if, unlike in the 1930s or the 1980s, business protectionism no longer threatens to dominate the trade-political process? And what if, by sliding over the benefits of imports, the tried-and-true line of argument puts its purveyors at a serious disadvantage in the now more public trade policy debate? Specifically, if one limits the debate to trade's impact on producers, how does one justify eliminating textile quotas and (hence) thousands of textile jobs? These workers are already at the margin economically—how can we risk pushing them over the edge?

The standard response has been the logic of comparative advantage—whatever hurt is suffered by particular groups, trade leaves the nation as a whole better off. And the victims could theoretically be compensated through redistribution of the gains. But as Dani Rodrik has noted, "Compensation rarely takes place in practice, and never in full."[2] Hence, abandoning textile quotas seems to be helping the richer at a cost to the poorer—unless and until one adds the fact that trade liberalization can offer disproportionate gains to the poor as consumers. Edward Gresser has shown this for tariffs—they apply disproportionately to low-end garments, footwear, etc., which are bought mainly by those with limited incomes. For example, the tariff for garments made from synthetic fibers is typically 6 to 17 times that for comparable garments made of silk.[3] William R. Cline's more comprehensive analysis of the costs of textile protection in the mid-1980s found that the poorest Americans, taken as a whole, lost the most and the richest 20 percent actually gained because of transfers of quota rents to producers and retailers.[4]

Of course, the potential gains from import liberalization are not limited to the poor. For decades, purchasing power comparisons have shown that

1. Scott C. Bradford, Paul L. E. Grieco, and Gary Clyde Hufbauer, "The Payoff to America from Global Integration," in C. Fred Bergsten and the Institute for International Economics, *The United States and the World Economy* (Washington, DC: Institute for International Economics, 2005), chapter 2. This incorporates the impact of technological change and income elasticities as well as reduction or removal of trade barriers.

2. Dani Rodrik, *Has Globalization Gone Too Far?* (Washington, DC: Institute for International Economics, 1997), 30.

3. Edward Gresser, *America's Hidden Tax on the Poor: The Case for Reforming U.S. Tariff Policy*, Progressive Policy Institute Policy Report, March 2002, table 3. See also Gresser, "Toughest on the Poor: America's Flawed Tariff System," *Foreign Affairs*, November-December 2002: 9–14.

4. Cline finds that the lowest 20 percent lose an average of 3.64 percent of income, and the richest 20 percent gain an average of 0.32 percent. See *The Future of World Trade in Textiles and Apparel* (Washington, DC: Institute for International Economics, 2d ed., 1990), 202.

Americans live better, compared to Europeans and Japanese, than their relative incomes based on exchange rates would suggest. The apparent reason is the relatively greater openness of the US economy. Imports also contribute to productivity gains, as producers facing international competition are less free to enhance profits by raising prices and are driven to reduce costs instead. Finally, it appears from the experience of the late 1990s that with unprecedented openness to product and capital flows, the US economy can operate at lower levels of unemployment without triggering inflation. This means that marginal workers are more likely to get hired. Indeed, that was the one period in the past quarter century when US income distribution did not grow more unequal!

If consumers benefit from imports, so of course do businesses—well over half of what Americans buy from abroad does not enter the retail trade but goes to manufacturers in the form of industrial machinery or producer inputs to services industries.[5] Catherine Mann estimates, for example, that "global sourcing . . . of [information technology] hardware resulted in IT prices some 10 to 30 percent lower than they would have been." This in turn fueled investment and workplace restructuring that brought substantial gains in productivity and GDP.[6]

All of this suggests that trade advocates should make fewer concessions to mercantilist trade-speak and be more outspoken about the benefits of trade across the board. They should continue to highlight exports: J. David Richardson's analysis indicates that "worker wages are 10 to 11 percent higher at American plants that export" and that such plants "continuously grow 0.5 to 1.5 percent faster per year and enjoy 8.5 percent lower plant-closure rates than otherwise comparable locally focused plants."[7] But they should encourage import-dependent interests to make their case as well. They should speak out against pressure-diverting processes that are substantially skewed against imports, such as the antidumping laws as currently written and administered. "Contrary to popular wisdom, which celebrates exports and questions imports, economists attribute gains to *both* exports and imports. Indeed, imports are often a more important driver of economic growth."[8] Perhaps, as Brink Lindsey has argued, trade

---

5. In 2004, 51.4 percent of total merchandise imports were industrial supplies and equipment or nonautomotive capital goods. To these can be added substantial imports of auto parts, and of agricultural products imported for processing. (Percentage calculated from Department of Commerce, *U.S. International Trade in Goods and Services*, December 2004, issued 10 February 2005.)

6. Catherine L. Mann, "Offshore Outsourcing and the Globalization of US Services: Why Now, How Important, and What Policy Implications," in Bergsten et al., *The United States and the World Economy*, 299.

7. J. David Richardson, "Uneven Gains and Unbalanced Burdens? Three Decades of American Globalization," in Bergsten et al., *The United States and the World Economy*, 112–13.

8. Bradford, Grieco, and Hufbauer, "The Payoff to America from Global Integration," 66.

liberalizers should go "all out" for trade openness and abandon the notion that protectionist buyouts are necessary to sustain the policy.[9]

Yet before they abandon the old ways and highlight the two-way gains from trade, advocates of further liberalization must confront a troubling fact. The American public that so benefits from trade is underwhelming in its support of it.

Lukewarm Public Support for Trade Expansion

Fifty-nine percent of Americans see trade as good for the US economy and 73 percent find it good for consumers, but 64 percent view trade negatively in terms of "job security for American workers."[10] Sixty-seven percent support the reciprocal lowering of trade barriers, but 41 percent feel that the pace of liberalization has been "too fast," compared with just 18 percent who regard it as "too slow."[11] Pluralities typically back actual or prospective trade pacts like the North American Free Trade Agreement (NAFTA), the Central American Free Trade Agreement (CAFTA) signed in 2004, or the proposed Free Trade Area of the Americas (FTAA), but they generally see them as benefiting US trading partners more than the United States itself. By a 2 to 1 margin, Americans see "the growth of international trade" as negative rather than positive for American workers.[12]

Support is particularly weak among the less educated and, to a lesser degree, among those with low incomes. Only 22 percent of Americans with less than a high school education are positive about the growth of international trade, compared to 55 percent of those with at least a bachelor's degree. Similarly, just 27 percent of those with household income under $25,000 are positive, compared with 44 percent of those above $100,000.[13]

---

9. Lindsey, *A New Track for U.S. Trade Policy*, Cato Institute, Trade Policy Analysis 4 (11 September 1998).

10. Chicago Council on Foreign Relations, *Global Views 2004: American Public Opinion and Foreign Policy*, 41.

11. Steven Kull et al., *Americans on Globalization, Trade, and Farm Subsidies*, a Program on International Policy Attitudes (PIPA)/Knowledge Networks Poll, 22 January 2004, 11, 9. In the same survey, only 23 percent of Americans said government should "try to actively promote" trade, compared to 36 percent who responded "try to slow it down," 7 percent who wanted to "try to stop or reverse it," and 31 percent who said government should "simply allow [trade] to continue" (10).

12. Ibid. Forty-eight percent see the growth of international trade as negative for American workers, 25 percent positive, and 24 percent see the impact as neutral.

13. Ibid., 10. Respondents were asked to estimate, on a scale of 0 to 10, "how positive or negative do you think the growth of international trade is for the US overall?" Those above 5 (36 percent) were rated positive; those below (23 percent) were negative, while 38 percent chose 5, the halfway point. The education and income breakouts are not in the publication, but were provided by PIPA to the author upon request.

As Kenneth F. Scheve and Matthew J. Slaughter concluded from earlier data, "It is the less-educated, lower-income US workers who tend to be most concerned about globalization."[14]

Uneven Distribution of Gains from Trade Expansion

Those US workers may well be right. It is "a deeply troubling fact," in the words of former Treasury Secretary Robert Rubin, "that over the past 25 years the median real wages in the United States have been roughly stagnant, and median real incomes up a small fraction of real growth. . . . Thus, a large number of our citizens did not have wages or incomes that benefited much, if at all, from the great economic success of our country during that period."[15]

Over the past several years, the Institute for International Economics has been reviewing the societal impact of international engagement in its Globalization Balance Sheet (GBS) project. In his draft summary of its findings, project director J. David Richardson finds greater than anticipated gains for Americans "fit" for global competition—the well educated, with relevant skills, working in competitive firms. But "some global linkages have darkened the prospects for a large number of Americans." Though one cannot fully separate the impact of internationalization from other forces (technological change in particular), "it is hard to dismiss the possibility that typical, middle-class Americans have enjoyed only modest gains from global integration, and that lower-middle-class American workers have often suffered losses—exactly the perception that surveys and polls tend to reveal. And it is equally hard therefore to dismiss as alarmist the popular 'backlash' against *further* American moves toward global interdependence."[16]

Of course, the idea that trade can impact income distribution is hardly new. The classical Heckscher-Ohlin model noted that trade benefits a nation's abundant factors of production and penalizes its scarce factors. As elaborated by Stolper-Samuelson, this means that in a country where labor is scarce (relative to its availability in other nations), trade will hurt

---

14. Scheve and Slaughter, *Globalization and the Perceptions of American Workers* (Washington, DC: Institute for International Economics, 2001), 96.

15. Address at the Institute for International Economics, 15 February 2005. Measured in 1982 dollars, average weekly earnings for "private nonagricultural industries" peaked at $311 in 1977, fell to $258 by 1995, then rose to $276 in 2000 and have stayed at roughly that level since (*Economic Report of the President*, 2005, table B-47, 266). Average family income did better, as the number of workers per family rose and family size declined.

16. J. David Richardson, "Global Forces, American Faces: US Economic Globalization at the Grass Roots," Institute for International Economics, Working Draft, January 2005, 5, 6. Quoted with permission.

labor. In his comprehensive review of the issue, William R. Cline finds that this has happened in practice to American workers with limited skills: Expanded trade, he calculates, contributed about 6 percent to the increase in the gap between skilled and unskilled wage rates from 1973–93, and is projected to contribute 4 percent to the gap in the ensuing two decades.[17] When one adds technology to the mix,[18] as well as labor migration across US borders, it is the less technically proficient worker who is most disadvantaged. Indeed, drawing on the work of Lori Kletzer, the GBS project finds that "the personal capabilities of American workers seem to loom far more significantly in their labor-market woes than the exact sector in which they work."[19]

Globalization has also put pressure on organized labor. "Increased international trade has not been the major factor in the [sharp] decline" of unionization rates among American workers, concludes a GBS study by Robert E. Baldwin, but surging imports did contribute significantly to deunionization among workers with just a basic education (12 years or less).[20] Though an increasing share of organized labor works outside of trade-impacted industries, there is some reality to match the perception that trade has contributed to the decline of unions.[21]

And if the total US gains from trade expansion are enormous—around a trillion dollars in annual income—the costs to trade-displaced workers are not trivial. The same study that found trade-expansion benefits of a trillion dollars a year estimates that US workers displaced by trade in a given year lose a total of $54 billion in lifetime earnings,[22] while programs that explicitly address this loss total less than $2 billion annually.[23] And the broad societal trend has been against funding social programs that redistribute income among the nonelderly. When asked why the overwhelming majority of liberal Democrats had opposed President Clinton's fast-track legislation in 1997, Representative Barney Frank (D-MA) said,

---

17. William R. Cline, *Trade and Income Distribution* (Washington, DC: Institute for International Economics, 1997), table 5.1 (264).

18. Cline attributes a change of 29 percent to skill-biased technological change.

19. Richardson, "Global Forces, American Faces: US Economic Globalization at the Grass Roots," 38.

20. *The Decline of US Labor Unions and the Role of Trade* (Washington, DC: Institute for International Economics, 2003), 5. Baldwin finds this trade impact over the 1977–87 period. Overall, "the share of workers who were union members [fell] from 25 percent in 1977 to 14 percent by 1997." For manufacturing, it dropped from 38 to 18 percent (1).

21. On ways that globalization weakens union power, see Rodrik, *Has Globalization Gone Too Far?*, chapter 2.

22. The specific calculation is for 2003. See Bradford, Grieco, and Hufbauer, "The Payoff to America from Global Integration," appendix 2B, 106–09.

23. Ibid., 97.

less than half in jest, that they were "taking a hostage" in response to cuts in social programs.[24]

This tendency has been reinforced by deep partisan polarization in the House of Representatives. Under current political circumstances, most Democrats in that body are likely to be naysayers in any contested trade vote. Organized labor's strong opposition reinforces this position. But legislation normalizing trade with China in 2000 and entering bilateral free trade agreements in 2003 and 2004 won support from a significant number (from 73 to 120) of House Democrats, including senior members of the Ways and Means Committee. Nevertheless, the current style of House leadership—at the committee and chamber level—does not offer these Democrats what they need, substantively or politically, on the most controversial trade legislation.

To sum up, given the decline of traditional protectionism and the substantial (if unevenly distributed) societal gains from globalization, an unvarnished protrade agenda is within reach as never before. Most of the remainder of this chapter will set forth elements of that agenda. But its success requires softening the partisan divide in Congress and buttressing the shaky support among the public. The best path to both of these is a serious, comprehensive program of remediation, reflecting a societal commitment to address the needs of globalization's losers, with actions consistent with that commitment. Only with such a program can—and should—we complete the transition to globalization. What such a commitment implies will be spelled out later in this chapter. But first, let us address some of the basic elements of an open trade policy for the 21st century.

Two Key Preconditions: Macroeconomic Balance and Productivity Improvement

One fundamental prerequisite for sensible trade policy is *macroeconomic balance*. If a nation is consuming more than it is producing, if investment within its borders exceeds saving, it runs a trade deficit by definition. If that deficit is large and growing, it will affect balance of trade politics by increasing the number of producers hurt by imports relative to the number of those helped by exports. Moreover, a huge global trade deficit will inevitably incorporate even more one-sided trade deficits with some major trading partner. In 2004, US merchandise imports of $1.47 trillion were, astonishingly, almost double its merchandise exports of $808 billion.[25] With China, imports of $197 billion were almost six times US exports of $35 billion.

---

24 Quoted in Jeffrey J. Schott, ed., *Restarting Fast Track* (Washington, DC: Institute for International Economics, Special Report 11, 1998), 24.

25. If one adds trade in services, where the United States runs a modest surplus, total imports come to $1.76 trillion and exports to $1.15 trillion. The narrower merchandise balance

As noted in chapter 9, the rising US trade deficits from 1998 onward generated far less protectionism than did those of the mid-1980s. Nonetheless, they inhibit support for trade liberalization and spawn initiatives like the Schumer-Graham proposal, noted earlier, to impose a 27.5 percent temporary surcharge on imports from China.[26] Such a measure would, of course, violate US trade obligations under the World Trade Organization (WTO).

Thus, a large trade deficit exerts an undeniable impact on trade policy. However, the converse is not generally the case. Action specifically directed toward imports or exports has little effect on the balance between them. Trade measures can affect the volume of trade, and they can influence the composition of trade. But unless coupled with other measures, they will have little impact on the overall surplus or deficit of a nation. The reason is that macroeconomic forces will pull the overall imbalance back toward its level prior to the trade action.[27]

Rather, the appropriate remedies for a trade deficit are macroeconomic actions that increase saving relative to investment and production relative to consumption. For the United States, the most promising course by far is action to reduce the federal budget deficit, because that represents massive dissaving for the American economy. Under conditions of slack domestic demand, there can also be a role for exchange rate policy, meaning direct efforts to influence the value of the dollar.[28]

Within a condition of overall balance, the United States should expect to run surpluses with some trading partners—such as the European Union—and deficits with others—such as Japan and, above all, China. These bilateral imbalances are normal, even beneficial: They are one way that nations

is what is emphasized here because that is what trade politics is still overridingly about, notwithstanding the establishment of the General Agreement on Trade in Services (GATS) in the Uruguay Round agreements. But services are undeniably growing and, more importantly, growing as a share of trade and the US economy. See Mann, "Offshore Outsourcing and the Globalization of US Services," Bergsten et al., *The United States and the World Economy*, chapter 9.

26. The aim was to offset the estimated undervaluation of China's currency, the renminbi, pegged at 8.28 to the dollar since 1994. In the unlikely event it became law, such a surcharge would certainly reduce US imports from China but would likely have at least a partially offsetting effect on US trade balances with other nations. On China's currency, see Nicholas R. Lardy, "China: The Great New Economic Challenge?" in Bergsten et al., *The United States and the World Economy*, 134–37.

27. For example, a higher tariff on imports will reduce the need to convert dollars to foreign currency to purchase them. This will, all else being equal, raise the dollar exchange rate, which in turn will dampen overall exports and increase overall imports.

28. Under these circumstances, a decline in the value of the dollar will increase demand for exports and replace imports with domestic products, thus increasing production relative to consumption (and bringing the economy closer to full capacity). At full capacity, however, the main product of dollar depreciation will be inflation. See I. M. Destler and C. Randall Henning, *Dollar Politics: Exchange Rate Policymaking in the United States* (Washington, DC: Institute for International Economics, 1989), especially 10–11 and 148–49.

maximize the gains from trade. Measures that seek to regulate or eliminate them make no economic sense whatsoever, though it is appropriate to press partner nations running large global surpluses (or deficits) to pursue exchange rate and other macroeconomic policies that bring them into overall international balance.

Macroeconomic policy can help the United States balance its global trade account and thereby reduce pressures on trade policy. It cannot, however, determine the exchange rate at which balance will take place. Nor can it have much impact on another key variable: the rate of productivity growth. By this measure, the US economy has done very well over the past decade, reversing the productivity slowdown of the 1970s and 1980s. The main determinants here lie in the private economy, but *microeconomic* policy measures can improve the quality and profitability of economic activity in the United States. These policies include measures to enhance the quality of the workforce (education and training), strengthen the US economic infrastructure, increase private saving and investment, rationalize regulation of business, and encourage technological innovation and the efficient application of new ideas to the production process. The aim of such measures is to make the economy both more productive and more flexible. The result, if successful, is greater gains from trade and a higher living standard for Americans.

Trade policy is not an effective instrument for addressing these broad, economywide problems of international balance and domestic productivity growth. It can have two very important goals, however. Its "positive" goal is to help increase the volume of trade—and hence the gains from trade—by opening markets abroad and at home. As noted earlier, these gains to date appear to have been enormous—on the order of a trillion dollars a year in increased national output resulting from overall global integration. Its "negative" goal is damage limitation—that is, minimizing the harm to the overall US economy, and to the international trading system, from successful attempts by special interests to win import protection. In practice, the two goals are related. Damage limitation requires mobilization of counterpressure to offset the concentrated interests hurt by trade. And one of the best means of creating such counterpressure is through negotiations aimed at increasing export opportunities, because these bring the export interests that gain from trade expansion more actively into the political fray.

But if, over the past decade, concentrated interests hurt by trade have declined in political influence, this rationale for ongoing negotiations becomes less potent. The bicycle metaphor described in chapter 2—that the trade system needs to continually move forward (liberalize) or else it will fall (into new import restrictions)—may no longer be as apt. With the globalization of business, today's trade policy regime may have sufficient support to remain standing without steady forward movement. Instead, the argument for further trade liberalization must rest mainly on the additional welfare gains it will bring. These include, of course, gains for peoples around the world, particularly those in poor nations, and the gains in global stability that enhanced economic interdependence can bring. But the main argument, in US politics, must be the gains it brings to Americans.

The gains could be substantial. Bradford, Grieco, and Hufbauer, applying several methodologies, reach a "conservative" conclusion that "removing all remaining [global] barriers to trade would increase US production by approximately $450 billion to $600 billion annually."[29] Unlike their estimate of past gains of roughly $1 trillion, this comes from trade policy change alone. Any induced technological change or other effects would be icing on the cake.

Completing the Transition to Globalization

What would be required to bring this about? Essentially, the United States would have to remove its remaining barriers and induce other nations to do likewise. And the primary vehicle for achieving this objective remains global trade negotiations under the WTO. Bilateral trade deals bring some economic and geopolitical gains. They are useful in buttressing the leadership of the USTR in periods when global talks are flagging, like the early 2000s, and they can sometimes generate constructive pressure on broader negotiations via "competitive liberalization," But the real pay dirt is in the WTO's Doha Round (and succeeding negotiations, if Doha does not achieve its lofty goals).

USTR Robert Zoellick worked diligently and successfully to rescue the Doha talks at Geneva in July 2004 following the collapse at Cancún the previous September. He helped open the way not only to serious concessions on agriculture but also to the possibility of broader liberalization on goods and services. But much more work needs to be done if the round is to fulfill its promise and conclude successfully in 2006. Such a broad, globally liberalizing outcome would bring major new US gains from trade, not to mention the help it could provide the developing world.

For the United States, this will require reduction—and eventually removal—of entrenched barriers to imports. American trade barriers and distortions, taken as a whole, are relatively modest: the simple average tariff applied by the United States is 3.9 percent, comparable to the European Union (4.4 percent) and Japan (3.3 percent), but far below that of India (31.4 percent), Brazil (14.6 percent), China (12.4 percent), and Korea (12.4 percent).[30] As of 1 January 2005, the United States removed its textile quota

---

29. "Gains in this range," they add, "would increase US per capita income between $1,500 and $2,000 annually and US household income between $4,000 and $5,300 annually." See Bradford, Grieco, and Hufbauer, "The Payoff to America from Global Integration," 95.

30. World Trade Organization, *World Trade Report 2003* (Geneva: World Trade Organization), appendix table IIB.4, Most Favored Nation Applied Tariffs for All Products, 208–10.

restrictions as part of the phaseout of the Multi-Fiber Arrangement agreed to in the Uruguay Round—though some restrictions, especially vis-à-vis China, are being maintained for a transitional period. But tariffs on textile and apparel products remain relatively high, as do measures limiting imports and subsidizing exports on products such as sugar, cotton, dairy products, and orange juice.

USTR has made sweeping Doha Round offers to eliminate tariffs on industrial products and liberalize agricultural trade.[31] But real negotiations to date have involved more modest measures. This is due in part to the reluctance of other nations to reciprocate, including the European Union (agriculture) and advanced developing nations (import barriers in general). Still, the United States, for its part, has sent mixed messages. It seemed to back off its ambitious agricultural proposal in September 2003 when it joined with the European Union in putting a more modest initiative before the Cancún Ministerial Conference. Refusal to grant Australia *any* increased access to the US sugar market in the free trade agreement concluded with that nation in 2004 sent a very negative signal to Brazil and other countries seeking access to US agricultural markets at Doha, and in negotiations for an FTAA.

In the meantime, the United States has been under international attack for its enforcement of trade remedy laws, losing a number of WTO cases. Canada has successfully challenged US countervailing duties on softwood lumber. Japan and Korea have won cases against US enforcement of antidumping law. And no fewer than 11 nations (including the European Union) won a finding that the Byrd amendment (which channels the proceeds of antidumping duties into the coffers of the petitioning firms) violated US commitments in the Uruguay Round. More recently, on the agricultural front, Brazil won a WTO decision against US subsidies on the production of cotton, which is a particularly sensitive issue as well with sub-Saharan African producers.

The appropriate US response on cotton is to comply by cutting subsidies and decoupling them from production—as promised in the Doha negotiations.[32] Agricultural trade has become the linchpin for broader success in the talks, and both the advanced and the poorest developing countries have made it clear they will not approve an overall deal with-

---

31. For the 26 November 2002 proposal on industrial tariffs and the 25 July 2002 agricultural proposal, see www.ustr.gov/Document_Library/Press_Releases/2002/November/U.S._Proposes_Tariff-Free_World,_WTO_Proposal_Would_Eliminate_Tariffs_on_Industrial_Consumer_Goods_by_2015.html (accessed 6 April 2005) and www.ustr.gov/Document_Library/Press_Releases/2002/July/Administration_Unveils_Comprehensive_U.S._Trade_Proposal_to_Exp_American_Farmers'_Access_To_Overseas_Markets.html.

32. This could end up requiring the politically difficult step of compensating landowners, to some degree, for resulting declines in land value.

out substantial opening of rich-country farm markets. This opportunity should be exploited.

On the trade remedy front, the US response to losses in WTO dispute settlement has been piecemeal and minimalist: complying with specific WTO rulings where it was feasible but resisting broader concessions. This is understandable, since congressional resistance to changes in these laws is particularly stiff. A trade policy aimed at thorough liberalization would be much more ambitious, however, using these international rulings as a rationale for liberalizing proposals at Geneva and legislative changes at home. On antidumping and countervailing duty laws, the United States should take steps to make procedures better balanced between foreign and domestic producers of the products at issue, and between US producers and importers of the products. This should be part of a broader reshaping of the statutes governing administrative trade relief. Before the 1970s, it was too hard for firms to get action under these statutes; now it is too easy. The result is too much protection and too many cases diverted from consideration under the escape clause to the laws that highlight alleged foreign "unfairness" (see chapter 6).

Moreover, these laws are written as if the only domestic interests of concern are US-based producers of the specific products whose trade is at issue. But the real world has long since departed from this model. A firm's capacity to export may rest upon its capacity to import—as Caterpillar has argued in resisting restraints on steel imports. Yet US dumping laws ask only whether products priced below an arbitrarily set "fair value" hurt competing US producers (who do not have to follow the same pricing rules). They do not ask whether imposition of a duty will damage US firms that use the imported products as inputs—perhaps even forcing them to move operations overseas.

Current US practice also provokes foreign emulation, as the European Union and other trading partners impose mirror-image penalties on US producers. Finally, easy access to antidumping relief undercuts what is supposed to be the primary channel for import relief and adjustment: the "escape clause" (Section 201). For if dumping findings are quasi-automatic, why should a company seek action under a statute with a more demanding injury standard, a time limit for any protection, and a presidential right to deny relief even if statutory criteria are met?

The best solution would be an international agreement on competition policy, with rules on predatory pricing that apply equally to both foreign and domestically produced goods.[33] But absent such an agreement, the United States should adopt the following reforms as a package:

---

33. However, one should not assume that if antidumping law were placed in the competition policy framework, that framework would go unchanged. See I. M. Destler, "U.S. Approach to International Competition Policy," in Robert Z. Lawrence, ed., *Brookings Trade Policy Forum 1998* (Washington, DC: Brookings Institution), 395–418.

- Ease the threshold for proving injury under the escape clause (Section 201) and limit administration discretion, but tie relief to an explicit adjustment commitment by the petitioner;

- Toughen the threshold for proving dumping, returning to the original standard of comparing selling prices in the United States to selling prices in the producer's home market; and

- In dumping or countervailing duty cases in which dumping or subsidy and injury are found, create a follow-on procedure whereby users and other affected interests can seek a reduction in the assessed penalty duty by demonstrating that its full imposition would cause them serious economic harm.

Changes in Structure and Process

US trade policy would also benefit from changes in the structure of the executive branch and reinforcement of the processes for interbranch cooperation on trade. The Omnibus Trade and Competitiveness Act of 1988 moved to strengthen this system by buttressing the authority of the Office of the US Trade Representative. Congressional approval of landmark agreements in 1993 and 1994, along with the trade promotion authority (TPA, also know as "fast track") legislation of 2002, give testimony to the fact that the system continues to work. Still, it could be further strengthened by moderate reforms at both ends of Pennsylvania Avenue.

The reason to consider trade reorganization is *not* the fact that many federal agencies have fingers in the trade pie. This simply reflects the range of governmental concerns that trade policy affects. In any conceivable organizational arrangement, the United States would continue to have the State Department and the National Security Council stressing trade's importance to alliance relations, the Defense Department worrying about the defense industrial base, the Treasury Department and the Council of Economic Advisers responsible for linking trade policy to the overall domestic economy and global development, and the Department of Agriculture stressing the connection of grain exports to commodity programs and overall farm welfare.

All government activities that have a "trade" label do not require a common home. As a day-to-day matter, for example, export promotion through technical aid to firms need not be housed in the same agency that handles import regulation or trade negotiations. But if substantial dispersion of US governmental trade responsibility is inevitable, the current bifurcation of central trade responsibility is not. In fact, the current executive branch organization has at least four serious flaws:

- The USTR-Commerce division of labor invites conflict by assigning "policy," "coordination," and "negotiations" to the USTR and "nonagricultural operational trade responsibilities" to the Secretary of Commerce.

- This is exacerbated by the fact that international trade is the only subject in the Commerce secretary's portfolio that offers an opportunity for important policy leadership. Thus, any ambitious incumbent with decent White House connections becomes a rival of the USTR.[34]

- The numerical expansion of the Office of the USTR beginning in 1980 created an organizational hybrid, too large for a flexible coordinating-negotiating staff but too small to be the central executive branch repository of line expertise and responsibility. And the USTR's size makes it a target of White House reorganizers seeking to trim overall staff.

- Presidential support for the USTR, particularly important at times of trade policy crisis or major negotiations, has often been tenuous.

This situation has intermittently led legislators, such as former Senator William V. Roth, Jr. (R-DE), to propose replacing this "two-headed monster"[35] with a Department of Trade. In earlier editions of this book, this author expressed concern that a trade secretary would be "distant from the president" and "overly responsive to the protection-seeking complainers" in the business community. This led to a somewhat complicated counterproposal built on USTR and on moving Commerce's trade responsibilities under USTR's authority.[36]

Times have changed. Business community concerns over trade no longer have such a protectionist tilt. And the USTR office has become less an administrationwide policy broker and more like a trade department. The National Economic Council established under President Clinton has taken over, at least formally, the overall policy coordination function. Moreover, USTR's connection with the president has, in general, eroded, as illustrated by the shakiness of the incumbent's Cabinet-level status under President George W. Bush.[37]

On balance, therefore, a Department of Trade now seems a sensible solution. It would place trade leadership under a Cabinet member heading

---

34. This proved a serious problem in the Nixon and Reagan administrations. It could have become a problem in both Bush administrations, since in each case the president was closer personally to the Commerce secretary than to the USTR.

35. Roth is quoted in US Congress, *Trade Reorganization Act of 1983*, 2.

36. This option is spelled out in the previous (3rd) edition of this book, *American Trade Politics* (Washington, DC: Institute for International Economics, 1995), 300–01. Briefly, it involved transforming USTR into a small, elite presidential staff and moving the remaining USTR and Commerce trade officials and offices to a "United States Trade Administration" reporting to the USTR.

37. Prior to the appointments of both Robert Zoellick in 2001 and Rob Portman in 2005, Bush advisers indicated a desire to reduce the status of the position. Pressure from Congress and the business community kept this from happening, but the fact that it was known to be considered could only undercut USTR's credibility.

a familiar organizational structure. If accompanied, as it should be, by elimination of the Department of Commerce, it would remove the built-in structural conflict at the Cabinet level.[38]

If the president were to recommend and the Congress were to legislate such a reorganization, they should also consider instituting modest changes in the TPA process. The basics remain appropriate—the executive branch gets authority to negotiate and the promise of expeditious congressional action on the results, in exchange for close consultation with legislators and advisory groups throughout the negotiations.

The procedure was originally established for a limited time period for one specific negotiation—the Tokyo Round of 1973–79. Subsequent extensions have likewise been limited in time but have broadened in scope—to cover global deals, but also regional and bilateral free trade agreements. This has created two problems. One is that the authority can lapse for long periods, as in 1995–2002, weakening the US negotiating hand. The second is that it can be employed for agreements not contemplated when the extension was enacted (no one expected a NAFTA when fast track was renewed in 1988). This arguably gives the executive too much leeway.

An appropriate and balanced remedy would be for Congress to make TPA permanent but require prior legislative approval (either specifically or by category) for its application to negotiation of a particular trade agreement. It would also be desirable to enact into law the essence of the "nonmarkup" process, through which the trade committees, acting generally on a bipartisan basis, have made detailed recommendations (often amounting to full draft legislation) on what should be included in the nonamendable implementing bills submitted by the president. This could include a minimum time period (say 90 days) for this process.[39]

These substantive and process changes would do much to help the United States complete the transition to globalization. But their practicality remains in question. How can today's Congress, bitterly divided by party and barely able to enact trade-negotiating authority, support such ambitious objectives? How can today's public, ambivalent about trade and globalization, only a quarter of which wants government to actively

---

38. The nontrade staff in Commerce is mainly housed in a set of autonomous technical offices—the National Oceanic and Atmospheric Administration, Bureau of the Census, National Institute of Standards and Technology, and Patent and Trademark Office are the largest. These could exist as freestanding federal agencies.

39. For more detail on this idea, see I. M. Destler, *Renewing Fast-Track Legislation*, POLICY ANALYSES IN INTERNATIONAL ECONOMICS 50 (Washington, DC: Institute for International Economics, 1997), 41–43. A related change, suggested in the previous edition of this volume, would be to shorten the time period for committee consideration of the bill once submitted, since no changes are then permitted. This would reduce the threat from delaying tactics near the end of a Congress, such as those employed in 1994.

pursue further liberalization, be expected to support such an ambitious policy agenda?

It is hard to avoid negative answers—if the program is simply trade liberalization. But if leaders think more broadly and inclusively, there is a potential path forward. It is a path that may well not be taken in the fiscal and political climate of 2005. But before too many years, its logic may prove irresistible. It is a path both substantive and political. It consists of moving cautiously forward on the social issues that have exacerbated partisan differences over trade and moving aggressively to build what J. David Richardson has labeled "a new civic infrastructure" to spread the gains from globalization.[40]

What Americans Want in Trade Policy

In Washington, the most divisive trade policy issue since the 1990s has been the pursuit of labor and environmental objectives in trade negotiations. As depicted in chapter 10, this issue blocked agreement on fast-track authority under President Clinton, and it narrowed support majorities under his successor.

Yet the public is not divided on this matter at all. In survey after survey, Americans overwhelmingly support inclusion of minimum labor standards and minimum environmental standards in trade agreements, with over 90 percent typically approving.[41]

This does not, of course, make such standards easy to negotiate internationally. They are widely regarded in the developing world as stalking horses for protection, and have been largely excluded from the Doha Round. At home, many Republican lawmakers view them as anathema and fear in particular that trading partners could use them to influence labor and environmental regulations in the United States. Yet some compromise has proved possible, as in the 2002 TPA legislation and in bilateral free trade agreements. More might have been achieved had House Republicans taken up Representative Charles Rangel's offer to negotiate these issues in 2001 (see appendix A).

In a globalizing world, trade competition can affect a nation's capacity to maintain such standards in the absence of international cooperation. So it is reasonable to seek international action. Such action cannot be

---

40. See Richardson, "Global Forces, American Faces," 49.

41. The Chicago Council on Foreign Relations (CCFR) survey of June 2004 found that 94 percent of Democrats—and 93 percent of Republicans—favored incorporating minimum labor standards in US trade agreements. For environmental standards, support was 94 percent among Democrats and 91 percent among Republicans. The CCFR's survey of leaders found similar support among Democrats, but "just" 69 and 67 percent, respectively, for Republicans. See Chicago Council on Foreign Relations, *Global Views 2004: American Public Opinion and Foreign Policy.*

achieved overnight: The issues are not ripe for comprehensive international agreement. But serious international engagement on these issues, through trade and nontrade negotiating channels, would give moderate environmentalists and labor supporters a stake in the process. It would also give them a rationale for voting "aye." Hence, it could well increase support for trade liberalization among that substantial minority of House Democrats who remain conflicted on the issue. Such support could, in turn, provide a sufficient political margin to enable the USTR to confront remaining entrenched protectionist groups like sugar producers.

In the near term, however, these issues are mainly symbolic, in the sense that no plausible agreements on other nations' labor and environmental standards would provide much concrete benefit to the Americans who are currently globalization's losers. Helping them requires action here at home in the form of a range of mutually reinforcing measures to make Americans fit to be globalization participants and beneficiaries.

Completing the Transition to Globalization at Home

The explosion of international trade has been an enormous boon to Americans in general, but not to all Americans in particular. The same study that estimates annual US income gains at $1 trillion calculates that the lifetime wage losses to trade-displaced workers in a given year are around $54 billion.[42] In theory, they could be made whole by reallocating one-twentieth of the trade gains. Yet even with the reforms enacted in 2002, total annual federal spending specifically devoted to trade-displaced workers comes to just $2 billion.

In principle, there is public support for more. As noted in chapter 11, the Chicago Council on Foreign Relations poll of 2002 found 73 percent support for "free trade" if government help was available for workers who were hurt. (Sixteen percent supported free trade without such programs, and 9 percent opposed free trade.) Responses in 2004 were less positive, but they still indicated opposition to free trade limited to one-third, assuming such government aid was available. Another recent survey finds that the public believes that aid is *not* sufficiently available: 63 percent believe retraining support is "inadequate."[43] And in fact, aid for trade-displaced workers has received lukewarm support where it most matters—from the Department of Labor, which administers the programs, and from the union movement, which has regarded the programs as a second-best alternative to limits on import growth.

---

42. Bradford, Grieco, and Hufbauer, "The Payoff to America from Global Integration," appendix 2B (106–09).

43. Kull et al., *Americans on Globalization, Trade, and Farm Subsidies.*

The 2002 reforms in trade adjustment assistance (TAA) responded to this concern. They were pressed by Democratic Senators Jeff Bingaman of New Mexico and Max Baucus of Montana and embraced by then Majority Leader Tom Daschle as the price for broad Democratic support of TPA in the Senate. Authorized funding for the program was roughly tripled. The pool of eligible workers was expanded—to those whose plants sold inputs to manufacturers hurt by imports and to some of those hurt by shifts of production to other countries. A health insurance benefit was added, with government paying 65 percent of the cost. A new wage insurance program was established, allowing workers over 50 (as an alternative to regular TAA) to recoup up to half of the wage difference between their old and new jobs, for up to two years. There were also increases in job search and relocation assistance and in the overall time period over which workers can receive training and income support.[44]

Yet the results have been disappointing. Worker participation has remained low—about 48,000 workers in 2003, for example, out of about 200,000 certified as eligible. Training responsibility is delegated to state government agencies, which often use up their TAA money well before the end of the fiscal year. Very few workers eligible for TAA actually received the health insurance benefit in the first eight months it was available. Over that same period, just 42 workers enrolled in the wage insurance program![45]

Participation will surely expand with time, and program advocates have formed a new Trade Adjustment Assistance Coalition to speed this process.[46] Just as surely, the TAA program will prove inadequate to the need. One reason is limitations in its mechanisms: Government-managed retraining courses have a mixed track record at best. A larger reason is that labor displacement directly attributable to trade is hard to isolate from the much larger overall job losses generated by economic and technological change.

On balance, moreover, it is a mistake to try. For in welfare terms, the distinction is arbitrary. A displaced worker whose plant moves, downsizes, or restructures because of domestic competition or technological change suffers essentially the same losses as one whose plight can be

---

44. This and subsequent paragraphs draw substantially on Lori G. Kletzer and Howard Rosen, "Easing the Adjustment Burden on US Workers," in C. Fred Bergsten et al., *The United States and the World Economy*, chapter 10. Rosen, as staff aide and policy entrepreneur, played a key role in enactment of the 2002 reforms.

45. According to Kletzer and Rosen (ibid., 327), this was due to an arbitrary requirement inserted in the statute providing that petitioning firms or groups of workers must indicate interest in this program when they first apply for trade adjustment assistance, even though nothing in the process informed them of its existence.

46. See www.TAACoalition.com (accessed 6 April 2005). Senators Max Baucus (D-MO) and Norman Coleman (R-MN) are cochairs. Howard Rosen is executive director.

attributed to imports. If help for trade-impacted workers is appropriate, why not help for all who are displaced from their jobs? They are equally victims of a rapidly changing American economy.

Moreover, the political gains from a separate trade adjustment assistance program have clearly diminished. The 2002 reforms built Democratic support in the Senate, but (judging by the final tally) won exactly four converts to TPA out of 210 Democrats in the House of Representatives. For many, TAA is viewed as a backwater government program that gets attention only when an administration needs votes for trade legislation. This may be changing somewhat—several members of Congress have associated themselves with the new monitoring organization. But they are mainly legislators who support trade expansion to begin with. Liberal Democrats who have been voting "nay" are more concerned with the broader erosion of the social safety net and the rise of economic insecurity among the less well-off generally.

For such Democrats, the vision of a much stronger program for displaced workers should have real appeal. It would address the broad distributional costs of the market economy—as their party has sought to do since the Great Depression. It would, at the same time, leave that market economy free to flourish.[47]

A New Social Compact

Such a program could be built, in part, on the trade-specific programs of the 2002 act, and on the long-standing unemployment insurance program. Extended unemployment insurance benefits and worker retraining now available under TAA could be available to all workers with similar plights. Wage insurance could be broadened as an alternative, with removal of the arbitrary age requirement and counterproductive procedural hurdles that limit participation. The health insurance benefit could be made available to all displaced workers and easier to obtain. Job search aid could be similarly expanded.

But reform should not be limited by the TAA model. As J. David Richardson has suggested, the United States needs "creative innovation in *domestic* policies designed to empower large numbers of Americans . . . to prosper from global opportunity and technological dynamism."[48] This should include not just government retraining but incentives for firms to

---

47. According to Kletzer and Rosen, "Relative to five other major industrialized countries, the United States spends the least on active labor-market adjustment programs. . . . France and Germany each devote [relative to GDP and the unemployment rate] about five times more to their active labor-market programs than does the United States." See "Easing the Adjustment Burden on US Workers," 315.

48. See Richardson, "Global Forces, American Faces," 49.

provide on-the-job training, and for workers to seek out relevant educational, skill enhancement opportunities.[49] Labor unions should be brought into the process, so they can help their current and potential members cope with change rather than railing against it.[50]

Such a program would not be free. Kletzer and Rosen estimate that the cost of extending current trade adjustment assistance benefits to all displaced workers would be $12.1 billion.[51] Lael Brainard and Robert G. Litan calculate the costs of a general two-year wage insurance program at $3.6 to $7.52 billion a year.[52] If one added on new business tax incentives, such as the "human capital investment tax credit" proposed by Catherine L. Mann,[53] one could easily reach an annual budgetary price tag of $20 billion.

Within the broad globalization and fiscal context, this does not seem excessive. If Americans gain $1 trillion a year from international openness and stand to gain half a trillion more from further liberalization, if the current lifetime costs to workers displaced in a given year come to around $50 billion, and if total federal spending is projected at $2.57 trillion for fiscal year 2006, then a $20 billion program cost is modest: about 2 percent of annual globalization gains, and under 1 percent of annual government spending.

Trade advocates should embrace such a program. A broad social compact reaching all losers from economic change is a necessary and appropriate foundation for a policy that seeks full international openness in the 21st century. Extending adjustment aid beyond those specifically hurt by trade is a reflection of economic reality—as interdependence deepens, it becomes harder and harder to isolate the cause of specific economic misfortunes, and less and less reasonable to try. It is also the most plausible route to broadening public support for trade expansion, and for bridging the partisan divide.

Two short-run barriers loom large, however. First is the atmosphere of extreme budget stringency brought on by record budget deficits and President Bush's determination to maintain his huge tax cuts. This makes

---

49. The agenda could also address other sources of workplace insecurity, by providing pension stability, flexible schedule/day care/leave, raising the minimum wage, and enhancing the earned income tax credit. The focus here, however, will be mainly on maximizing the number of Americans who can compete successfully in the globalization job market.

50. Ideally, this program would be pursued as part of a "grand bargain" with organized labor, as suggested by C. Fred Bergsten, in which the major unions would withdraw or mute their opposition to further trade liberalization. But it should be pursued in any case.

51. "Easing the Adjustment Burden on US Workers," 333.

52. Brainard, Litan, and Nicholas Warren, "A Fairer Deal for America's Workers in a New Era of offshoring," in Lael Brainard and Susan M. Collins, eds., Brookings Trade Forum, 2005 (forthcoming).

53. See Mann, "Offshore Outsourcing and the Globalization of US Services," 306–7.

nondefense and non–Homeland Security programs the prime targets for spending restraint. The second is the continuing fractious atmosphere in the House of Representatives. The comprehensive program advocated here might be attractive to protrade Republicans—*if* they were seeking to maximize support from Democrats. But the 2001 experience on trade, and the process since then on all contentious issues, suggests that the dominant strategy of the current House leadership is to build consensus within their own party and then use their modest 30-vote majority to press legislation through. Minority votes are welcome, of course. But the procedure does not welcome minority participation in the consensus-building process, much less substantive adjustments to broaden minority support.

The barriers to building a comprehensive domestic infrastructure for globalization are daunting. And so are those to full global trade liberalization. Robert Rubin has cited former President Bill Clinton's observation that trade liberalization "needed to be inextricably combined with a parallel agenda of domestic programs," but that, "too often, those who support trade oppose the domestic agenda, and those who support the domestic agenda oppose trade. . . . [T]he right answer was to combine the two, but bringing together those two conflicting groups makes for difficult politics."[54]

Yet advocates should not despair. Changes in American trade politics make this dual agenda plausible for the first time in American history. The positive but mixed impacts of globalization make it necessary.

---

54. Address at the Institute for International Economics, 15 February 2005.

Appendix A
Trade Promotion Authority in 2001:
The Bargain That Wasn't

On 6 December 2001, the US House of Representatives passed the Bipartisan Trade Promotion Authority Act by a vote of 215 to 214. It was the closest vote ever on a major piece of trade legislation. And notwithstanding the title, it marked the most partisan congressional vote on such a bill since the 1930s. Just 21 of 210 Democratic votes were recorded in favor. Only 23 of the 217 Republicans casting ballots said "nay."

In the broad political context, this was not entirely surprising. Increasing attention to foreign labor and environmental standards had been exacerbating interparty divisions on trade legislation as Democratic constituencies pressed these concerns and Republican business allies resisted them. Moreover, as set forth in chapter 11, broad political forces—particularly the drawing of "safe" congressional districts that promote election of liberal Democrats and conservative Republicans—had been making Capitol Hill a more and more polarized place. Hair's-breadth victories won by holding the floor vote open until that last Republican arm was twisted into the fold would become a trademark of the House in the 2000s under Speaker Dennis Hastert and his hard-driving deputy, Tom DeLay. So would processes designed to marginalize the Democratic minority.[1]

---

1. In November 2004, Hastert went so far as to refuse to bring to the floor the conference report on the major intelligence reform bill that both he and President George W. Bush supported, because the issue was splitting Republicans and victory would have depended on a substantial number of Democratic votes. In the end, dissenting Republicans were appeased and the bill enacted.

But winning this way was costly for trade policy. Since the victory was built on a number of Republicans voting against their convictions and their constituencies, it cast doubt on the ability of the US Trade Representative (USTR) to win approval of controversial trade agreements in the future. It inflated the leverage of the entrenched interests (such as steel or sugar producers) determined to resist liberalization of their markets. (If your mandate is narrow, any organized group can threaten it.) For USTR Robert B. Zoellick, winning by a narrow, partisan margin was certainly a lot better than not winning trade promotion authority at all. But it gave him a far weaker negotiating mandate than the parallel trade legislation of 1962, 1974, and 1988 had provided his predecessors.

Winning this way may also have been unnecessary. In 2000, a bipartisan coalition, including 71 House Democrats, had approved the terms of Chinese entry into the World Trade Organization (WTO). Among the supporters were the three senior trade Democrats on the House Ways and Means Committee—ranking member Charles Rangel (D-NY), ranking trade subcommittee member Sander Levin (D-MI), and long-time liberal trade supporter Bob Matsui (D-CA).

This important trio ended up bitterly opposed to the 2001 trade legislation. In the month before the vote, Rangel had sent Hastert a summary of their position that seemed a plausible basis for compromise negotiations with the bill's chief sponsor, Ways and Means Chair Bill Thomas (R-CA). But neither Hastert nor Thomas replied, and negotiations never took place.

This short chronicle explores why. Was a compromise in fact possible? If so, what mix of issues and personalities kept it from happening? Was one side to blame? Or did the roots lie in issues that were too dicey to bridge? In the end, no clear answers may be possible. But seeking them will still prove illuminating.

■ ■ ■

It was only on 13 December 2000 that George W. Bush laid claim to the presidency, following the closest US national election since 1876. But in the first half of January, key elements of the trade drama of 2001 were falling into place. On the 4th, the House Republican Conference chose Bill Thomas as Ways and Means chair over his more senior colleague, Phil Crane (R-IL).[2] On the 8th, the president-elect's press secretary declared that Bush would seek renewal of fast-track negotiating authority. On the 11th, Bush announced his choice of Zoellick to serve as US Trade Representative and declared that the position would remain at the cabinet level. (Members of his transition team had suggested earlier that the job might be downgraded, eliciting the predictable protests from organized business and Capitol Hill.)

---

2. In fact, Thomas ranked third in seniority, behind Crane and Clay Shaw (R-FL), but the latter did not enter the contest for the chairmanship.

The Senate confirmed Zoellick unanimously on 6 February, and he promptly set to work trying to build support for renewal of fast-track authority. He found the going hard. His initial idea was to bundle that authority in a comprehensive bill that would include such other measures as the recently completed free trade agreement (FTA) with Jordan and the bilateral trade agreement with Vietnam. A broad range of House Democrats objected, arguing instead for "taking up the key trade issues in progression" in order to form "building blocks toward reaching common ground."[3] Other senior administration officials objected also, partly because of the Democrats' resistance. Zoellick backed away from the package approach.

The Democrats wanted—and eventually got—separate House votes on Jordan and Vietnam, both of which passed easily. The Democrats also achieved their goal of keeping intact the labor and environmental provisions of the Jordan FTA, which were negotiated under President Bill Clinton.[4] But their main interest was in the content of fast-track legislation, which Zoellick had relabeled "trade promotion authority" (TPA). To formulate a consensus, they met through the spring and into the summer under the leadership of Levin, ranking Democrat on the Trade Subcommittee. But the process was slow. Meanwhile, moderate "New Democrat" Cal Dooley (D-CA)—a participant in the meetings—was also circulating an outline proposal, which became known as the "Dooley Principles." Its central thrust was that labor and environmental provisions in a trade agreement would receive parallel treatment with other provisions in terms of the means of enforcement.

Through the spring and summer, the Democrats refrained from submitting a bill—one reason was to leave the door open for negotiations with the Republicans, another was that they had not yet reached a consensus among themselves. On 13 June, however, Crane and 62 largely Republican cosponsors introduced a fast-track bill (HR 2149) that excluded labor and environmental issues entirely. The House Republican leadership immediately endorsed the bill, and began talking about bringing it to the floor before the August recess. House Democrats reacted angrily. Minority leader Dick Gephardt (D-MO) said it represented "the most extreme view on the other side" of labor and environmental issues. Levin said the approach had "close to zero" chance of gaining Democratic support. And the administration expressed caution. Zoellick declared, "The formal legislative process has begun, and I look forward to working with members of both parties in the Congress as we move ahead." And White

---

3. Letter to the president from Rangel, Levin, Matsui, Nancy Pelosi (D-CA), Cal Dooley (D-CA), Steny Hoyer (D-MD), and 21 other House Democrats, 16 March 2001.

4. But in a bow to Republicans opposed to enforcement of such provisions with trade sanctions, Zoellick and his Jordanian counterpart exchanged letters declaring that they "would not expect or intend" to employ trade sanctions to enforce any provisions of the agreement. Ways and Means Democrats saw this as unnecessary and a harbinger of future trouble on these issues.

House legislative director Nick Calio indicated that it was important to count the votes before proceeding.[5]

Also cautious in his response was the new Ways and Means chair, Bill Thomas. He had been instrumental in moving Bush's tax bill through his committee on a party-line basis, to the unhappiness of his Democratic colleagues. But he wanted to move carefully on trade—and to play the central role in the process. He was determined to be a strong chair, and felt that Archer, his predecessor, had let some power over trade issues slip to other House Republicans, including the able chair of the House Rules Committee, David Dreier (R-CA). So while Thomas formally cosponsored Crane's bill, he emphasized—in language similar to Zoellick's—that its introduction was just "the beginning of the process."[6]

Thomas had been elevated over his Ways and Means colleagues because he was smart, strong, and substantive. He was not chosen for popularity—he had, in the words of a former colleague and supporter, "no interpersonal skills." A headline in a feature story two years later would label him "smart as a whip, and almost as subtle."[7] His insensitive and noncollegial style would generate friction time after time with Republican as well as Democratic members. In particular, there was a striking incompatibility between his approach to issues and that of Rangel, his Democratic counterpart. The New Yorker liked first to establish interpersonal trust and agreement on process and broad principles, moving from there to fleshing out the details. Thomas' style was to focus on the substance from start to finish—he saw "process" as an excuse for ducking or deferring hard choices.

Looking at the substance, Thomas seems to have concluded early on that he could not find common ground with Rangel and Levin, and when the latter reportedly approached the chairman informally, he was rebuffed. The trade press reported Thomas as indicating in July that "he would only work directly with Levin if it became clear that he needed to pick up a large number of Democrats"—that is, more than the 40 he then estimated he could get without the Ways and Means trio.[8]

But as that same report made clear, Thomas knew he needed *some* Democratic support. His party had only a 12-vote House margin, and there had been at least 50 negative House Republican votes on every trade-liberalizing bill from the Uruguay Round/WTO legislation onward. Having a Republican president would presumably bring that number down.

---

5. Quotes and information from *Inside US Trade*, 15 June 2001.

6. Ibid.

7. *Washington Post*, 27 July 2003, D1. This article was triggered by a bizarre incident nine days earlier in which Thomas had summoned the Capitol police to go after Democratic members who had walked out of a contentious Ways and Means session on pension reform. Thomas apologized on the House floor the following week.

8. *Inside US Trade*, 27 July 2001.

But how much? In 2000, 33 Republicans had even backed a resolution to have the United States withdraw from the World Trade Organization.

Meanwhile, on the Democratic side, Dooley was getting impatient. He had received some positive feedback for his "principles" from a range of trade policy professionals, including some in the business community, and he thought they might offer a basis for substantive compromise. But neither party's members seemed to be moving in that direction. So he sounded out some of his Democratic colleagues on their willingness to approach Thomas directly. Two junior members of Ways and Means agreed to do so: William Jefferson (D-LA) and John Tanner (D-TN). Dooley then contacted Thomas and suggested they explore possible compromise legislation. Thomas agreed.

Dooley's California congressional district bordered on that of Thomas, and they had worked together before. And the Democrat had a straightforward, substantive approach that proved quite compatible with the style of the chairman. So Dooley, Jefferson, and Tanner began to submit compromise suggestions to Thomas, particularly on labor and environmental issues. The three were careful to keep Rangel informed about what they were doing. By late summer, they had reached broad agreement on a formula that was more labor- and environment-friendly than the unsuccessful Clinton-era proposal or the Crane bill. The legislation reported by Ways and Means, in 1997, for example, had excluded all but a narrow range of trade-related labor and environmental issues from inclusion in a fast-track implementing bill.[9] The Thomas-Dooley draft had no such exclusion, though its stated negotiating goals were modest—enforcement of existing national laws and ensuring that trading partners' labor and environmental practices did not "serve as disguised barriers to trade." And regarding the enforcement of trade agreements, it did not explicitly distinguish between labor-environment and other provisions, though it allowed for some distinction in practice.[10]

As members returned from recess in early September, there was talk of rapid introduction and Ways and Means consideration of the Thomas-Dooley bill. Then came the 9/11 terrorist attacks, which shocked the nation and focused congressional energies on immediate, direct legislative responses. There was a new mood of bipartisan cooperation that some hoped would extend to TPA. But the general mood proved short-lived. The attacks did prompt several long-time Republican opponents of fast track, such as Duncan Hunter of California and Frank Wolf of Virginia, to back the president on this issue as a matter of national security. But when

---

9. HR 2621 (105th Congress) did so by including broad objectives ("preserv[ing] the environment," "promoting respect for worker rights") in a separate subsection (102[c]) of the bill, outside of the "principal trade negotiating objectives," which explicitly excluded them from "use of the trade authorities [fast-track] procedures."

10. HR 3005 (107th Congress), Section 2(b)(10).

Zoellick championed national security arguments for TPA in a 24 September speech (originally scheduled for the 11th) at the Institute for International Economics, Rangel responded angrily to what he labeled an attempt to make support of the bill a test of "patriotism." Matsui also declared himself "offended."[11]

On 25 September, Thomas released a summary of what he labeled the "bipartisan compromise" on trade promotion authority. Dooley declared it "monumental" and said, "For the first time, it includes enforceable labor and environmental standards in a trade promotion authority plan."[12] The next day, however, Rangel, Levin, and Matsui responded with a "Dear Democratic Colleague" letter with a heading, "Thomas' 'Bipartisan Compromise' Is Neither" and expressing "significant concerns" in three areas: labor standards, environmental protection, and the role of Congress. A week later, Thomas and Dooley introduced the Bipartisan Trade Promotion Authority Act, which became HR 3005. The next day, 4 October, the Democratic trio put into the hopper their alternative, HR 3019, labeled the Comprehensive Trade Promotion Authority Act.

The rhetoric was sharp from both sides, but on substance, as the *Washington Post* editorialized, "The differences do not seem insurmountable."[13] The specific points in the Democrats' letter of 26 September, for example, did not seem unreasonable: emphasis on core International Labor Organization (ILO) labor standards, reconciling multilateral environmental and trade agreements, and strengthening the oversight role of Congress. After Thomas had scheduled a Ways and Means markup for Friday, October 5—signaling a plan to roll the Democrats in a party-line vote—he surprised friends and foes alike by announcing at that session that he would postpone the markup—and vote—so that staffs on both sides could meet over the weekend and explore possible compromise. As noted in chapter 11, Rangel responded graciously: He had been "relieved from having to read a very painful statement that . . . I have worked all night on."[14] And while Thomas reacted rather grumpily to this statement, his action seemed to signal a search for common ground.

But compromise was not to be, and the opportunity went unexploited. And so did another, one month later, that involved President George W. Bush.

When the Ways and Means Committee reconvened on 9 October, nothing had changed. The staffs had met over the weekend in a session described by participants on both sides as contentious and unproductive. With no one tasked to lead toward compromise and no apparent instruc-

---

11. *Inside US Trade*, 28 September 2001.

12. Quoted in Paul Blustein, "Trade Compromise Proposed," *Washington Post*, 4 October 2001.

13. "A Chance for Trade," *Washington Post*, 2 October 2001.

14. Statement of 5 October 2001, released by Rangel's office.

tions in that direction from members on either side, the aides could only reiterate entrenched positions. As Rangel told the committee, "What was missing from these talks was what can only be done with members and not staff . . . negotiation to see whether we can find some common ground that would allow Fast Track to pass the House with . . . broad, bipartisan support."[15] So Thomas presented his bill, essentially unchanged from the version he had introduced. Rangel's motion to substitute the Democratic alternative failed, 26-12; the chairman's bill then prevailed 26-13. Just two committee Democrats, Jefferson and Tanner, voted in favor. It was the most partisan committee vote in memory on major trade legislation.

Had Ways and Means been a mirror of overall House sentiment, a two-to-one margin would have been reassuring. But it was not such a mirror. Its membership was disproportionately Republican, and disproportionately protrade. So the vote was not encouraging. The day after, White House spokesman Ari Fleischer declared that TPA "certainly can't pass without a healthy dose of bipartisanship." Yet few other Democrats were coming on board. Dooley arranged a meeting with the president, and hoped to attract at least 20 Democrats—but only 13 came, and just two of them declared their support. In all, fewer than 15 of the chamber's 211 Democrats appeared to be in favor. The White House was well aware of this. So were business community advocates of the legislation.

So the scene appeared ripe for compromise. It seemed possible. And it seemed necessary.

Around this time, Zoellick contacted ex-President Jimmy Carter through his long-time associate, Bob Pastor, a professor at Emory University and the Carter Center who had worked with the former president on his initiatives for democracy and human rights. The aim was to secure Carter's endorsement of TPA, and thus replicate the united front of former presidents that had buttressed Bill Clinton's campaign for the North American Free Trade Agreement (NAFTA) eight years earlier. Carter was very much a free-trader and hence favorably disposed. But where were the House Democrats? he wondered. Learning that senior Ways and Means Democrats had been shut out of the bill's drafting, Carter—through Pastor—pressed for a new effort. The Georgian wrote President Bush on 29 October to encourage him to meet with Democratic leaders and lend his influence to a compromise.

This led, with Zoellick's encouragement and facilitation, to a short White House meeting about the trade stalemate on 1 November involving Bush, Rangel, and Nick Calio, the president's assistant for congressional relations. The meeting apparently went well. Bush and Rangel were personally simpatico. When Rangel complained of the Democrats' exclusion, the president expressed regret and asked what the New Yorker thought should be done. Rangel responded that Bush should call the

---

15. Statement of Charles B. Rangel, 9 October 2001, released by his office.

House Speaker, Dennis Hastert (R-IL), and ask that he set up a process for a compromise negotiation. Bush said he would.

After some further back-and-forth, Bush did phone Hastert. This led to a meeting six days later involving Hastert, Thomas, Rangel, and Representative Rob Portman (R-OH), a committee member with ties to the president.[16] Portman also met jointly with Republican and Democratic staff members, exploring compromise possibilities. In the meantime, aides had managed to draw from the Democrats' 134-page bill a one-page statement highlighting differences in four areas: core international labor standards, multilateral environmental agreements, investment, and the role of Congress. This was delivered to Hastert on 8 November, with a handwritten note from Rangel noting that staff members "were not able to resolve key differences." The ranking Democrat also had another short meeting that day with Hastert and Portman that he characterized as "helpful." All the while, Calio and other administration officials were signaling their openness to changes in the Thomas bill.

In describing the meetings, Rangel declared his flexibility. "I never insisted that my bill or any bill be the basis for negotiations or fully incorporated."[17] His one-page summary set forth issues that needed to be resolved, but it was not a take-it-or-leave-it proposal. It did not put forward any draft legislative language other than (by reference) that in the Democratic alternative. Still, it was a genuine overture. If it reflected the Democrats' actual bargaining position (and Levin and Matsui had been consulted), it certainly represented a reduction in differences when compared with the full Rangel bill.

But the initiative failed. Worse, Rangel did not get the courtesy of a response. Thomas was resistant throughout, offering no encouragement in the 7 November meeting and not joining the meeting the following day. So the four issues were never joined. On 15 November, Rangel joined a press conference with Gephardt denouncing Republicans for failure to engage with Democrats on airline security and economic stimulus as well as trade.

From then until the House vote on 6 December, the game was played mainly on the Republican side. Process leadership moved from Thomas to DeLay, and the Republican Whip, known as "The Hammer," pressed reluctant colleagues to join him. Speaker Hastert leaned on members particularly responsive to calls of party loyalty. Rules chair Dreier, whose role Thomas had limited in earlier stages, played a key lobbying role on substantive issues. DeLay doled out favors as needed—and drove the overall process. The White House was nervous and skeptical: as late as noon on the day of the vote, it urged House leaders to withdraw the bill to prevent

---

16. In March 2005, Bush would designate Portman as Zoellick's successor as US Trade Representative.

17. Rangel quotes are from the statement of 9 November 2001 released by his office.

its being voted down. But DeLay stood firm. Reportedly, he had a list of Republicans in order of increasing difficulty they had with the bill, and planned to go as far down that list as necessary.

When the normal time period ended with more nays than ayes, DeLay had the Speaker hold the vote open until he could reach the member whose switching would put the bill over the top. Finally, as reported in *The Congressional Record*, 37 minutes after the 15-minute roll call began, "Mr. DeMint changed his vote from 'nay' to 'aye.'" The South Carolina Republican's price was a concession to the textile industry. He won a letter promising future legislation mandating that Caribbean and Andean beneficiaries of US trade preferences would have to use, in their apparel products, yarn and cloth dyed in the United States.[18] It was signed by Hastert, DeLay, and Majority Leader Dick Armey (R-TX)—noticeably *not* by Thomas, who like Rangel was bitter about this dilution of preference laws.[19]

Washington Post columnist David Broder called it "a shaky victory."[20] It was followed by a much more constructive, bipartisan process in the Senate, highlighted by a comprehensive expansion and reshaping of trade adjustment assistance laws that brought a substantial number of Democrats there on board. Then came a tumultuous conference process, in which Thomas first insisted on rewriting the House bill entirely for bargaining purposes, then fought over who would chair the proceedings, and finally offered—at the eleventh hour—a constructive compromise that led to agreement and final enactment. President Bush signed it into law on 6 August 2002.[21]

"They wanted fast track in the worst possible way, and they got it." So stated this author the day after the December House vote. But was another "way" possible? Had Thomas and the Republicans accepted Rangel's invitation and sat down with the senior Democrats, would this have led to agreement? Were the Democrats really serious? Aside from the interplay triggered by Carter and Pastor, the Democrats had been reluctant to take the initiative—out of resentment over their treatment, and also in the expectation that, in the end, the Republicans would lack the votes and have to come back to them. (In the meantime, it would not help their bargaining position if they seemed too eager to deal.)

We cannot know, of course, and the lack of an aggressive senior crafter of compromise on either side of the aisle made no small contribution to

---

18. The existing requirement (the "yarn forward rule") was that it be spun and woven in the United States.

19. Representative Robin Hayes (R-NC), also credited with the deciding vote in some accounts, received a statement from President Bush praising Hayes' devotion to textile industry trade interests and endorsing those interests to some degree.

20. "A Shaky Victory on Trade," *Washington Post*, 12 December 2001.

21. For more detailed treatment of these events, see chapter 11.

the interparty impasse. One way of assessing prospects, however, is to examine the specifics in Rangel's one-page summary. Essentially, it contained five proposals under its four headings, examined here in order of increasing difficulty.[22]

One proposal regarding labor standards was to create a WTO Working Group on Trade and Labor. This essentially replicated a goal already specified in existing law (albeit unsuccessfully pursued by the Clinton administration). One of the two environmental issues was to negotiate a WTO rule allowing a nation to use trade measures to enforce a multilateral environmental agreement against a nation party to that agreement. This should have been easy for Republicans to accept: it would apply only to a narrow range of cases, and it is substantively appropriate for the WTO to defer to multilateral consensus on issues like the environment. The other environmental issue, of great importance to environmental groups, was to correct a flaw (apparently inadvertent) in NAFTA that gave foreign investors greater rights in member countries than domestic investors. This problem was in fact addressed in a House floor amendment. So none of these should have been difficult for Thomas and other Republicans to accommodate.

The Rangel proposal on the role of Congress was more problematic. Its core provisions were, first, a structured biennial review of trade negotiations allowing one-third of a chamber's members to bring a resolution of disapproval to the floor for a vote; and second, a new requirement that a group of congressional trade advisers concur with the president's certification that negotiating objectives had been met. Either of these could have proved troubling in practice, and while these hurdles could likely be surmounted by a reasonably adroit USTR, one could see why the administration would be wary here. However, Rangel had made a point of signaling flexibility in this area, and plausible and acceptable modifications of each of these provisions are easy to envisage.

The hardest issue was the Rangel bill requirement that "FTAA countries . . . implement and enforce five core ILO standards in domestic law."[23] This went beyond the "Jordan formula" fashioned under Clinton and employed in subsequent free trade agreements—that parties would enforce their existing labor laws—by establishing a minimum level of pro-

---

22. The undated and unpublished document provided by Rangel to Hastert was entitled "Fast Track—Four Key Differences Between Rangel and Thomas Bills." The section of the document labeled "Core International Labor Standards" included two distinct provisions for FTAA and the WTO, hence the above reference to five proposals.

23. In the Rangel bill, these were listed (without explicitly naming the ILO) as "the right of association, the right to bargain collectively, and prohibitions on employment discrimination, child labor, and slave labor" (HR 3019, Section 2(c)(9)(A)).

tection that their laws should provide.[24] The standards themselves were not controversial—in 1998, members of the ILO from around the world had adopted, by consensus, a "Declaration on Fundamental Principles and Rights at Work," specifically (a) freedom of association and the effective recognition of the right of collective bargaining; (b) the elimination of all forms of forced or compulsory labor; (c) the effective abolition of child labor; and (d) the elimination of discrimination with respect to employment and occupation.

But Republicans were wary, particularly about the requirement for collective bargaining, and because a US commitment to ILO standards might be used by other nations to challenge US labor laws. In general, GOP legislators were not in favor of anything that might strengthen regulation of labor practices in the United States. The Rangel summary stressed that it "does not require countries to sign ILO conventions" (and the United States has never ratified most of the basic ones). But it would have been difficult nonetheless for Republicans to accept this commitment—in fact, Senator Phil Gramm (R-TX) was lobbying against the Thomas bill that very month because he thought its lesser language opened the door to attacks on, or changes in, US labor laws.

If Hastert or Thomas had responded constructively to Rangel's initiative, and, to employ his words, "the members [had gotten] together to have substantive discussions to . . . resolve some of these issues in a broadly bipartisan way," core labor standards could well have proved the deal breaker. Nor was there any guarantee that, once such talks began, the Democratic trio would not have pressed other provisions of the Rangel bill—such as its much more demanding general standard for an agreement to qualify for TPA procedures.[25]

Yet it seemed astounding at the time that the House Republican leadership, encouraged by the president and badly short of the needed votes, did not respond positively to Rangel's overture and put the senior Ways and Means Democrats to the test. At a minimum, Republicans could have discussed the specific points in the Rangel summary—which ones they might accommodate, which ones caused them major problems. Or they could have responded by accepting, say, half the points and asking if the Democrats would yield on the rest.

---

24. Democrats did not see it this way—in fact, in developing that formula, the Clinton administration had stressed that Jordan did in fact have the basic labor standards incorporated in its laws.

25. The Rangel bill allowed an agreement to be submitted under fast track only "if such agreement *substantially achieves* the applicable objectives described in [the sections spelling out negotiating objectives]" HR 3019, Section 4(B)(1)(c)(2). The Thomas bill required only that "such an agreement *makes progress in meeting* the applicable objectives . . . " HR 3005, Section 3(b)(1) (C)(2). Emphasis added. Prior fast-track laws had employed the "makes progress" standard.

If the Democrats did not in fact raise additional hard issues, and a middle way could be found on core labor standards, the result would have been the real bipartisan agreement that both sides said they wanted. If, on the other hand, agreement in the end was simply not possible, the Republicans would have visibly walked the extra mile, and would have been in a far better position to ask other Democrats to join them. And the opposition of Rangel, Levin, and Matsui to the legislation might have been less intense.

For most of the year, to be sure, the Democrats had been difficult, complaining about exclusion but not putting forth an alternative that would encourage the administration or the Republicans to respond. Through October, for some combination of personal, substantive, and tactical reasons, the two sides stayed apart, in a sort of Alphonse and Gaston routine. But in November, Rangel took an important step to break the impasse. It was just a first step—but his Republican counterparts never even responded. An opportunity was lost.

Three years and some months later, at this writing, the costs of this failure are manifest. The second Bush administration faces the daunting task of winning House approval of the Central American Free Trade Agreement (CAFTA). Democrats are overwhelmingly opposed, citing labor and environmental concerns very much like those advanced by Rangel and his colleagues in 2001. Administration hopes for victory seem to rest on replicating that year's partisan vote, which will require putting the squeeze on an even larger number of reluctant Republicans.

Such a narrow margin has once again inflated the power of special interests. Exploiting CAFTA's frail condition, the US sugar industry has leaped into the fray, declaring all-out war against the tiny increase in sugar market access that the agreement provides to Central American nations. If the Bush administration cannot turn this attack aside, how will it be able, credibly, to negotiate the much larger reduction sin US sugar protection that a serious Doha agricultural agreement will require? There could hardly be a more graphic illustration of how ongoing partisan rancor undermines the administration's capacity to pursue the serious trade liberalization to which it is committed.

Glossary

Alternative Trade Adjustment Assistance. See "Wage insurance."

Antidumping (AD) investigation. An investigation instituted by an importing country in response to a claim that a foreign supplier is selling merchandise at "less than fair value" (see "dumping.") In the United States, if the Department of Commerce finds dumping has occurred, and the US International Trade Commission finds that US firms have been materially injured, the law provides that customs officials levy an additional import duty equal to the calculated price discrepancy. GATT Article VI authorizes such measures. The Uruguay Round antidumping code, signed in 1994, aims to standardize and discipline national government practices.

Appellate Body. The WTO entity in the dispute settlement process that adjudicates appeals from panel decisions. The body is composed of seven individuals and functions when either the complaining or responding country appeals the decision of a dispute settlement panel report. Three of the seven individuals hear the appeal and can elect to modify, overturn, or accept the panel findings.

Asia Pacific Economic Cooperation (APEC) forum. An informal grouping of Asian and Pacific Rim nations that provides a forum for discussing economic and trade issues. The members as of the end of 2004 were Australia, Brunei, Canada, Chile, China, Hong Kong, Indonesia, Japan, Malaysia, Mexico, New Zealand, Papua New Guinea, the Philippines, Singapore, South Korea, Taiwan, Thailand, and the United States. At the 1994 APEC summit, the leaders of member countries agreed to eliminate barriers to trade and investment among industrialized members by 2010 and among all members by 2020, but implementation has lagged.

Bipartisan Trade Promotion Authority Act of 2002. Legislation that granted the George W. Bush administration authority to negotiate the Doha Round and regional and bilateral trade agreements under fast-track procedures (relabeled "trade promotion authority"). The law also expanded trade adjustment assistance. Notwithstanding the law's title, the House vote was more divided along partisan lines than for any such bill since the 1930s.

Byrd Amendment. Also known as the Continued Dumping and Subsidy Offset Act, the amendment directs that the antidumping and countervailing duties collected by US Customs be distributed to the companies that supported the original petitions in these cases. Previously, these duties were deposited with other government revenues in the general treasury. In 2000, Senator Robert Byrd (D-WV) quietly added the amendment to the agriculture appropriations bill in the conference committee. In January 2003, the WTO Dispute Settlement Body found that the Byrd amendment conflicted with US obligations under the antidumping agreement, and called for its elimination.

Cancún Ministerial Conference. The September 2003 WTO meeting intended to achieve a breakthrough in the Doha Round. It broke up in disagreement, after the Group of 21 (led by Brazil, China, and India) challenged US-EU proposals on agricultural market access and a "group of 90" developing countries, mostly from Africa, demanded immediate concessions (especially for their cotton producers).

Central American Free Trade Agreement (CAFTA). This agreement removes trade barriers among the United States and five Central American countries: Costa Rica, El Salvador, Guatemala, Honduras, and Nicaragua. The agreement was modeled after the North American Free Trade Agreement (NAFTA). It was signed on 28 May 2004 in Washington, DC. The Dominican Republic has since been added, making it CAFTA-DR. As of the end of 2004, the agreement had not been submitted to Congress for approval.

Comparative advantage. Relative efficiency in production of a particular product or class of goods. Trade theory holds that a country should export those goods in which it has the greatest comparative advantage and import those goods in which it has the greatest comparative disadvantage, regardless of its general level of productivity or its absolute labor costs relative to other countries.

Competitive liberalization. The Bush (43) administration policy, pursued by US Trade Representative Robert B. Zoellick, involving negotiation of free trade agreements with selected countries at the same time that the United States engages in regional and global trade talks. The theory is that these narrower deals will generate pressure to emulate them, thus improving prospects for reducing barriers in broader trade talks.

Countervailing duty (CVD) investigation. An investigation instituted by an importing country when given evidence that foreign goods sold within its borders are subsidized by the government in the country of production. If a subsidy is found by the US Department of Commerce, and the US International Trade Commission finds that US firms have been materially injured, US law generally requires imposition of a duty to offset the subsidy. The Uruguay Round code on subsidies and countervailing measures, signed in 1994, aims to standardize and discipline national practices on subsidies and offsetting duties.

Current account balance. A measure of a country's international transactions that includes trade in goods and services and unilateral transfers. A "negative" balance on a current account, or a current account deficit, means that outflows of currency resulting from these transactions exceed inflows. (A current account deficit is offset and financed by a capital account surplus, representing a net inflow of investment funds.)

Customs value. A method of valuing imported goods; in traditional US practice, it excludes shipping costs from the price of the goods.

Dispute settlement mechanism (DSM). Considered one of the major advances made in the Uruguay Round negotiations, the dispute settlement mechanism was created to ensure uniform application of all WTO agreements and rules. Under the GATT, each country involved in the dispute process—even the defendant country—had to agree with the final panel decision. This made the process nonbinding. Under the WTO, a negative consensus is required to reject a panel's determination. The DSM is activated when a country requests consultations regarding another country's trade practices on the grounds that they violate that nation's commitments under existing agreements. At that point, the countries involved can come to a mutually agreeable solution or a WTO panel will be created to hear the facts of the case and make a determination. All panel reports are subject to appeal to the WTO appellate body (see "Appellate Body").

Doha Round. The comprehensive WTO negotiation launched at the fourth ministerial meeting of the WTO in Doha, Qatar in November 2001. Also known as the "Development Round," its focus has been on agriculture, market access in industrial products, trade facilitation, and services, with special emphasis on the needs of developing countries. Progress was stalled at the Cancún Ministerial meetings in September 2003, which broke up in disagreement over agricultural trade issues. It was resumed the following summer, resulting in adoption of a "July package," which established modalities for agricultural and other topics and committed advanced nations to the elimination of export subsidies on farm products. The talks have continued past their original December 2004 deadline, with much work remaining.

Domestic content requirement. A requirement that firms selling a particular product within a particular country must use, as a certain percentage of their inputs, goods produced within that country.

Dumping. The sale of a commodity in a foreign market at "less than fair value." Fair value is usually considered to be the price at which the same product is sold in the exporting country or in third countries, but under US law dumping can also be established by comparing the export price to the estimated costs of production of the merchandise in question. When dumping occurs, the legal remedy is imposition of a special duty equal to the "margin" of dumping, defined as the difference between fair value and the actual sales price. (See also "Antidumping investigation")

Escape clause (Section 201, Article XIX). A provision of the GATT articles, and of US law, authorizing import relief as a temporary "safeguard" for domestic producers injured by import competition. Originally limited to those whose losses resulted from prior US trade concessions, escape clause eligibility was extended in Section 201 of the Trade Act of 1974 to all who could establish that imports were "a substantial cause of serious injury, or the threat thereof." The Omnibus Trade and Competitiveness Act of 1988 stipulated that the goal of any relief must be "positive adjustment." If the US International Trade Commission finds injury and recommends relief, the president must grant it or report to Congress why, after reviewing the "national economic interest of the United States," he has decided there is "no appropriate and feasible action to take." Congress may then override his decision through enactment of a joint resolution, imposing thereby the remedy recommended by the USITC.

Fast-track procedures. Legislative procedures set forth in Section 151 of the Trade Act of 1974, stipulating that once the president formally submits to Congress a bill implementing an agreement (negotiated under the act's authority) concerning nontariff barriers to trade, both houses must vote on the bill within 90 days. No amendments are permitted. The purpose of these procedures is to assure foreign governments that Congress will act expeditiously on an agreement that they negotiate with the US government. The procedures were generally in effect from 1975 through 1994. At that time, President Clinton failed to win renewal for these procedures and they lapsed. They were renewed in 2002 under President Bush and renamed trade promotion authority (TPA) procedures.

Free trade agreement (FTA). An arrangement between two or more nations to remove barriers to the trade they conduct with one another. An FTA also usually addresses trade-distorting practices such as government subsidies. Under such an agreement, concessions are not on a most favored nation basis but only to the parties to the FTA. Such agreements were first authorized by the Trade and Tariff Act of 1984.

Free Trade Area of the Americas (FTAA). The goal of negotiations launched in 1994 among 34 Western Hemisphere nations. The January 2005 target date for completing the negotiations and launching the FTAA was not met.

General Agreement on Tariffs and Trade (GATT). The early postwar multilateral agreement on trade rules completed in 1947 as an interim arrangement pending establishment of the projected International Trade Organization (ITO). After Congress failed to ratify the ITO agreement, the articles of the GATT agreement became the basic rules of international trade, and the GATT organization at Geneva became the central institution supporting international negotiations and the reduction of trade barriers. As part of the Uruguay Round agreement, the GATT was superseded by the World Trade Organization (WTO) on 1 January 1995, with all bodies and rules of the GATT as modified by the Uruguay Round agreements becoming part of the WTO.

General Agreement on Trade in Services (GATS). Established in 1995 pursuant to the Uruguay Round agreements, the GATS seeks to liberalize—and develop agreed rules for—services trade as the GATT has done for goods.

Generalized System of Preferences (GSP). A system under which industrial nations give preferential rates of duty on imports from less developed countries without receiving trade concessions in return. The United States began extending preferences in 1975 and renewed them in the Trade and Tariff Act of 1984 and subsequent legislation.

Group of 21 (or 20, or 22). A group of developing nations, led by Brazil, China, and India, active in the Doha Round negotiations. The Group formed in September 2003 in response to the perceived inadequacy of US-EU proposals to reduce agricultural subsidies. It contributed to the failure of the Cancún Ministerial of September 2003, and also to the stronger advanced-country commitments made the following summer.

Industrial policy. Governmental actions affecting, or seeking to affect, the sectoral composition of the economy by influencing the development of particular industries.

Industrial targeting. The selection by a national government of industries important to the next stage of that nation's economy, and encouragement of their development through explicit policy measures. A frequent goal of such targeting is competitiveness in export markets.

Injury. The requirement, under GATT, that an industry seeking trade relief establish that it has been hurt by foreign competition. In the United States, a finding of injury has always been required for escape clause relief, and since 1979 for the bulk of countervailing duty and antidumping cases as well.

Intellectual property. See TRIPS.

International Trade Commission. See US International Trade Commission.

Kennedy Round. The popular name for the sixth round of trade negotiations under the aegis of the GATT, conducted during 1963–67. The round produced major cuts in tariffs.

Macroeconomic policy. Policy geared toward influencing the overall aggregates of the economy, such as employment, production, and the rate of inflation, through measures affecting the fiscal balance and the supply of money and credit. It has an important influence on a nation's balance of trade.

Mercantilism. Historically, an economic philosophy that equates national wealth with the accumulation of gold or other international monetary assets, and hence with running a trade surplus. In today's world, mercantilism refers to a belief that running a consistently positive trade balance contributes to a nation's economic strength and moral virtue, and also to policies aimed at this goal.

Most favored nation (MFN). See normal trade relations (NTR).

Multi-Fiber Arrangement (MFA). An international trade compact, in effect from 1973 through 2004, that established a framework for negotiating bilateral orderly marketing agreements under which exporting nations undertook to limit their shipments of textile and apparel products. Under the MFA, importing nations could impose quantitative import restrictions when unable to negotiate such agreements or to counter market-disruptive import surges. The MFA succeeded the Long-Term Arrangement (LTA), which took effect in 1962 and applied only to cotton textiles. The MFA broadened controls to include products made from wool or synthetic fibers. The Agreement on Textiles and Clothing (ATC) concluded in the Uruguay Round provided for phased elimination of all textile and apparel quotas over 10 years, ending 1 January 2005.

Multilateral trade negotiations (MTN).   Technically, any of the postwar series of barrier-reducing negotiations under the auspices of GATT; however, "the MTN" commonly refers to the Tokyo Round of 1973–79.

National Economic Council (NEC).   An interagency, cabinet-level committee and staff in the Executive Office of the President that coordinates US domestic and international economic policy, including trade policy. President Clinton established the NEC by executive order in 1993. His successor, President Bush, continued it in 2001.

Newly industrialized countries (NICs).   Developing countries (for example, Hong Kong, Korea, Singapore, and Taiwan) that have experienced rapid industrial development and, hence, expanding exports of their industrial products.

Nonmarket economy.   An economy that relies on forces other than the market, such as state intervention, to determine the allocation of goods and resources in the country. This has a distorting effect on prices and costs within the economy. US trade remedy laws include special procedures for dealing with products of nonmarket economies.

Nontariff barriers (NTBs).   Government measures other than tariffs—i.e., import quotas, buy-national procurement regulations, product standards, and subsidies—that impede or distort the flow of international commerce. The Tokyo Round was devoted primarily to limiting and disciplining national use of nontariff barriers.

Normal trade relations (NTR).   The principle of nondiscrimination in international trade, formerly known as "most favored nation" (MFN) status. A nation receiving this treatment from another is assured that the products it exports are subject to tariffs no greater than those imposed on imports from any other country. The United States extends this status to all WTO member countries as well as to many other nations. Trade preferences (GSP) constitute an exception to MFN, as do free trade agreements (FTAs) between two or more nations.

North American Free Trade Agreement (NAFTA). Agreement establishing free trade among the United States, Mexico, and Canada. Negotiated by President George H.W. Bush and signed on 17 December 1992, NAFTA removes barriers to trade and investment and improves the protection of intellectual property rights. Prior to seeking congressional implementation of NAFTA, President Clinton negotiated side agreements on labor and environmental issues. Congress approved implementation of NAFTA in November 1993.

Omnibus Trade and Competitiveness Act of 1988. This act was the first comprehensive trade legislation initiated by Congress since before the Smoot-Hawley Act of 1930. Its important features included the strengthening of unilateral trade retaliation instruments, particularly Section 301, provision of fast-track negotiating authority for the Uruguay Round of GATT negotiations, and enhancement of the authority of the US Trade Representative.

Orderly marketing agreement (OMA). A formal agreement in which an exporting nation undertakes to limit its sales of specified "sensitive" products to specific levels, so as not to disrupt, threaten, or impair competitive industries or workers in an importing country or countries.

Organization for Economic Cooperation and Development (OECD). An organization of 30 advanced European, North American, and Asia-Pacific market democracies whose members consult regularly on issues of economic policy. Established in 1961, the OECD grew out of the Organization of European Economic Cooperation formed in 1947 to administer the Marshall Plan.

Permanent normal trading relations (PNTR). Ongoing nondiscriminatory trade treatment (not conditioned on annual renewal). Refers specifically to the US grant of PNTR to the People's Republic of China in legislation enacted in 2000. See also "NTR."

Plaza Agreement. An agreement in September 1985 among the "Group of Five" advanced industrial nations (France, Germany, Japan, the United Kingdom, and the United States) to encourage depreciation of the US dollar.

Protectionism. The imposition of substantial tariffs or other limitations on imports in order to insulate or "protect" domestic producers from foreign competition; hence, support of the imposition of such import barriers.

Quasi-judicial procedures. Procedures through which law is made by regulatory agencies applying general statutes to specific cases. On trade, procedures administered by the US International Trade Commission and the Department of Commerce determine the eligibility of petitioners for import relief under the escape clause, countervailing duty, antidumping, or other trade statutes.

Quota. A limit on the quantity of a product that may be imported by (or sold to) a country. Import quotas are enforced by the receiving nation, export quotas by the country of origin.

Reciprocal Trade Agreements Act of 1934. The law that initially provided authority for the US government to enter into bilateral agreements for reciprocal tariff reductions. Through successive extensions and amendments, it also authorized US participation in the first five GATT rounds of multilateral trade negotiations. It was superseded by the Trade Expansion Act of 1962.

Reciprocity. The general principle or practice of nations negotiating mutual reductions in import barriers. See also "sectoral reciprocity."

Retaliation. Import-restrictive action taken by a country in response to similar measures by a trading partner. WTO rules permit a country whose exports are hurt by unjustified new restrictions to retaliate by imposing trade barriers on products sold by the nation taking the initial protectionist action. In principle, the value of trade affected by retaliation should be comparable to that affected by the measures against which it is targeted.

Rules of origin. The criteria used to determine where a product was made. These rules are a necessary part of free trade agreements that do not impose a common external tariff. Globalization has meant that many products can have value added in several countries before going to market.

Safeguards. See "Antidumping investigation," "Countervailing duty investigation," and "Escape clause."

Section 201. See "Escape clause."

Section 301. Under this provision of the Trade Act of 1974, as amended by the Omnibus Trade and Competitiveness Act of 1988 and subsequent legislation, the US Trade Representative is required to take all appropriate action, including retaliation, to obtain the removal of any act, policy, or practice of a foreign government that violates an international agreement or is unjustifiable, unreasonable, or discriminatory, and burdens or restricts US commerce. In practice, Section 301 has been employed on behalf of American exporters fighting foreign import barriers or subsidized competition in third-country markets. The Uruguay Round weakened Section 301 by subjecting unilateral US retaliation to challenge under the WTO dispute settlement mechanism. Since 1995, most Section 301 cases have been pursued through the WTO.

Sectoral reciprocity. The principle or practice of comparing the openness of national markets to imports sector by sector, and negotiating restraints sector by sector, rather than across entire economies. US advocates of a sectoral reciprocity approach to trade in telecommunications or wine, for example, propose to compare the levels of US and foreign barriers to imports of these products, and to equalize them, either by negotiating reductions in foreign restraints or by raising our own. A modified version of sectoral reciprocity was enacted into law as Title III of the Trade and Tariff Act of 1984.

Smoot-Hawley Act. The Tariff Act of 1930, which raised US tariffs on over 20,000 dutiable items to record levels and contributed to the deepening of the Great Depression.

Special Representative for Trade Negotiations (STR). See "US Trade Representative."

Special 301. This clause in the 1988 Omnibus Trade Act requires the US Trade Representative to investigate countries determined to have a history of violating existing laws and agreements dealing with intellectual property rights. Such countries must have their current practices reviewed each year, and if they are not found to be improving, are subject to mandated retaliation under Section 301.

Subsidy. A bounty or grant conferred upon the production or exportation of an article or merchandise by the government in the country of origin. Foreign subsidies affecting trade are subject, under US law, to countervailing duties.

Super 301. Under this amendment to Section 301 of the 1988 Trade Act, the US Trade Representative was required in 1989 and 1990 to designate "priority foreign countries," chosen for the "number and pervasiveness" of their "acts, policies or practices" impeding US exports, and for the US export gains that might come from the removal of these practices. The law called for retaliation if foreign action was insufficient or not forthcoming. In March 1994, President Clinton issued a so-called Super 301 executive order targeting "priority foreign country *practices*." Its provisions were codified in the Uruguay Round implementing legislation.

Targeting. See "Industrial targeting."

Tariff Act of 1930. See "Smoot-Hawley Act."

Tokyo Round. The GATT negotiations formally initiated by the Tokyo Declaration in 1973 and completed in 1979. The Tokyo Round, also called the multilateral trade negotiations (MTN), differed from previous GATT rounds in its primary focus, which was on reducing and regulating nontariff barriers. It yielded a number of multilateral codes covering, among other areas, subsidies and countervailing measures, antidumping, customs valuation, government procurement, and technical barriers to trade. Participating nations also agreed to substantial further reductions in tariff rates.

Trade Act of 1974. Legislation signed into law on 3 January 1975 that granted the president the authority to enter the Tokyo Round and negotiate international agreements to reduce tariffs and nontariff barriers (see also "Fast-track procedures"). The act also amended US law governing the escape clause, antidumping, and countervailing duties; expanded trade adjustment assistance; established guidelines for granting most favored nation status to East bloc states; and granted limited trade preferences (GSP) to less developed countries.

Trade Adjustment Assistance (TAA). Originated under the Trade Expansion Act of 1962, this program is designed to provide retraining and financial benefits to workers and firms that are injured as a result of increased imports. Eligibility and funding were cut back sharply after Ronald Reagan took office in 1981. TAA benefits were expanded modestly with the passage of NAFTA in 1994 and substantially in the trade act of 2002.

Trade Agreements Act of 1979. Legislation, adopted under the fast-track procedures, that approved and implemented the trade agreements negotiated during the Tokyo Round. It made US law consistent with the MTN agreements, while at the same time rewriting the countervailing duty and antidumping laws, extending the president's authority to negotiate nontariff barrier agreements, and requiring the president to reorganize executive branch trade functions.

Trade and Tariff Act of 1984. An omnibus trade bill whose provisions included extension of the president's authority to grant trade preferences, authorization for negotiating bilateral free trade agreements, and authority to enforce export restraint agreements on steel.

Trade balance. The total value of a nation's merchandise exports minus the value of its merchandise imports, globally or vis-à-vis specific countries or regions. A "negative" trade balance is one in which imports exceed exports.

Trade Expansion Act of 1962 (TEA).   Legislation that authorized the Kennedy Round of trade negotiations amended US escape clause procedures, and established the trade adjustment assistance program.

Trade Promotion Authority (TPA).   See "Fast-track procedures."

Trade-Related Aspects of Intellectual Property Rights (TRIPS).   Issues involving nations' treatment of intellectual property owned by foreigners. The United States has focused on preventing the piracy of intellectual property in foreign nations. Specific areas covered by the Uruguay Round agreement on TRIPS include copyrights, patents, trademarks, industrial designs, design of integrated circuits, and anticompetitive practices in licensing.

Trade-Related Investment Measures (TRIMs).   Issues involving restrictions on the operations of foreign firms—requiring, for example, foreign firms to produce a certain percentage of the final product locally or export a certain percentage of their output. Although the TRIMs agreement was less ambitious than the TRIPS agreement, the Uruguay Round did produce the first GATT agreement on investment measures. The Uruguay Round agreement on TRIMs focused on providing national treatment and eliminating quantitative restrictions.

Trade remedy procedures.   See "Quasi-judicial procedures"; "Section 201"; "Antidumping investigation"; and "Countervailing duty investigation."

Triple transformation test.   Also known as the "yarn forward rule," it is a three-step rule of origin included in NAFTA. To be considered a North American apparel product, the fiber must be created, woven into cloth, and made into clothing in North America. This created a huge incentive for Mexico-based apparel operations to use cloth made in the United States. The same basic rule has been included in other US free trade agreements and trade preference arrangements.

UN Conference on Trade and Development (UNCTAD).   A quasi-autonomous body within the United Nations system that focuses its attention on measures that might be taken to accelerate the pace of economic development in developing countries. The conference was first convened in Geneva in 1964, and has met quadrennially since then.

US International Trade Commission (USITC).   An independent, fact-finding and regulatory agency whose six members make determinations of injury and recommendations for relief for industries or workers seeking relief from increasing import competition. In addition, upon the request of Congress or the president, or on its own initiative, the USITC conducts comprehensive studies of specific industries and trade problems, and of the probable impact on specific US industries of proposed reductions in US tariffs and nontariff trade barriers. The USITC was created by the Trade Act of 1974 as the successor agency to the US Tariff Commission, which was created in 1916.

US Tariff Commission.   See "US International Trade Commission."

US Trade Representative (USTR).   An official in the Executive Office of the President, with cabinet-level and ambassadorial rank, charged with advising the president, working with Congress, and leading and coordinating the US government on international trade negotiations. ("USTR" also designates the governmental unit that the trade representative heads.) Established by the Carter administration in 1980, the USTR was given increased authority in the Omnibus Act of 1988. The USTR succeeded the Special Trade Representative (STR), created (at congressional insistence) in the Trade Expansion Act of 1962, whose status and authority were strengthened in the Trade Act of 1974.

Uruguay Round.   The comprehensive GATT negotiations initiated by the Punta del Este Agreement of September 1986. The negotiations were originally to be completed by the end of 1990; however, a final agreement was not reached until December 1993, with the formal signing in April 1994. Substantial new agreements were reached on general tariff reduction, agricultural subsidies and quotas, textiles, safeguards, antidumping and countervailing duties, trade-related investment measures (TRIMs), rules of origin, standards, services, trade-related intellectual property rights (TRIPS), and government procurement. An unprecedented number of nations adhered to the major Uruguay Round accords—123 as of mid-1994. The Uruguay Round also created the World Trade Organization to supersede the GATT structure.

Voluntary export restraint (VER).   An arrangement under which exporters voluntarily limit exports of certain products to a particular country. Such restraints (also known as voluntary restraint agreements, or VRAs) are typically undertaken under threat of that country's imposition of import restrictions. VERs circumvent the GATT most favored nation principle and the obligation on the part of the importing country to provide compensation to the exporting country when it imposes new import restrictions. The Uruguay Round agreement on safeguards bans the use of VERs.

Wage insurance. Also known as alternative trade adjustment assistance (ATAA) and established in the 2002 Trade Act, wage insurance is provided to certain workers who have lost their jobs or are displaced because of trade-related economic forces. The workers are offered a wage subsidy of 50 percent of the difference between the old and new wages, up to $10,000, for up to two years. The legislation limited wage insurance to workers over age 50 and required that they select it as an alternative to regular trade adjustment assistance.

World Trade Organization (WTO). A global organization created by the Uruguay Round agreements that came into being in 1995. The WTO oversees the global trading system and ongoing trade negotiations and monitors implementation of trade accords. It also administers a strong dispute settlement process. The WTO succeeded the GATT; however, unlike the GATT it was explicitly established to play this role. The WTO encompassed and extended the GATT structure. As of 31 December 2004, there were 148 WTO members.

Index

APEC. *See* Asia Pacific Economic Cooperation (APEC)
apparel products. *See* textile industry
appellate body, definition of, 343
apples, 244
Archer, Bill, 216, 290, 334
  and fast-track authority, 263–64, 288
  and NAFTA, 261, 261n
  and Uruguay Round implementation, 222
  and US-China relations, 276, 276n
Armey, Dick, 339
Asia Pacific Economic Cooperation (APEC)
    forum, 193, 205, 206–8, 237, 299
  definition of, 343
Askew, Reubin, 115
ASP. *See* American Selling Price (ASP)
Association of Federal, State, County, and
    Municipal Employees (AFSCME), 257
Australia, free trade agreement with, 299, 301,
    304, 320
automobile industry
  escape clause petition, 144–45, 148n
  and Japanese trade relations, 77–79, 81, 88,
    144–45, 215, 243
  and NAFTA, 204–5
  protection for, 25, 77–79, 88, 119, 121, 195
auto parts agreement with Japan, 207, 215, 243

Bahrain, free trade agreement with, 299
Baker, Howard H., Jr., 60n, 85
Baker, James A. III, 91, 93, 122–23, 134
Baldrige, Malcolm, 104, 116, 117, 122, 154
Baldwin, Robert E., 315
bananas, 244–45
bargaining tariff, 16–17, 34–35
Barshefsky, Charlene, 207, 236–37, 263–64, 275
Bator, Francis M., 106
Baucus, Max, 228, 295, 296, 297, 298, 298n, 327
Bayh, Evan, 309
beef hormones case, 244
Bello, Judith, 92, 128n
Bentsen, Lloyd, 67
  and fast-track renewal, 99
  and HR 3, 94
  and NAFTA, 100, 174–75, 200, 260
  and omnibus trade legislation, 92, 93
  and partisan politics, 287
  relations with USTR, 128n
  and trade relations with Japan, 81, 89, 207
  and Uruguay Round implementation, 217, 222n
Bereuter, Douglas, 255, 276
Berger, Samuel ("Sandy"), 222n, 263–64
Bergsten, C. Fred, 27n, 84, 183, 295n, 329n
Berkeley Roundtable on the International
    Economy (BRIE), 180–81
Berman, Jason, 265
Bethlehem Steel, 155
bicycle theory, 18
Binder, Sarah, 282

Bingaman, Jeff, 280, 327
bipartisanship. *See also* partisan politics
  decline of, 287–90
  and fast-track renewal, 305
  and free trade agreements, 302
  and trade adjustment assistance reform, 297
  and Trade Promotion Authority Act, 290–98,
    332, 337–42
Bipartisan Trade Promotion Authority Act of
    2001, 282, 290–98, 302, 331–42
  definition of, 344
Black Monday, 93
Blumenthal, W. Michael, 20, 105
Bolivia, free trade agreement with, 299
Bolling Committee, 68
Bolton, Josh, 93
Bonior, David, 201, 204, 267
Bork, Robert, 221
Bowles, Erskine, 264
Branson, William H., 47
Brazil
  free trade agreements with, 300, 320
  informatics case, 124
  steel cases, 155
  as Super 301 target, 130
  trade imbalance with, 89
Breaux, John, 279
Bressand, Albert, 183
Bretton Woods system, 42–43, 57
BRIE. *See* Berkeley Roundtable on the
    International Economy (BRIE)
Brittan, Leon, 135, 208
Brock, William E., 78–79, 83, 102, 104, 115–16,
    116n, 198
  versus Commerce Department, 115–18
  congressional relations with, 305
  free trade initiatives, 119–20
  and the Generalized System of Preferences,
    84–85, 86n, 87
  presidential relations with, 119
  as secretary of labor, 120
  and steel cases, 156–57
Broder, David, 339
Brown, Ron, 236
Bryant amendment, 91, 93–94
Buchanan, Patrick, 175, 221, 226
budget deficits, 247n, 317, 329
budget issues, Uruguay Round, 217
Burke-Hartke quota bill, 81, 187
Burns, Arthur F., 60
Bush administration (George H. W.)
  agriculture measures, 131
  and human rights issues with China, 208, 211
  and Japan trade relations, 234
  and Mexican free trade agreement, 98
  and NAFTA, 98, 132
  and special-interest politics, 189
  and steel industry case, 157–58
  and Super 301, 129–31

textile case, 191
and trade as political issue, 133–34
trade policy initiatives, 83
Bush administration (George W.)
budget deficit, 247n, 317, 329
and competitive liberalization, 298–302
and fast-track renewal, 279–81, 290–95, 298, 306, 310, 332
and NAFTA, 260
and partisan politics, 10, 279–306
second, 303–4
steel protections, 233, 244, 245, 248, 250, 303
tax cuts, 290, 296, 329
and Trade Promotion Authority Act, 336–37
USTR for, 280, 294n, 299–300, 304, 309, 323, 332
WTO cases, 244n, 244–45
Business Coalition, 212
Business Coalition for US-China Trade, 211
business community
benefits of free trade for, 312
consultation with, 109–10
globalization of, 249–52
and loss of fast-track authority, 265, 266, 268, 269
and NAFTA, 260–61
polarization on trade, 289
and social issues, 271, 280
support for free trade, 249, 310, 323
and Uruguay Round implementation, 226–27
and US-China trade relations, 211–12, 275
business productivity, 235, 312
Business Roundtable, 184, 188, 220, 265
"buy America" campaign, 134, 134n
Byrd, Harry F., Sr., 19
Byrd, Robert, 90, 92, 97, 226, 242
Byrd amendment, 242, 320, 344

Cabinet Council on Commerce and Trade, 116
CAFTA. *See* Central American Free Trade Agreement (CAFTA)
Cairns Group, 209
Calio, Nick, 334, 337, 338
Canada
free trade agreement with, 54, 95–96, 299 (*See also* North American Free Trade Agreement)
wood products case, 149, 320
Cancún Ministerial Conference, 250, 302–3, 319–20, 344
Cannon, Joseph G., 28
CAP. *See* Common Agricultural Policy (CAP)
captive production, 163
Cardin, Benjamin L., 304
Carter, Jimmy
support for free trade, 32, 337
and trade promotion authority, 337, 339
Carter administration, 20n
automobile case, 78
and fast-track renewal, 74
Panama Canal treaties, 200n
shoes industry case, 144

special trade representative, 103, 107–11, 118–19, 119n
steel industry cases, 26n, 146
textile case, 70, 70n
and Trade Act of 1974, 147
trade adjustment assistance, 150
trade policy success, 111
trade reorganization proposal, 114–15
and US-China trade relations, 274
Cassidy, Robert C., Jr., 73
CEA. *See* Council of Economic Advisers (CEA)
cellular telephones, 214, 225
Central American Free Trade Agreement (CAFTA), 250, 250n, 270n, 299–301, 304, 306, 313
definition of, 344
CFA. *See* Consumer Federation of America (CFA)
Chadha case, 97n, 141n
Chafee, John H., 173
Chamber of Commerce, 188
Charnovitz, Steve, 270
child labor, 257n, 341
Child Labor Deterrence Act, 257n
Chile
copper industry, 189
free trade agreement with, 237, 255, 262n, 270n, 299–302, 300n
China
entry into WTO, 233, 237, 273, 275, 277, 332
most favored nation status, 274
and human rights issues, 193, 208, 211–13, 255, 276–77
permanent normal trade relations status, 255, 273, 276–77, 280
textile restraints, 154–55, 188–89, 320
trade imbalance with, 249, 274, 309, 316
trade relations with, 274, 309, 317
during Clinton administration, 207–8, 211–13, 253
normalization of, 274–77, 288, 316
"China lobby," 212, 212n
Christopher, Warren, 212
Chrysler, 77
CIEP. *See* Council on International Economic Policy (CIEP)
Citizens' Trade Campaign, 225
citrus industry, 205
Clayton, Will L., 19
Cline, William R., 311, 315
Clinton, William J.
presidential campaign, 135, 135n–36n, 197–99
on trade liberalization, 330
Clinton administration
antidumping investigations during, 162, 240, 240n–41n
and antidumping law reform, 217–19
and China trade relations, 207–8, 211–13, 253, 275, 288

de minimis requirements, antidumping, 161, 163
DeMint, Jim, 295, 339
Democrats. *See also* partisan politics
  and congressional reform, 68
  distribution of, 282, 283*f*, 284–85
  and fast-track renewal, 281, 291–95, 305, 310
  and free trade versus protectionism, 170–75, 289–90
  and Japanese trade imbalance, 89
  and loss of fast-track authority, 220, 267, 268, 269, 315
  and NAFTA, 197–98, 199–200, 203–4, 206, 217, 260–61, 281
  and trade adjustment assistance reform, 296–98, 305, 327–28
  trade policy stance, 31, 316, 325–26
  and Trade Promotion Authority Act, 331–42
  and Uruguay Round implementation, 222–27, 287
Department of Agriculture, trade responsibilities, 114
Department of Commerce
  antidumping investigations, 162
  enforcement of administrative trade remedies, 148
  trade responsibilities, 114, 322–24
  unfair-trade practices statutes, 151–52
  versus USTR, 115–18
Department of International Trade and Industry, 103, 117
Department of State, trade responsibilities, 19, 105, 114
Department of Trade, proposal for, 113–14, 117, 120, 122, 323–24
Department of Treasury
  authority to waive countervailing duties, 145–46
  and countervailing duty investigations, 142–43
  enforcement of administrative trade remedies, 148
  trade responsibilities, 114
depoliticization of trade issues, 138, 144, 148, 152
Depression, 12
Dewey, Thomas E., 171
digital tape recorders, 91
Dillon, C. Douglas, 19, 105*n*
Dillon Round, 23, 105
Dingell, John D., 80, 158, 225
dispute settlement mechanism (DSM)
  definition of, 345
  GATT, 243
  Uruguay Round, 209–10
  WTO, 243–46, 321
diversionary input dumping, 160
Doha Development Agenda, antidumping laws in, 297
Doha Round, 280
  agriculture under, 302–3, 320
  Cancún Ministerial Conference, 250, 302–3, 319–20, 344

description of, 345–46
  and globalization efforts, 319
  social issues during, 254*n*
Dole, Robert J., 67, 78
  and committee competition, 83
  and loss of fast-track authority, 267
  and partisan politics, 288
  and special-interest politics, 188
  and textile quotas, 89
  and Uruguay Round implementation, 222–28, 226*n*, 228*n*
  and WTO, 221, 245
dollar. *See* exchange rate
dolphins, 259
domestic content requirement, 79, 346
domestic economic policy
  versus free trade, 35–36, 310–13
  reform of, effect on trade policy, 8–9
  and trade expansion, 326–30
Dominican Republic, free trade agreement with, 299, 304, 306
Dooley, Cal, 280, 291, 333, 335, 336
Dooley principles, 280, 291, 333
Downey, Thomas J., 80
Dreier, David, 204, 334, 338
DSM. *See* dispute settlement mechanism (DSM)
dumping. *See also* antidumping (AD) investigations
  definition of, 137, 346
  diversionary input, 160
  non-market-economy, 160
Dunkel, Arthur, 161, 209, 218
Dunkel text, 208–9
dynamic random access memories (DRAMs), 125–27, 127*n*

East Asian "tigers," rise of, 53
Eberle, William D., 20, 106, 119
ECAT. *See* Emergency Committee for American Trade (ECAT)
economic decline
  effect on trade policy, 9, 113
  postwar, 48–51
economic growth
  effect on trade policy, 234–36, 318–19
  of Japan, 48, 51–52
    effect on US trade policy, 9, 63, 186
  as multiplier of trade pressures, 36
  rate of, and stagflation, 56
  and trade deficits, 248
economic policy, domestic
  versus free trade, 35–36, 310, 313
  reform of, effect on trade policy, 8–9
  and trade expansion, 326–30
Economic Policy Council, 122
Ecuador, free trade agreement with, 299
Eisenhower, Dwight D., 19
Eisenhower administration
  inflation during, 55
  textile case, 25

Matsui, Robert, 200n, 201, 212n, 216, 266, 267, 268, 281, 288, 292, 332, 336
  and Trade Promotion Authority Act, 332, 336, 338
McDermott, Jim, 212
McDonald, Alonzo L., 107
McDonald, David J., 23
Mchumo, Ali, 273n
McKinley Tariff Act of 1890, 16n
McLarty, Mac, 204
Meany, George, 172
Medicare prescription drug plan, 302
Meese, Edwin, 117, 122
MEFTA. See Middle East Free Trade Area (MEFTA)
mercantilism, definition of, 348
merchandise trade, 194, 194n–95n, 235, 246, 250, 316
  benefits of, 312, 312n
  deficits in, 49–51, 50n
Mexico
  free trade agreement with, 98, 132 (See also North American Free Trade Agreement)
  1943 agreement with, 22
  steel cases, 155
Mexico City policy, 268, 268n
MFA. See Multi-Fiber Arrangement (MFA)
MFN principle. See most favored nation (MFN) principle
microelectronics, Japanese negotiations on, 125–27, 127n
Middle East Free Trade Area (MEFTA), 299
Mikulski, Barbara, 229
Milliken, Roger, 223
Mills, Wilbur D., 19, 28–30, 33, 106
  scandal involving, 66–67, 67n
minivans, tariffs on, 198, 198n–99n
misery index, 55
Mitchell, George, 97, 208, 213, 224
Mitterrand, François, 132
Moffett, A. Toby, 75
Mondale, Walter F., 86, 87, 172–73, 173n
money managers, effect on exchange rates, 59–60
Moore, Michael, 272, 273n
Moran, Theodore H., 218, 238, 240n
Morocco, free trade agreement with, 299, 301, 304
Mosbacher, Robert, 129
most favored nation (MFN) principle, 17. See also normal trade relations (NTR)
  and China, 193, 208, 211–13, 254–55, 274
  definition of, 349
Motorola, Inc., 186, 214
Moynihan, Daniel Patrick, 217, 220, 274
Multi-Fiber Arrangement (MFA), 26, 70n, 76
  definition of, 348–49
  phaseout of, 209–10, 224, 233, 248, 249, 320
  renewal of, 89, 190–91
Multilateral Agreement on Investment (MAI), 265–66

multilateral trade negotiations (MTN). See also specific round of negotiations
  definition of, 349
  during postwar period, 12–13, 17
  role of special trade representative in, 107–11
Murayama, Tomichi, 215

Nader, Ralph, 188, 221, 226
NAFTA. See North American Free Trade Agreement (NAFTA)
Nakasone, Yasuhiro, 88, 120, 125
National Association of Manufacturers (NAM), 188, 211
National Bureau of Economic Research (NBER), 180
National Economic Council (NEC), 199, 264, 323, 349
National Electrical Manufacturers Association, 189
National Journal, on party polarization, 282
national security, and trade issues, 62, 183
national sovereignty
  and nontariff barriers, 36
  and WTO, 220–21
natural resource subsidies, 159
Neustadt, Richard E., 118, 285
newly industrialized countries (NICs), 54, 63. See also specific country
  definition of, 349
  and the Generalized System of Preferences, 84–88
  steel industry cases involving, 155
New Zealand, 300
Nippon Telephone and Telegraph (NTT), 109
Niskanen, William A., 156n
Nixon, Richard, support for free trade, 32
Nixon administration
  China trade relations, 274
  and interest-group politics, 187
  nontariff commitments, 72–73, 142
  special trade representative during, 103, 106, 118–19
  and stagflation, 55
  textile wrangle, 26, 29–30, 31, 34, 106, 170–71, 190
  trade adjustment assistance during, 141
Nixon shocks, 41–44
  and dollar misalignment, 57
  and trade balance, 49
nonconferences, 73–74, 96, 222
nondiscrimination principle, erosion of, 54
nongovernmental organizations (NGOs), anti-fast-track coalition of, 265–66, 281
nonmarket economy, definition of, 349
nonmarkups, 73–74, 76, 96, 238, 287
  abandonment of, 301–2
  under Uruguay Round, 216, 216n
nontariff trade barriers (NTBs), 71–72, 141–42
  definition of, 349

Persian Gulf War of 1991, 133
Peru, free trade agreement with, 299
Petersen, Howard C., 19
Peterson, Peter G., 106
pharmaceuticals, Japanese negotiations on, 125
Plaza Agreement, 58, 91, 194, 196
    definition of, 350
political response
    avoidance of, 138, 144, 148, 152
    to China trade relations, 276
    creation of FTAs on basis of, 300
    to currency misalignment, 62
    forcing of, 153–55
    to globalization, 253–54
    to post–Cold War trade issues, 62–63
    to trade deficit, 49–51, 50n, 246–49
    to trade expansion, 45, 47
political system. *See also* partisan politics; *specific party or agency*
    and creation of trade policy, 5–6, 8, 169–70
    and interest groups, 4–5, 24–27, 169–70, 185–92
polluter pays principle, 259
Portman, Rob, 280, 294, 294n, 304, 305, 309, 338
presidential trade authority, 9, 12, 14–17, 16n, 35, 103–36. *See also* fast-track authority
    and escape clause petitions, 143–45
    and executive broker role, 18–21, 66, 105, 111–14
    reassertion of in 1980s, 196–97
    restructuring of, 322–25
    and support for free trade, 32
    and textile case, 25
Pressler, Larry, 228n
Prestowitz, Clyde V., Jr., 53, 181, 181n
price averaging requirements, antidumping, 161–62
principal negotiating objectives, 261
private sector. *See* business community
procedural openness, changes aimed at, 148n
process protectionism, 90
productivity, 235, 312
    improvement in, and open trade policy, 316–19
Program on International Policy Attitudes (PIPA), 290
protectionism
    decline of, 102, 230, 233–54, 309, 316
    definition of, 350
    domination of policy process by, 4–5, 90
    versus free trade, 4, 119–20, 310–13
    and globalization, 250, 251
    institutional collaborations against, 189–90
    interest-group initiatives as, 169–70, 185–92
    and partisan politics, 170–75
    political role of, 31–32
    right to, 21–24
    rise of, 82–83, 88–91
    and special trade representative, 104
Public Citizen, 258, 261, 265
Public Law 100-418. *See* Omnibus Trade and Competitiveness Act of 1988

public opinion
    of fast-track renewal, 281
    of free trade, 6–7, 9, 175–78, 280–81, 281n, 313–14, 326
    of globalization, 258–59, 314, 325
    of NAFTA, 203–4, 258, 261, 313
    partisan divide of, 284
    of social issues, 280–81, 325
    of trade policy, 325–26
    of WTO, 245–46

quasi-judicial procedures, definition of, 350–51
quota, definition of, 351

Randall, Clarence B., 19
Randall Commission, 23
Rangel, Charles, 269, 277, 281, 292, 293, 301n, 325
    and Trade Promotion Authority Act, 334, 336–42
Rashish, Myer N., 20
Rayburn, Sam, 25
Reagan, Ronald
    fair trade speech, 196–97
    and free trade versus protectionism, 173n, 173–74
Reagan administration
    agriculture measures, 131
    automobile case, 78–79, 145
    budget deficit, 247n
    and Canadian free trade agreement, 95
    damage limitation during, 127–29
    escape clause use during, 148–49
    and fast-track renewal, 76
    first, 115–18
    free trade versus protectionism during, 119–20, 122, 128–29
    inflation during, 55–56
    and Japan trade relations, 125
    microelectronics case, 127
    second, 120–23
    and semiconductor agreement, 242–43
    shoe industry case, 149, 189
    and special-interest politics, 188–89
    special trade representative during, 103, 104, 115–18, 118–19
    steel cases, 156–58, 248
    textile cases, 70, 155, 188–89, 190–91
    trade adjustment assistance during, 150
    trade deficit during, 247
    trade policy initiatives, 66, 83–90, 196
Reaganomics, and exchange rates, 60
recession, and trade as political issue, 172
reciprocal noninterference, 185n
Reciprocal Trade Agreements Act of 1934, 3, 12, 14n, 15n, 17, 22, 71, 172
    definition of, 351
reciprocity
    definition of, 351
    sectoral, definition of, 352
redistricting, 285–86

Regan, Donald T., 120
Reich, Robert B., 181, 190
Reifman, Alfred, 82
Republicans. *See also* partisan politics
    distribution of, 282, 283*f*, 284–85
    and fast-track renewal, 279, 291–95
    and loss of fast-track authority, 220, 262–63,
        266, 267, 268, 269
    and NAFTA, 197–98, 201–4, 206, 260–61
    and protectionism versus free trade, 170–75,
        289–90
    and social issues, 270, 280
    and trade adjustment assistance reform, 296–98,
        330
    trade policy stance, 31, 325–26
    and Trade Promotion Authority Act, 331–42
    and Uruguay Round implementation, 222–27,
        287
    and WTO, 221
resource input subsidies, 160
Retail Trade Action Coalition (RITAC), 189
retaliation, definition of, 351
Reuther, Walter, 251
Ribicoff, Abraham A., 69, 114
Rice, Condoleezza, 304
Richardson, Bill, 201
Richardson, J. David, 236, 312, 314, 328
Rivers, Richard R., 74, 107
Rockefeller, Jay, 298*n*
Roderick, David M., 155
Rodrik, Dani, 311
Rongji, Zhu, 275
Roosevelt, Franklin D., election of, 171
Roosevelt administration
    partisan politics during, 8, 31
    presidential role in trade policy during, 18
Rosen, Howard, 280
Rostenkowski, Dan, 67
    and committee competition, 80, 82
    and fast-track renewal, 98–99
    and the Generalized System of Preferences,
        86–87
    and HR 3, 94
    and Japanese trade imbalance, 89
    and NAFTA, 100, 201, 260
    and omnibus trade legislation, 92, 93, 95
    and partisan politics, 287–88
    relations with USTR, 128*n*
    support for NAFTA, 174–75
    and Uruguay Round implementation, 216
Roth, William, 20, 105–6, 108, 113, 119, 274, 323
Rove, Karl, 250
Rubin, Robert, 263, 275, 314, 330
Ruggiero, Renato, 272
rules of origin, 248–49
    definition of, 351

Salinas de Gortari, Carlos, 98, 100, 131–32, 134, 197
Santos, Leonard, 93
Schattschneider, E. E., 3, 5, 13, 30

Scheve, Kenneth F., 314
Schnietz, Karen E., 14*n*, 15*n*
Schott, Jeffrey J., 272
Schultze, Charles L., 181–82
Schumer, Charles, 309, 317
Schwab, Susan, 93
Scott, Bruce R., 181
Scowcroft, Brent, 134
Seattle Ministerial Conference (WTO), 230, 253,
        271–73
Section 201. *See* escape clause
Section 301, 95, 123–24, 196
    automobile case, 243
    Chinese labor practices case, 277
    definition of, 351–52
    dispute settlement provisions, 243*n*, 243–44
    semiconductor case, 125–27, 243
sectoral reciprocity, 186
    definition of, 352
security, and trade issues, 62, 183
Semiconductor Industry Association (SIA),
        125–27, 186, 189
semiconductors, Japanese agreement on, 125–27,
        127*n*, 166*n*, 181*n*, 196, 207, 242–43
Senate, and trade adjustment assistance reform,
        297–98, 305
Senate Finance Committee, 27–30
    chairmen, 67
    and countervailing duty investigations, 142–43
    and fast-track renewal, 72–74, 76
    and Japanese trade issues, 108–9
    and loss of fast-track authority, 266*n*
    and material injury test, 147
    and partisan politics, 279, 287
    and Trade Authority Promotion Act, 295–98
    USTR relations with, 128, 128*n*
Sensenbrenner, James, 255*n*
September 11th terrorist attacks, 279, 335
services, trade in, 209–10, 316*n*
Shaw, Clay, 304
shoe industry
    alliance with textile industry, 186–87
    escape clause petitions used by, 121, 144, 149
    protection for, 89, 189
shrimp, 259
Shultz, George P., 21, 60, 119
Singapore
    economic growth of, 53
    free trade agreement with, 237, 255, 262*n*, 299,
        300*n*, 301–2
    trade preferences for, 87*n*
Slaughter, Matthew J., 314
Smith, Adam, 178
Smoot-Hawley Tariff Act of 1930, 3, 6, 8, 11, 13,
        16, 18, 54*n*
    definition of, 352
social issues. *See also* environmental issues; labor
    during Doha Round, 254*n*
    effect on trade policy, 253–54, 269–71, 280,
        328–30

social issues. *See also* environmental issues;
    labor—*continued*
    and globalization, 253–59, 316
    and loss of fast-track authority, 263–69, 310, 316
    and NAFTA, 98, 100, 201–2, 220, 255, 259–62,
        270
    and partisan politics, 284–85, 289
    public opinion on, 280–81, 325
    during Tokyo Round, 254
    and WTO, 220–21
Social Security, restructuring of, 304
Southern Africa, free trade agreement with, 299
sovereignty
    and nontariff barriers, 36
    and WTO, 220–21
Soviet Union, disintegration of, 61–62
Special 301, definition of, 352
special cases, deals for, 24–27, 76, 195–96
special interests, political power of, 4–5, 21, 24–27,
    169–70, 185–92
special representative for trade negotiations
    (STR), 103, 105–7 *See also* Office of the US
    Trade Representative (USTR); *specific
    representative*
    creation of, 20–21
    and fast-track renewal, 72–74
    organization of, 112
    role of, 105n, 107, 112–13
specificity test for subsidies, 160n
Sperling, Gene, 264, 275
stagflation, 44, 55–57, 62–63
standard of living, 312
standing requirements, antidumping, 161, 163
Stans, Maurice H., 106, 117
start-up requirements, antidumping, 161–62
static comparative advantage, 179n, 179–80
steel industry
    antidumping investigations, 146, 162, 233, 239,
        240, 241t
    countervailing duty investigations, 163
    escape clause petitions, 233, 244
    and newly industrialized countries, 155
    1982 cases, 153n, 153–58
    protection for, 24, 26, 26n, 76, 195, 303, 321
    and special-interest politics, 187, 189
    and trade balance, 43, 250
    voluntary restraint agreements, 85–88, 119,
        157n, 157–58, 248
Steel Trade Liberalization Program, 158
Stockman, David A., 150
stock market, fall of, 93
STR. *See* special representative for trade
    negotiations (STR)
Strauss, Robert S., 20, 20n, 70, 198
    congressional relations with, 305
    and fast-track renewal, 73–75
    and multilateral trade negotiations, 107–11
    presidential relations with, 119, 119n
    and Trade Act of 1974, 147

Structural Impediments Initiative (SII), 130
subsidies. *See also specific product*
    definition of, 352
    resource input, 160
    specificity test for, 160n
sugar industry, 195, 205, 250, 250n, 304, 306,
    320
Summers, Lawrence, 263–64
sunset requirements, antidumping, 161–62, 240
Sununu, John, 129
Super 301, 92, 93, 192, 197
    definition of, 129, 352
    and Japan, 101, 215, 215n
    and USTR, 129–31
suspension of investigations, 152–53
Sutherland, Peter, 209, 209n
Sweeney, John J., 263

TAA. *See* trade adjustment assistance (TAA)
Taiwan
    economic growth of, 53
    and the Generalized System of Preferences,
        84–88
    and Super 301, 97, 129
    trade imbalance with, 89
Talent, James, 268
Talmadge, Herman E., 72
Tanner, John, 291, 335, 337
Tariff Act of 1930. *See* Smoot-Hawley Tariff Act of
    1930
Tariff Commission. *See* US International Trade
    Commission (USITC)
Tarullo, Daniel, 264
tax cuts, 290, 329
TEA. *See* Trade Expansion Act of 1962 (TEA)
telecommunications, 214, 225, 237
    Japanese negotiations on, 109, 125
    reciprocity agreements on, 89
    Section 301 case, 124
temporary quantitative indicators (TQIs), 207
terrorist attacks, 279, 335
textile industry
    alliance with shoe industry, 186–87
    Chinese cases, 154–55
    congressional committee action on, 29, 69–70
    and interest-group politics, 185, 188–91, 191n
    and NAFTA, 204–5, 205n, 248–49
    and partisan politics, 31, 91
    protection for, 170–71, 233–34, 311, 320
    quota restrictions, 89, 119, 195–96
    special case, 24–26, 33–34, 76
    and Tokyo Round, 69n, 69–70
    and trade balance, 43, 248–49
    and Uruguay Round, 209–10, 223–24
    and WTO, 221
Thailand, free trade agreement with, 299
Third World nations. *See also specific country*
    and the Generalized System of Preferences,
        84–88

Truman, Harry S.
  election of, 171
  trade remedies order, 22
tuna, 259
turtle-excluding devices, 259
Tyson, Laura, 199, 199n

Ullman, Al, 67, 288
UN Conference on Trade and Development
    (UNCTAD), 354
Underwood Act, 16
unemployment, 235, 312
  and inflation rates, 55–56
unemployment insurance, 328
unfair trade practices, 137
  new legislative initiatives on, 158–60
  upsurge in cases involving, 151–53
unilateralism
  aggressive, 123
  steps toward, 90
United Auto Workers (UAW), 78, 79, 148n, 172,
    187–88, 251
United States Steel, 155
United Steelworkers, 155
Uruguay Round
  agriculture under, 131, 209, 210, 216
  antidumping agreement, 161–62, 217–19
  completion of, 198, 208–11
  and creation of WTO, 193
  definition of, 355
  dispute settlement provisions, 209–10
  and economic tripolarity, 61
  enforcement procedures, 54
  and fast-track authority, 95, 98, 99–100, 128
  financing of, 217
  implementation of, 216–17, 222–29, 287
  innovations created by, 193–230
  intellectual property rights, 254
  and NAFTA, 131–34, 205n
  politics of, 135–36
  and Super 301, 130
  textile industry under, 209–10, 223–24
  timetable for, 97
  versus Tokyo Round, 210
  worker rights under, 187
USA-NAFTA, 203, 203n
US International Trade Commission (USITC), 78,
    141, 354–55
  and antidumping laws, 218
  and escape clause criteria, 143–44
  and interest-group politics, 185
USTR. See Office of the US Trade Representative
    (USTR)

Valenti, Jack, 209
Vanik, Charles A., 76, 77, 78, 145, 274
Veneman, Ann M., 299
Vietnam, bilateral trade agreement with, 291,
    333
Volcker, Paul A., 55, 60

voluntary export restraints (VERs), 26–27, 27n, 33,
    195
  declining use of, 164, 165t
  definition of, 355
  and nondiscrimination principle, 54
  outlawing of, 209–10
voluntary import expansion (VIEs), 207

wage increases, and stagflation, 56
wage insurance, 327–28
  definition of, 356
Washington Post
  on Bill Thomas, 334, 334n
  on Reagan administration, 120
  on Trade and Tariff Act of 1984, 85, 86, 86n
  on Trade Promotion Authority Act, 339
  on Uruguay Round implementation, 225, 227
White House trade office. *See* Office of the US
    Trade Representative (USTR)
Wignot, Mary Jane, 96
wine equity, 86, 87n
wine gallon concession, 74n
Winham, Gilbert R., 110
wireless telephone services, 214, 225
Wofford, Harris, 133, 174
Wolf, Frank, 335
Wolff, Alan Wm., 74, 107
wood products
  Canadian negotiations on, 149, 320
  Japanese negotiations on, 125
Woodward, Bob, 200
workers
  displaced, assistance for, 328–29 (*See also* trade
    adjustment assistance)
  rights of (*See also* labor unions)
    and Trade Promotion Authority Act,
      340–41
    and Uruguay Round, 187
World Trade Organization (WTO), 9, 242–46. *See
    also* Doha Round
  China's entry into, 233, 237, 273, 275, 277, 332
  creation of, 193, 209–10
  definition of, 356
  dispute settlement provisions, 243–46, 321
  Hong Kong Ministerial Conference, 303
  labor standards, 219–20
  NAFTA and, 193–30
  organization of, 302
  partisan politics and, 221, 227–28, 289
  public opinion of, 245–46
  Seattle Ministerial Conference, 230, 253, 271–73
  social issues and, 220–21
  structural imbalance in, 246
  US compliance record, 245, 245n, 320–21
  and US sovereignty, 220–21
  Working Group on Trade and Labor, 340
  as "world government," 221
World War II, trade policy during and
    immediately after, 6–8, 12–13
Wright, Jim, 91, 94, 95, 96, 191n, 287

Yerxa, Rufus, 92, 198, 216
Yeutter, Clayton, 91, 93, 102, 121*n*, 196
    appointment of, 122–23
    congressional relations with, 128*n*
    damage limitation by, 128

Zoellick, Robert B., 280, 282, 304
    and Cancún Ministerial, 302–3
    and competitive liberalization, 298–302

congressional relations with, 298*n*, 298–99,
    301*n*, 305
and Doha Round, 319–20
and fast-track renewal, 290–91, 298
success of, 299–300, 332
and Trade Promotion Authority Act,
    332–33
use of trade promotion authority, 299–300
Zysman, John, 181

Other Publications from the Institute for International Economics

Why Exports Really Matter!* ISBN 0-88132-221-0
Why Exports Matter More!* ISBN 0-88132-229-6
J. David Richardson and Karin Rindal
July 1995; February 1996
Global Corporations and National Governments
Edward M. Graham
May 1996 ISBN 0-88132-111-7
Global Economic Leadership and the Group of Seven C. Fred Bergsten and C. Randall Henning
May 1996 ISBN 0-88132-218-0
The Trading System after the Uruguay Round*
John Whalley and Colleen Hamilton
July 1996 ISBN 0-88132-131-1
Private Capital Flows to Emerging Markets after the Mexican Crisis* Guillermo A. Calvo, Morris Goldstein, and Eduard Hochreiter
September 1996 ISBN 0-88132-232-6
The Crawling Band as an Exchange Rate Regime: Lessons from Chile, Colombia, and Israel
John Williamson
September 1996 ISBN 0-88132-231-8
Flying High: Liberalizing Civil Aviation in the Asia Pacific*
Gary Clyde Hufbauer and Christopher Findlay
November 1996 ISBN 0-88132-227-X
Measuring the Costs of Visible Protection in Korea* Namdoo Kim
November 1996 ISBN 0-88132-236-9
The World Trading System: Challenges Ahead
Jeffrey J. Schott
December 1996 ISBN 0-88132-235-0
Has Globalization Gone Too Far? Dani Rodrik
March 1997 ISBN cloth 0-88132-243-1
Korea-United States Economic Relationship*
C. Fred Bergsten and Il SaKong, editors
March 1997 ISBN 0-88132-240-7
Summitry in the Americas: A Progress Report
Richard E. Feinberg
April 1997 ISBN 0-88132-242-3
Corruption and the Global Economy
Kimberly Ann Elliott
June 1997 ISBN 0-88132-233-4
Regional Trading Blocs in the World Economic System Jeffrey A. Frankel
October 1997 ISBN 0-88132-202-4
Sustaining the Asia Pacific Miracle: Environmental Protection and Economic Integration Andre Dua and Daniel C. Esty
October 1997 ISBN 0-88132-250-4
Trade and Income Distribution William R. Cline
November 1997 ISBN 0-88132-216-4
Global Competition Policy
Edward M. Graham and J. David Richardson
December 1997 ISBN 0-88132-166-4

Unfinished Business: Telecommunications after the Uruguay Round
Gary Clyde Hufbauer and Erika Wada
December 1997 ISBN 0-88132-257-1
Financial Services Liberalization in the WTO
Wendy Dobson and Pierre Jacquet
June 1998 ISBN 0-88132-254-7
Restoring Japan's Economic Growth
Adam S. Posen
September 1998 ISBN 0-88132-262-8
Measuring the Costs of Protection in China
Zhang Shuguang, Zhang Yansheng, and Wan Zhongxin
November 1998 ISBN 0-88132-247-4
Foreign Direct Investment and Development: The New Policy Agenda for Developing Countries and Economies in Transition
Theodore H. Moran
December 1998 ISBN 0-88132-258-X
Behind the Open Door: Foreign Enterprises in the Chinese Marketplace
Daniel H. Rosen
January 1999 ISBN 0-88132-263-6
Toward A New International Financial Architecture: A Practical Post-Asia Agenda
Barry Eichengreen
February 1999 ISBN 0-88132-270-9
Is the U.S. Trade Deficit Sustainable?
Catherine L. Mann
September 1999 ISBN 0-88132-265-2
Safeguarding Prosperity in a Global Financial System: The Future International Financial Architecture, Independent Task Force Report Sponsored by the Council on Foreign Relations
Morris Goldstein, Project Director
October 1999 ISBN 0-88132-287-3
Avoiding the Apocalypse: The Future of the Two Koreas Marcus Noland
June 2000 ISBN 0-88132-278-4
Assessing Financial Vulnerability: An Early Warning System for Emerging Markets
Morris Goldstein, Graciela Kaminsky, and Carmen Reinhart
June 2000 ISBN 0-88132-237-7
Global Electronic Commerce: A Policy Primer
Catherine L. Mann, Sue E. Eckert, and Sarah Cleeland Knight
July 2000 ISBN 0-88132-274-1
The WTO after Seattle Jeffrey J. Schott, editor
July 2000 ISBN 0-88132-290-3
Intellectual Property Rights in the Global Economy Keith E. Maskus
August 2000 ISBN 0-88132-282-2

**Australia, New Zealand,
and Papua New Guinea**
D.A. Information Services
648 Whitehorse Road
Mitcham, Victoria 3132, Australia
tel: 61-3-9210-7777
fax: 61-3-9210-7788
email: service@adadirect.com.au
www.dadirect.com.au

United Kingdom and Europe
(including Russia and Turkey)
The Eurospan Group
3 Henrietta Street, Covent Garden
London WC2E 8LU England
tel: 44-20-7240-0856
fax: 44-20-7379-0609
www.eurospan.co.uk

Japan and the Republic of Korea
United Publishers Services Ltd.
1-32-5, Higashi-shinagawa,
Shinagawa-ku, Tokyo 140-0002 JAPAN
tel: 81-3-5479-7251
fax: 81-3-5479-7307
info@ups.co.jp
**For trade accounts only.
Individuals will find IIE books in
leading Tokyo bookstores.**

Canada
Renouf Bookstore
5369 Canotek Road, Unit 1
Ottawa, Ontario KlJ 9J3, Canada
tel: 613-745-2665
fax: 613-745-7660
www.renoufbooks.com

India, Bangladesh, Nepal, and Sri Lanka
Viva Books Pvt.
Mr. Vinod Vasishtha
4325/3, Ansari Rd.
Daryaganj, New Delhi-110002
India
tel: 91-11-327-9280
fax: 91-11-326-7224
email: vinod.viva@gndel.globalnet. ems.vsnl.
net.in

Southeast Asia (Brunei, Burma, Cambodia,
Malaysia, Indonesia,
the Philippines, Singapore, Thailand
Taiwan, and Vietnam)
APAC Publishers Services
70 Bedemeer Road #05-03
Hiap Huat House
Singapore 339940
tel: 65-684-47333
fax: 65-674-78916

**Visit our Web site at:
www.iie.com
E-mail orders to:
orders@iie.com**